Innovative Reward Systems for the Changing Workplace

Innovative Reward Systems for the Changing Workplace

Thomas B. Wilson

McGraw-Hill, Inc.

New York   San Francisco   Washington, D.C.   Auckland   Bogotá
Caracas   Lisbon   London   Madrid   Mexico City   Milan
Montreal   New Delhi   San Juan   Singapore
Sydney   Tokyo   Toronto

Library of Congress Cataloging-in-Publication Data

Wilson, Thomas B.
    Innovative reward systems for the changing workplace / Thomas B.
Wilson.
            p.   cm.
    Includes bibliographical references and index.
    ISBN 0-07-070960-2
    1. Incentives in industry—United States.   2. Compensation
management—United States.   3. Organizational change—United States.
I. Title.
HF5549.5.I5W45   1994
658.3′14—dc20   94-22541
                                                                              CIP

  2 3 4 5 6 7 8 9 0   DOC/DOC   9 0 9 8 7 6 5

ISBN 0-07-070960-2

*The sponsoring editor for this book was James Bessent, the editing supervisor
was Jim Halston, and the production supervisor was Donald F. Schmidt. It
was set in Palatino by McGraw-Hill's Professional Book Group composition
unit.*

Printed and bound by R. R. Donnelley & Sons Company.

This book is printed on recycled, acid-free paper containing
a minimum of 50% recycled de-inked fiber.

To Fran, Robert, and John, who provide my life with continuous rewards.

And to my parents, Lawrence and Helen, who made my life possible.

Contents

Foreword

Tom Wilson's book is timely, insightful, comprehensive, informed by first-hand experience, and above all, useful. Wilson crystallizes the experience of the best companies, showing how these leaders link their reward systems to effective business strategies. He presents a comprehensive array of innovative incentives and shows managers how to choose and implement them. He goes behind the system to the people, showing what actually drives human behavior. He provides nuts-and-bolts, top-to-bottom, start-to-finish advice on performance management for organizations in the midst of change.

And as if all that were not enough, Wilson does one more thing: he issues a wake-up call to companies everywhere *to change their assumptions about the design of effective organizations.* The revitalization of American business rests increasingly on the delegation of more responsibility to more responsible people. It requires workforce professionalism to use the disciplines of total quality management or to permit the empowerment of frontline service workers to better care for customers. It means encouraging entrepreneurial initiative—managers and workers behaving like owners. To get there, we have to undo almost a century of management theory and practice.

Traditional reward systems were defined by hierarchy. Rewards were tied to level or position, not to performance.

Positions were evaluated in terms of staff or assets controlled, not in terms of strategic contributions to building the future. Behavior was controlled by procedure manuals and supervisors who watched closely, monitoring activities rather than measuring results. People were evaluated by their immediate boss and were thought to be motivated by the hope of a promotion. In fact, as befit hierarchical structures, rewards were largely linked to promotion. Without promotion to a higher rank, people soon reached ceilings in terms of salary or wages, influence and responsibility. While such systems controlled performance, they also encouraged behaviors that could constrain the achievement of high levels: building organizational empires, focusing on getting promoted rather than achieving results, doing the least to meet minimum standards, following internal rules rather than producing excellent results for customers.

Today, the fault lines in this costly, slow moving, bureaucratic system have been exposed from inside and outside: from inside, by the declining performance of aging, giant U.S. industrial corporations; and from outside, by the explosive growth of newer, high-technology firms that work integratively to produce rapid innovation. In the 1980s, America's small-business job-creation engine, led by high technology companies, created new models, less hierarchical and more flexible. Increased global competition, which threatened rigid and parochial large corporations in once-secure industries such as autos and steel, made companies more receptive to new models. Large American companies began to emulate the innovative and team spirit of smaller ones as well as to look beyond their organizational boundaries for ideas about how to be competitive. The process of change, seeded in the 1980s and accelerated in the 1990s, is loosening structures and breaching boundaries, tearing down the walls between levels, functions, departments, divisions, suppliers, and customers.

The most successful organizations today are characterized by what I call the "4 F's" of strategy and management.[1] They are more *focused* on fewer lines of business and fewer activities that they perform with greater depth and skill; they are *faster*, quick to innovate and speedier in their ongoing operations; they are *more flexible*, crossing traditional boundaries of departments, functions, and levels to put teams together to get results; they are *friendlier*, engaged in alliances and partnerships with customers, suppliers, and external collaborators.

These four strategic "F's" imply important shifts in the emphasis for workplaces and people:[2]

- *From fat to lean: the new staffing principle*. Empowerment assumptions have moved away from "bigger is better" to "smaller is beautiful"— and more flexible. Increasingly, the desire for "fat" organizations that relied on redundancy, encouraged overstaffing, and could afford to waste people on nonessential tasks, has been replaced by a preference for "lean" organizations with focused efforts. Such organizations are willing to try outsourcing and external suppliers for internal services; they expect existing staff to do more before they add others.

- *From vertical to horizontal: the new organization*. The hierarchical emphasis of classic American corporations inhibits their ability to act like entrepreneurs, create change, or produce innovation. Because companies need to encourage higher performance by making rewards more contingent on actual contributions, compensation is more likely to fluctuate rather than rise steadily year by year as individual or team performance changes and company fortunes ebb and flow. In short, *companies need creative new reward systems because the old ones cannot work in today's competitive business environment*.

To compete effectively in the global economy, businesses must attract, retain, motivate, and utilize effectively the most talented people they can find. But people do not want to invest their talents without feeling that they are getting something in return. In the 1990s, it is harder to get the balance right using assumptions from the hierarchical, bureaucratic model of the 1970s. As Wilson shows, companies today must use a wide variety of innovative rewards linked closely to business strategy and supported by multiple, frequent measures of performance.

The rhetoric about valuing human capital is increasingly in place; leaders speak of "core competence," and "competing on capabilities," or say "our most important assets walk in and out the door every day." But accounting systems have not caught up with the shift that is needed from measuring only the use of financial capital to measuring the building of human capital. And reward systems have not yet fully translated strategic goals into concrete performance incentives and measures that give people and their managers the tools to take effective action in a demanding competitive environment.

So Tom Wilson's book is a wake-up call to American business. It is also a wake-up call to America's human resource managers and professionals—those who design and implement performance management and reward systems. For all the talk of the last decade and more about a "strategic" role for the HR departments, HR managers have been laggards, not leaders. It was not human resource executives but engineering and statisticians advocating total quality management who led the redefining of performance management and reward systems. (The expert whom Wilson quotes frequently in this book is the quality guru W. Edwards Deming.) It was not compensation professionals but corporate raiders, institutional investors, economists, and other shareholder rights activists who led the rethinking of managerial pay levels, incentives, and stock options. It was not HR departments but market pressure to better respond to customers that raised the need for redefinition of performance measures.

But this book gives human resource managers another chance. With the comprehensive approach outlined here, the dream of marrying business strategy to human resource policies and practices can become a reality. I hope managers throughout American industry and the world read this wise book, absorb its messages, and use its helpful tools.

Notes

1. Kanter, R. M., *When Giants Learn to Dance: Mastering the Challenges of Strategy, Management, and Careers in the 1990s.* New York: Simon and Schuster, 1989.

2. Kanter, R. M., "The View from the 1990s: How the Global Economy Is Reshaping Corporate Power and Careers," in *Men and Women of the Corporation.* New York: Basic Books, 1993.

Rosabeth Moss Kanter, Ph.D.
Class of 1960 Professor of Business Administration
Harvard Business School

Preface

Companies throughout the world are attempting to implement fundamental changes in their organizations. Some of the reasons include increased competition, changing regulations, the emergence of new technologies, and the changing needs of customers. They employ a variety of initiatives, such as total quality management, re-engineering, cycle time reduction, downsizing, empowerment, strategic alliances, and focused customer service.

Many of the leading advocates of organizational change stress the importance of changing the reward systems in order to sustain desired improvements. They point out that if reward systems are not changed, people will soon return to old patterns of behaviors. As reported in numerous surveys, this fear has a basis in reality, for many companies are indicating that they're dissatisfied with the results they've realized from their investment in change. Clearly, if the results from change efforts are to be realized and sustained, people need to employ different behaviors or practices.

This means that people need do some things differently. For some, change offers an opportunity for something new, something better. For others, change is associated with losing something they currently enjoy (like status, power, or control), concerns about the future, or feelings that past activities are no longer valued. So why would people do anything differently?

Should they do it to protect their jobs? Should they do it because they are told to? Should they do it so that the organization and its major shareholders will prosper?

Reward systems can give people a reason to take desired actions by providing something positive for achieving a desired result. However, there are many problems with the current approaches to reward systems. Most of today's reward systems are based on principles of command and control, not customer focus; on competition, not collaboration; on "one size fits all" rather than on personalized rewards. If reward systems are to reinforce desired changes in behaviors, they need to be redesigned from the ground up.

There are many approaches to designing reward systems. Those that attempt to focus rewards solely on business strategy and organizational objectives have a weak link to human behaviors. Those that focus on external competitiveness, legal compliance, and costs spend more time seeking control than supporting the process of change—ignoring the important process of reinforcing collaboration and achievements on a daily basis. Finally, those that challenge the use of rewards as simply "carrot-and-stick" systems offer few constructive alternatives.

Innovative Reward Systems for a Changing Workplace picks up where the advocates of change leave off. It provides an understanding of why current attempts to recognize and reward performance don't work, the fundamental theory and concepts necessary for effective reward systems, and many practical action steps. The book doesn't just provide superficial descriptions of what companies are doing, should be doing; it gives specific alternatives and a framework for selecting and developing a portfolio of reward programs.

I wrote this book to show executives, managers, and other leaders how to use reward systems to encourage and reinforce change. We do not need to be held captive to the paradigms that surround current thinking about rewards systems, but we do need to understand the conditions that impact human behavior and know how to design systems to marshall these forces. This book is intended to provide both the why and the how.

This material is for anyone facing the challenge of fostering change in an organization. It is the first book to comprehensively examine all reward systems, formal and informal, short-term and long-term, cash and noncash, that exist in today's organizations. The concepts and tools are drawn from a wealth of established research in the behavioral sciences, organizational change and business management, as well as from wide personal experience in a variety of best practices. It does not attempt to provide a single method but enables readers to tailor their own answers to the specific issues of their organizations. This book should become a resource book, a guidebook, or simply a source to stimulate workable ideas and purposeful actions.

Traditional compensation practices often link pay systems to employee benefits. Benefit programs can be effective in attracting and retaining people, but because they are not based on performance they have not been dealt with directly in this book. They are not performance-based because benefits programs apply to everyone and cannot be made contingent on certain results.

My challenge in writing this volume was to chart a course between the principles of human behavior and the practical application of techniques. You do not need to read this book from start to finish. You should read the first three to four chapters to gain an understanding of the conceptual frameworks. Then select the specific chapter in which you are interested: base pay, variable pay, equity programs, special recognition programs, or performance appraisals. Once you have an understanding of one area, go to the next logically related area based on the concerns in your organization. You may also want to understand how to improve your performance measures or develop strategies for implementing change; there are chapters on each of these subjects. Then examine several of the case studies to see how these plans can be applied to an organization. To conclude, read the final chapter to review why it is important to do what you are doing. Hopefully, this book will help you create and sustain meaningful change in your company and bring a clearer purpose to your mission.

The job of developing this material was not undertaken alone. There were many who aided in the development of these concepts, and others who have contributed directly to the production of this book. Most notably, there are many individuals who have helped create and shape these ideas. Ned Morse, Jim Hillgren, and I have together developed perhaps most of the new ideas and concepts presented in this material. Ned brought a strong understanding of strategy and organizational change; Jim brought fresh insights and creativity in how to look at traditional practices. In addition, Amy Armitage provided a continual focus on the customer and an understanding of related theories. Dave Cheatham provided me with very useful insights and an awareness of how much classic literature has to offer. Lauren Sagner and John Somatican have continued to ask the tough questions and offer clear answers. Finally, Aubrey Daniels has provided many conceptual frameworks and scientific principles of human behavior presented in this book. I hope that these ideas will be further developed and enhanced in the years to come.

Many of the ideas, concepts, and processes outlined in this book were developed in real-world settings with my clients. They have given me a forum in which to expand and apply these ideas, and in turn I have helped them become more competitive and attractive places to work. These companies, many of whom are described in this book, have made the ideas presented here possible.

Finally, I could not have completed this book without the assistance of Fran Grigsby. She is my best critic, my personal consultant, my advisor for trying out crazy ideas, and my wife. As a line executive she has added both practical experience and valuable advice in how to structure, apply, and communicate these concepts.

This book is about how to make change a reality and how to create conditions of high performance within the organization. There are very many companies experimenting with innovative ideas to achieve these ends. I am always looking for programs that work, not to replicate them in some other location, but to understand why. By understanding why things work, we are in a strong position to develop and implement programs that do work. Therefore, if you know of an organization that has implemented programs or practices that are reflected in this book, please contact me. I would be very interested in learning more and sharing new ideas with you. Please contact The Wilson Group, Inc. in Concord, Massachusetts.

I hope that this material will prove valuable to you and your organization. We face the challenges of turning the organization into a highly competitive force in a global marketplace. Our task is to create an environment in which each person feels a sense of responsibility and ownership of the organization. Only by creating a stake in the results can we truly achieve this. Only when people understand and feel reinforced for their actions can the organization continually excel. You will learn throughout this book that when people take the initiative to go beyond expectations, we all realize tremendous gains. Our task is to create the conditions that make an organization become more competitive and more successful and enable its employees to feel more valued and more rewarded for their achievements.

Thomas B. Wilson

1
The Changing Workplace

An invasion of armies can be resisted, but not
an idea whose time has come.
                    —VICTOR HUGO
        Histoire d'un Crime, 1852

George and Martha had been working together for more than 12 years. They operated lathing and finishing equipment in the division of a large industrial manufacturing company. They used separate equipment in the same work function and location. They were both on the company's piece-rate incentive system and had achieved reasonable overall production levels. George had worked for the company three years longer than Martha, and both had many years of seniority in this relatively stable company.

They were good friends and enjoyed discussing many of their outside activities. They would often seek and offer advice from each other on the trials and pressures of parenting young children and laugh at the funny things kids do. The families would periodically get together socially, as their youngest boys were in the same Cub Scout den.

George and Martha were very good employees and seldom caused trouble for their supervisors. On the setup and grinding process for a major product, however, Martha always had significant difficulty. She would scrap at least 30 percent of the materials in the operation. This frequently led to delayed orders because parts would need to be replaced and the operation reworked. Her supervisor would frequently yell at her when these errors threatened to cause the department to miss the weekly production goals. As hard as she tried and as angry as she got, Martha kept scrapping many of the materials in the setup process.

George didn't have this problem. He knew just how to tighten the clamps, how to carefully bring the cutting tools into the operation. He always exceeded his production quota and was able to reap the benefits of this performance. He was reluctant to tell Martha his special secrets because the industrial engineering group might reset the performance standards and that would cut his earnings. While George felt sympathetic about Martha's problem and often gave her moral support, he did nothing. When the supervisor asked George to teach Martha how to do the operation, he said he would, but he never did. He knew it was important to keep these and other techniques to himself so as to not jeopardize his performance ratings. He wanted Martha and the business to succeed, but not at the expense of his personal livelihood.

While George felt torn by this dilemma, Martha was reconciled to the problem and considered it normal. The supervisor didn't know what to do except to keep a watchful eye on the situation. The plant manager didn't know anything about the problem. This situation and many other similar problems throughout the plant continued.

Searching for the Answer

This brief story illustrates a situation common to many organizations worldwide. George and Martha and millions like them in other organizations are responding normally to the conditions they face. Supervisors and managers have resigned themselves to believing that this is the normal state of affairs. Executives are watching macrolevel results and seeking to implement change efforts that will reshape their organizations, unaware of opportunities that exist in their own organizations. Programs like reengineering, self-managed teams, and corporate restructuring are being implemented on top of other programs like total quality management, cycle time reduction, and employee empowerment. Executives feel an urgent need to make dramatic changes in the competitiveness of their organizations; managers feel overburdened by commitment after commitment; and employees feel pulled in multiple directions and question where all this is going. We are facing an environment in which the response is ever-expanding change.

- Why are we doing this?
- Where is it heading?
- Why isn't it working?
- Why isn't it working fast enough?

Our challenge is quite simple: *We need to build organizations that are highly competitive and highly attractive to desired customers by creating an environment where people take the initiative to do what is needed.* This challenge will require a fundamental change in the way we structure, build, and lead organizations. To truly understand the nature of the required changes, we need to review how we got to where we are. As with George and Martha, we got there because we were responding normally to increasingly abnormal situations.

Learning from the Past

In the beginning...man (as was customary then) created the organization because he could not do all the work himself. Whether he was producing shoes, clothing, houses, or automobiles, the increasing demand for products or services resulted in the entrepreneur hiring people to assist in doing the work. As demand grew and the business became successful, more and more people were hired.

At first people did the routine jobs the entrepreneur did not want to do. Then they began doing more value-added work, actually creating new elements for the product that increased its value to the customer. (See Figure 1-1.) As demand increased, they began to hire people themselves. Success came from growth, and growth meant more hiring.

Success and growth also meant more conflict, confusion about roles, and concerns about how to keep people performing. What should be done so that people could continue to satisfy customers and increase

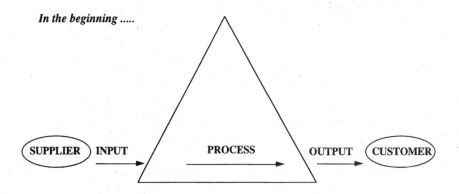

In the beginning .....

SUPPLIER INPUT PROCESS OUTPUT CUSTOMER

..... the organization was created to transform inputs into outputs
that met the needs of a customer.

Figure 1-1. A historical context of work systems.

the success of the enterprise? What would motivate people so that they would continue to work to their fullest potential?

In searching for solutions, the entrepreneur turned to the only successful and enduring models for managing people at work: the military, Adam Smith, and the Catholic Church. In these organizations, the chain of command was clear; the power and authority rested with the superior. Hence, the purpose of the organization's design was to provide a process of directing and controlling work. The organizational chart displaying lines of authority, power, and accountability, was constructed and communicated so that people would understand the rules of authority. People then saw themselves as having roles within this organizing concept.

The entrepreneur who had become a manager looked for management concepts that would prove reliable and effective in addressing the critical needs of the organization. This led many to the teachings of Frederick W. Taylor, an engineer who invented carbon steel machine tools. He became the leading authority on management at the turn of the century.[1] Taylor asserted that there was a best method for organizing work. Organizations that adopted these principles did, in fact, prosper. His principles included:

1. *Simplify work by specialization.* By identifying the basic tasks involved in work, reducing any unnecessary movements, and structuring them into related tasks, organizations could achieve incredible efficiencies. This enabled companies over the next 50 years to employ workers with limited skills, and achieve efficiencies as the workers mastered the skills. Further, this simplified the process of supervision, because work would be organized into discrete functional elements.

2. *Establish predetermined rules to govern work methods.* This involves determining the standard operating procedures and work rules necessary to complete the needed tasks. The work process could be controlled to minimize variance. When integration was needed, it would be accomplished by adding managerial levels or changing the organization's hierarchy.

3. *Monitor work activities to assure compliance.* The principal role of management was to oversee that employees were following the prescribed rules. They established sophisticated management information systems to achieve this. The process of planning and organizing work was separated from those performing the work—brains would be separated from brawn.

These principles of organizing work helped organizations to achieve a critical advantage—the production of a high volume of standardized products or services. Our success as a nation from the 1920s to the 1970s was based on this. Our output per worker during this period grew at an average rate of 2.3% per year, far faster than any other industrialized country. The basic driver of this success was our ability to take inventions and resources and to mass produce and distribute them to a major market. American society embraced this method of production by purchasing the products, which in turn fueled this growth.[2]

In this earlier era the purpose of the organization was to control work so that customers received the desired products when they needed them, and at an appropriate cost. Customers exerted significant influence on the people who served them. People listened to their customers because there were so few of them and because, if they lost a customer, the consequences could be devastating.

However, as organizations became more successful, the voice and influence of single customers (and, in fact, the voices of most customers) became indistinct to the people controlling these firms. Executives concerned themselves with the organization's structure, lines of authority, span of control, personnel policies, and financial reporting systems. They sought to assure that the work was being done properly and at minimal cost. This organizational concept worked especially well when the ultimate focus was still on the customer. Demand for products grew, the firm remained competitive, and the shareholders and managers gained a great deal of wealth. (See Figure 1-2.)

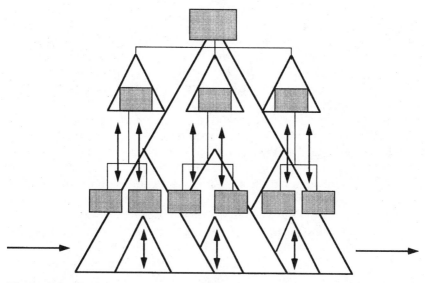

Figure 1-2. The bureaucratic organization emerges.

The Rise of the Hierarchy

The hierarchical organization philosophy was very effective in handling people and work activities of smaller organizations, in which technology was relatively simple and the workforce primarily uneducated. However, problems began to emerge as the focus shifted from the customer to the organization's hierarchy. Managers, supervisors, and employees became more interested in satisfying the needs of their superiors than of their customers because the consequences of not doing so were more instantaneous and dramatic. As long as the organization grew and the products or services were being acquired in the market, they were viewed as successful. But, as organizations became larger, people became more insulated from the external customer, and consequently the customer exerted less and less influence. The only real power the customer had was the relatively indirect one of choosing to purchase or not to purchase the goods/services of the organization. Compared with the customer's indirect influence, the superior's power over the producers of the goods and services was immediate and intense. Ultimately, this fact had the effect of turning the superior into the primary customer.

The Rise of the Supervisor

The position of supervisor was created as a reflection of this organizational model. Rooted in the job of "over-seeing," the main element of the position was "super-vision." The supervisor was supposed to know what was going on at all times and had the power to command and control the activities of assigned people. In some work settings the supervisor was located on a platform or high above the work area so that he or she was literally able to see more than anyone else. In other locations, the supervisor had an office with glass walls, not so that people could see whether he or she was in, but so that he or she could see out. The supervisor's duty was to direct and control operations in terms of what senior management wanted. The supervisor spent most of his or her time watching for mistakes so that immediate actions could be taken to return the operation to control. (Even many of the total quality management efforts have been focused on keeping operations in control.)

The person to whom people reported was often referred to as the *superior*. This implies, like the word *supervisor*, that the person had extraordinary abilities like higher technical know-how, more knowledge about the organization and customers, and greater authority. Furthermore, a supervisor had greater control over company resources and could use them to reward and punish those within his or her control. The result was that the organization's overall hierarchy reflected mounting levels of knowledge, understanding, and power that were very attractive to aspiring employees.

Within this context mid-level managers spent most of their time making sure supervisors were directing and controlling their operations efficiently. They continually sought ways to gain greater productivity and satisfy the needs of their senior managers. In turn, the supervisor's role was to meet the needs of his or her superiors and make sure his or her people did as the superiors wanted. Employees realized that their security depended on keeping the supervisor "off their backs" because the supervisor usually took action only when there was problem.

Gradually, organizations' response time began to slow. Even if customers' needs changed, organizations tended not to respond until the people in positions of power understood the changes and directed actions. If the change challenged the executive or manager's traditional authority, beliefs, or paradigm, the pressure was ignored. Action was finally taken only when the negative consequences far outweighed the benefits of inaction. Employees continued to respond more to the wishes of their superiors than to those of their customers because their supervisors had more immediate control over their lives. Hence, organizations became very resistant to change or late in acknowledging change in the environment.

Given this framework, it is easy to see why executives in the U.S. automobile, steel, and consumer electronics industries were so slow to respond to changes in the marketplace. One can also understand why U.S. steel manufacturers and other major industry heads sought to protect themselves rather than respond to changes in the external marketplace. This process was a natural by-product of the fact that the decision makers were high up in the organization's hierarchy, and that the higher up they were, the more insulated from the customer they had become. Conflict emerged when the needs of the customer were not matched by the needs of the superior. Competitors arrived in the market and customers started going to them. The response by many executives was to slash prices and "buy" customers or marketshare. In many industries this change was not immediate. Like a disease, it was slow, steady, and deadly.

The Emergence of Compensation Systems

As a further reflection of this philosophy of management, compensation systems grew to support the values and organizing concepts of the company. In the mid-1950s and 1960s, compensation systems were created because people felt pay practices were out of control. The "let's make a deal" pattern of determining compensation had become destructive to the sense of internal control and harmony many executives sought. (This will be discussed in more detail in Chapter 4, Developing a Reward Strategy.) Consequently, systems like National Metal Trades, AAIM and The Hay System emerged as a way of rationalizing why some people were making more money than others.

Compensation systems began to focus on the job as the primary unit of value. Job descriptions, a common element in many pay programs, sought to capture the unique, specialized content of the job as well as the authority and accountability assigned to it. They became a process for controlling the allocation of compensation dollars and defining status and power in the organization. Job descriptions were customarily used to clarify job responsibilities in the context of the superior's responsibilities. The focus of one's work was on satisfying the needs of the supervisor.

The use of incentive plans was frequently reserved for the top executives or high operations jobs. Usually focused on individual effort, they were either formulaic (i.e., awarded for the number of pieces produced over a standard minimum) or discretionary (i.e., how the top executive judged the value of one's performance).

Compensation systems became both a reflection of the organization's hierarchy and a way of reinforcing it. As the internal dynamics of organizations became ever more removed from a focus on the customer and the marketplace, power and influence became ever more centered *within* the organization. Because pay systems were often related to hierarchical control and power, they reinforced organizational values and philosophy in ways very significant to the individual. Managers were reluctant to implement change until they could see how the new "points," or job levels, would impact their people. Additional organizational layers were created to give people an opportunity to earn more, whether or not the work could actually be justified.

Hierarchical organizations were very appropriate at a time when people were rather unskilled and the focus of work was on simple production. Pay systems that reflected these principles were quite common and accepted in industry. These pay systems were reflections of their times, and were accepted as the natural order of things in the workplace.

Then Things Began to Change

The processes of hierarchical organization design and compensation worked well for many years. Then something began to happen. Though the change was not immediate or extensive, it led to a growing sense that traditional patterns of management, organization, and rewards were no longer working. Many organizations began to experience a conflict between the old emphasis on stability, efficiency, and control, and the new pressure for speed, simplicity, flexibility, quality and cost. (See Figure 1-3.)

The push for change is driven by many factors: increasing competition, especially from non-U.S. or cross-industry companies; the liquidity crisis; the aging population; the high cost of capital and the rising debt at the personal and governmental level; changing regulatory pressures; a growing concern about the environment; fraud and abuse in the financial markets; merger-mania; the real estate crisis; greater workforce diversity; the increased speed and scope of communication technology; the rise of the niche player and the erosion of market share in small bites; total quality management and reengineering; the new tax laws; employee empowerment and self-managed work teams; the decline of communism and the opening of the Iron Curtain countries; international trade agreements; and on and on and on. The root causes were many and diverse. But one thing was certain: the practices that had led to success in the past would no longer provide the formula for success in the future.

Today, every industry and company is facing major challenges. Although competitive pressures have always been present, they seem more real, more powerful, and more threatening today. At this writing we are still embroiled in this transition, this process of change. No single new model of management has yet replaced the hierarchical, direct-and-control approach, but there are some widely recognized

Intense Pressure by Regulators

Workforce Diversity

Re-Engineering

Values Shift

Total Quality

New Tax Laws

Customers Seek Personalized Service

Aging Population

Rising Concern for the Environment

Merger-mania

Downsize Rightsize

Competition
Competition
Competition

The New World Order

Liquidity Crisis

Real Estate Crisis

Niche Players

New Technology

Fraud & Abuse in the Securities Markets

Capital Formation Crisis

Oil Price Uncertainty

Global Competition

Figure 1-3. Something began to happen, and the requirements for success changed.

principles that should guide us. Six of the most important of these principles are discussed below (see Figure 1-4):

1. *Focus on what is valued by the customer.* The primary emphasis on total quality can be summed up as continually seeking ways to do things that add value for the customer. This can involve reduced costs, more accurate and timely deliveries, elimination of errors, custom-designed programs or products, partnering with the customer to anticipate needs and prevent problems, and so forth.

2. *Break down the walls that impede responsiveness and change.* Jack Welch, the CEO of General Electric, stated in the GE 1990 annual report that "Our dream for the 1990s is a boundaryless company...where we knock down the walls that separate us from each other on the inside and from our key constituencies on the outside." He went on to say that GE must remove barriers created by traditional practices, "recognize no distinctions" between levels and operations, and "ignore or erase group labels such as 'management,' 'salaried,' or 'hourly' which get in the way of people working together."

The traditional bureaucratic organization has people working for their superiors and those superiors working for their superiors, on up until a point is reached at which cross-functional work can occur. Then the directives or decisions work down again through the layers, each layer adding some special spin on the message or nature of the work. This takes time, and the messages are often distorted along the way. We cannot continue to operate in this manner and expect to be successful in a rapidly changing and challenging marketplace. The new workplace requires people to talk and work and achieve together. This requires building partnerships and using collaboration and teamwork to achieve desired ends.

3. *Build strong partnerships with suppliers and customers (internal and external).* In the traditional organization, unless you had direct contact with the external customers, you had no primary customer other than your immediate superior. In the new organization, people need to feel the influence of the horizontal customers and focus on efforts that add value to meeting their needs. This approach is being followed in organizations as diverse as Ford Motor Company and Ocean Spray Cranberries, Inc., each of which is seeking to reduce the number of its suppliers to 20 percent of previous levels. After such reductions, the suppliers have a closer understanding of the customer's needs for products and services and know that they must provide error-free products or they will not be on the short list. This process is also reflected in the rise of the so-called internal customer and a call for greater teamwork within organizations.

Perhaps the most radical change in this new paradigm of organiza-

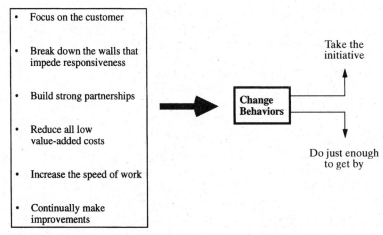

- Focus on the customer

- Break down the walls that
  impede responsiveness

- Build strong partnerships   Change
                                               Behaviors

- Reduce all low
  value-added costs

- Increase the speed of work   Take the
                                               initiative

- Continually make   Do just enough
  improvements   to get by

Figure 1-4. Fundamental changes in the way we manage our business
mean that people need to do some things differently.

tions is the role of the manager. Earlier we discussed the hierarchical organization and the manager as the customer of the employee. In this new context, the employee is the customer of the manager; the manager is the supplier. The primary purpose of the manager is to provide those services that enable the customer-employees to succeed in their tasks. This includes providing the employee-as-customer with the information, tools, resources, coaching, action, and opportunities needed to achieve ultimate customer satisfaction. The power is shared more and focused more on achieving results when the employee is viewed as the customer serving other customers, within or outside the organization's formal boundaries.

4. *Reduce low value-added activities.* Bureaucratic organizations create waste as a natural by-product of their existence. Authors as diverse as W. Edward Deming[3], Rosabeth Moss Kanter[4], and Tom Peters[5] describe the process at length. In the hierarchical organization, systems, staffing, and procedural controls are all needed to direct and control others. Work activities are delayed until the deadline is near. One set of procedures is established to control the work process; another set of procedures is established to assure that the initial set of procedures is followed.

Systems are established to verify that these controls are working. However, many of these activities add little value to the product or service and contribute little to the organization's ability to compete in an increasingly intense marketplace.

But how does one determine what is low value-added once one gets beyond the obvious needless tasks, reports, and committees? Work reengineering seeks to concentrate on this need, but such projects are often conducted in a manner that intensifies the bureaucracy's cultural hold on the organization. The behaviors initiated to reduce costs are seldom honored, valued, or reinforced (either publicly or privately). People who offer to eliminate their work often find themselves out of work or somehow placed in a waiting situation. So people rightfully fear such reengineering efforts, suspecting that, like many of their predecessors—downsizing, overhead value analysis, delayering—they will do little to benefit them or the organization over the long term. As many a veteran of organizational overhaul will recognize, such tactics can be futile exercises unless real fundamental behavioral changes take place.

5. *Increase speed in all aspects of work.* Given that all the strategies so far discussed are aimed at serving the customer in a more efficient and effective manner, one of the organization's most pressing needs is the ability to respond more quickly. Responsiveness means bringing new products to market faster; answering new competitive challenges more forcefully; decreasing the cycle or lead times in operations; and increasing the yield on human, material, and capital investments. In many competitive situations, speed will determine the winners and losers. However, speed without quality, partnerships, and value may turn into mere foolish actions, ultimately leading to lowered success. Speed coupled with quality and appropriate cost will win in almost every game.

6. *Continually seek improvements.* The total quality movement has brought a new and important concept to management: continuous improvement. This is rooted in the Japanese principles of kaizen.[6] Nearly everyone believes that continuous improvement is important (except for those technologists who want to wait until the product is perfect before it is released). However, this is not enough. As in the past, future competitive advantage will not only depend on continuous improvement, but also on the *rate* at which improvement occurs.

A case in point: The American automobile industry in 1960 virtually controlled the U.S. marketplace and was the dominant player in the world. Japanese automobiles were regarded as cheap, unsafe, technically inferior, too small for the American body, and hard to maintain. Over the next 20 years the U.S. automobile industry continued to make improvements in its automobiles. Although the improvements may have been more oriented to meeting the needs of senior managers (i.e., crome content, horsepower, and style obsolesence, etc.), improvements were being made. However, Japanese manufacturers were making changes at a faster *rate* and targeting their changes to the needs and wants of the buying customer. They redefined the expectations of the car-buying market by giving customers a vehicle with features they valued and quality they appreciated.

The understanding of the needs of the American consumer, the incorporation of new manufacturing technologies espoused by W. Edward Deming, Joseph Juran, and others, and the ability to analyze, develop, and execute enabled Japanese automobile manufacturers to achieve a rate of change faster than that of U.S. automobile companies. These changes were not only more focused on the true customers, but were implemented more effectively. Hence, in the mid-1980s the Japanese superseded American companies as the quality car manufacturers preferred by U.S. consumers. Their market share, though less than the total of all American manufacturers, is still growing. But U.S. companies have refocused and increased their rate of change for customer-centered improvements and may be turning the corner in this highly competitive marketplace. This trend is also starting to be seen in the electronics and computer industries.

Robert Reich stated in *The Next American Frontier*, "Since the late 1960s, America's economy has been slowly unraveling."[7] We are emerging with a new paradigm for the successful management of a business. Focusing on the customer, improving internal communications, building partnerships, reducing low value-added activities, speeding up responsiveness, and increasing the rate of improvement will become the principles by which our organizations live or die.

People Need to Do Some Things Differently

Examining each of these new requirements for success, reveals common threads of collaboration and responsiveness in serving the needs of the customer. To transform an organization in this direction, people will need to start doing some things, stop doing others, and change some of their practices.

Hence the primary unit for achieving desired organizational change is human behavior. Not just any human behavior, but those behaviors that enhance customer focus, communication, and responsiveness. This involves *collaboration*—between customer and provider, manager and employee, staff and line management, engineering and hourly workers, executives and clerical workers, sales and engineering staff, marketing and manufacturing employees—all across the organization.

Collaboration is the central theme in all change efforts. Collaboration, as a fundamental concept, is a set of specific human behaviors that creates the best possible win for all parties concerned. This concept is depicted in the diagram in Figure 1-5, which defines two dimensions of interest. One focuses on the self, seeking to maximize personal self-interest. The other focuses on the other party, seek-

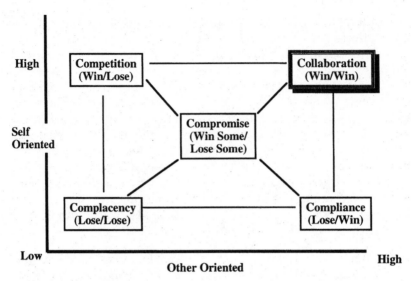

Figure 1-5. In order to do what this new model of management requires, systems need to be founded on principles of collaboration.

ing to assure that they achieve what they want. Taken together, they describe the two extremes of the ways people work together.

In the first situation, each party is totally self-oriented and has little regard for the other. This is called *competition.* In this situation, each strives to win and/or do better than the other person. It is quite effective when there is truly a zero-sum game with clear winners and losers. But one of its unfortunate side effects is that the one who loses will in most cases seek restitution. This means that the strategy requires a continuing vigilance for continued winning.

The second situation is the opposite of the first. This is called *compliance.* In this case one party seeks to satisfy the needs and wants of the other with little or no regard to his or her personal interest. Such "accommodators" go along with what is expected of them and seek little personal gain from the effort. But while the situation works in indentured servitude, it has only short-term benefits in business. By pleasing only the other party, accommodators tend to place themselves in powerless and submissive positions that may result in their feeling humiliated and seeking to get even. The compliant mode is also a win/lose situation, with the other party the winner and the accommodator the loser.

In the third situation, there is little regard for either self-interest *or* the other party's interest. This is the *complacency* mode, a lose/lose situation with by-products that affect future relationships. This situation may occur when there are external events that render the task unattainable or not under the control or within the influence of the participants. Neither party sees any possibility of personal gain or makes any effort to assist the other in achieving anything. Both simply do what is necessary to get by.

In the fourth situation, both sides seek to make trade-offs. This process involves *compromise*; both parties win some *and* lose some. This can be a satisfactory strategy when the conditions that define the task cannot be reformulated to allow both parties to get what they want. Compromise is used best when each party can get essentially what they want and enable the other to get elements essential to them as well. Here, a portion of something is better than a lot of nothing. Traditional labor-management contract negotiations fit this mode of transaction.

The fifth situation is called *collaboration*. Collaboration is achieved when both parties achieve what they want. It defines an exchange process that is attained through problem solving, looking for new approaches, and redefining the problem so that a new kind of resolution can be obtained. This situation truly defines "win-win" because both parties walk away from the engagement better off than they were before.

People cannot be made to collaborate. The management methods of command-and-control do not work well to increase collaboration and responsiveness. To illustrate, the chief executive of a large technology company sent a memorandum to all employees extolling the virtues of teamwork and directing all employees to start communicating and cooperating with each other. Needless to say, the action not only had no effect on people's actions, it reduced the credibility and respect of the top executive.

In another situation, a manufacturing company put people into specific work teams. They were trained in team building but they had little desire to work together. People sat in their weekly meetings, wasted time, and did little to integrate their work. They had a long history of emphasis on individual performance and competition within the workplace. When the management fad of teamwork faded, they returned to their traditional habits a little more skeptical about the senior leadership of the firm. People will only collaborate when they *want to*, when they view the value to be derived from collaborating as greater than the value to be derived from competing.

The challenge is how to create conditions in which people *want* to focus on the customer, *want* to collaborate, *want* to perform only value-added activities, *want* to increase the speed, responsiveness, and innovations needed by the customers. An executive can in essence direct people to collaborate or cooperate, but unless this process becomes inherently satisfying, workers will only do it as long as the threat remains. When people take those actions needed by the organization to become or remain highly competitive, when they are valued for doing so, and when the organization achieves the desired results, they are contributing to a truly *win-win* environment.

Facing Up to the Paradox

There has been much written and espoused about the new requirements for success. Experts in organizational change, such as Deming, Hammer, Kanter, Peters, Senge, etc., all say that unless reward systems are changed, people will return to their traditional habits. We are facing a contradiction between what we expect people to do and how we reward them. Traditional hierarchies, reflected in pay systems and practices, have become impediments to achieving desired change. This book picks up where others leave off. Its primary purpose is to provide specific strategies to achieve the behavioral changes needed in today's organizations.

To establish a definition, a reward system is any process within an organization that encourages, reinforces, or compensates people for taking a particular set of actions. It may be formal or informal, cash or noncash, immediate or delayed. We will examine a comprehensive array of reward systems and explore how to transform them into systems and practices that create conditions that bring out more desired behaviors. This book is about focusing the efforts of people and utilizing reward systems effectively so that people contribute, work, and achieve more, *because they truly want to.*

This chapter has examined how we got to where we are now, and what is emerging around a new paradigm for management. The focus, however, needs to be not on specific programs, but on understanding and implementing the principles of behavioral change that work over time. We do not need more gimmicks in our organizations, especially when it comes to people's pay. We need systems that work, can be replicated, and are founded on principles that have demonstrated results.

This book is based on the belief that the success of an organization lies in the hands of its people. Managers can plan, strategize, direct, and provide the leadership so needed by many firms. But it is what people do on a daily basis at all levels of the organization that will determine how competitive and successful the organization can be. This means that we need to create conditions that inspire and reward people for their achievements in ways that utilize their talents forcefully and creatively. We need to help them contribute to building more competitive organizations because they themselves feel valued and share in this success. This is the essence of collaboration and the root condition for achieving lasting success.

Epilogue to the Story of George and Martha

The company took a bold and risky step. It eliminated the piece-rate incentive system, then developed and implemented a team-based incentive program along with a management process to guide and reinforce desired behaviors. Once the new pay systems were implemented, George took 15 minutes to explain to Martha his special secrets to prevent scrapping the operation. A problem that had existed for 12 years was gone in less than an hour. George was honored for his assistance by Martha, his coworkers, and the supervisor. Similar situations occurred throughout the organization. As a result, over the next 10 months the scrap rates of this division were reduced from over 12 percent to less than 3 percent. Further, delivery schedules improved dramatically to 97 percent on-time shipments; lead times were reduced by 40 percent; and profitability increased by 300 percent.

Achieving these results is not enough. We need to understand why this occurred and how its successes can be replicated in all sectors of the organization. In this way, this division became a stronger competitor in a global marketplace, and people enjoyed contributing their full talents and abilities. And they did it because they wanted to.

References

1. Taylor, F. W., *The Principles of Scientific Management.* New York: Harper and Brothers, 1911.

2. Reich, R. B., *The Next American Frontier.* New York: Penguin Books, 1983.

3. Deming, W. E., *Out of the Crisis,* Cambridge, Mass.: MIT Press. 1986.

4. Kanter, R. M., *When Giants Learn to Dance: Mastering the Challenges of Strategy, Management, and Careers in the 1990s.* New York: Simon and Schuster, 1989.

5. Peters, T., *Thriving on Chaos.* New York: Alfred A. Knopf, 1987.

6. Imai, M., *Kaizen: The Key to Japan's Competitive Success.* New York: Random House, 1986.

7. Op cit., Reich.

2
Why Be Concerned about Reward Systems?

If you always do what you've always done,
you'll always get what you've always gotten.
　　—A FAMOUS OLD SAYING I HEARD SOMEWHERE

The employees of the Precision Metals Company were called into the cafeteria for an announcement. They knew that they had just finished an outstanding year. Sales and profitability were up, and their customers were singing their praises. The charts that adorned the workshop area and all the offices spoke of their achievements. It was an exciting time, but they didn't know what to expect at this meeting.

After a few moments, Lawrence Cate, the president, called the meeting to order. His expression was serious. He announced, "As you all know, this was the best year in the company's history. In every measure that is important to our competitive strategy, we have scored wins. You did this. Each one of you contributed in incredible ways to bring us this moment. Our customers are as excited as we are about the changes we have been able to implement. They want to do business with us. But *you* made it happen." His seriousness was washed away by a big grin and sparkling eyes.

"As you know, about a year ago we instituted the Performance Sharing Program, which enables us to share the results of our achievements." He went on to review the performance in each area of the program. He discussed the quarterly progress payments and then summarized the annual results. He concluded by saying, "So I have here a small but important recognition of this success." He held up a stack of envelopes bound together with green ribbon. He said, "There is an envelope here with your name on it, and there is a check inside. This payout is a symbol of what we can achieve when we do it together.

"I am going to pass out the checks now, but I will not give you yours. I will give you an envelope with somebody else's name on it. Your task is to find that person and give them their check. As you do this, tell them something specific that they did that helped you or the company over the last year. If you don't know them, ask someone who they are. If you don't know what they did, just say 'Thank you.' It is because of each one of your contributions that we are able to share these dollars and this time together."

With that, Lawrence went through the crowd passing out checks to different people. The group began laughing and hunting for the person belonging to the check. They told stories of major achievements over the last year. They kidded each other. Someone who received Lawrence's check wanted to keep it, but didn't. There were refreshments and a lot of people got to know each other in new ways. The celebration lasted only about an hour, but the memory lasted for years. Each person was looking forward to what they could do to celebrate in this way again. It was a memorable moment.

In the previous chapter we examined how the philosophy of the hierarchical model of management, using command-and-control methods, has now become an albatross around the neck of many organizations. While this approach was effective in an environment that was stable, predictable, and in need of control, it is now inhibiting many organizations from responding effectively to a changing world. Our focus in this and following chapters will be on how to create and sustain the changes that organizations need to make in order to survive and prosper.

In this chapter we will examine current reward systems and whether or not they should be used to support the change process. Along the way, we will examine the purpose and role of such systems and explore a variety of ways in which they can be focused and improved.

The Intent Versus the Reality of Today's Reward Systems

All organizations have reward systems today. Without them, people would probably not come to work or perform at any reliable level. Even voluntary groups create opportunities for individuals to be val-

Reward Program	Original Focus	Current Focus
Base pay	Jobs and markets	Reduce costs
Merit pay	Pay for performance	3 percent to 4 percent or less
Management bonus	Reward performance	Pay to retain
Promotions	Reward high performers	Delayering
Employee recognition	Recognize high performers	Apply only to top 5 percent
Equity related programs	Retain employees	"Uncertain"

Figure 2-1. Traditional programs to reward performance have become mere distribution systems for cash or are in conflict with change efforts.

ued for their contributions. These programs have become the tools by which managers reward their employees. Many of these reward systems were established with sincere performance-oriented objectives. However, for a variety of reasons, they have lost some of their desired characteristics or functions. Let's briefly review what they have become in today's organization. (See Figure 2-1.)

Base Pay

This is the stable, regular income that people receive for coming to work. It is sometimes called "show-up pay." Traditionally, this remuneration reflects different levels of responsibility and accountability as well as what the marketplace pays people with similar responsibilities or capabilities. The problem in many organizations today is that base pay has become a major fixed expense. When firms need to reduce costs, they cut head count in order to reduce payroll expenses. Furthermore, companies are seeking to minimize the base pay they provide in order to control costs. Having the highest pay level in the marketplace is no longer desirable. Hence, the current focus of base pay programs is to reduce the costs associated with human resources.

Merit Pay

Traditionally, this is the annual increase people receive that reflects their performance or rise in cost of living. Many organizations adjust pay increases to reflect the performance of each individual employee, with the idea that those who perform better receive higher pay increases than those who function at average or below average levels. The problem today is that the merit pay budget for many organizations is small—around 3 percent to 4 percent of payroll—and it is very difficult to give an individual an increase above 5 percent without denying pay increases to a large number of other people. Furthermore, the actual range of merit increases used tends to be so narrow—just 3.5 percent to 4.2 percent, that the differences are basically meaningless from the employees' standpoint. Finally, many of the gurus in the total quality management arena, like W. Edwards Deming, indicate that firms should not differentiate individual.performance with merit increases. However, people have grown to expect their annual pay increase. Hence, merit pay has lost much of its ability to reward individuals (if it ever had any to begin with).

Management Bonuses

These constitute the annual incentive pay program awarded to executives and managers. The dollars do not get added into their base pay, but are given in lumpsum payments. Many managers have grown to expect and live on their annual bonus. The payout is often determined by overall company financial performance and the achievement of individual objectives. In today's organization, however, these bonuses have become an expected part of the overall compensation program. If the results are not achieved, some bonuses are provided anyway because firms are afraid of losing their key talent. Furthermore, since bonuses are usually tied to individual performance and goals are seldom formally written or made public, these programs have become a discretionary reward in many firms. Hence, if the manager achieves what the executive wanted, the manager will expect the bonus award. Bonuses have become another entitlement program, one necessary in order to prevent unwanted turnover in the managerial ranks of the organization.

Promotions

This is the most common form of effective recognition. If a person excels in his or her job, the organization promotes the individual to bigger responsibilities and challenges. Men and women naturally seek to climb the ladder of success. In many firms, if people remain in their current role for more than three years, they are seen as being stuck and their potential is questioned. Traditional organizations have created levels just so that people can have a sense of progress in their careers. The problem today is that many firms are delayering their organizations, expanding the span of control, and reducing the opportunity for promotions. Furthermore, an increasing number of firms are reducing the number of job grades (i.e., broad-banding), further limiting the ability to differentiate individuals with promotions. Finally, while large numbers of baby boomers occupy management and senior technical levels, there are fewer chances for people to find higher-level jobs. Hence the opportunities for promotion in many organizations are declining, not increasing.

Employee Recognition

Programs to recognize individual top performers have gone in and out of favor in American businesses. Employee-of-the-month, key-contributor awards, and special-achiever programs abound as ways to recognize the contributions of individuals above and beyond traditional pay or promotion rewards. The problem is that these programs are often limited to so few of an organization's employees that they have little true impact on overall performance. If employees don't know what they have to do to be eligible for an award (because the selection criteria is vague and subjective), or if they feel they have little chance of winning an award, such programs will have little impact on general behavior. They are often effective only for the executive who wants to give them out and do nothing for the majority of employees who have to watch while a few receive lavish praises.

Equity-Related Programs

These reward programs are given to select employees, usually in managerial or highly technical roles, and include company stock or stock options. Frequently the selection criteria are vague. The amount of the equity made available is often discretionary. Restrictions are usually placed on the acquisition or sale of the stock. Finally, the value of the award is based on the performance of the firm in the eyes of investors. These programs are often intended to give employees the feeling of having a stake in the firm. They are also designed to retain employees (i.e., they loose the gain if they leave the company). But unless they are very large (to catch the attention of the shareholders and the media), such reward programs are more symbolic than real.

Conclusion

While conditions vary in different organizations, the compelling conclusion of this brief overview is obvious: Current reward programs no longer serve their original purpose. They have either become ineffective in achieving their desired impact or they have changed their focus and now have a mostly negative consequence on employees. (Each of these programs will be examined in greater detail in subsequent chapters of this book. We will explore how they usually operate and why they either do or do not impact behavior in desired ways. We will then examine how to redirect or reshape them to enhance their positive impact.)

Should Reward Systems Be Used?

Why should organizations be concerned with reward systems? If they have become so misdirected or ineffective, would not it be better just to ignore them or eliminate the emphasis on rewards? Should we not just let the intrinsic value of the work or the workplace itself provide the necessary rewards to employees, managers, and salespeople?

If the American culture were able to boast of a centuries old code of social conduct accepted by one and all across the land, then reward systems would not be necessary. Social conditioning and workplace procedures would guide behavior. Executives would just need to dictate desired actions and a compliant workforce would follow. However, we enjoy a culture of immense diversity and complexity. The entrepreneurial foundations of many of our organizations and the opportunity to receive rewards for one's achievements have long been cherished principles of American industry. We are a culture founded on individual effort, and we admire our heros. We honor the John Waynes and Amelia Earharts of our culture. We simply do not have a tradition of social control and conformity.

The six primary guidelines for management described in the last chapter (focus on customer needs; improve communication; build strong partnerships; keep only value-added activities; increase speed; continually seek improvements) require enhanced coordination within and across organizations. We face a conflict between traditions that value individual effort and pressures that call for increased collaboration. We have reward systems that honor the hierarchy, differentiate the individual, and seek to control costs. But utilizing team-oriented rewards will not necessarily be effective if individuals do not see such efforts as being in their self-interest. The foundation of this change, as stated earlier, is human behavior. We therefore need to develop conditions in which individuals *want* to take new actions. We can tell them, we can train them, but will this be sufficient to achieve lasting desired change?

There is a long-standing controversy in the behavioral sciences between those who believe that desired behaviors are best reinforced by the work itself (i.e., *intrinsic reinforcement*) and those who believe that rewards and recognition are a necessary condition to achieving desired behaviors (i.e., *extrinsic reinforcement*). Many of the intrinsic-reinforcement arguments have become popular in light of research indicating that rewards and punishments lower self-esteem, lower creativity, and are not effective in improving organizational performance. Citing numerous studies, those who favor intrinsic reinforcement insist that external rewards (like praise, money, or special awards) consistently produce negative results. According to this group, extrinsic reinforcements tend to:

- Reduce creativity and risk-taking because they encourage people to do only what is needed to get a reward, while regarding the work itself as distasteful. (Otherwise why would the organization pay extra money to have it done?)

- Create competition and reduce cooperation among people, especially when the rewards are scarce (as in merit-pay programs or other winner-take-all incentive or recognition programs)

- Create only temporary compliance and ultimately leave people feeling they are being punished when a reward is taken away or not given.

Those who support this view find the carrot-and-stick or the reward-and-punishment approach to management distasteful and ultimately dehumanizing. They often cite research studies showing that desired behaviors decrease when certain rewards are removed.[1] Such studies demonstrate that when a reward is associated with a particular task, people tend to focus on it to the detriment of other tasks. Ultimately this group is against rewards, they say, because of fundamental concerns about manipulation, social engineering, and the destruction of the human spirit.

Their alternative to providing rewards is to make the work process inherently fulfilling. They advise companies to design jobs and workplace conditions so that people will receive value from the work itself and place minimal or no emphasis on external recognition. According to their models, the workplace should give individuals room for self-determination and provide them with personal fulfillment. If people do not perform as expected, they argue, workplace systems should be examined to see whether the proper procedures are in place. Systems, not people, are the problem, they maintain. (This argument has the added appeal of eliminating personal blame and fault-finding). Proponents of the work process seldom see the value of providing any visible, personalized, or tangible forms of recognition for job performance.

In contrast, those who support recognition-and-rewards argue that behavior is a function of its consequences, whether the source is internal or external to the individual, positive or negative. Behavior will continue only if the external rewards confirm its value or if the behavior becomes naturally fulfilling to the individual (i.e., intrinsic). Their research studies indicate that reinforcement does in fact influence behavior, the main principle being that positive reinforcement is the only true consequence that achieves and sustains desired behaviors.[2] (The reward systems that will be discussed in this book are founded on the principles of positive reinforcement as they are applied in the workplace. Chapter 3 will discuss related research concepts in more detail).

The controversy between those for and against reward systems is not about whether reinforcement impacts behavior; there is common agreement that it does. Both agree that behavior is influenced by internal and external consequences, although they differ about the degree of impact. The issue seems to be how one achieves the optimal behaviors.

Let's examine how personal fulfillment would be achieved in the workplace. If the requirements for work are not inherently fulfilling to the individuals, the organization has a choice: either change the work or change the people. If the tasks themselves cannot be fulfilling (certain mining, forging, assembling, packing, distributing, billing, collecting, and servicing activities come to mind), the organization needs to employ people who will find this work meaningful. If this cannot be achieved, the organization is left without answers.

In contrast, by using external rewards, including team celebrations, positive reinforcement practices, special awards, and compensation, the organization can create conditions in which people associate the work they do with being valued. Their work then becomes paired with positive feelings and thereby becomes intrinsically fulfilling. This means that intrinsic motivation can be created through the selective, precise, and effective use of external rewards. We can create workplace conditions in which people are valued for work that needs to be done. The ultimate goal is to achieve a balance between intrinsic and extrinsic reinforcement. People will then take the initiative to do necessary tasks because they *want* to.

Intrinsic Versus Extrinsic Reward Strategies

To explore the process advocates' viewpoint more fully, we should examine their three primary concerns about rewards and determine if there is merit to their arguments.

Do Rewards Work?

First, rewards do gain the attention of most people, especially if the rewards are meaningful, timely, and associated with specific performance. Those opposed to rewards argue that laboratory research has shown that people limit other actions in order to achieve a specific goal associated with a reward. This research is more a demonstration that rewards act to stimulate desired behaviors than evidence that they drive out creativity. It shows that rewards encourage people to focus on what is being reinforced and not on extraneous activities. In fact, creativity is a more complex process than just the provision of rewards for certain behaviors. Behavioral research shows that creativity is stimulated by a dynamic pattern of frustrations and successes.[3] Their argument is an oversimplification of an array of contingencies. Furthermore, behavioral research indicates that other behaviors return once the experimental conditions cease.[4]

Do Rewards Discourage Collaboration?

The second argument centers around the loss of cooperation by those participating in incentive programs. Those opposed to rewards cite studies on the failure of current merit-based pay systems or executive compensation plans to encourage collaboration. They say that when rewards are limited to a fixed pool or when only a small number of participants is eligible, collaboration is discouraged. This is a reflection of current flaws in reward programs. As stated earlier, many such programs have become too restrictive or too discretionary. The intrinsic and extrinsic behavioral scientists, as well as most line managers and compensation professionals, agree that this is a major problem in today's current reward systems. However, the process advocates have concluded that, because of these flaws, we should eliminate all reward programs.

This is a "guilt by association" argument. A far better strategy would be to examine why these programs do not work, find the root causes of the conditions, and fix the problems. If we eliminate the use of rewards, we may be inflicting a solution that is worse than the problem. We need, then, to explore alternative solutions based on sound, established behavioral principles.

Do Rewards Punish the Performer

The final argument postulates that rewards create only temporary compliance and that, once they are gone, people feel punished. This argument holds that rewards and punishments are actually part of the same process—an attempt to dehumanize the workplace. It is an argument with both behavioral research and philosophical components.

From a behavioral standpoint their citations do not provide a complete review of the scientific findings. People engage in certain behaviors when rewards are contingent on their success. Rewards that are noncontingent—handed out merely for participating in a task—tend not to yield high performance nor interest in the activity once the rewards cease. This is true of any entitlement-based compensation program, like cost-of-living increases, annual bonuses, etc. If and when these rewards are removed, people do feel punished and their interest in the task goes away. However, behavioral research also indicates that if people receive rewards contingent on their *improving* their *performance,* their interest in the activity actually increases and the rewards reinforce this process.[5] People respond well when rewards are contingent on performance and don't lose interest in an activity if they do not always achieve the desired levels. (It may be hard for them to understand, however, why rewards are not currently being given if they were given unconditionally in the past). Hence, in order to sustain interest and full efforts, rewards need to be contingent on achieving improved performance.

From a philosophical viewpoint, the advocates of process reinforcement are concerned about manipulation, social engineering, and workplace control. When a manager uses the power of reinforcement as an instrument of manipulation—"Do this. Now do that."—people experience the process as aversive. People naturally react negatively when they are being treated in an exploitative and control-oriented manner. Behavioral research has further shown that when aversive rewards are removed, performance declines rapidly. But rewards given in this manner are not considered a positive element by performers. Indeed, this manipulative use of rewards is characteristic of the worst form of command-and-control management practices.

I both understand and support this view. However, I believe that when rewards are given out of a sincere desire to share the fruits of success, to encourage participation in a market-competitive organization, and to bring the workforce into the process as partners, a desirable workplace environment is created. This is the essence of collaboration between the organization and its workforce and a demonstration of the sincerity of management intentions. However, if we remove all reward systems simply because some organizations use them in a manipulative manner, we are left with only superficial symbols of true partnership in organizations. If the organization is highly successful and only the shareholders share in the benefits, the workforce is being exploited. If all members and stakeholders of an organization can share in its success, we create a common basis of interest and achievement. Then the process of reengineering work, decreasing low value-added activities, and increasing the satisfaction of customers can be accomplished with faith that the outcomes of these efforts will benefit everyone. The ultimate objective is to create a workplace environment that is filled with both natural work reinforcers (intrinsic) and external rewards and recognition, all directed to those behaviors necessary to achieve results that make a difference.

What Are the Alternatives?

So far, we have examined how current reward systems have become ineffective in driving desired behavioral change. We have explored the reasons why it is important to develop systems in a manner that reinforces desired behaviors. But what alternatives does the organization have to address this situation?

1. *Ignore the reward systems.* Many of the concerns about reward systems expressed by organizational change gurus are about current practices. They rightfully identify the way in which these systems cause people to "suboptimize" team achievements in order to protect personal gain. This was illustrated directly in the story of George and Martha at the beginning of this book. Without any guidelines about what to do differently, their conclusion is understandable: eliminate any relationship between pay and performance or what people do. This would involve:

- Minimizing the pay differentials between individuals
- Eliminating all incentive pay
- Recognizing only total group achievements
- Eliminating performance appraisals and merit pay

One strategy for change would be to focus on the structure of work, eliminate unnecessary levels of control and management, hire only the best people, communicate results, and invest heavily in training the workforce. The differentials and contingencies in reward systems would be minimized and pay systems would be regarded purely as an infrastructure to the organization.

This alternative is the easiest to implement, but it may result in unintended consequences. While such efforts can initiate much-needed change, they do not address the basic personal issue of "What's in it for me?" Why should employees do as the organization commands? Is the threat of losing one's job the only compelling reason to conform?

2. *Make modest incremental improvements.* This strategy simply means implementing a program, like a team incentive plan or a special recognition program, or making modifications to existing programs, like expanding salary ranges (e.g., broad-banding). This is a programmatic approach to change and involves investments related to the scope of the desired program. These change efforts can serve limited purposes but often expose issues in related systems. The process can begin to look like a never-ending series of "fixes" to existing reward programs and systems. Furthermore, such change efforts address the systems within the organization but often do little to change the practices or capabilities of managers to utilize these programs. The emphasis is often on communication about the program, not on changing the fundamental elements that influence human behavior. This is the strat-

egy most preferred by executives because they believe that if the program is developed and implemented well, the "presenting" problem will be solved. The solution, they believe, will come quickly with limited real investment or commitment to personal change.

3. *Develop and implement a behavioral framework for rewards.* This strategy involves rethinking the reward systems—both formal and informal—that exist within the organization. The process entails viewing reward systems as supporters, if not drivers, of change and modifying the concept that pay programs are just an infrastructure to the organization. It goes beyond making sure that people are getting paid and includes understanding the messages that are being sent and the behaviors that are being reinforced. Furthermore, this approach involves establishing a strategy for building and integrating a set of systems, programs, and practices that reinforces the behaviors necessary for the implementation of the firm's goals.

The task is a challenging but necessary complement to the new directions undertaken by the firm to maintain survival or continued prosperity. The process cannot be acquired from another company; it needs to be unique and designed to fit a particular situation. Nor can the process be accomplished in a short time period, although specific programs can be implemented quickly as long as they are in concert with an overall game plan. In this way, change efforts can achieve early wins and establish a continuous developmental process into the fabric of the organization.

What the Reward Systems Should Do

If the current reward systems do not positively impact desired behaviors and the organization chooses to implement a strategy for change, what should new reward programs do? Throughout this book several recurring themes define the operating principles necessary for effective reward systems. We will examine each of the themes outlined below in the context of specific applications and design guidelines. (See Figure 2-2.)

---

1. Reward systems need to have a positive impact on behavior
2. Reward systems need to focus efforts on serving the customer.
3. Reward systems need to enhance collaboration within the workplace.

Figure 2-2. Critical requirements of the new reward systems.

1. *Reward systems need to have a positive impact on behavior.*   To accomplish this, we have learned that rewards need to be:
   - Contingent on achieving desired performance levels rather than on merely doing certain tasks
   - Meaningful and valuable to the individual
   - Based on objective and attainable goals
   - Open to all, and not based on a competitive struggle within the workplace
   - Balanced between conditions in the workplace (extrinsic) and fulfillment of individual needs and wants (intrinsic)

2. *Reward systems need to focus efforts on serving the customer.*   In the new, successful organizational model the customer, not the hierarchy, will be the primary focus for all activities. Reward systems need to support and drive this process throughout the organization. This will be reflected in the performance measures as well as in the determinants for payouts. Furthermore, the employee of the organization will be viewed as the customer for reward programs based on serving their needs. Identifying the customer and understanding the customer's needs will become an essential element of the reward systems of the future.

3. *Reward systems need to enhance collaboration within the workplace.* Competitive struggles need to be focused on acquiring and retaining new customers, not on the methods by which the organization works. This can be accomplished by creating a stake in the business for workers and providing opportunities for people to earn and feel part of the solution. Furthermore, we cannot just reward team performance; we need to reinforce individual actions that lead to team results. It is through the combination—the blending of reward and recognition into a process of reinforcement—that the desired results will be achieved.

   In short, we are seeking to use reward systems to support, if not lead, the process of change within the organization by creating conditions in which employees themselves take the initiative to achieve the results needed by today's organizations.

The Organization of This Book

Essentially, this book is intended as a resource for the reader. It does not need to be read from beginning to end, but rather should be used as a source for examining current practices and developing new approaches. Overall, it is organized as follows:

- *Chapters One and Two* summarize the thinking and concepts by which many organizations are reformulating their core business strategies.

- *Chapter Three* discusses the core behavioral science principles necessary in developing an effective system of rewards and outlines the five criteria for an effective reward system.

- *Chapter Four* shows how new reward systems need to be based on a strong strategy linking the actions of people within an organization to the firm's core requirements for success. The chapter shows how to develop such a strategy, assess current conditions, and give new direction to the primary reward systems within the firm.

- *Chapters Five through Nine* explore specific reward programs within the organization, examining everything from base pay systems to special recognition to performance management. These chapters explore why these systems no longer serve their intended function and how they can be reshaped into an influential force within the organization.

- *Chapter Ten* focuses on measures of performance as an essential element in any behavioral reinforcement system. The chapter describes how to develop performance measures so that efforts can be focused on serving the customer and reinforcing collaboration.

- *Chapter Eleven* concentrates on what the firm needs to do to understand change, plan and address resistance, and implement a strategy that will yield the highest level of performance in the shortest time possible.

- *Chapters Twelve through Fourteen* are the application chapters. Chapter Twelve examines a comprehensive case study that makes full use of the primary elements of rewards. Chapter Thirteen examines reward systems as they pertain to emerging, growing businesses. Chapter Fourteen examines the reward systems necessary to help a large organization implement change.

- *Chapter Fifteen* recaps the primary learning points presented and examines the factors necessary to make the change process succeed. It presents not a closure, but a call to action.

Understanding Human Systems

The reader will not be presented with a simple answer or single course of action. The real challenges facing today's organization do not lend themselves to easy, single solutions. Rather, the reader will be guided through a set of principles, guidelines, ideas, and applications that hopefully will spur ideas appropriate to particular circumstances. As

Peter Senge, director of the systems thinking and organizational learning program at the MIT Sloan School of Management, states in *The Fifth Discipline*, "It is poorly designed systems, not incompetent or unmotivated individuals, that cause most organizational problems."[6]

This discussion, then, challenges us to understand the systems that drive human behavior as a process within an organization. To reengineer only on the content of work is to ignore the systems that have the greatest impact on human, and ultimately on organizational performance. This book seeks to offer useful insights into these systems and to provide the foundation for implementing much-needed change.

References

1. Perhaps the most cited reference for these research studies is in Deci, E. L. and R. M. Ryan, *Intrinsic Motivation and Self-Determination in Human Behavior*. New York: Plemum Press, 1985.

2. Daniels, A., *Bringing The Best Out of People: How to Apply the Astonishing Power of Positive Reinforcement*. New York: McGraw-Hill, 1993.

3. Epstein, R. "Bringing Cognitive and Creativity into the Behavioral Laboratory," *Approaches to Cognition: Contrasts and Controversies*, T. J. Knapp and L. Robertson, editors, pp. 91–109, Hillsdale, N.J.: Erlbaum Publishers, 1986; and Koestler, A., *The Art of Creation*, New York: Macmillan, 1964.

4. Dickinson, A. M., "The Detrimental Effects of Extrinsic Reinforcement on 'Intrinsic Motivation'," *The Behavioral Analyst*. Spring, Vol. 12, No. 1, 1989, pp. 1-15.

5. Bandura, A., *Social Foundations of Thought and Action*. Englewood Cliffs, N.J.: Prentice-Hall, 1987.

6. Senge, P., *The Fifth Discipline: The Art and Practice of the Learning Organization*. New York: Doubleday, 1990.

3

The Fundamentals of Reward Systems

*Be careful what you reinforce—You will surely
get more of it*
—DR. AUBREY DANIELS

People used to believe that human behavior was a function of the good and evil spirits within us. Today we know that certain behaviors can be significantly shaped by external factors. Managers have tried many ways to get people to do things; some have been successful and others have not. To separate superstition from reality, fad from fact, we need to understand the science of human behavior. Only then can we understand how best to encourage the workplace behaviors that make for efficient, successful companies and proud, productive staff.

In previous chapters, I outlined the changing requirements for organizations facing today's challenges. Not adapting to new conditions is to risk possible extinction or certain decline. Despite this threat, not all challenges are the same for every industry or every company in a given industry. There is no single answer out there, and an organization's attempts to emulate other companies may result in its misjudging what it needs to do to be successful. However, there is one element that is fundamental to all pressures for change: *people need to do some things differently.*

In this chapter we will focus on understanding the fundamental principles of reward systems and examine what makes them effective in reinforcing desired behaviors. In later chapters we will show how to apply these principles to several selected compensation and recognition programs and to various organizational situations. In a sense we will examine the fundamental "operating system" which determines the efficiency and success of the "application programs" like base pay, special recognition, incentives, etc. Our task will be to go beneath the results of reward systems and fully examine the process that makes them fail or succeed. The central question is not what people are rewarded but how.

The Roots of Human Behavior

Human behavior lies at the heart of any change process we are seeking within an organization. Executives and managers who try to bring about organizational change are really calling for a change in the way people do things. What is needed is a foundation for examining, developing, and managing a new paradigm of rewards based on human behavior. Strong and enduring behavioral change will not occur until we are able to provide people with reasons for making the change, for doing things differently from the way they've always done them. Programs attempting to bring about change that are not based on an understanding of the principles that drive human behavior are seriously at risk. If they are successful, you never know why; if they are not, you never know why. Hence, you may needlessly repeat flawed programs or fail to learn from programs with potential.

Imagine for a moment that a ship from outer space is hovering over your place of work. Then imagine that it "freezes" all your employees like statues. Machines continue to run, but people do not. The telephone rings, but no one answers. Computer systems still communicate, but no one listens. How long will it be before your business is affected negatively? Or imagine a more realistic situation. A major snowstorm hits your town and all roads are closed for five days. No one is able to come to work. How long will it be before your business is affected negatively?

Robert Herrnstein, the Edgar Pierce professor at Harvard University, says that the business of business is behavior. Gary Hamel of the London Business School writes that the key to the global conquests by Japanese firms in the 1970s and 1980s was their ability to create an organizational environment that merged the knowledge, skills, and abilities of their workforce with the needs of their customers. Organizations able to utilize systems and practices that maximize human performance are at a significant competitive advantage.

At the core of this change process is behavioral change. To define our key term, *behavior* is something somebody does or says. Traditional thinking in the world of total quality management holds that people are not the problem in quality; all we need to do is focus on the work process and people will respond appropriately. Many organizations attempt to implement self-managed work teams by supplying training. The expectation is that if we simply "get out of the way," people will become productive and teams will excel. When people don't respond as we expect, we blame it on management or problems in our work systems. We become frustrated when people don't respond as required. Organizations try more training, give more speeches, restructure jobs, continue downsizing, or implement information systems that will monitor performance. But, as the chief executive of a large technology company said to a group of senior managers after their strategic planning retreat, "For us to implement this strategy, we need to either change the people or change the people!"

By understanding what *drives* human behavior, we can create the conditions necessary to encourage *desired* behaviors. These principles can be employed as systems and practices focused on customers, innovation, and collaboration. Our challenge will be to create those conditions that encourage people to collaborate because they *want* to, not because they *have* to. The task will be to understand the forces that drive human behavior and to apply these principles to the redesign or better management of the organization's reward systems—the resources and processes we use to recognize, encourage, and compensate individuals.

The advantage of this approach is that it works. The 1992 report by the American Compensation Association on the effectiveness of incentive compensation plans reported that the plans with the highest return on investment were those viewed as a process to *lead* organizational change, rather than just ensure that people were paid fairly. This confirms the importance of viewing reward systems as instruments of change rather than merely as distribution systems for compensation dollars.

Using Science to Understand Behavior

To fully understand the principles of effective reward systems, we need to base our work on sound research evidence. This leads us to the primary field of science that addresses behavior: Applied Behavior Analysis (ABA). The roots of ABA lie in the research of Ivan P. Pavlov, John B. Watson, and B. F. Skinner. The work of Dr. Aubrey Daniels[1] has translated some of their scientific concepts into practical applica-

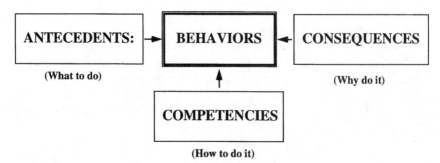

Figure 3-1. The forces that drive human behavior.

tions, tools, and skills that can be implemented by the average supervisor, manager, or executive. ABA research helps us understand the forces that drive human behavior and permits us to develop core concepts of reward systems in a new and powerful way.

Fundamentally, there are three major elements that drive human behavior and shape the habits we possess: antecedents, competencies, and consequences. (See Figure 3-1.)

Antecedents are those things that prompt us to take an action. In the business world these include policies, goals, directives, announcements, training programs, procedures, vision statements, organizational structures, accountabilities, and so forth. They are very important because they tell each person what to do in his or her job. They encourage certain actions—hopefully the ones you want taken. Antecedents are intended to get people to start doing something by providing them with reasons, plans, skills, or information to do it. They are directed at encouraging the desired actions. If they are effective, they will get a behavior started. (See Figure 3-2.) However, whether or not people continue with it depends on what happens when they do it.

The second element is made up of the *competencies*—the knowledge, skills, and abilities that enable people to perform certain tasks. These attributes may be genetic traits, such as speed, dexterity, or strength characteristics. Competencies are not behaviors; they are the abilities that enable a behavior to occur. Further, traditional ABA science does not include competencies in its research, but views them as a function of antecedents and consequences. For purposes of understanding behavior in the context of reward systems, it is important to view competencies as a factor for examining behaviors in the workplace. But technically speaking, most knowledge- or skill-based competencies come from this history of antecedents and consequences of the individual. The experiences and responses each of us has encountered have shaped certain of our abilities. These are the habits and skills

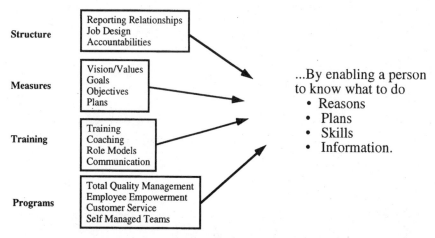

Figure 3-2. Antecedents get a behavior started. Whether it is sustained depends upon what happens to the person when they do it.

ANTECEDENTS are key to building success ...

Structure	Reporting Relationships Job Design Accountabilities
Measures	Vision/Values Goals Objectives Plans
Training	Training Coaching Role Models Communication
Programs	Total Quality Management Employee Empowerment Customer Service Self Managed Teams

...By enabling a person to know what to do
 • Reasons
 • Plans
 • Skills
 • Information.

COMPETENCIES

**The set of learned knowledge and skills necessary
to perform a given function or task.**

 • **Developed over time**

 • **A product of good antecedents and positive consequences**

 • **The focus for most selection and training strategies**

Figure 3-3. Competencies enable the person to do the task. Whether it is sustained depends upon what happens to the person when they do it.

each individual brings to the workplace. They can change and develop over time, depending on other forces that impact human performance. (See Figure 3-3.)

The third element is *consequences.* Consequences are those things that happen to the person when certain actions or behaviors are performed. They always occur after a behavior. They may be positive or

CONSEQUENCES

- Are **what happens to the person** when they perform a certain action,

- Occur after every action, **whether or not** planned or intended,

- **Provide the reason** for repeating (or not repeating) a specific behavior **again.**

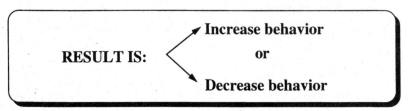

RESULT IS: → **Increase behavior**
or
↘ **Decrease behavior**

Figure 3-4. Consequences drive human behavior.

negative and, depending on their impact, will determine whether a person will repeat an activity.

To provide a simple illustration, let's examine an everyday activity. What is the speed limit on a major U.S. highway? Answer: 55 or 65 mph. How fast do people drive? Answer: 65 or 75 mph! What do you do when you approach a signal intersection and the light is red? Answer: Stop. Both situations have clear antecedents: posted speed limit signs and a signal light. One knows how to operate the car and what the sign means. Why is one obeyed and the other ignored? Answer: The consequences. There are potentially more serious consequences (e.g., an accident) to running a red light than to exceeding the speed limit. Conclusion: Consequences drive human behavior. (See Figure 3-4.)

When we apply this framework to the desire to increase teamwork, antecedents, competencies, and consequences can be understood more fully. Let's start with a group of people being trained in how to conduct a meeting. If the training is well conducted, the team members will learn a great deal and most likely want to apply their new knowledge in their first meeting back on the job. If the supervisor (who probably did not participate in the original training) controls the agenda, monopolizes the discussion, answers the questions, and directs the conversations (as supervisors used to be *expected* to do), the team members will quickly learn that the consequences of their training are negative. Further, they will feel that the training has been a total waste of time and money. Management's credibility will drop another notch. All the previous training experienced by the team members may be wiped out in one brief encounter because the employees are not reinforced for their actions.

If, on the other hand, positive consequences are experienced, the participants will feel different. What if the supervisor provides the space and other resources for the meeting, assists the group in defining its agenda, and helps them establish roles for the meeting (e.g., notetaker, timekeeper, etc.)? The team will learn a different lesson. If the meeting is successful and the team members feel they are able to develop a good action plan, the consequences they experience will be positive. If the supervisor takes an interest in what the team has done and helps them gain approval for what they want, their teamwork will be further reinforced. If the team members are then able to make major improvements in their work areas as a result of their team work, the positive lessons will be still further reinforced. In contrast, if their ideas are ignored, rebuffed, or assigned to others outside their area, the team members will quickly learn that teamwork is just another fad of management.

The antecedent–competencies–consequences dynamic applies to the supervisor as well. If you want a supervisor to manage teams, he or she first needs to know exactly what needs to be done differently. Just saying "You need to empower your people" is not specific enough for most supervisors. A good antecedent is needed to start a new behavior. This might include guidelines for coaching a team, a list of "ways you can be helpful" from the team, or a good role model for managing teams. (Note that all these are antecedents). But, if the results the supervisor is ultimately held accountable for (i.e., rewarded or punished for) remain unchanged, there will be no incentive for him or her to do anything different. Only when the teams produce better results and the supervisor is rewarded for his or her management of them will he or she change, because all behaviors are a function of their consequences. Antecedents like training or management directives may get certain behaviors started, but the consequences experienced by the performers will always determine whether the behaviors increase or decrease, continue or cease.

If the performers experience mainly negative consequences for doing something, they will do only enough to get by or merely present the appearance of operating as a team. By *appearing* to conform to policy, they will escape punishment and/or minimize any threat to themselves. The result will be mere window dressing rather than real substantive change. Further, if positive consequences are not sustained over time, the habits you are seeking from the supervisors and employees will not take hold. Hence, there will be no sustained return on investment.

When organizations attempt change, the traditional pattern is to address the first two drivers: antecedents and competencies. They conduct programs to tell employees about the importance of changing certain things and what the company must do to survive and prosper. They conduct training sessions on quality, customers, feedback, teamwork, problem solving, decision making, etc. But in fact, approximately 80 percent of the effort is spent on antecedents and competency development; consequences are viewed as difficult to manage, so only 20 percent of the effort is applied in that area. One can understand this process when one realizes that antecedents and competencies may achieve an initial increase in the desired activity. Every good antecedent should. But whether the effort will ultimately be sustained and grow in importance will depend on the consequences.

When organizations grow larger, the customer's direct impact tends to fade. Employees focus less and less on customer needs and more and more on pleasing their supervisor, who uses positive or negative consequences to achieve compliance and control. They look to their supervisor for recognition, attention, and rewards because their supervisor exercises immediate control over the consequences of their work. The end result is that the customer—and then the company—suffers.

The Four Types of Consequences

Understanding how consequences impact behavior positions us to redesign and manage reward systems in ways that are fundamentally different from the command-and-control method. There are more than just positive and negative consequences, and they impact behavior in predictable ways. In fact, there are four basic types of consequences. Two types of consequences work to encourage behaviors, the other two, to discourage them. (See Figure 3-5.)

Positive reinforcement (R+) occurs when people receive something of value for what they have accomplished. Outward examples of R+ can include letters of praise or appreciation from an executive, team celebrations, special notices, promotions, access to executives, spot awards, or a simple "thank you." Positive reinforcement can be limited to such external, or extrinsic, rewards. But it can also take the form of inner, or intrinsic, rewards. Intrinsic positive reinforcement occurs when the conditions of performance enable people to feel pleased or proud of what they have accomplished. Positive reinforcement is the only consequence that encourages people to take actions because they *want* to. They want to because they get something of value (internally or externally) for doing it.

The second consequence that increases behavior is *negative reinforcement* (R−). Negative reinforcement comes into play when a person

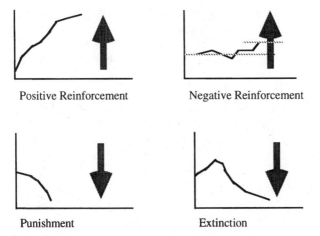

Positive Reinforcement   Negative Reinforcement

Punishment   Extinction

Figure 3-5. How the four forms of consequences affect behavior.

does something only to avoid something unpleasant—to prevent an adverse consequence. The unspoken but implied possibility of unpleasant consequences is probably the most widely used form of negative reinforcement used in business today.

If a manager wants a performer to turn in certain reports on time, he or she may use a message that implies "do this, or else." The employee responds according to the manager's wishes, and the report is turned in on time. Another example of negative reinforcement might include a supervisor's writing a complimentary performance appraisal in order to avoid dealing with the anger or conflict of one of his or her employees. Still another example might be a manufacturing plant working many hours of overtime in order to make its quarterly shipment targets. In each case, an action is taken to avoid something undesirable.

Two other consequences result in discouraging certain behaviors. The first is *punishment.* When people are punished, they receive undesirable attention for something they have done or failed to do. Punishment can take the form of a verbal reprimand, a warning, or actually firing an employee who has violated some code or standard. Punishment can also take more subtle forms, like sarcasm, belittling the employee in public, or assigning him or her to undesirable duties. When punishment is effective, the person usually stops doing whatever it was that caused it. Punishment can be used appropriately when an employee is doing something that is either unsafe or against company policies. It can also be used to put teeth into a policy. Sometimes, people will not believe a threat of negative consequences unless the threat is backed up from time to time with appropriate action.

The final consequence that reduces a behavior is called *extinction.*

Extinction occurs when people do not receive something they were expecting from an action they have taken. When an employee gets no reinforcement for taking certain actions, he or she is less likely to continue that behavior. Extinction usually occurs when a behavior that has been reinforced in the past begins to be ignored. One example would be when an employee puts considerable effort into a special project or research study, only to find that his or her manager is taking little or no interest in the work. Another example would be when a salesperson expends considerable effort and overcomes major competitive pressures to close a deal, only to find that management is too busy with other matters to notice. Finally, when companies remove management layers, or opportunities for promotion, employees who sought career progressions become discouraged. The behavior may not decline immediately. In fact, it may increase for a period. Eventually though, the employee, no longer seeing any benefit in a particular action, will alter his or her actions. Extinction occurs when we see the enthusiasm and excitement of a new employee gradually dissipate as he or she conforms to the same patterns of behavior as all the other employees. (See Figure 3-6.)

In the work environment all four consequences exist in a complex array of forces. The actions of people in all kinds of roles and functions provide consequences that impact on others. In fact, all the behaviors in organizations are perfectly aligned to the pattern of their existing consequences. People are taking actions today because of the consequences they expect to receive. However, only one consequence can truly capture the optimal performance of employees: positive reinforcement. It is the only one that offers a positive pull to performance

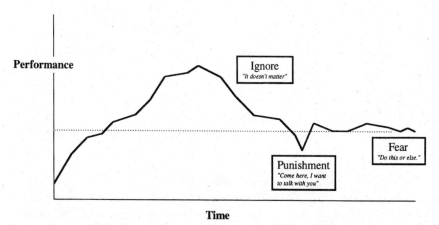

Figure 3-6. Most of the consequences in organizations today result in people doing "just enough to get by" or feeling "I can't work any harder."

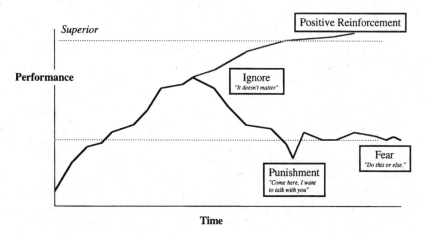

Figure 3-7. Systematic reinforcement provides the "pull" necessary to achieve superior performance.

and encourages people to take desired actions because they will receive something of value for doing so. The other three consequences lead the organization to suboptimal performance. (See Figure 3-7.)

The Story of the New Employee

To illustrate the impact of consequences, let's explore the experiences of a new employee. Let's say Jim has just been hired by your company for an important technical job. After he has completed all the necessary orientation activities, filled in the forms, and received all the company literature, he goes to see his new supervisor, Debby. Debby welcomes Jim to the work team and takes him for a tour of the work area, introducing him to different people along the way. Then Debby sits down with Jim to discuss his responsibilities and his job activities. She may assign a more senior person to work with him to help him learn the ways things are done. She probably also gives Jim an assignment, provides him with an overview of how the work is to be performed, and lets him try it. If he has problems with it, she is very responsive. She reviews his progress, giving him encouraging compliments about his work. If she discovers a problem, she tactfully points out the error and shows him how to do it right. When he masters one task, she gives him a bigger task.

This process of ever-increasing tasks and greater and greater freedom is part of the learning process in most jobs. Jim learns what to do through periodic reviews, and he probably feels good about the work he is doing. His coworkers support him and give him praise when he performs an important task correctly. Debby does the same. The result of this process is that Jim learns the job well, feels good about the workplace, and steadily improves his performance.

If Jim really learns fast and becomes a star performer, he is likely to experience certain other consequences. First, his coworkers may not be so thrilled about how he is advancing past them. They may make subtle comments to him about working so hard or continually seeking to please the boss. They may question his motives or enjoy watching him struggle with a problem they know how to solve. His supervisor may occasionally notice Jim, but to her, he has progressed so well that she can pursue other problems in the department. Jim experiences "extinction" from the supervisor; he may also experience extinction or punishment from his coworkers. His performance gradually levels off and may actually decline to the same level as that of his coworkers.

If Jim's performance continues to decline, it may reach a point where he becomes a problem employee. He may make important errors, miss deadlines, or start complaining about the workplace to others. He may feel "burned out" and believe that his efforts are neither recognized nor appreciated. At some point, his supervisor may decide to have a disciplinary discussion with him, during which he will probably feel punished. His performance may improve at that point, at least to a level above that at which he received his performance discussion.

But Jim's performance will then exist in an equilibrium. While there will be little or no positive reinforcement to achieve higher-than-normal performance, there will be a certain amount of fear to keep him from slipping behind. And so his employment status will continue, because Jim is an average worker responding normally to a common situation.

If we simply understand what was happening *in his early days of employment*, we may find some important general insights for managing people. In his early days with the firm he received steady, positive reinforcement from his peers and his supervisor. When he made mistakes, they were treated as opportunities to learn and improve. When he tried new things, he saw the benefits. He felt proud of his work, and others were proud of him as well. His working days were filled with positive consequences. If this could only continue, imagine how high Jim's performance could go.

Consequences in the Workplace

Punishment convinces a person not to take certain actions. It may be administered by a supervisor or by fellow employees (as in the case when a high achiever receives peer pressure to reduce performance so not to make the other employees look bad). The ultimate punishment for poor performance was reported in the *Los Angeles Times* on October 17, 1989, when a headline read: 18 CHINESE MANAGERS EXECUTED FOR SHODDY QUALITY.

In the United States we are more subtle. We tend to use sarcasm, ridicule, and talking down to people as a means of punishing them for behaviors we do not like. But these actions tend to encourage compliant or competitive responses rather than collaborative ones. Collaboration can only be achieved when positive reinforcement is used, either directly or in combination with the punishment/extinction of undesirable, noncollaborative behaviors. The reason is that people cannot be *forced* to communicate or cooperate fully with others. We can only create conditions in which people find it in their self-interest to collaborate.

Negative reinforcement is also pervasive. In fact, most managers use negative reinforcement when they set deadlines, stretch goals, or issue commands. The message is simply: "Do this, or else." Managers tend to use this method with great frequency because they are reinforced for using it. When managers need something done they simply tell their employees to do it. The employees know that if they *don't* do it, they may experience some reprisal. Knowing this, they do as they are told, which simply reinforces the manager's "do this or else" approach. Naturally, when a similar need arises, such managers repeat that pattern of behavior. Experience has taught them that threats of punishment work effectively to get people to do what they want (i.e., they received positive reinforcement).

Habits are created by a history of similar consequences associated with similar actions. They continue until the consequences change. Punishment and negative reinforcement become habitual tools of management, therefore, because they yield results quickly and predictably.

For their part, employees (and other managers) have learned some equally effective coping strategies. They know how to negotiate so that their goals appear difficult to achieve, even when they are not. They learn to only just meet deadlines, to produce goods that only just meet standards. Because they seldom get rewards for achieving results higher or sooner than expected, they function in a work environment ruled by the ethos of "just enough to get by" and "nothing in it for me to do more." This produces suboptimal performance. Only positive reinforcement provides the reasons for performers to focus on doing their very best. (See Figure 3-8.)

Dr. W. Edwards Deming, the first guru of the total quality movement, advised executives to "drive fear out of the workplace."[2] He meant that we should eliminate negative reinforcement from the workplace because of what it produces: fearful compliance. However,

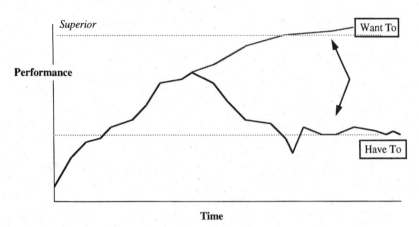

Figure 3-8. Positive reinforcement creates superior performance by motivating "discretionary effort" and creating a win/win outcome (collaboration).

if we only reduce negative reinforcement, extinction will be the primary consequence in operation, and when extinction occurs, performance declines. Consequently, negative reinforcement needs to be *replaced* by positive reinforcement in order to encourage desired behaviors and achieve superior performance. The difference lies in focused, discretionary effort. People begin to excel in their tasks because they want to. The positive reinforcement they receive makes them feel valued and appreciated for their contributions.

Reward systems and practices provide positive reinforcement with great impact if used effectively. But what types of positive reinforcement are really effective in encouraging desired behaviors? Dr. Aubrey Daniels has identified five elements[3] essential to effective positive reinforcement. Whatever form it actually takes, he points out, any consequence must be:

1. *Specific* Participants need to know exactly what they did well in order for the consequence to have the desired impact. Performance measurement and feedback are essential in this connection, enabling the reinforcement to be keyed to measurable before-and-after data.

2. *Personalized* The consequence needs to be meaningful to the individual. There are many types of reinforcers; if they are to be effective they need to reflect the needs, wants, and expectations of the participants. The key objective is that the people involved feel valued for their achievements in terms that have real meaning for them.

3. *Contingent* Reinforcers need to be *earned*. Participating individuals must achieve some action or result in order for them to draw the

correct connection between action and reinforcement. And, of course, in order for the reinforcer to be effective, the performance level must be achievable.

4. *Sincere*   The consequence needs to be honest, deserved, and "from the heart." Employees can easily see through responses that are scheduled, calculated, and/or manipulative. When reinforcement is delivered sincerely, it can have a very powerful impact on both the receiver and provider.

5. *Immediate*   The consequence should be given to participants either during the new behavior or as soon after their achievement or new behavior as possible. This timeliness enables the performer to draw the connection between what he or she did and what was received.

Using Multiple Reinforcers

All five of these criteria must be met if a reinforcer is to have the desired impact on people's behavior. They determine the power and effectiveness of the consequences. There are a great number of possible positive reinforcers. The practices listed in Figure 3-9 fall into the following four categories:

VERBAL/SOCIAL	WORK-RELATED
Specific Compliments	Promotions
Recognition	Special Development Programs/Projects
Commendation Letters	Increased Decision Authority
Award Dinners	Increased Control Over Resources
Celebration lunches/activities	Access to Top Executives
Take an Interest in Their Work	More Challenging Assignments
TANGIBLE/SYMBOLIC	**MONETARY**
Trophies/Plaques	Special Recognition Awards ($)
Special Recognition Clubs	Individual Bonuses
Work Related Tools and Equipment	Group Incentives/GainSharing
Office Equipment (e.g. computer, furniture)	Pay Increases Based on Merit
Personal Items of Interest (e.g. trips, time off, wine, etc.)	Stock Related Rewards

Figure 3-9. What systems and practices do we have to provide positive reinforcement?

1. *Verbal/Social*   These reinforcements consist of things said or done to make participants feel valued for their accomplishments or actions. Such verbal or social rewards can come from the participants' immediate supervisor, or from customers, peers, other staff members, or upper level management. Research has shown that positive reinforcements of this type are usually the most powerful because they most easily meet all five criteria.

2. *Tangible/Symbolic*   This form of reinforcement involves giving participants something of value for something they did. The value of such rewards lies not in their financial worth, but in their emotional meaning to the participants. (There will be more discussion in Chapter 8 of how apparently simple items can have great symbolic value).

3. *Work-Related*   This type of reinforcer includes promotions, special professional development opportunities, or desirable assignments. It can also include seeing one's ideas implemented, one's recommendations accepted, or one's concerns or issues resolved.

4. *Monetary*   While money is perceived as the universal reinforcer, it often fails to have a powerful impact on behavior because it is limited in terms of immediacy, sincerity, and personal meaning. Hence compensation systems have inherent drawbacks.

The focus of this book is on transforming compensation and recognition systems into true reward systems. The key is to apply the knowledge of what drives human behavior to reward-related systems and practices, and to find and use the right combination of them as reinforcers.

One can find out what is meaningful by: (1) asking participants what they would find most valuable; (2) trying different ideas until participants respond favorably; or (3) observing what participants themselves do. In other words, if you want to know what people find reinforcing, observe what they do when they have the freedom to choose.[4]

Making a Reward System Work

Many organizations see their compensation programs as defacto reward systems because they believe they are "paying for performance." But, in reality most employees do not feel they are rewarded for their performance. These systems fail because many of them are neither designed or managed with an understanding of the forces that drive human behavior. An understanding of these forces can help such companies design reward systems and practices that work as new and powerful "consequence" systems within the organization.

Like positive reinforcers, reward systems must have certain key characteristics. Effective reward systems are:

1. *Specific* Performance measures and feedback systems need to define what people should do to contribute to the organization's success. There needs to be a clear line of sight between the results desired and the behaviors required to achieve them. The reason that performance measures are so key to any reward or recognition system is that they provide specific data about the results or actions at issue. (Chapter 10 discusses strategies and techniques for developing effective performance measures.)

2. *Meaningful* Rewards need to make people feel valued for their achievements from their own point of view. Traditional assumptions about "how much financial incentives (e.g., bonuses) it will take" for people to perform as required ranges from 10 percent to 20 percent.[5] However, behavioral research on this question indicates that the true leverage point may be closer to 3 percent and 5 percent, given other supporting practices related to performance measurement, feedback, and reinforcement.[6]

3. *Achievable* The desired actions or results need to be within the participants' control or influence and attainable through reasonable effort. Traditional assumptions about goal setting indicate that high performers set "stretch goals" (i.e., these are goals which are very difficult to achieve). Therefore, to gain maximum advantage, managers need to set tough goals for their people. But research shows that people achieve better results, sooner, and with more continued vigor if the goals are perceived as achievable. The research of David McClellan, formerly of Harvard University, on goal setting and motivation indicates that achievable goals are more characteristic of high performers.[7] If goals are too difficult, people are less likely to achieve them, or will only achieve them far in the future. This can lead to the process of extinction, reducing, rather than increasing, the behavior desired.

4. *Reliable* The system needs to be designed and operated in a fashion consistent with its purpose. Not only should rewards be contingent on the achievement of desired results; the whole process must be managed in a cost-effective manner.

   A growing services company was known to provide profit-sharing payouts to all its employees regardless of whether or not it was achieving a profit. The employees came to expect the annual payouts and saw the bonus as an entitlement. The system had no effect whatsoever as a way of reinforcing company efforts to achieve profits. Payouts tied to actual performance would have had far more impact on the employees' performance.

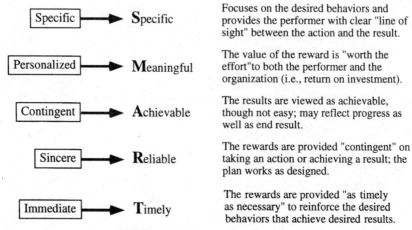

Figure 3-10. What makes a compensation system a true "reward system"?

5. *Timely*   Feedback, reinforcement, and rewards need to be provided as soon after the achievement and/or behaviors as possible. An examination of employee performance in relation to most annual incentive plans shows that employees make a concerted effort to achieve goals toward the end of a performance period. It seems clear that people work harder to achieve their goals when they can see a clear alignment between the effort necessary to achieve the goals and the timing of the reward. Timing has a significant impact on the pace of activities, the sense of urgency, and the focus on priorities.

Taken together, the five criteria for a successful rewards system—Specific, Meaningful, Achievable, Reliable, Timely—make up the acronym SMART. (See Figure 3-10.) In subsequent chapters we will further examine these criteria and apply them to different reward programs, always with the idea that a properly designed and managed reward system can drive an organization's change process by effectively reinforcing desired behaviors.

Successful reward systems are designed to encourage the collaborative behaviors needed to serve the customer's needs at a level better than the competitors'. To impact behavior in positive ways, reward systems must create conditions in which people *want* to take the initiative needed by the organization because they receive something of value from doing so. Money is not the only answer, nor objects, nor announcements. By understanding what reinforcements are meaningful to employees and providing opportunities for them to earn reinforcement and rewards (both extrinsically and intrinsically), we can create win/win situations. This is the true essence of collaboration and the foundation of any effective system of rewards.

Notes

1. Daniels, A., *Performance Management: Improving Quality Productivity through Positive Reinforcement.* Tucker, Ga.: Performance Management Publications, 1989.

2. Deming, W. E., *Out of the Crisis.* Cambridge: MIT Press, 1986.

3. Daniels, A., op. cit.

4. Premack, D., "Toward Empirical Behavior Laws: I. Positive Reinforcement." *Psychological Review,* Vol. 66, 1959, pp. 219–233.

5. Lawler, E., *Strategic Pay.* San Francisco: Jossey Bass, 1990.

6. Dickinson, A. M., "Exploring New Vistas: Performance Management Research Laboratory at Western Michigan University." *Performance Management Magazine,* Vol. 9, No. 1, 1991, pp. 27–31.

7. McClellan, D., *The Achieving Society,* Princeton, N.J.: Van Nostrand, 1961.

4

Developing a Reward Strategy

The A implementation of a B strategy is better
than the A strategy with a B implementation.
—MICHAEL PORTER
Competitive Strategy, 1980

We have examined some of the new behaviors needed to address today's complex challenges and we have seen how the forces that drive human behavior provide the guiding principles for the design and management of reward programs. In this chapter we will show how to focus reward programs on the aspects of human behavior where they can have the greatest positive impact. We will also present a game plan for redirecting an organization's reward programs to support, if not lead, its change effort.

A reward strategy is a plan of action for the way an organization can direct and invest its resources to reinforce desired behaviors. Its resources can include compensation dollars, special recognition awards, and celebrations in honor of high achievers.

The reward strategy provides the organization with a framework for determining how and where to invest its reinforcement dollars. This reflects a strategy of investment in the human resources of the organization.

Within this context, there are three primary types of reward programs. They are:

1. *Base Pay* This is the secure, stable income given to individuals every pay period. It reflects what an organization needs to pay in

order to get employees to show up for work. It provides workers with some base of economic security so that they are not overly concerned about primary needs.

2. *Variable Pay* This is compensation received in addition to base pay, and it varies depending on the performance of the individual, team, company, etc. By its very nature it is not guaranteed, although many organizations have allowed such programs to become entitlements, like base pay. Variable pay is usually received in a lump sum check, and does not become part of base pay. Variable pay can also take the form of cash payments or equity-related investments (e.g., stock grants, restricted stock, stock options, etc.).

3. *Performance Management* This is a systematic process of measurement, feedback, and reinforcement that represents appropriate consequences for a person's actions. It is executed between the periods in which base pay is adjusted or variable pay is awarded. While performance appraisals (see Chapter 9) are viewed as annual or time-based events, performance management occurs in relation to the work performed and the needs of the performer. It can include verbal/social reinforcers; tangible/symbolic reinforcers; work-related reinforcers; and financial, spot, or special recognition awards.

Taken together these three primary elements form a system of rewards that can be very powerful in reinforcing desired behaviors (see Figure 4-1). As a system they impact each other and gain their strength from their alignment and effectiveness. To illustrate, the base and vari-

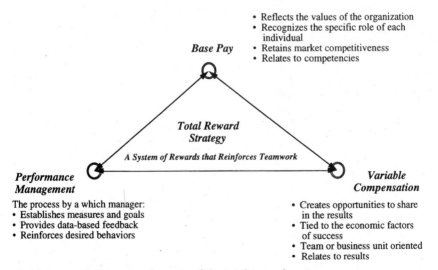

Figure 4-1. The primary elements of the total reward system.

able compensation components often enable the organization to attract the talent it needs to do its business. They can offer a portfolio of pay programs that are attractive to the people needed by the firm. The base compensation and performance management form a basis to shape behaviors in specific ways. Base pay can encourage people to learn and apply new skills, and this learning can be reinforced by the performance management process. The performance management and variable compensation components can drive specific performance issues by providing incentives for achievements and immediate recognition for progress.

These three elements functioning as a system provide the framework for understanding and integrating a firm's approach to rewards. This model provides the conceptual context of this book and encourages the organization to examine all three elements in a systematic, strategic, and synergistic way.

As stated earlier, understanding the desired behaviors forms the heart of this system. The strategy defines the behaviors needed for successful performance, and the focus, design, and management of these three elements will reflect the implementation of this strategy. In this manner, the organizaation can target and allocate its resources as most needed for success.

The Drivers for Success

In order to understand the use and integration of these rewards from a strategic viewpoint, we first need to understand the primary drivers of an organization's success and how it allocates its resources. Every organization has a strategy, regardless of whether or not it is articulated or understood throughout the organization. (Here the reader may want to refer to current thinking on strategy in the works of M. Porter,[1] R. H. Hamilton,[2] or J. Galbraith.[3]) A strategy can be viewed as having two primary leverage points for implementation: (1) the economics of the organization; and (2) the values of the organization (see Figure 4-2).

The *economics of the organization* boil down to the way it allocates and utilizes its resources to serve customers and achieve a competitive advantage. A firm's economics include how it makes its money, how it invests its resources (in people, equipment, materials, technology, and/or partnerships with other organizations, for example), and how intensively it uses capital and labor in the work process. Performance measures that relate to the firm's economics are usually financial (e.g., return on investment, variance to budget, gross margins, revenues to goal, etc.) or operational (e.g., productivity, reject/scrap rates, on-time delivery, cycle time, accuracy rates, etc.).

The *values of the organization* are reflected in an organization's determination of which behaviors get reinforced and which get punished.

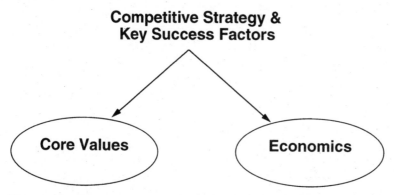

Figure 4-2. The importance of an organization's economics and values to its overall strategy.

An organization's culture is a reflection of its actual values, not necessarily of its espoused values. Standard definitions of corporate culture include the norms and beliefs of an organization. If norms are patterns of behaviors, and behavior is a function of its consequences, therefore, we can conclude that culture is the product of the consequences at work within the organization.

When seeking to change the culture of an organization, one must first analyze what reinforcements are in use, and then change them to encourage desired behaviors. This is how values become a reality to the members of the organization. When a firm's stated values are congruent with the behaviors it rewards, its values are aligned with its actions. The degree to which this is so will also indicate the degree of trust and credibility senior management has in the organization.

If we view an organization's economics and values as the primary leverage points for implementation of its strategy, we can then focus on the purpose of various reward programs and determine how they can best be used to support the strategy. Most incentive compensation plans, for example, include financial or operational measures. If there is real gain in financial or operational areas, the incentive plans provide a payoff. If there is poor performance in these areas, the incentive payout will be small or nonexistent. Hence, these pay plans tend to be best aligned with clear economic measures of the business. Incentive pay programs should reinforce what was done or the results that were achieved by the individual or team.

If the focus of the reward programs is chiefly on results, the values of the organization will be left to managers to interpret. A conflict may result between the organization's stated values and those it reinforces with its practices. When this disparity exists, employees feel the difference between the "talk" and the "walk" (i.e., between the antecedents and the consequences), and learn to ignore whatever is said to them. The antecedents reflecting the firm's stated values are weakened because they are disconnected from any meaningful consequences.

A view held by many line managers is that the current base pay program is not effective in paying for performance. Despite efforts to rank individuals for determining pay increases, allocate smaller amounts of budget salary increases, and link pay with performance ratings, salary programs have generally become ineffective in making people feel truly rewarded. When we focus a base pay system on results, we complicate the measures associated with an incentive pay plan.

Many organizations go to great lengths to communicate their corporate values. They create training programs, make videos featuring their CEOs, hang banners, and provide employees with lucite obelisks with the "magic words" inscribed in gold. Recently, for example, a large industrial manufacturing company in the northeast spent $2.5 million on a campaign to change the firm's culture (i.e., values), only to find that very few employees were working any differently from the way they had always done. After the process was completed, the CEO pronounced the effort a waste. He said that instead of investing so much money, time, and effort in conveying values, his organization should have put its resources into encouraging and reinforcing behavioral changes.

This firm's expensive values campaign produced few results because there was little meaningful translation of its values into everyday activities and because there were few attempts to reinforce behavior that exemplified these values. This was a very costly lesson, one that is too often repeated by American companies. Enter a new role for the base pay system and the performance management process.

By translating values into desired behaviors that reflect of the role of each individual within an organization and then providing reinforcements, we can create conditions in which people *want* to do what the organization needs them to do. The process includes unlearning certain old behaviors (through extinction or punishment) and learning new behaviors (through positive reinforcement).

We can focus the base pay in several possible areas. First, we can use the pay program to reward individuals who acquire new skills or competencies and apply them to the work setting. We can also use pay to reinforce specific actions people take to encourage innovation, reduce low value-added costs, and contribute to the success of a team in the work area. The next chapter will examine alternative approaches to base pay programs in more depth. Here, the primary conclusion is that we can use various pay systems to reinforce desired actions. (See Figure 4-3.)

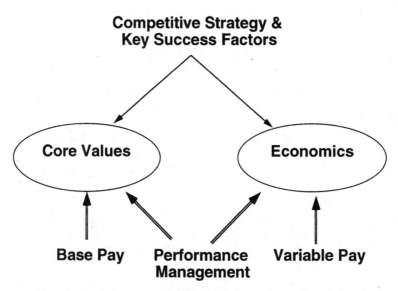

Figure 4-3. The relationship between the three primary reward systems and an organization's economics and values.

Reward Programs: The Next Generation

Adopting a systematic approach to reward systems means that we can change the purpose, application, and impact of each reward element to reinforce desired behaviors within the organization. Systems of this kind, developed in line with the SMART design criteria outlined in the previous chapter, are part of a new generation of reward programs. In fact, if we understand the evolutionary stages of various programs, we can see that the time has come for a fundamental change in the paradigms we use to reward people in organizations.

Compensation systems have evolved through a series of stages. Each stage was fitting for the management philosophy of the time or the needs of the particular businesses involved. In many ways this evolution reflects the management concerns of various periods and provides a useful framework for looking at the current, versus the desired, state of particular compensation systems. Today, we are witnessing the emergence of a customer-focused philosophy of management, and can view previous reward systems in a totally different light. They have set the stage for the next generation. The four evolutionary stages are shown in Figure 4-4 and described below.[4]

Stages of Development for Compensation Systems

Dimensions	I. Discretionary Process	II. Job-Based System	III. Objectives-Based System	IV. Customer-Focused System
Determinants of pay:	Needs of the individual and the manager.	Accountabilities of the incumbent.	Capabilities/performance of individuals.	Value-added role of the individual or team.
References for pay adequacy:	Reaction within the organization to pay decisions (fairness).	Market pay levels (external) needed to attract and retain talent.	Market competitiveness and company performance. Tied to compensation strategy.	Performance and degree of reinforcement achieved. Comp. strategy linked to HR and business strategy.
Use of multiple pay programs:	Usually simple system (base pay plus discretionary bonus).	Primarily base pay. Uses incentives in specialized areas (sales, exec.s).	Use of two predominant systems—base pay plus structured incentive.	Integrated reward systems: • Base pay, Pay for Skills • Team/group incentives • Co. incentives ($/Stk) • Special recognition
Focus of control:	Discretion of the senior most manager. Ability to pay.	The budget or pay increase guidelines. Fixed merit pool.	Performance sharing guidelines. Planned and fixed merit pool.	Performance guidelines. Variable merit pool.
Accountability:	Line manager	Compensation department.	Compensation department	Partnership: Management and Compensation department.
Linkage with other systems:	Seldom if ever.	Tied to organizational structure. Hopefully neutral to change.	Tied to performance of the organization. Supportive of change.	Tied to strategic programs (TQM, SMWT, etc.) and on-going management practices and reinforcement. Leads or links directly with change process.
Payout timing:	Usually annual, but depends on the issues to be addressed.	Annual	Primarily annual, but may have other time based payouts (Qlty, multi-year).	Schedule tied to performance plans, payouts tied to when achievements occur.
Nature of measures:	At discretion of the manager usually unknown by the performer.	Usually based on policies, budgets and individual MBO's.	Objectives are tied to annual operating plans.	Operating plans, strategic initiatives and critical behaviors.

Figure 4-4. The four stages of development for compensation systems.

Stage 1: The Discretionary Process—Let's Make a Deal

In the days when most organizations were small, the employer decided on each employee's compensation arrangement, the employees came to work, and hopefully the business prospered. The manager and the employee determined what was a fair and appropriate fit between the needs of the business and the work and talent of the individual. The process was relatively simple to administer, and only the "deal" needed to be documented. The level of pay was a function of what the individual wanted in order to work for the organization and of the firm's ability to pay. The measures of performance were dependent on the judgment of the manager. And pay increases, if there were any, depended on what was necessary to keep the employee satisfied and working for the organization.

This practice worked well until employees began talking to each other about pay. When they compared pay levels, heated eruptions and cries of "unfair" were often heard by managers and human resource professionals (who in those days were known as personnel managers). As managers within the organization began to make their own deals, great inconsistencies emerged. People who performed the same basic function received sometimes vastly different levels of pay. The compensation system was seen as out of control. There were no guidelines for hiring rates, pay increases, or promotional increases. Pay became a major political issue within the organization and lessened the commitment felt by many employees.

Stage 2: The Job-Based System— The Worth of the Job

This chaos gave rise to the need to establish a pay system based on an employee's level of responsibility and the value of his or her work within the organization. During this stage, companies sought to rationalize pay levels based on some criteria that would support past decisions, with minimal disruptive cost impact. In most cases the organization began the process by preparing job descriptions that asked people to document their reporting relationships, staffing and budgetary control or impact, primary accountabilities or duties, decision-making authority, and the like. These descriptions were then used to analyze or measure the job according to a series of job evaluation factors. The factors frequently included such dimensions as knowledge, effort, responsibility, and working conditions. In the beginning, these factors were developed as a reflection of the current pay levels. Today, sophisticated, computer-based statistical processes are used to determine the relationship between similar factors and existing pay levels.

Companies that minimized the impact of internal job evaluation systems used pay levels based on external market information for jobs of similar responsibility. When sufficient external market data was not present, the compensation professional would make an educated guess based on similar roles within the organization.

Salary administration systems were then established to handle the preparation of job documentation, reevaluation of job content, and changes in pay. There was minimal use of incentive pay below the most senior management levels. Salary increases were planned, budgeted, and controlled with a fixed merit pool. The compensation department was modeled on the command-and-control philosophy of the overall organization, and was often used by senior management as the focal point for actions necessary to reign in the discretionary process.

While the system worked well to control compensation costs, it raised other problems. The primary issue was that the organization was spending a lot of money on pay increases without being sure that there was performance to justify it. Managers found ways to game the system. The key challenge was to keep someone low in the salary range so that high pay increases could be justified. Periodic job upgrades and promotions became the major tactic to accomplish this goal. Managers felt that they needed to provide high pay increases to their top performers in order to retain them and keep them motivated to do superior work. Promotions or job upgrades became a major tool to accomplish this task. But there was nothing built into the process that directly related pay to performance.

Stage 3: The Objectives-Based System—Pay for Performance

The pay-for-performance philosophy emerged as an answer to this problem. The primary purpose of this process was to ensure that the highest performers received the highest rewards. This approach to rewards assumed a zero-sum game and sought to distribute rewards to individuals who clearly distinguished themselves from others. The rationale was that giving relatively higher pay increases to top performers would keep them motivated and loyal to the organization. The process was frequently managed through salary increase guidelines that related people's job performance to their position within a certain salary range. Those with high performance ratings and low salary-range positions received the highest pay increases. Those with high positions in the salary range received lower pay increases, unless they were extremely high performers, in which case exceptions might be made for them.

This process created several interesting dynamics. The rise of management by objectives (MBO), made it possible for an employee to negotiate easily achievable performance targets in order to appear a star. Since the performance was evaluated on an individual basis, employees who had strong relationships with their managers always did well. Furthermore, if one individual were to get more than the average, another person had to get less. Budgets were established a year in advance and the game was essentially a zero-sum process. As a result, there were few positive consequences for making one's teammates look like star performers. Because performance ratings were a primary determinant of one's pay, both the manager and the employee prepared extensively for the performance appraisal meeting in order to present the best case possible. (Performance appraisals will be discussed extensively in Chapter 9). Finally, organizations sometimes required managers to distribute performance ratings according to a predetermined allocation formula. It was felt that this would force managers to pay for performance. The reality was that only spending controls were achieved; people did not feel they were being rewarded for performance.

With the rise of total quality management (TQM) and the philosophy of W. Edwards Deming, Joseph Juran, and others, individually focused work and evaluation systems were revealed for what they had become—inherently competitive struggles with peers, with supervisors, and with the work itself. Today, as teams increasingly become the preferred organizing concept, individual performance evaluation and pay are frequently seen as inimical to the goals of sharing, collaborating, and focusing on the customer. As downsizing continues to occur and many management levels are eliminated, opportunities for promotion are becoming more limited, employees' time with their managers is becoming more rare, and managers are using less and less firsthand information as a basis for their performance judgments.

In light of the way consequences impact human behavior, the implications of these developments are clear. If employees depend on their managers for a significant amount of support and reinforcement, the removal of this layer of management is likely to cause a decrease in their performance over time. This is the impact of extinction on human behavior. If the reinforcement process is not replaced by one's peers, one's customers, or the work itself, performance is likely to decline overall.

Finally, extensive employee opinion surveys, both public and within organizations, point to the failure of this approach to really pay for performance. In fact, it has become a mere financial distribution system. The process tells who should get what level of pay, but does not operate as a system of rewards.

Stage 4: The Customer-Focused System—Personalized Rewards

The next generation now beginning to emerge is a fundamentally different view of how we understand and use compensation systems. An organization has several resources to achieve its basic mission and serve its customers; people represent the major one. The actions and behaviors of people determine whether an organization achieves results and establishes a competitive position in the marketplace. The key driver to creating the conditions in which desired behaviors are realized is positive reinforcement. Compensation and other reward programs must be consistent with the principles that determine the effectiveness of consequences (SMART).

The new philosophy will utilize a broad portfolio of reward systems within the organization. Managers will be skilled in understanding how to create conditions for effective positive reinforcement—measurement and feedback—and be able to use a portfolio of reinforcers with precision. In this way the compensation system will become personalized. By *personalized,* I mean that individuals will understand not only what they need to do but also how well they are doing it. Rewards will be contingent on their progress. Furthermore, rewards will come in many shapes and sizes, depending on what is important to the individuals and the organization. The next generation of compensation systems will be based on collaboration and positive reinforcement. They will provide the flexibility to adapt to individual needs and provide opportunities for all to participate. It will reinforce those behaviors that enable an organization to be successful and at the same time offer opportunities for individuals to feel valued and appreciated for their contributions.

Developing a Reward Strategy

This new philosophy is fundamental to a reward strategy that enables an organization to use its resources to reinforce desired behaviors. Such a plan of action needs to be based on an understanding of the customer, the business goals, and the core competencies or key success factors of the firm. To arrive at this understanding, we need to answer five groups of questions:

1. What are the organization's key success factors? What does the firm need to do to be successful in fulfilling its mission or achieving the desired position in its marketplaces?
   - What is the organization—company, division, department, etc.?
   - What is the strategy of the organization?

- What are the key success factors of the business?
- What are the primary indicators that will demonstrate progress on the success factors?
- What are the primary issues or barriers facing the organization in accomplishing this goal?

2. What are the behaviors or actions needed to successfully implement this competitive strategy?
   - What do people need to start doing, do more of, do less of, or stop doing to achieve these results?
   - What needs to be done by all members?
   - What needs to be done by specific groups of members?
   - To what extent do people know how to do these things?
   - To what extent do people know it is important to do these things?

3. What programs should be used to reinforce these behaviors for each specific target group? What should be the purpose of each program in reinforcing desired behaviors?
   - Base pay program
   - Merit-based pay program
   - Variable or incentive pay program
   - Equity-based variable pay program
   - Performance management program
   - Special recognition or key contributor program
   - Other programs

4. What requirements should each program meet to be successful in fulfilling its purpose?
   - Should it be individually based or team focused?
   - How competitive should it be in the marketplace?
   - Should it be highly leveraged or highly secure?
   - Should it support or lead change efforts?
   - Should it apply to everyone or be tailored to each group?
   - Should it be kept separate or be integrated with other compensation programs (e.g., benefits)?

5. How well do the current reward programs match up to these requirements?
   - Where does each program meet or exceed the requirements?
   - Where do the programs fall short? Why?
   - Where should the change process begin?
   - Is the organization (and management in particular) prepared to invest the time, effort, and resources to achieve the desired changes?
   - How critical are these changes to the strategic and current issues facing the business?

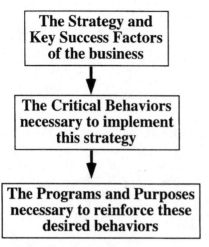

Figure 4-5. Developing the total reward
strategy.

The answers to these questions will aid in building a reward strategy for the organization. In defining the purpose and basic requirements of each program, the reward strategy will support and energize
the change process, in line with the emergence of a new philosophy of
management. The emphasis will not be on paying at a predetermined
level in the marketplace, but on doing what is necessary to achieve
success in implementing the firm's strategy. The overall framework
will emphasize *how* dollars are invested, not how *much* money is
spent or how well the company "keeps up with the Joneses." (See
Figure 4-5.)

Reward Strategy Case Studies

After this overview, let's examine several situations that reflect different reward strategies.

The Case of the Turnaround Company

Jackson Electronics Company (a real company but a fictitious name) is
fighting for its life. Over the last several years it has faced increased
competition, primarily foreign, for its markets. The competitors have
been able to introduce similar products at costs that are 15 percent to 20
percent below those of Jackson which is the last remaining company
in the United States to produce these products. The challenge it
faces now is a competitive fight for survival.

The overall business strategy calls for multiple efforts to regain Jackson's market leadership. The attention will be on meeting the changing needs of its customers and on reducing costs to the customer. This will be accomplished through introducing new products in specific areas that round out the product line, reducing prices (and costs) on the current lines, and strengthening face-to-face relationships with customers. Further, by increasing services, improving the quality of the products, and lowering prices, Jackson seeks to reduce all costs to customers of doing business with them. The implementation of this strategy will involve many members of the organization, not just management, sales, or customer service.

The implications of this strategic change for individuals at Jackson will be significant. First, there has to be an increased sense of urgency and responsiveness among staff members. Waiting for someone else to do something will not lead to success. Second, people need to focus on the core competitive issues facing Jackson and concentrate on those areas that will lead to overcoming the current situation. This will require translating the competitive strategy into measures and directives to which each individual can relate. Third, employees need to drive out any waste or low value-added activities. This will reduce costs and speed up the process of work. Reports or meetings that are not necessary will have to be dropped. Materials and supplies will have to be used carefully to minimize loss. Fourth, people need to treat each other—and especially outsiders—as customers. From now on, everyone will be viewed as a customer or someone to serve and appreciate. Finally, while the task of a turnaround is massive, people need to see their accomplishments and feel valued by others. In this way, Jackson plans to create a spirit of change and winning that will motivate their people and enhance performance as an organization.

As an element of this business strategy, Jackson has decided to make specific changes in its reward systems. These changes are focused on driving the changes needed in the way Jackson conducts business. The reward strategy will include the following goals:

- Identify and focus performance measures on the key factors of the competitive strategy that people can impact: product costs, delivery performance, the quality of customer service, and introduction of new products.

- Use the reward strategy to emphasize variable compensation for organization-wide and team performance. Use base-pay increases to identify and reward individuals who make major contributions to the team or company. Use performance management to measure factors that contribute to overall goals, chart improvement in critical areas, and celebrate any major achievements that strengthen Jackson's relationship to current or new customers.

- Be less concerned about the external competitiveness or internal equity of the company's pay rates as long as they remain within generally accepted levels in the marketplace.

- Increase the payout frequency of the incentive system to four times a year in line with the increased sense of urgency. Restructure the incentive plan so that each quarter stands on it own and there are no payments for cumulative performance. Make each quarter a battle that has to be won.

The Case of the Rapidly Growing Firm

Dutch Beverage Products (a real company but a fictitious name) is enjoying the benefits of a market that is coming to its door. Dutch's products began as specialty items in convenience and grocery stores, but changes in consumer demand have made them increasingly attractive, and the company is experiencing record-setting growth.

The challenge to Dutch is that competition is also increasing, particularly from major market players (Coca-Cola, Pepsi, etc.). Dutch does not have the marketing resources to withstand a direct attack on its market position, so it needs to remain flexible, responsive, and quality-focused. It also needs to develop a reward strategy that will retain the qualities of its current culture while enabling it to attract, retain, and manage new people.

The essence of this challenge is to support the firm's growth while retaining its core values. Dutch's key success factors require a continual focus on the customer and continual improvement in the work process, the maximizing of current resources and the minimizing of new costs, the assimiliation of new people into the firm's culture, an emphasis on individual efforts, and a focus on teams that work strongly together and produce desired outcomes. The corporate culture itself needs to adapt and change without creating the weight of traditional bureaucratic practices.

Dutch's reward strategy seeks to accomplish two major objectives: First, it must be sufficiently competitive to enable Dutch to attract and retain the talent it needs. This will entail creating a combination of base pay, incentive pay, and equity-related programs tailored to attract the expertise needed and make the firm clearly superior in the marketplace. Dutch needs to provide average levels of base compensation but significantly higher incentive opportunities than its larger competitors. (Its environment of growth, opportunity, and involvement will certainly be a major competitive advantage to attract and retain the desired talent.)

Second, Dutch needs to ensure that the base pay program and the incentive program do not reinforce a bureaucratic philosophy of management. Its measures must focus on the customer's requirements, not on the needs of managers. The feedback process must be real-time, not delayed to tie in with annual events. The data must provide people with the information necessary for them to respond to rapidly changing conditions. The decision criteria need to be established before the performance period, so that management discretion is minimized. Finally, the firm needs to reinforce people who take actions that enhance its competitiveness. This effort will primarily focus on special teams, but must ensure that individuals are valued by their team members. In this way Dutch can leverage all the talent potential of the firm to compete aggressively with others who may be larger or have deeper pockets. The competitors' processes will be slowed by bureaucracy and control; Dutch will be different.

The Case of the Renewal Company

The Steele Manufacturing Company (a real company but a fictitious name) has a long history of quality products and industry leadership. It is a large company with manufacturing and customer centers located throughout the world. Although it enjoys a dominant share of its primary markets, an erosion is emerging in many of its key market segments. Competition is appearing within its industry as well as from new entrants to the market. Steele's top executives are realizing that if the firm does not increase the rate of improvements, it will soon face major issues. Although the firm has an established vision statement and has made significant investments in total quality management efforts, there have been only modest improvements in results.

To meet the challenge, Steele's executives have developed, in combination with several special task forces throughout the organization, a strategy to improve the competitiveness of the firm, to move the company back to its position as a market leader. The strategy entails focusing on core strategic business units (SBUs), and developing specific investment, marketing, and organizational plans around them.

The executives have decided that a new reward strategy is necessary to reinforce these change efforts. The implications of this strategy for behaviors will be quite important. First, corporate executives need to let go of their traditional patterns of control. They need to focus on encouraging the SBUs to formulate and execute strategies to rebuild their business. Investment decisions need to be made according to what will benefit the units and in turn create synergy across lines of business. Second, managers need to take greater risks and challenge the assumptions of past practices. If the firm is to regain its competitive strength, some actions must be retained and others changed. Each SBU needs to determine this difference and support the changes required. Finally, the firm must integrate new investments in technology or work processes to build their competitiveness quickly. This means reducing the walls that divide divisions, minimizing internal competitiveness, and focusing on serving the changing needs of Steele's internal and external customers.

The firm's executives have decided to decentralize the current control-oriented pay system to the divisions. Each division will develop its own reward strategy to support its business plans. The corporation will manage general employee benefits, such as in health and retirement plans, but each division can be as creative as it wants around special benefit programs, such as child care centers, special leave policies, etc.

Although each SBU will create its own reward strategy, there will be some common themes. First, incentive plans will be developed around the key success factors of each SBU. In most cases the measures will include factors related to product quality, customer satisfaction, and expense control. Some divisions will create incentive plans for new product introductions, delivery times, and customer service. Second, the base pay plans will seek to address the performance of the individual. While most divisions will refocus merit pay around individual contributions to team performance, a few divisions will develop pay-for-competencies-employed programs. In these cases the firm will seek to

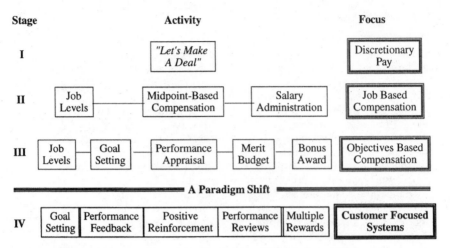

Figure 4-6. A fundamentally new approach to compensation is emerging: the next generation will focus on the behaviors needed to serve customers.

reinforce employees for increasing their skills as new technology, process manufacturing, and new product development strategies are implemented. Finally, the performance management process will become the centerpiece for managing performance on a day-to-day basis. The focus will not be on appraising performance, but rather on providing people with the measures, feedback, and reinforcement they need to excel in their work. In this way Steele is making the process of change and renewal real, positive, and meaningful to their employees.

Summary

The reward strategy is the process by which the firm translates its competitive business strategy into a series of programs and investments that will positively impact human behavior. A reward strategy that only focuses on establishing a desired position in the external marketplace will not be effective in driving needed change. Only when the strategy defines what new behaviors are needed and builds systems and practices to reinforce these behaviors will desired change become real. The reward strategy provides an overall architecture or blueprint to guide changes in pay and performance systems. In this way, people can both see and feel a difference in their world. The change in performance, coming about from a change in daily actions, will produce the results necessary for the firm to survive and prosper. Behaviors are the raw materials for implementing a competitive strategy, and reward systems are the core tools needed to create the conditions where people take the initiative to change. Reward systems help employees know what to do and why they should do it. Reward systems help an organization marshall the resources of its people to create a win/win situation for all.

Notes

1. Porter, M., *Competitive Strategy.* New York: The Free Press, 1980.

2. Hamilton, R. H., "Scenarios in Corporate Planning." *Journal of Business Strategy*, No. 2, Summer, 1981, p. 82.

3. Galbraith, J. *Designing Complex Organizations.* Reading, Mass.: Addison-Wesley Co., 1973.

4. Many of the concepts presented here were developed initially by Edward N. Morse of Aubrey Daniels and Associates. Ned has an amazing ability to see patterns of transitions where others see only chaos.

5
Building a Foundation with Base Pay

The greatest waste in America is failure to use
the abilities of people.
　　　　　　　—W. EDWARDS DEMING
　　　　　　　Out of the Crisis, 1986

Virtually every organization has a base salary program for compensating its employees. These programs provide employees with paychecks of a fixed amount at regular intervals. Base salary programs are the foundation of the economic contract between individuals and their employers.

The salary/wage is a primary element of the discussion when a new employee is hired and when a person is promoted to a new position. This frequently defines the size of the job in relation to the new employee's previous experience. The pay levels are often set through a system of market pricing, job evaluation, and salary administration. Base pay accounts for most of an organization's compensation expenditures—as high as 50 percent to 70 percent of its total costs in some companies. Hence these programs are marbled into every facet of the organization.

In this chapter we will examine how current base pay systems function, assess their effectiveness using the SMART criteria, and examine alternatives to enhance or reform them. Among these alternatives there will be both simple and sophisticated approaches to addressing the fundamental flaws in base pay systems.

There is perhaps no other reward system within an organization that has caused more pain and agony than base pay. In many organizations no one seems truly satisfied with his or her current pay level. There are continual pressures to increase them, either to keep pace with inflation or to increase the economic well-being of employees. There are equal pressures to reduce them, through headcount reductions, minimal increases, or the establishment of a fixed amount to distribute to members of a division or company. Increases in pay outside of normal adjustments often become a political process in which work is reorganized merely to justify a desired upgrade. There are often bitter internal struggles over granting such raises, including controversies with other units that are seeking similar increases.

Increases in base pay become annuity costs to the organization; they compound year after year. Figure 5-1 shows how a $30,000-a-year salary can grow to $38,289 in just five years. At an annual increase rate of 5 percent; this is a 28 percent increase in costs and represents the effects of compounding pay increases. If the productivity of the organization is not increased by the same amount, the process will require the firm either to increase prices or to live with lower gross margins. Both options will reduce its ability to compete in the global marketplace.

There *are* solutions to this complex array of issues. But to find them, we need to understand how base pay systems work. We can then target specific strategies to enhance their potential use as a collaborative reward system from which both the organization and the individual can reap benefits.

Year	Base Pay	Pay Increase (5%)	% Differences
0	$30,000	$1,500	—
1	31,500	1,575	5.0%
2	33,075	1,654	10.3%
3	34,729	1,737	15.7%
4	36,466	1,823	21.6%
5	38,289	—	27.6%

Figure 5-1. The compounding impact of base pay increases.

Overview of Traditional
Base Pay Systems

The basic purpose of the salary program is to enable the organization to attract and retain the employees it needs to conduct its business. (It is sometimes referred to as "show up" pay, because without it, people would most likely not show up for work.) The programs are often based on the pay levels of the marketplace. Salary surveys provided by consulting companies and industry associations offer much of this information. The market price for a job is then established, based on a comparison of the levels paid by other companies for jobs of similar scope, the organization's desired level of competitiveness, and the amount the organization can afford to pay. Consideration of these pay levels is particularly important for organizations hiring a great number of people or vulnerable to losing talent to other companies.

Edward Lawler of the Center for Effective Organizations at the University of Southern California and author of many books on compensation systems, voices a commonly held belief that employees value themselves in relation to the marketplace.[1] If a competitor organization offers more money to an individual, the employee will change companies. While people do often have a sense of their worth in dollars, Lawler assumes that employees have a full understanding of the marketplace pay rates and frequently seek to test the waters regarding pay opportunities. Hence, he recommends that base pay levels be based on a careful competitive market data.

In reality, employees use a variety of sources to determine the fairness of their pay. Some people always compare themselves to someone who is higher up or paid more, and then use these data points to feel dissatisfied. Others see how far they have come or compare themselves to their parents, and feel satisfied (sometimes). While pay satisfaction is interesting, there is no clear evidence it has any impact on behaviors (except at extremely low levels). Instead, pay dissatisfaction is often more a reflection of the lack of reinforcement in the workplace than the absolute dollar levels. Many managers and compensation professionals address the wrong problem when they provide more pay to reduce dissatisfaction. A more effective approach would be to increase the degree and impact of reinforcement and recognition systems to more directly solve the problem.

The conventional wisdom is that if an employee is generally satisfied with his or her job, a competitor needs to offer between 10 percent and 15 percent more pay to get him or her to switch jobs. If this conventional wisdom is correct, the effective application of reinforcement can give an organization a competitive advantage in attracting and retaining employees. If the organization succeeds in helping its employees feel valued for their work, it can spend less to *keep* them than does the firm that has to "buy" its people. The level of reinforcement will define the costs necessary to attract and retain desired talent. If employees are very dissatisfied or feel stuck in their current functions, the cost to retain them will be high; if employees feel reinforced and valued by the organization, the costs will be less.

In addition to market data, many organizations use some form of internal pricing of jobs based on a job evaluation and salary administration system. Chapter 1 discussed the way traditional systems of job evaluation tend to mirror an organization's command-and-control or bureaucratic values. Organizations usually implement a job evaluation system in reaction to a compensation system that is viewed as out of control. The compensation system is then designed to ensure that pay practices will be seen as fair from an internal perspective, and enables the organization to relate external market pay practices on an internally rational basis.

The Need for a Structured Pay System

Let's examine how base pay systems operate by reviewing two brief case studies. They will describe different situations with different issues but essentially the same approach to base pay.

Case Number One

Walden Widgets Co. (a fictitious name but a real company) has been growing rapidly. In the past three to four years alone, its employee population has grown from 125 people to over 350. When the company was small, the president herself interviewed and made the final selection decision on every employee. As the firm grew, her managers interviewed and hired employees for her. As the organization grew still further, *their* managers interviewed and hired employees. With each hiring decision, compensation was established on the basis of what the individual wanted and what people were currently paid in the same department.

In the last few years employees have began comparing their pay levels with each other, and many have become very angry. In some departments employees have been hired at rates equal to or above others who have long service with the company. The marketing and sales people have all received higher pay than others in operations, finance, and development functions. As the organization has grown, people have been promoted into supervisory levels, and in some areas have received large pay increases (as much as 15 percent to 20 percent), while others have received much less (3 percent to 6 percent). The employees have come to know which senior managers offer big raises to their employees and which ones don't.

The frequency and severity of the complaints have increased. Employees have sought transfers or threatened their managers with quitting. In some cases, the managers have responded with pay increases; in others, they have not. Salary grades have been created, but there has been no rationale for why people are put in any particular grade except that it reflects their current pay or it is the same as for others performing the same function. The company is still seeking to find and implement a compensation system that is rational and that provides some control over the compensation program.

Case Number Two

Security National Bank (also a fictitious name but an actual organization) is made up of a confederation of 12 small to midsize banks. The chairman is seeking to merge the affiliate banks into a single organization in order to increase their overall ability to compete with other major financial institutions. The integration will involve a functional-based organization structure, the centralization of operations, the centralized setting of rates and credit policies, and centralized advertising and promotions. In addition, a single job evaluation and salary administration system is being sought to provide a common structure for all organizational units within the newly merged banking organization.

How It Usually Works

In both these cases the organization is trying to provide a single system of compensation in which the emphasis is on internal equity. By *internal equity* I mean that individuals with similar levels of responsibilities and impact on the organization have similar compensation opportunities. The job evaluation process defines levels by applying a common set of criteria to a representative sample of jobs. This measurement process is in terms of points or grade levels. For example, jobs with 500 points are at a similar level, and that level is lower than jobs with 800 points.

The evaluation of the job is usually based on information contained in the job description, which is commonly prepared by the supervisor or manager of the position or someone in the compensation department. Some organizations have adopted questionnaires which are completed by the job incumbent(s) and reviewed by the supervisor. The intention is to decentralize the effort required for this task.

Most job descriptions require the following information:

- Title of the job
- Title of the position to which the job reports
- Summary of responsibilities
- Budget, staffing, and other dimensions that the job controls/impacts

- Primary accountabilities and responsibilities
- Primary areas with which the job coordinates work
- Decision-making authority
- Overall requirements for knowledge, skills, or certifications

Using the job evaluation criteria, this information is then used to determine the level of the position. The job description can also be used for clarifying performance expectations, identifying dimensions for performance evaluation, developing selection tests, and describing career paths. However, few organizations use job descriptions for more than communicating general accountabilities of the job and determining the salary grade level assignments.

The criteria used in most of these job evaluation systems fall into four basic areas:

1. Knowledge and Skills

   Technical know-how
   Specialized knowledge
   Organizational awareness
   Educational levels
   Specialized training
   Years of experience required
   Interpersonal skills
   Degree of managerial or supervisory skills

2. Performance Effort

   Diversity of tasks
   Complexity of tasks
   Creativity of thinking
   Analytical problem solving
   Physical application of skills
   Degree of assistance available

3. Scope of Responsibility

   Decision-making authority
   Scope of the organization under one's control
   Scope of the organization where one has impact
   Degree of integration of work with others
   Impact of failure or risk associated with work
   Ability to perform tasks without supervision

4. Working Conditions

   Potential hazards inherent in job
   Degree of danger which can be exposed to others (e.g., handling toxic materials)
   Impact of specialized motor or concentration skills

Degree of discomfort, exposure, or dirtiness in doing job
Impact of work on personal relationships (i.e., travel)

The job evaluation process involves applying a set of dimensions for a selected number of these factors to the position and determining an overall score for each. These scores are then added or weighted in a prescribed fashion to reach a final score. This process occurs in a variety of settings: (1) a group of people in a committee; (2) a small team of experts from the compensation department; or (3) through a computer scoring of a questionnaire.

Regardless of the method used, all jobs are scored using the same criteria. This makes possible the establishment of a rank order of positions. The rank ordering or clustering of the positions into a series of grades or levels, is then compared to current pay levels and market pay levels for similar positions to determine the range of pay most appropriate to individuals at similar levels.

Finally, salaries are administered using a variety of decision tools. The first is the salary range. This range defines the minimum and maximum the organization is willing to pay for work of a specific nature. Based on the analysis of the marketplace and job evaluation criteria, the position is usually assigned to a grade level with a predetermined salary range. Positions with a similar job evaluation and marketplace reference have the same salary range. This salary range provides the guidelines necessary for the organization to manage compensation costs. Individuals at the lower end of the salary range are considered *learners,* and individuals at the upper levels are considered *high performers,* in that the organization is paying a discount or a premium, respectively, for their efforts. Individuals paid around the middle of the range (also known as the midpoint) are generally considered as *fully competent.*

Problems often emerge when the actual performance of the individual is not consistent with their position in the salary range. The customary practice is to make a salary adjustment if the person is paid below an appropriate level for their performance, or freeze or limit pay increases for the person who is considered overpaid for his or her performance or job function. In this way, the salary range can serve to control compensation costs relative to a midpoint or control point level.

Many organizations use a salary increase matrix to administer salary increases. This matrix (see Figure 5-2) is usually divided into 3 or 5 vertical and horizontal sectors, with one dimension being zones within the salary range and the other being levels of performance. As shown in the exhibit, individuals who are paid low in the salary range but who are high performers receive the largest pay increase. Individuals who are high in the range but are performing below standard receive no or little pay increase. Consequently, the matrix manages compensa-

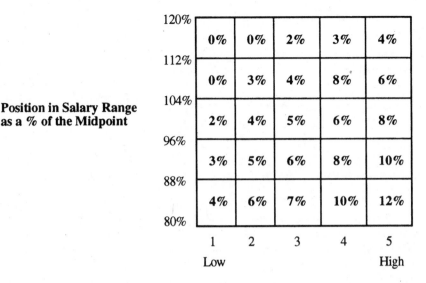

Position in Salary Range as a % of the Midpoint

120%					
	0%	0%	2%	3%	4%
112%					
	0%	3%	4%	8%	6%
104%					
	2%	4%	5%	6%	8%
96%					
	3%	5%	6%	8%	10%
88%					
	4%	6%	7%	10%	12%
80%					
	1	2	3	4	5
	Low				High

Individual Performance Rating

Figure 5-2. Traditional salary increase guide.

tion relative to the midpoint levels by providing controls relative to the level of salary increases permitted. This process of relating the salary increase to the performance and the position within the salary range is referred to as *pay for performance.*

If an individual is promoted to a higher level or a new job is created that results in a higher job evaluation, the individual is moved to a higher salary range. The position in the salary range declines as the individual's current pay is compared to the new salary range. Depending on the number of levels the promotion reflects (frequently there is a one- or two-level difference), a promotional increase is usually provided. If after this change in pay, the individual remains in the lower portion of the new salary range, he or she receives a higher salary increase at the next performance review, depending on the performance rating.

These tools—job description, job evaluation, salary ranges, salary increase guides, etc.—comprise the elements of traditional base pay systems. While many organizations have added new features to many of these, the fundamental premise reflects the following:

- The organization pays for the job, not the person.
- Internal equity is determined by a common set of job evaluation factors or internal comparisons of responsibilities.

- External competitiveness is determined by the level of salary ranges.
- Salaries are administered relative to the midpoint of the salary range, reflecting this level as the appropriate price for a job that is performed in a fully competent fashion.
- The job description is the foundation for the system, and the salary increase guidelines and job evaluation process control the compensation expenditures of the organization.

What Is Wrong with This Picture?

This summary describes the traditional process for determining and managing base salaries. These practices were established during the 1950s and 1960s and are used by thousands of organizations. The Wyatt Company, a compensation and benefits consulting firm, reports that over 98 percent of the *Fortune* 500 companies have a similar form of merit-based compensation system. An entire industry of compensation consulting has grown up around these principles, and organizations spend millions of dollars each year on services to support such systems. Given the amount of money that organizations spend on compensation for their employees, it is no wonder that internal expertise is developed and external expertise sought to ensure that dollars are spent wisely. But are they? Let's examine some issues that have emerged as a result of current practices.

In the first chapter we discussed the emergence of a new philosophy of management that places the customer at the center of work activities. Whether the customer is the external user of products or services or an internal user, more and more organizations are creating opportunities for the customer to have more impact on the actions of people. Yet traditionally, bureaucratic organizational structures have reinforced the manager as the customer, and in so doing have fragmented work, increased oversight functions, and emphazied control. As organizations attempt to realign their activities with a customer-oriented, horizontal rather than vertical perspective, conflicts have arisen with the compensation systems that once supported traditional structures.

To understand many of these conflicts, one needs to look at each element in the traditional compensation system. The first is the job description. The standard description asks people to document certain aspects of their job that reflect the command-and-control paradigm. These include:

- Whom you report to—strengthening the idea of hierarchy
- What resources (people, budgets, etc.) you control—reinforcing the

point that the more you direct and control, the more valuable your job

- The responsibilities of your job—implying that the more responsibilities are yours alone, the more important your job
- The decision-making authority—reflecting the idea that the more decisions you control, the more important your job is.

So, from the very start, the next-level manager is designated as the customer and the job is fulfilled by performing a set of upwardly focused responsibilities. Where is the customer? What is the value-added nature of the function? How can the talents of the individual be reflected in valuing the importance of the position?

In many organizations job descriptions are viewed as a necessary evil to get a job into the level desired by the manager. One frequently finds people searching for the magic words that will provide the desired result or using impressive-sounding phrases merely to comply with policies or regulations. At best job descriptions can become good antecedents to the performer, but few meaningful, immediate consequences are associated with them (except for job evaluation). Overall, job descriptions are either insufficiently used or associated with negative reinforcement (i.e., "do just enough to get by").

The job evaluation criteria are usually based on a theoretical paradigm that jobs form the basic economic unit of the organization and need to be highly differentiated from one another for their scope to be effectively measured. This is rooted in the Frederick Taylor approach to scientific management developed in the early 1900s.[2] The more independence and control over resources that reflect a job, the more valuable to the organization it is seen to be. Is this consistent with a customer-focused organization? Increasingly, as organizations seek to reduce unnecessary levels of management, delegate decision-making authority to the lowest possible level, and create teams with accountability for critical functions, we find a direct conflict with the system of rewards that uses traditional job evaluation as its foundation.

For example, when ATT was undergoing its massive cultural change efforts in the 1980s, and sought to remove layers of management and increase the use of cross-functional teams, many managers fought the change because they thought it implied a reduction in their job evaluation points. These point levels had become a yardstick for measuring the status one held in the organization and had for a long time been associated with management perks and authority. Hence, the job evaluation system reinforced, along with many other bureaucratic practices, the idea that power and status were associated with the hierarchy of the organization.

An examination of the salary administration system, reveals several very interesting, competition-oriented practices. First, the salary increase guide provides pay increases based on individual performance and the level within the salary range. Since few people are rated at the highest level, and fewer people are rated below competent or midlevel, most employees are rated at average or above-average performance. Therefore, if one wants to maximize pay, the strategy is to continually seek upgrades or promotions so that one remains in the lower quadrant of the salary range. Employees and managers in a large publishing company with such a system, for example, were often heard to remark that once you went above midpoint, you were dead in the water when it came to salary increases.

Second, because there is usually a fixed budget for salary increases, when any individual receives more than the average, someone else in the group has to receive less. For example, if an average pay increase budget for a group of ten people is 5 percent, and one person gets $7\frac{1}{2}$ percent, the extra $2\frac{1}{2}$ percent will have to come out of one or more of the others' increases. Hence, people in the team will be in competition with each other to protect their standing in the group. This win-lose game reflects an inherently competitive pattern of management that subtly undermines the spirit of collaboration required by most of today's organizations.

Ned Morse refers to this as the "Pie-Comp" system, which divides a static amount of money among a group of employees. As he states:

> Organizations need innovation, calculated risk-taking, teamwork, and a spirit of idea and information sharing to surmount today's economic challenges, but Pie-Comp programs reinforce information hoarding, CYA maneuvers, risk aversion, and competition among employees at all levels."[3]

Finally, the performance is typically evaluated on the basis of individual achievements. This assessment should reflect a full year's performance, but in most cases it takes into consideration only the critical incidents in the preceding two to three months. The value of earlier achievements is often forgotten or discounted. Furthermore, the achievements of the individual are often weighed more heavily than the achievements of the group of which the performer is a member. Individuals seek recognition, and managers frequently seek to use salary increases to recognize their top performers.

If salary increases are out of guidelines, the manager often needs to justify this action to some higher authority. If no salary increase is provided, then documentation is necessary in order to protect the organization from being sued by the employee for wrongful treatment. Therefore, in order to avoid an adverse consequence in either situation (i.e., negative reinforcement), the manager will provide pay increases within a moderate range and attempt to explain to the higher performers that the system will not allow a larger pay increase but that they will be recommended for a promotion or job upgrade.

As organizations reduce levels of management, combine salary ranges to create broad bands, and reduce the amount of money available for merit increases, the salary administration program has lost its impact on performance. Employees continue to want and expect regular pay increases, and managers seek to do what they can. We find ourselves with an engine that is without gasoline and unable to drive performance.

Applying the SMART Criteria

Let's examine the traditional base salary program against the criteria of an effective reward system presented in Chapter 3 on the fundamentals of reward systems.

Specific

Most base salary programs have few areas in which a clear line of sight can be established. First, the level of pay needs to be sufficient so that the performer does not seek employment alternatives elsewhere. The range is frequently dependent on what one views as primary references for value/worth. This is frequently a very personal decision. Second, while managers often seek to manipulate the system through the job description and job evaluation process, these practices often undermine the collaboration and customer focus of one's activities. Third, the salary increase process is usually well known, although employees frequently don't know what they need to start doing or do differently to receive higher performance ratings and associated higher pay increases. (There will be more on this in Chapter 9.)

Meaningful

Job promotions are often the only significant reward an individual receives from the salary administration system. Not only is the money a higher amount than received in merit increases, the promotion often places the person at a level in the new salary range at which increased opportunities are the greatest. However, as organizations remove layers or broaden the salary ranges, opportunities for promotion are decreasing. Hence, base salary programs are offering fewer and fewer meaningful rewards.

Achievable

If the salary system can be easily manipulated, the desired results can be achieved. But results in this context undermine the intent and design of the salary administration system. From a performance standpoint, if the employee clearly understands the performance expectations and perceives them as achievable, there is an opportunity to reward desired performance. The fallacy is that the performance is often only evaluated on an annual basis, encouraging participants to apply extra effort only as they approach the review date. Results achieved earlier in the performance cycle are often forgotten or considered not sufficiently challenging to be worth a reward. Clearly, the messsage is that one must look very busy, act as if the assignment were monumental, then make it in time so that the evaluation of performance can be "properly" considered.

Reliable

Much has been said about how current salary administration systems are being undermined by the practices of managers. What is quite interesting in many companies is that this practice is reinforced. Compensation departments are required to be customer focused and many line managers are interpreting this to mean that they now have the authority to do what they want. The challenge is to redesign the system so that it works to meet the needs of its customers, line managers, employees, and shareholders.

Finally, current practices require a significant number of staff to keep job descriptions and evaluations up to date, analyze market survey data, and plan/budget/control the salary increases. As compensation staffs are reduced, the process of administering pay in the traditional manner is becoming more difficult.

Timely

Because most salary administration systems are built on an annual cycle, it is difficult to view them as timely. When jobs are documented, evaluated, and repriced on a frequent basis, the systems reinforce actions to upgrade or market price jobs. Since the focus needs to be on enabling the organization to be more competitive and successful, salary administration systems as currently configured do not provide sufficiently frequent awards.

In summary, the question is not why current base salary programs are not effective, but why we ever believed they would work to drive desired performance. Based on this analysis, it seems clear that base salary programs are not effective at reinforcing the desired behavior. In many cases they actually undermine the process of change; at best, they are neutral. Thus, pay for performance, using this type of system, simply does not exist—as managers and employees have been telling executives and compensation professionals through various employee opinion surveys for some time. This leads us to two questions:

- If base salary programs don't work to reinforce desired performance, what is their purpose?
- How can we make base salary programs more effective in reinforcing desired behaviors?

Redefining the Purpose of Base Salary Programs

Given the challenges facing today's business and the changes they are instituting, the fundamental requirement is to redefine the purpose of the base salary program. In Chapter 3 I outlined the critical decisions involved in developing a rewards strategy. Within this context we need to formulate the purpose of the base salary program. Once it is identified, we can select and develop an alternative system that reflects not only the fundamental requirements of the organization, but those of the people whose behaviors we seek to reinforce—and in the process makes them the customers of the system.

To review briefly, there are two basic elements necessary to a firm's ability to implement its strategy: the *economics* of the firm (i.e., how it makes its money and performs its services) and the *values* of the firm (i.e., the particular behaviors and culture that make the organization a special place). The base salary program is best suited to support the values of the firm because the nature of the rewards can focus on the behaviors and contributions of the individual. The base pay program can be *personalized*, and the differences in base pay can reflect the unique contributions of each individual. While an individual may make an economic contribution to the firm (e.g., a salesperson making a sale), these actions are often best handled with the variable pay program (e.g., sales incentive plan).

Therefore, the purpose of the base pay program within the context of a total reward system will be to: *Provide a method for reinforcing the value-added contributions of each individual through the application of their talents, the growth of their capabilities, and the performance of their actions consistent with the key success factors of the organization.*

This fundamental purpose carries several critical messages. First, the base salary program provides a method for reinforcing desired behaviors. We can use the base pay system to reinforce *how* results are achieved, not just *what* results are achieved. Second, the focus is on the individual. Although the performance of teams may have a direct bearing on one's compensation and pay opportunities, the focus is on providing a base salary that is keyed to the individual. Third, individuals impact the success of the organization in three ways: (1) in the application of their talents; (2) in the growth of their capabilities; and (3) in the results of their actions.

Hence, the focus will be on how the individual applies his or her talents to the organization and how those talents grow and develop. Peter Senge's work on defining the learning organization is reflected here in creating reinforcers by which people learn, continue to learn, and strengthen the capabilities of the organization to meet ever-changing and challenging external situations.[4]

Finally, the organization's key success factors form the foundation for the base salary program. Each organization serves a customer and has a unique set of competencies and strategies to give it a competitive edge. Some experts in the field refer to this as the *core competencies* of the organization: those things that the firm does particularly well and that provide it with an advantage in the marketplace.[5]

It will be important to go beyond the core competencies and reflect the requirements of the organization to implement its basic business strategy—*how* it will be successful. While key success factors are usually conceptual and strategic in nature, they need to be translated into a set of criteria that will form the basis for the allocation of compensation dollars. In this manner compensation becomes the investments made by the organization in its human resources to gain market leadership or fulfill its basic mission.

When compared to traditional thinking about base salaries, one should note the absence of the external marketplace or the emphasis on internal equity. An organization that is not able to provide an attractive place to work for a reasonably competitive pay level will not be able to acquire the talent it needs to do its business. Consequently, it will not be able to have the talent necessary to be successful. In my experience with consulting to hundreds of companies, the external market needs to be a centerpiece of the pay system only when the firm desperately needs to attract or protect its human resources. When the attraction and retention of human resources is a key success factor, pay levels should operate well above the norm. This means that the firm needs to be aggressive in hiring or retaining talent. When the firm has to operate with minimal costs, pay levels should be below average market values. Hence, the marketplace is really a tertiary reference for the base pay system and for the employees. In contrast, the pay system needs to be geared more to the individual and to the organization.

Further, internal equity is not a primary focus for the new requirements of reward systems. When people complain about the lack of fairness in the current compensation program, they are generally reflecting either a lack of understanding of the requirements of others or a sense of not being valued and reinforced by the organization. Traditional compensation systems seldom satisfy either of these concerns. In a reinforcement-enriched environment, people are not concerned about what others get; they feel valued for what they personally do.

Further, as will be discussed later in this chapter, new approaches to establishing base salary levels need to be highly visible and well understood by managers and employees. Internal equity need not be an issue if it is defined in a manner in which it can be understood or solved.

The old thinking holds that internal equity is based on seniority and job responsibility. The new thinking, based on concepts of performance and reinforcement, holds that internal equity is based on individual contributions and accomplishments. With this purpose in mind, let's examine some alternative approaches to developing a reward-oriented base salary program.

Turning Base Salaries into Reward Programs

A basic premise of this model of compensation design is that there is no single, perfect system for every organization. Therefore, we will discuss several alternative approaches, each with particular advantages and disadvantages. The task for the reader is to select an approach that best fits the needs of his or her organization, then modify and adapt it to the organization's particular requirements using the SMART principles outlined earlier.

Team-Based Salary Increases

Perhaps the easiest change to make is in how salary increases are determined. While traditional approaches compare the individual's performance to the level in the salary range (note the salary increase guide described earlier), an easy alternative is to change the dimensions on the decision matrix. Instead of using the salary range position, use the performance of the team. (Individual performance indicators should examine how well the individual contributed to making the team successful.) The actual increase may be adjusted if a person is particularly low or high in the salary range, but this is done for an equity adjustment, not based on performance (see Figure 5-3).

In addition, the decision-making process can be expanded to include the team as well as the manager. This is sometimes referred to as a

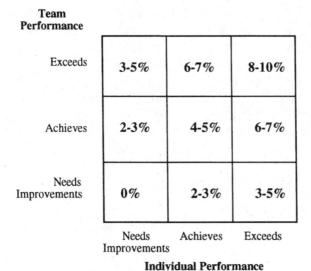

Figure 5-3. Team-based salary increase guidelines.

360-degree review or multi-rater reviews, in which feedback on an individual's performance is gathered from all those affected by the individual's actions. While traditional practices place the manager in the sole decision-making role, an alternative would be to empower the team to make salary increase recommendations or decisions for members of the team. Obviously this step requires a team that can honestly and with integrity differentiate among the performances of individual members and reinforce those that have truly made a difference. This decision can be made as input to the manager who has final decision-making authority or delegated entirely to the team. Another alternative is to use the manager to coordinate the collection of assessment feedback from multiple sources, and share all this with the performer. The conclusion will be a clear performance standing that is not based solely on the judgment of the manager. The decision on salary increases should be made after the *team's* performance has been evaluated, and the range of pay increases is known.

This matrix has several simple advantages. First, it uses the performance of the team directly in the considerations on salary increases. This encourages the individual to work for the team's success as well as his or her own success. Second, it removes the salary range as a major determinant of an employee's pay increases. This reduces the pressure to seek promotional increases in order to provide pay increases. Equity adjustments can still be made, but as a separate decision independent of the reward decisions.

The primary disadvantage is that the matrix does not control compensation expenses. Expense controls need to be put in place so that pay increases do not become excessive, particularly when salaries approach the maximum of the salary range. Although this may be viewed as a drawback, it does have the advantage of removing decisions about rewards and reinforcement from decisions about cost control. The author feels strongly that one should use the correct tools for the correct application and not seek to use a single tool for multiple, conflicting needs. Or stated another way, one should not use the salary increase process to both reward performance and control costs. Use it to reward performance and use the budget and financial control process to manage costs.

Variable Merit Pool

One of the principal problems with current merit pay systems is that they are fundamentally a zero-sum game. If one member of the team is to get more than the budget, then someone else has to get less. This basically competitive situation seldom leads to encouraging superior performance, but rather encourages individuals not to find ways to help others be successful. This is based on the assumption that the amount of money available for merit pay increases is fixed. Why does it need to be fixed?

An alternative is to make the merit pool variable. Based on the performance of the team, division, or company, the merit pool can be increased or decreased. Then individuals can receive a share of this pool as their merit pay increase based on individual and\or team performance. This makes for a mutual interest in increasing the size of the pool through the improved performance of the whole. Increases in pay that are not allocated are not automatically redistributed to other teams because to do so would be to create inappropriate competitive struggles within the organization. But savings can be generated by reducing pay increases to units that are underperforming.[6]

A midsize manufacturing division of a large industrial company adopted this concept. The company planned and budgeted for a 5 percent average pay increase. It established specific performance measures for the four key divisions, and adjusted merit pay increases based on both company and divisional performance. Every employee was adjusted to a common salary increase date 45 days after the end of the fiscal year. Overall, the company achieved its goals slightly ahead of target, and therefore the merit pay increase was adjusted to 6 percent. Of the four divisions, two fell below the target, and their merit adjustments were reduced to 4 percent. Another was on target and received 6 percent. The fourth was significantly above target and received an average of 8 percent. The pay increase for each person was figured at this planned level.

(Another alternative would have been to provide people with pay adjustments when they achieved a predetermined level of performance. This could be less than 1 year for those early achievers or beyond a year for those slow starters. This could have been at either the team or the individual level, and would have linked the pay increase to the goal achievement, rather than to an arbitrary time period. The system requires careful performance measures and goal setting and needs to reflect a process of continual improvement. Pay increases don't have to be the same as traditional annual increases, but they do have to be meaningful to the performers.)

The primary lesson to be learned from this company's experience is that the merit pay program is tightly aligned with the success of the company and each division. At this firm, the opportunity for pay increases was generally known to be 5 percent if the organization and its various parts were able to achieve desired performance levels. Divisional objectives and performance were well understood across the areas of the company—a fact that contributed to the acceptance of the diversity in merit increases. Actual pay increases ranged from 0 for the team and individuals who simply did not perform well to 12 percent for the high performing team and individuals. This process significantly reduced the we/they condition operating among employees and between managers and the human resources compensation department.

Market Price Jobs within a Broad Band

The current approach to job evaluation reinforces the concept of command and control. In order to increase one's pay opportunities, one needs to expand the scope of resource control as well as decision-making authority. Obviously, this runs counter to what many firms are attempting to implement in order to increase their flexibility and competitiveness.

An alternative is to change the basis on which jobs are priced and pay opportunities are determined. This approach involves establishing a market price for a job, based on the rates of pay for similar positions as well as on the rates necessary to attract the talent needed. Then, based on strategic considerations, this rate is adjusted, increased, or decreased. The pay rates become guidelines to managers for administering salaries. Further, the number of grade levels are reduced, providing salary ranges geared more to fundamental differences in roles within the organization. The result is a broad salary range or a specific target rate of pay for each position.

The following will illustrate this briefly. A large technology company reduced the number of grade levels for their exempt, professional employees from 12 to 3. The salary ranges were increased from 50 percent (from minimum pay level to the maximum pay level for the range) to up to 200 percent. The levels were defined as:

- Basic, entry level contributor
- Seasoned contributor or team leader
- Business unit\team managerial or senior professional contributors

Then within these levels, managers hired and calibrated pay levels based on market information for individuals with similar backgrounds and responsibilities. The managers were given market data and charged with the responsibility of making salary adjustments as appropriate to attract, retain, and reward their staff. They had to operate within a designated payout cost budget, but how these dollars were allocated was based on managerial judgments.

In order to provide pay target guidelines, the market for capabilities needs to be defined based on a variety of sources. First, the external market can be defined as what other organizations pay people with similar roles and responsibilities. Second, the external market can be segmented to target on what level of pay is needed to attract the quality of talent desired. In organizations experiencing rapid growth, understanding the competition and establishing a competitive advantage are key to attracting the talent needed for the firm. Third, while the external market may be a useful benchmark, another consideration is to examine where people come from and where people go. This analysis can be performed by developing a human resource movement matrix as shown in Figure 5-4.

The human resource movement matrix is rather simple to conceptualize, but requires sound data to construct. First, one defines the target group of employees, such as engineers, marketeers, skilled technicians, etc. Second, one defines the scales for describing movement within the group. The most frequent method is to use salary grade levels, although other forms of assessment may be useful. Third, one needs to define the time period for assessing the movement of people; usually this is between one and three years. Finally, the matrix is constructed by indicating the number of people who started in one level and ended in another level during the prescribed period. There are columns for noting the levels at which people were hired and left the organization (through transfers, exits to competitors, exits to others). What this presents is a analytical map of the movement of people in the organization.

The analysis of this data can provide several very valuable insights.

The number of employees that started in grade level:		The number of employees that ended in grade level:						
Grade	No. Empl's.	21	22	23	24	25	26	Terminated
21	24	18	3	1				2
22	60		45	12	1			2
23	82			60	15	2		5
24	58				46	2		10
25	22					17	3	2
26	7						6	1
	Hired	6			12	6	1	
	Ending Total	24	48	73	74	27	10	

Figure 5-4. Human resource movement matrix.

First, one can clearly identify the sources of new employees, where they entered the system, and where they were promoted to higher levels. Second, one can clearly identify where the most vulnerable leaks are in the system. Are the terminations desired or undesired by the organization? Third, one can identify where the stuck jobs are (that is, which people are not moving beyond a certain level) and even pinpoint organizations that are a frequent source of talent. The extent of the analysis can go as far as one needs to go to answer the key questions about the flow of human resources.

This human resource movement matrix has been used by companies active in the areas of human resource planning. The implications of compensation design are very powerful both for defining the marketplace for talent and for understanding how competitive compensation levels need to be. Based on this data, the market price can be established in a more strategic and systematic manner.

Case History

A large aerospace technology company became concerned about retaining its engineering staff. Its immediate response was to raise the salaries of all the technical staff by up to 15 percent, costing the organization an additional $2.5MM. When a human resource movement matrix was completed, some interesting findings emerged. First the company had recruited a large number of entry level engineers, and over 80 percent of them had left within three years. Then the firm had hired a large number of midlevel engineers from competing companies to replace the new recruits and many of this *second* group of engineers had left within five years. Meanwhile, the upper-level, highly seasoned engineers had remained in their positions for many years with only few terminations. But the pattern that had emerged was one of a revolving door when it came to career progression for newcomers. This pattern was further verified through employee focus groups and interviews with terminated employees. The employees felt the firm offered them little career advancement opportunity or serious development. The only career paths open to them lead directly into program management or unit supervision. There was little recognition of strong technical expertise. By understanding these reinforcers and creating new career paths, pay opportunities, and training processes, the company was able to solve its problem. Not only did it not spend additional compensation dollars to retain much-needed talent, it was able to achieve greater performance from the unit because of the increased stability of its professional workforce.

The second aspect of this approach is to identify the strategic spin on the pricing of jobs. By this I mean that once the price of talent in a given marketplace is understood, senior managers need to assess whether this will support the strategic requirements of the organization. The primary factors to consider may involve:

- *The requirements for new products/services and processes.* Does this position have a direct and significant impact on the firm's ability to compete in the future?

- *The impact on resource utilization.* Does this position have a special and significant impact on the firm's ability to develop, control, or utilize resources within the organization, whether or not they are within direct control?

- *The impact on customer relationships.* Does this position provide a vital link between the organization and its external customers, creating the kind of close, integrated, and sustained partnership essential to the success of the enterprise?

- *The impact on supplier relationships.* Does this position provide a vital link between the organization and its external suppliers so that the firm receives the materials, resources, and information in the most efficient manner so that the competitive advantage is sustained?

- *The impact on the culture and values of the organization.* Does this position provide a broad and significant impact on the organization's culture and facilitate the translation of its values into practice?

An assessment of the degree to which the position has an impact in any or all of these areas will determine its strategic importance to the organization. Then the market price should be adjusted to reflect its importance to the firm. This combined practice will enable the company to establish salary levels sufficient to attract and retain the talent it needs, while adjusting the levels for those areas that have a strategic role within the context of the firm.

Job Evaluation that Reflects Core Values

Companies that adopted job evaluation systems developed in the 1950s, 1960s, and 1970s were buying the philosophy of management that was prevalent in those days. But as we move into the twenty-first century, the requirements for success have changed, and we need to question the philosophical principles on which these systems were based. Today we see a management philosophy emerging that is focused more on creating what is value-added for the customer and promoting an organizational commitment to quality, flexibility, and speed. Retaining the philosophy of command and control, of job specialization, and of hierarchical relationships is keeping many of today's organizations from being truly successful. Even many Japanese companies are instituting changes that enhances decision-making authority and accountability at the lowest levels.

Another approach to redesigning an organization's job evaluation systems is to analyze the factors that reflect the firms's values, core competencies, and economic value-added functions. This involves asking new questions about the structure of work tasks and determining worth from a customer-focused, value-added framework.

The methodology begins with a different approach to job descriptions. Instead of asking the standard questions (whom do you report to? What resources/people do you control/impact? What is your decision-making authority?), you ask:

- Who are your customers and what do they need?
- Who are your suppliers and what do you receive from them?
- What value-added activities do you perform to produce what end results?
- What are the key requirements for your success?
- What are the primary indicators or measures of your performance?

These questions provide a method to define roles within a customer-focused context and may serve as an important antecedent to new behaviors. This information can also be used to support a role assessment process, not a job evaluation system, which reflects the factors truly important to the firm's competitive success.

The development if this assessment process can take many different forms. One of the simplest involves three steps. The first is to define the activities and behaviors that best reflect the values, core competencies, and key success factors of the business. The more they can be measured in actual results, the easier the assessment process will be. Examples may include the following:

- Integrates with customers

  Understands needs of the external customer
  Utilizes a sense of urgency to meet customer needs
  Integrates feedback from customers into operations
  Positively impacts customer's ability to achieve/retain competitiveness

- Integrates with critical suppliers

  Translates firm's needs to external suppliers
  Ensures that suppliers' services are aligned with firm's needs
  Integrates capabilities and performance of suppliers into operations

- Establishes focus

  Ensures work has a clear purpose and is linked to primary objectives/mission of unit
  Exercises discipline to keep activities working in concert with unit objectives
  Communicates to others the purpose, rationale, and requirements for success

- Utilizes resources effectively

  Determines priorities in relation to customer needs, organizational goals, and operating values
  Assures that resources are utilized in the most efficient manner possible
  Establishes clear, specific measures to track progress
  Positively impacts firm's ability to serve customers
  Anticipates and determines resource requirements necessary to achieve key goals

- Empowers others

  Verbally expresses trust and confidence in the abilities of others to succeed
  Encourages others to take calculated risks to achieve desired ends
  Encourages individuals and teams to set their own goals and align them with overall unit goals

Allows others to decide how tasks will be accomplished after delegating them

- Focuses on continuous improvement

  Sets, maintains, and monitors work activities
  Implements strategies to develop capabilities
  Seeks innovative ways to achieve objectives with fewer resources or less time

- Collaborates and integrates work with others

  Works collaboratively with related functions
  Participates in interdisciplinary efforts to achieve goals
  Keeps others informed of key events in a timely fashion

The second step is the assessment process, which should be carried out by a panel of experts using a paired comparison or delphi decision-making methodology. In this technique, a set of core positions is evaluated by comparing each factor to each of the role definitions or positions. The task is to determine whether the position in question is the same, higher, or lower than a comparable position for a given factor. This process is best implemented with a computer decision-making system to expedite the decision-making process, retain the decision records, and make it fun for the evaluator. The result is a rank order of all the positions based on the critical criteria. Not only is the order important; so is the relative scaling of the positions in dimensions.

The third step involves analyzing and clustering the ranking of the positions into levels consistent with their patterns. The positions are reviewed for quality assurance, and additional positions are integrated into the system by comparing job families or positions with similar functions. No attempt is made to draw cross-functional comparisons beyond the core benchmark positions. The end result is a set of levels that reflects the values and philosophy the organization needs to support its strategic direction.[7]

There are several risks inherent in this approach. First, the factors need to be clearly defined and understood by the panel of experts. Second, the source documents for the assessment—customer-centered role definitions—need to provide the information necessary to make a sound judgment. Third, because the process does not attempt to address marketplace pressures but instead reflects the unique value structure of the organization, the actual pricing of jobs needs to become a separate decision-making activity once the ranking is completed.

Case History

A large southwestern bank introduced new role assessment criteria based on core values required by its new competitive business strategy. When the function of customer service representative or CSR (i.e., the traditional teller function) was reviewed, it was priced at approximately 20 percent above the market rates for standard CSRs. While the difference was shocking, the reasoning became clear. The bank had transformed this role from one centered on transactions and accuracy into one focused on service and relationships. The bank was making extensive use of automated teller machines and so standard transactions had declined considerably. Those who used the services of a CSR had a real need, or an opportunity, for sales. Relationships were very important to these customers, and it was important for the bank to retain its key staff. Fewer CSRs were needed by the bank than in previous, transaction-oriented years, but the quality and importance of their work had increased. These changes had not yet been reflected in the rates of pay of the bank's competitors. This gave them a competitive advantage to attract and retain desired talent and the role definition gave them clearer recruitment and selection criteria.

In summary, this approach offers the advantage of rebuilding the foundation for a base compensation program grounded in translating core competencies and values into the structure of the organization and its investments in its people. It is more extensive than changes to salary increases, but may offer an attractive alternative to the stranglehold of current job evaluation systems.

Pay for Competencies Employed (PACE™)

However they are configured, job evaluation systems allocate pay based on the content of the job. There is little or no value placed on the talent or people performing the function unless the system is manipulated or interpreted to reflect the talents of the people in the jobs. An increasing number of companies are experimenting with pay systems based on the talents of the individual and the way they are employed within the work setting. I refer to these as pay-for-competencies-employed (PACE™) plans. They are similar to pay for skill plans, pay for knowledge plans, and career-based pay plans in that they focus on the talent of the individual but are different because we need to examine the application of that talent to work.

The American Compensation Association (ACA) recently conducted a study of these plans and discovered that although they had been developed for operational (usually manufacturing) employees, their underlying concepts were being employed in professional service functions like information systems, engineering, legal services, consulting, and accounting.[8]

Companies seek this form of compensation when the skill mix of its workforce is not consistent with the emerging requirements for being competitive. In many cases they seek cross-training by employees so that several individuals can do the same job. This is most appropriate when the firm can and should move its human resources to reflect the volume of work and when flexibility is essential. Often, bottlenecks develop in operations as work waits for people to get to it. PACE-type pay programs serve to reduce these bottlenecks by rewarding people who have and apply cross-functional skills.

Companies also seek this form of compensation when they are undergoing significant technological change and when jobs of a routine nature are being eliminated. Employees are then encouraged to expand their knowledge, skills, and abilities in order to perform more advanced jobs.

Case History

A funds accounting operation of a large financial services company was instituting a variety of computer-based systems that would eliminate transaction-related functions. Rather than terminating large numbers of people and hiring more skilled ones, the transition plan included implementing a competency-based pay program along with specialized skills training. The new tasks upgraded skills from routine accounting and transaction processing to analyzing transactions for errors or unusual trading patterns and preventing errors before they appeared on the customers' statements. This strategy resulted in the firm's discharging a minimal number of employees, experiencing a smoother transition in operational functions, retaining staff with the know-how to run manual systems if the computer systems malfunctioned, and increasing the level of its services to fund managers.

The primary advantage companies seek with PACE-type programs is an increased flexibility by the workforce to respond to changes in the way work is performed. Companies are also seeking cost reductions, because with Pace-type programs fewer people are usually needed to perform the same functions. While this is often the way such programs are sold to senior management, the ACA study concluded that few firms realize significant cost saving through downsizing.[9] Perhaps the greatest advantage of PACE-type programs is that they enhance employee performance so that a firm gains greater return on investment from its compensation dollars.

The disadvantages of PACE-type programs are often built into the way they are designed or a company raises its expectations for continual pay increases. First, the cost savings stated above are seldom realized. The firm may experience higher actual labor costs in the effort to gain greater productivity, but unit costs may decline. If such performance improvements are not soon realized, this type of pay program is not a worthwhile investment. This is the first reason why most of these forms of pay programs are disbanded.

Another is that these systems require the organization to invest in training and development opportunities for employees to use the skills they've acquired. If the nature of work does not provide or even require these new skills on a regular and extensive basis, the system may not be appropriate. Further, once the pay system is in place, employees tend to want to receive the necessary training and development. This training may come from more seasoned employees or from special programs conducted by the organization. Regardless of how it is provided, employees want to take advantage of the opportunities presented to them to expand their contributions and increase their earnings.

Finally, administering such systems with integrity and reliability is frequently a major undertaking. Depending on the extent of the assessment process, records will need to be kept on each employee's evaluation and development. Management will need to ensure that the program is applied consistently to all employees and that employees who clearly demonstrate the application of their abilities on the work receive their rewards. This investment will need to be considered in the overall cost and return on investment requirement of the system.

One application used by some companies is to pay the individuals more while they are performing the higher-skilled job, and then return them to a base rate when they perform their basic job. But companies like Pepsi-Cola, Motorola, and Texas Instruments have dropped such requirements. The primary reason is that this administrative requirement proved cumbersome, low value added, and not cost justifiable. Furthermore, it created confusion on the part of the employees and tended to strain their relationships with management. Frequently tasks were called some thing new, but performed in the same old way. The audit and control functions created more barriers among employees than they were ensuring fairness. The method now used by these companies is to increase a worker's pay after he or she has clearly learned and applied the new skill over an extended time period (three to nine months). Hence, these pay plans differ from promotions because they pay people *after* they have demonstrated the skill, where in promotions, people are paid *before* they become fully competent in a new role.

How are such plans developed? Much has been written on this subject, so I will only attempt to highlight the primary steps. This process is reflected in the flow chart shown in Figure 5-5 and in the list of elements shown in Figure 5-6. To define a range of alternatives I will describe a basic process and provide a case illustration of a more simplified version.

The first step is to identify the critical competencies necessary to perform the work. Frequently these competencies are described in terms of specific but categorical dimensions. These competencies need to reflect the critical business requirements of the organization, function, or business unit. Examples are as follows:

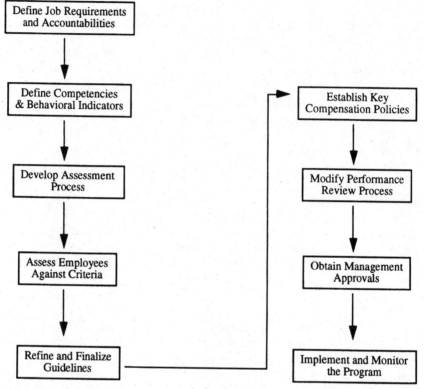

Figure 5-5. Overview of the steps for developing a pay-for-competencies-employed (PACE) plan.

- Establishes focus to assignments
- Assures quality of results
- Remains current in specialized know-how
- Demonstrates concern for work effectiveness
- Fulfills commitments and achieves results
- Contributes to the training and development of staff members
- Effectively influences others
- Contributes to the innovative resolution of work assignments
- Maintains relationships with customer/suppliers
- Participates in the selection and staffing of the unit

Next, these competencies are described in a series of levels using knowl-edge, skills, and behavior statements. These statements provide indica-

1. DEFINED LEVELS OF COMPETENCIES
   - To fulfill task requirements
   - To perform specific behaviors
2. AN ASSESSMENT PROCESS (CERTIFICATION AND MONITORING)
   - The tools to be used
   - The decision-making process
3. PRICING OF PAY LEVELS
   - To link pay levels with the value-added levels of work
4. INDIVIDUAL DEVELOPMENT PLANNING, FEEDBACK, AND REINFORCEMENT
   - To manage the developmental process
   - To reinforce desired behaviors
5. PROGRAM MANAGEMENT PROCESS
   - To provide opportunities to learn new skills
   - To provide opportunities to use new skills
   - To provide ongoing recertification and updating of requirements
   - To ensure that compensation events occur according to policies
   - To track and reinforce adherence to program guidelines.

Figure 5-6. Elements of the competency-based pay program.

tors of whether this competency is being performed consistent with the level within the organization. These indicators form the basis on which the individual will be assessed, they will be the basis for a development plan, and determine whether the additional compensation is warranted.

Earlier in this chapter I described three levels used to form broad bands for compensation. In order to develop meaningful descriptions of the competencies, defining three to four levels within the organization is often very helpful to the process. The levels may be defined as follows:

1. Entry—The emphasis is on learning the functions and skills of the work unit.

2. Contributor—The emphasis is on performing the scope of tasks needed for the unit to be successful, including team leadership.

3. Leadership—The emphasis is on guiding an operation, project, or unit, and taking full accountability for development of the people and the functions of the unit.

In this context, the competencies can be defined with two to three specific statements that characterize the level within the organization.

1. Establishes focus to assignments
   - Able to articulate the purpose and key objectives of assignments
   - Ensures that team members understand tasks and assignments
   - Ensures that the work of the team contributes directly to the company's goals
   - Establishes objectives and milestones that focus activities
2. Assures quality of results
   - Follows routine procedures and guidelines
   - Checks and validates the accuracy of own work
   - Identifies and resolves work process exceptions
   - Ensures the quality and accuracy of a group of staff members
3. Remains current in specialized know-how
   - Attends internal and selected external training programs
   - Discusses current developments and advances in own specialized field
   - Participates in assignments that expand the acquisition of new skills
   - Prepares papers and presentations reflecting continued development of skills
4. Demonstrates concern for work effectiveness
   - Sets, maintains, and monitors work activities
   - Continually seeks ways to save time, effort, and resources
   - Organizes and uses personal time to achieve project objectives
   - Seeks innovative ways to achieve objectives with fewer resources
5. Fulfills commitments and achieves desired results
   - Determines priorities in relation to business objectives
   - Establishes clear schedules and work priorities
   - Monitors progress to ensure that goals are achieved
   - Demonstrates full commitment to meeting desired goals
6. Contributes to the training and development of staff members
   - Suggests areas where training is needed for the unit
   - Offers advice when requested by others
   - Provides training, usually one to one, for less experienced staff members
   - Participates in the delivery of training to unit's staff members

Figure 5-7. Selected competencies for the engineering and development department.

The more specific and relevant these descriptions can be to the work environment, the more useful and credible they will become. An example of descriptions by competency is shown in Figure 5-7. Each statement is associated with a level within the organization.

7. Effectively influences others within and external to the unit
   - Actively listens for the needs and concerns of others
   - Establishes relationships that build mutual trust and confidence
   - Involves others in task assignments that impact their area of work or expertise
   - Persuades others to support own opinions or viewpoints
8. Contributes to the innovative resolution of work assignments
   - Defines solutions once the problems assigned are clear
   - Defines the problem/task once broad parameters/objectives have been developed
   - Defines assignments and develops strategies to achieve primary results
   - Defines key objectives and specifications in relation to the needs of customers
9. Maintains relationships with customers and/or suppliers
   - Knows the primary units with which the group interfaces
   - Provides information and assistance to others outside the unit
   - Serves as the primary liason among selected customers/suppliers
   - Establishes new relationships with customers/suppliers
   - Assists in improving/enhancing relationships with others
10. Participates in the selection and staffing of the unit
    - Provides general guidance to new staff members
    - Participates in individual and group interviews of job candidates
    - Suggests staffing needs and skill level required
    - Participates greatly in the selection and assimilation process of new staff members

Figure 5-7. (*Continued*).

The second step is to create an assessment process that answers four questions:

1. What will you focus on (priority competencies)?
2. How will you test for the competency (measures)?
3. What will you use/look at (data)?
4. How will you decide the assessment (decision-maker)?

Some organizations use independent staff to conduct the assessment, while others use the supervisory/managerial, or senior technical staff, or expert panels. A few companies are experimenting with using data direct from customers in the assessments. The individuals who make the assessment need to have the critical knowledge and objectivity to ensure that the evaluation judgments are accurate.

The decision tree shown in Figure 5-8 depicts the process for the assessment, which begins when the indicators for the examination of each competency are selected. These assessment indicators can best be applied either by examining work as it is being performed or by examining the end product of the work. The indicators can also be applied by conducting such techniques as "in-basket/bench exercises," simulated programs, case studies, etc.

One of the shortcuts sometimes used is to key the assessment to the performer's successful completion of a training program. This factor, however, may be easy to measure but is not very reliable. The performance needs to be compared to established criteria of demonstrated capability so that the degree of competency/ability attained can be determined. Then, the assessment can be categorized as follows:

- *Basic*:   Able to perform the general functions of the required tasks

- *Proficient*:   Able to perform all functions with appropriate speed and accuracy

- *Mastery*:   Able to perform the functions at a level that reflects a complete knowledge of the concepts, principles, and applications

The assessment tools and process need to be tested and validated in a variety of applications to ensure that they are valid, nondiscriminato-

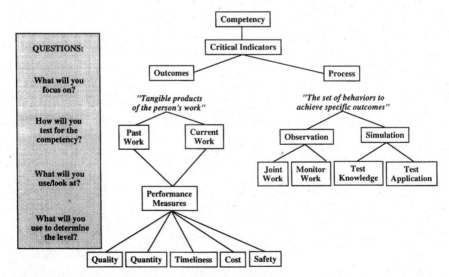

Figure 5-8. Decision-tree for the assessment process.

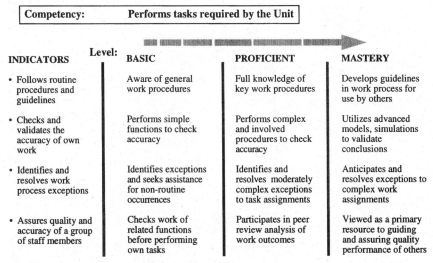

Competency:	Performs tasks required by the Unit		

INDICATORS	Level: BASIC	PROFICIENT	MASTERY
• Follows routine procedures and guidelines	Aware of general work procedures	Full knowledge of key work procedures	Develops guidelines in work process for use by others
• Checks and validates the accuracy of own work	Performs simple functions to check accuracy	Performs complex and involved procedures to check accuracy	Utilizes advanced models, simulations to validate conclusions
• Identifies and resolves work process exceptions	Identifies exceptions and seeks assistance for non-routine occurrences	Identifies and resolves moderately complex exceptions to task assignments	Anticipates and resolves exceptions to complex work assignments
• Assures quality and accuracy of a group of staff members	Checks work of related functions before performing own tasks	Participates in peer review analysis of work outcomes	Viewed as a primary resource to guiding and assuring quality performance of others

Figure 5-9. Illustrative competency assessment criteria.

ry, and cost efficient. An illustration of these proficiency levels is shown in Figure 5-9 for one of the competencies: "Performs tasks required by the Unit."

Once the levels have been defined, the third step is to price them. Once again, an examination of the marketplace and a determination of the economic value of each level is necessary. This establishes the range of pay appropriate for various functions as well as the level of pay adjustment appropriate for each achievement.

The organization needs to define the trigger for the salary adjustment that indicates when an individual is due an increase in compensation. In some organizations such salary events occur when workers demonstrate mastery of a given *skill block* or a set of competencies. This method is depicted in Figures 5-10 and 5-11.

Utilizing the competencies illustrated earlier, the skill block is defined by the mastery of different levels of competencies. As the individual demonstrates capability in certain prescribed skill block dimensions, he or she is viewed as competent in the specific level. Although an individual may show competencies in several other skills levels, he or she needs to progress through all the stages of the skill blocks in order to receive the associated increases in pay. Because the skill blocks are of increasing value to the company, they are associated with higher and higher rates of pay.

An illustration of this pay system is shown in Figure 5-12. As individuals demonstrate their competencies, they are eligible for increased pay levels. They become more valuable to the organization and their performance should demonstrate a clear return on investment.

Skill Block #1	Skill Block #2	Skill Block #3	Skill Block #4
BASIC	**BASIC**	**BASIC**	**BASIC**
Establishes focus	Fulfills Commitments	Maintains C/S relations	—
Performs required tasks	Conducts training	Participates in staffing	
Retains specialized know-how	Influences others		
Works effectively	Seeks innovative solutions		
PROFICIENT	**PROFICIENT**	**PROFICIENT**	**PROFICIENT**
—	Establishes focus	Fulfills Commitments	Maintains C/S relations
	Performs required tasks	Conducts training	Participates in staffing
	Retains specialized KH	Influences others	
	Works effectively	Seeks innovative solutions	
MASTERY	**MASTERY**	**MASTERY**	**MASTERY**
—	—	Establishes focus	Fulfills Commitments
		Performs required tasks	Conducts training
		Retains specialized KH	Influences others
		Works effectively	Seeks innovative solutions
			Maintains C/S relations
			Participates in staffing

Figure 5-10. Skill-block mastery assessment. Skill blocks are defined by competencies and the demonstrated level of performance.

STAFF MEMBERS	Skill Block #1			Skill Block #2			Skill Block #3			Skill Block #4		
	Basic	Proficient	Mastery	Basic	Proficient	Mastery	Basic	Proficient	Mastery	Basic	Proficient	Mastery
J. Johnson		X										
L. Peterson		X										
T. Iams												
I. Peters												
W. Collis				X								
E. Krembs				X								
W. Kellough				X								
C. Wilson					X							
P. Scarborough					X							
H. Anderson												
R. Harrison							X					
T. Webster								X				
S. Steele								X				
L. Bates								X				
B. Andrason										X		

Figure 5-11. Staffing level assessment summary.

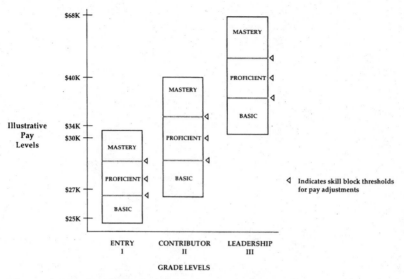

Figure 5-12. Illustrative base pay salary range.

The fourth and final phase is the administration of the plan. As stated earlier, there are three key requirements:

1. Each individual needs to have a *personalized development plan* that summarizes his or her assessments and outlines what he or she is working on.

2. The organization needs to provide *learning opportunities,* either through formalized training or on-the-job mentoring. This investment in training will yield increased capabilities, which will provide return on investment in direct and meaningful ways. In addition, *work opportunities* need to be provided to ensure that people can integrate the use of their new capabilities into the workplace. This performance improvement is where the greatest return on investment is realized.

3. *Record keeping systems* are needed to ensure a continuity of assessments and reliability in the system. Although at times judgments are made, they are based on preestablished criteria and can be reviewed and validated by external parties.

The basic premise of this form of compensation is that the organization needs capabilities that its employees do not yet possess. While some individuals may be inclined to continue their development on their own, most need outside encouragement, structure, testing, and rewards to improve their skills and learn new ones. Hence, the organization engages in this effort with the purpose of developing a system to reinforce people for learning and applying new skills to the workplace. The need must justify the effort in order for the return on investment to be realized.

Case History

A light manufacturing company implemented a simplified Pay-for-Competencies-Employed program as a support to broadening the skill base of their workforce and reinforcing the collaboration across all functional and operating areas. They adopted a relatively simple approach that would establish the foundation for further development of the criteria and assessment tools over time. The program included the following elements:

1. They established three broad grade levels, with the entry level having a 70 percent range from minimum to maximum pay, and the next two levels having a range spread of 120 percent and 200 percent, respectively. This was accomplished by collapsing existing grade levels into these new salary range spreads. They defined each of the grade levels in terms of Entry, Contributor, and Leadership as indicated above.

2. They define eight competencies that were important to the organization. These competencies included:
   - Focuses on the customer
   - Contributes to specialized tasks
   - Assures quality of results
   - Contributes to the development of others
   - Effectively influences others
   - Contributes to continual improvements
   - Utilizes resources effectively
   - Understands the business/products/services

   Descriptive statements were prepared for each of the competencies as they reflected level or role within the organization (e.g., Entry, Contributor, Leadership). This was done with a cross section of experienced individuals and managers/team leaders, facilitated by an external consultant. Once the competencies were defined, they tested them in focus groups of managers and staff. As part of these meetings, they examined certain individual roles within the organization, and tested the reliability of this framework. This process enabled them to ensure that the criteria worked when assigning people to levels. They were very pleased that there was a consensus on the factors once they were explained and clarified.

3. The assessment process included the manager or team leader collecting data from a variety of sources on each individual. The data was summarized and discussed with the individual. The assessments concluded that the person was at one of three zones within an overall grade level. These zones were:
   - Basic—Able to understand the minimum requirements and adapt to situations of a minimum diversity.

- Proficient—Able to perform the functions with a high degree of expertise and effectiveness.
- Mastery—Able to train others within the work context, and determine innovative, effective solutions to problems facing the unit.

4. When individuals demonstrated significant improvements in their abilities, according to the competency criteria, they were considered for a salary adjustment. At the Entry level, the manager could make the decision with minimal reviews. At the Contributor level, the management team over the work area needed to concur with any salary adjustments. At the Leadership level, the senior managers of the division needed to approve all salary actions. In all cases data was needed from multiple sources and clear improvements were needed. The market data was used as a supporting source of information, and adjustments in pay were occasionally made based solely on market conditions.

The emphasis of the program was on managing an inventory of talent and developing the abilities of their people consistent with the business requirements of the organization.

There are several primary advantages to this approach. First, the process enables the compensation system to be very personalized. People sense a greater control over their pay levels, know the rules, and associate the measurement with the opportunities for reward. As managers reinforce individuals for their learning and use the system to provide focus and objective feedback, the system works to motivate people to excel in their development. As work is then completed in a fashion more reflective of the defined dimensions, increased performance by the organization is realized. The return on investment from PACE-type programs is realized through improved performance, decreased unit costs, or reduced turnover. This enables the firm to be more competitive.

The first disadvantage of this form of compensation lies in the requirements of development and administration. To develop a highly reliable competency-based pay plan requires a lot of effort and expertise from both the line and human resources functions. The competencies need to relate to core business requirements and be clearly understood and validated. Second, the program requires managers to become more active in managing the assessments and developmental opportunities of their employees. Employees need regular review sessions in which they can see their progress and plan new activities to acquire new skills. Third, there are risks of discrimination for people of diversity; the competencies need to be available and fairly applicable to all. Fourth, these plans do not fit well in functions that are highly specialized in which there are few employees. For example, corporate legal functions (not private law firms) or other specialized functions within the firm may have difficulty justifying the costs of this kind of plan. Such PACE programs are also difficult to create for managerial roles unless the firm is committed to developing the role of general manager within the organization. Finally, there may be situations in which the skills established in the various blocks are no longer needed by the organization because of changes in technology or the marketplace. In such cases, the firm has high priced help that is capable of performing functions the firm no longer needs. A period of retrenchment and retraining may be required.

Summary of Alternatives to Base Salary

I have described five alternative tools for a base pay system. They range from very simple programs to plans requiring extensive development and implementation. Each is more effective than traditional methods as a reinforcement for desired behaviors, and each supports the new philosophy of management. By using the SMART criteria (Specific, Meaningful, Achievable, Reliable and Timely), they transform base pay systems from mere cash delivery systems into actual reward systems for desired performance. Each of the alternatives presented changes the basic premise of management and targets pay delivery as a process to reinforce those behaviors that lead to the firm's success. The primary advantage of these techniques is their ability to make pay systems more personalized and more directly supportive of the organization's key success factors. The responsibility of the organization is to create the opportunities and reinforce the process. The responsibility of the individual is to seize the opportunities and make ever growing contributions to the organization. In so doing, base pay systems can form the foundation for a comprehensive system of rewards.

Notes

1. Lawler, E., *Strategic Pay*, San Francisco: Josey Bass, Calif., 1990.
2. Taylor, F. W., *Principles of Scientific Management*, New York: Harper & Brothers, 1911.
3. Morse, E., "Contingent Compensation: Pay for Performance as Pie Comp." *Performance Management Magazine*, Vol. 6, No. 2, pp. 21–31, Spring, 1988.
4. Senge, P., *The Fifth Discipline: The Art and Practices of the Learning Organization*, New York: Doubleday/Currency, 1990.
5. Prahalad, C. and Harnel, G., "The Core Competence of the Corporation," *Harvard Business Review*, May–June, 1990, pp. 79–91.

6. This concept was developed by Edward Morse of Aubrey Daniels and Associates.

7. The basis for this process was developed by James Hillgren, Ph.D., of Aubrey Daniels and Associates.

8. "ACA: Skill-Based Pay—Practices, Payoffs, Pitfalls, and Prescriptions." A study sponsored by the American Compensation Association, Scottsdale, Ariz., 1992.

9. American Compensation Association, op. cit.

6
Making Pay Contingent on Achievements

If you are trying to change the way you run a company, one of the most visible things you have to change is the way you compensate, reward and recognize people.

PAUL ALLAIRE,
CEO XEROX CORP.
HARVARD BUSINESS REVIEW
OCTOBER, 1992

The landmark 1986 study on variable compensation programs, "People, Performance and Pay," by the American Productivity Center (APC) and the American Compensation Association (ACA),[1] reported that a total of 75 percent of American companies use some form of nonbase pay as part of their compensation programs. This conclusion, based on a survey of nearly 1600 companies, is substantiated by a recent compensation survey by Hewitt Associates[2] of over 2000 U.S. companies. The Hewitt survey shows that 68 percent of U.S. firms give some form of variable or incentive compensation to all salaried employees. (This figure is up from 47 percent in 1988). Such programs include companywide profit-sharing plans, individual incentive programs for executives and managers, and special incentive programs for sales personnel.

Other studies report that an increasing number of companies are experimenting with incentives farther down the organization that involve group/team or gain-sharing programs. A 1993 survey of companies by The Hay Group[3] indicated that approximately 19 percent of the reporting firms had some form of group incentive program, while 25 percent were considering the development of such programs within the next 18 months. Some 12 percent already had gain-sharing programs, while another 19 percent were considering their implementation.

The focus of this chapter will be to examine the key decisions involved in developing variable or incentive pay plans. The terms *variable* and *incentive* will be used interchangeably. The focus will be on building variable pay plans that enhance collaboration within the organization.

Alternative Types of Variable Pay Plans

Variable pay programs come in many forms. The next few pages provide definitions of the most commonly used plans.

Profit Sharing Plans: Perhaps the oldest and most widely used method, this type of plan comes into play when a company shares a portion of its profits (above certain planned levels) with its employees. The APC/ACA study[4] indicated that 32 percent of U.S. companies have this form of pay program in place. Profit sharing has great appeal because of its simplicity and the extent to which it reinforces the positive role of the top executives. Many of the larger firms use the payment as a funding method for contributions to employees through defined contribution retirement plans or 401(k) plans. In such plans, the profit sharing goes to fund the employer's contributions to retirement accounts and is not given as cash to employees. Usually these programs work best when the organization is small and people can directly relate their performance to the profitability of the organization.

Executive Annual Bonus Plans: In these plans, senior managers receive a payment based on their own and the company's performance. Such programs are separate from equity-based programs that use stock or stock-related payments instead of cash.

Management Bonus Plans: In these plans, mid- and upper-level managers receive annual payments based on their performance, which is usually determined by a set of objectives or discretionary assessments of performance by the top executives.

Sales Incentive Plans: These are incentive programs keyed to the tasks of the sales force within the organization. The payouts may be based on the dollar volume of units sold, on the revenues of specific products or services, or on other performance measures. The salesperson may receive a commission (i.e., a predetermined percentage of every unit/dollar sold), or a bonus based on achieving a certain level of sales or other performance objectives.

Sales Management Incentive Plans: Such programs link the manager's incentive payout directly to the performance of his or her sales staff. This can include an override based on the production levels of the staff, combined with longer-range more strategically focused objectives like marketshare, introduction of new products, etc. The overall advantage lies in tying the consequences felt by the manager to the success achieved by the staff.

Individual Piece Rate Incentives: These incentive programs focus on the tasks of operational employees and involve their receiving a predetermined amount of money for every unit of work they produce. The units of work can range from products made, like the number of golf balls produced by an assembly line, to operations performed, like the number of orders processed by a mail-order company.

Team Incentives: In these incentive programs, the payout is based on the work of a group of individuals, usually working in teams or departments. The performance measures may vary from units produced to the achievement of specific performance objectives.

Gain Sharing/Productivity Sharing: These programs usually involve operational and support employees (i.e., direct and indirect labor) and provide payments based on the achievement of performance levels above a predetermined baseline. These programs are sometimes referred to as Scanlon plans, Rucker plans, Improshare, and Gain sharing[5], among others. The payouts are usually based on a direct economic outcome, such as units of output, increased profitability, or decreased unit costs.

Key Contributor Incentive Plans: These programs often focus on individuals regarded as special talent to the organization. For example, a professional service company recently acquired another professional service firm in a related field. To retain the staff that managed key client relationships and provide technical guidance to others, the acquiring company developed a three-year cash incentive program for selected individuals. If certain profitability targets were achieved, the selected *key contributors* would receive cash compensation equal to one year's total compensation. In other settings, companies have used special incentive plans for new-product development teams, scientific and technical staff, and others whose talent as individual contributors is viewed as an essential asset of the company.

Excluded from this list are discretionary bonus plans in which there are no predetermined performance expectations and spot award programs in which employees are not told in advance that there will be an award. Both types of programs, while variable, do not imply a predetermined performance relationship to the award. Further excluded from the foregoing definitions are programs that relate to providing equity or company stock based on performance; the next chapter is dedicated to these incentive plans. The focus is on what it takes to effectively design a variable pay plan that links performance directly with rewards.

The Reasons and the Concerns

The purpose of variable pay programs is usually to:

- Shift more compensation costs from fixed to variable expenses
- Provide additional pay to employees for extra achievements
- Share the risks and fortunes of the enterprise

There is clearly a growing interest in instituting variable pay programs, but there are several very serious concerns. First, some executives argue, "Why pay more?" In other words, employees are paid a base salary to perform a certain job. Therefore, why should they receive additional compensation? The answer to this question can be philosophical or practical. From a management values perspective, variable plans can, if designed and managed effectively, provide a reward tied to performance levels that most likely would not be achieved otherwise. They can reinforce new behaviors by offering employees an opportunity to participate in the growth and success of the company. If the same performance can be achieved without such plans, the firm should pursue that course. In many firms such plans dramatically facilitate the performance improvement process.

The second concern usually centers on the task of setting or tracking performance measures. While there are many jobs that on the surface appear difficult to measure, a customer measures the results of the work on every encounter. It is perhaps more precise to describe this as a concern about the cost-effectiveness of performance measures. The administrative process needs to be judged in relation to its value-added contribution. Is tracing and providing feedback to performers worth the effort? The organization should be clear about what it believes is necessary to drive desired performance and establish priorities accordingly.

A third issue is the general resistance to incentive plans because of bad previous experiences with such plans. While this concern is important, one needs to examine what were the primary points of learning from the past experiences. If an executive has an essentially positive experience with incentives, this, too, needs to be examined for its learning points. Without such examinations, we may be unnecessarily avoiding using a process to support critical organizational change. Hence, change may be slowed at a time when it is needed, and the tools we have to perform a necessary function may be limited.

Other concerns tend to focus on the issue of control and the impact on employee relations issues. There is a belief that eventually the performance will reach a limit, and that the absence of incentive payments will make employees angry. The counter to this concern is to quote Willie Wanka, from Charlie and the Chocolate Factory, when he said: "Be careful of what you wish for, Charlie. It might come true!"

Another area of concern is the impact on management relationships when employees do not feel that measures are in their control or that their ideas for achieving improvements are listened to. This concern may be founded on past experiences in which employees sought to make changes in the business process but managers and supervisors did not support them. To have implemented such suggestions might have required additional investments when funds where not available or changes in procedures when the cost of change was perceived as greater than the potential benefit. Often a very important constituency to the successful implementation and management of a variable pay plan is the managers, who need to act like leaders and not like controllers. The responsibility for this change rests with senior managers and not with the supervisor or manager, who may not feel part of the change process.

Finally, there may be a concern that people will become fixed on earning their incentives and will not implement changes or take actions that do not directly support the incentive program. This concern about a single-minded focus on a few measures is an important consideration but is more reflective of the lack of other reinforcements in the work environment. One of the primary reasons for an incentive program is to drive organizational and cultural change. The management process to support a variable pay plan is large, important, and consistent with many of the change efforts most organizations are seeking to employ. This is not *additional* work; this is *the* work of the management team.

Case Study of a Typical Management Incentive Program

A midsize consumer products company has had a management incentive program for over ten years. The purpose of the program is to reward individual achievements in key performance dimensions. All middle-and-above managers participate in the plan. The payout opportunity varies according to the individual's level in the organization, as shown below:

- Chief executive officer: 60 percent of base salary
- Vice presidents: 40 percent of base salary
- Directors: 25 percent of base salary
- Managers: 15 percent of base salary

The company needs to reach at least 95 percent of its planned profit levels in order for the incentive plan to be funded. Once this threshold is achieved, each manager is eligible to receive the payout associated with his or her level, modified by a ± 25 percent based on individual performance. Individual performance is tied to management by objectives as established between each manager and the executive or to an after-the-fact assessment of the individual's performance. In some cases the objectives are statements of projects to be completed or financial objectives (growth in revenues, expenses to budget, etc.) for an individual's own functional area. If a manager is not able to prepare objectives or if conditions change significantly, the performance assessment is based on a judgment by the senior manager. Finally, the performance assessments and bonus calculations are determined at the end of the fiscal year, reviewed extensively, and approved by the chief executive of the company. The CEO uses this authority to modify the payouts, based on his personal experience with the performers.

One of the interesting characteristics of this company's executives is that they are reluctant to extend incentives farther down in the organization. They highlight many of the issues noted above but believe that their incentive program is an important pay-for-performance and pay-at-risk element of their compensation strategy. Each person agrees that the plan is important to him or her personally.

The plan is regarded by the participants as discretionary, in that they feel they have little control over the payouts. In terms of payout results, the bonus plan has paid out eight of the last ten years. Most managers receive within 5 percent of their target level. Over 90 percent of the participating managers receive their bonuses annually. While there is always concern about whether the 95 percent threshold is met, especially during the third and fourth quarters, most managers have come to expect their incentive payment. Finally, these payouts have enabled the company to achieve a sixtieth percentile in the marketplace for total compensation.

What's Wrong with This Picture?

This is a typical management bonus plan. It could really be called an *entitlement* bonus plan. The plan is set to pay out when the company can afford it, regardless of the contributions or efforts of these managers. The SMART criteria developed in Chapter 3 will help us to understand several critical issues regarding this plan.

Specific

While performance objectives may exist, they are not consistently applied to all participants nor are they necessarily related to the key factors of the firm's performance. The objectives are based on personal negotiation between the manager and the supervisor. This reflects the boss-as-customer or command-and-control philosophy discussed in Chapter 1. Furthermore, because the profit budget has been established as a primary measure, most executives do not see a direct relationship between their efforts and the specific actions necessary to achieve that goal. This common fate feature of the plan, therefore, is not likely to have any significant impact on their performance. The real determinant of the payout is the evidence the manager can produce to demonstrate his or her achievement of personal goals.

Meaningful

While the levels of payout are probably meaningful, the company is not getting a desired return on investment. In this organization the incentive compensation payout exceeds $2 million. If a midlevel manager asked to spend a similar amount of money on a project, the top executives would require a lot of hard evidence to justify the expense. Yet they do not demand the same level of rigorous return-on-investment analysis for their incentive plan. In no other areas of the business's expense do the top executives act so cavalierly about spending so much money.

Achievable

The performance objectives are achievable; in fact, they may actually reflect a slam-dunk level of challenge. Allowing managers to negotiate with their supervisors on performance objectives, creates an inherent conflict in which each one is trying to gain something from the other—more performance or more rewards. To what extent does this process reinforce collaboration and teamwork? Given the history of performance payouts, it seems clear that these incentive payments do not drive rigorous levels of performance. Yet increasing the payout will probably not improve performance. The CEO's reviews, especially when he relies on his personal judgment to modify the recommended payouts, further undermine the pay and performance relationship.

Reliable

The system is easy to administer and is handled only once a year. The executives rarely discuss progress on the key objectives (i.e., feedback), and yet the plan has provided a payout in eight out of the last ten years. In this case the plan is not perceived to be broken, yet does it truly drive desired performance? For the participants, this has become a standard element of their compensation. While it may be described as a pay-at-risk plan, the reality is that there is little if any actual risk. The only risk is that the executive may loose what he or she has grown to expect.

Timely

By providing reviews on an annual basis only, the plan is nonoperative for approximately three-quarters of the year. Serious attention to the objectives occurs only in the last quarter, after the executives determine whether or not the 95 percent profitability target will be met. The rest of the time there is little sense of urgency about the performance requirements of the plan. So, in terms of the timeliness, the annual plan has little impact on performance.

The key issue in this discussion is not why the plan does not work, but rather, whatever made us believe that it would. Like many organizations, this company established its plan as a way of retaining market competitiveness with other companies. But it avoided whatever complications might have made it directly address the issues facing the organization. Its plan is simple to understand—ultimately too simple to drive desired behaviors. Baldly stated, the company is not getting what it is paying for. The task is not to eliminate the plan, but to modify it, both in design and in how it is managed.

Managers who have grown accustomed to the plan will experience a degree of risk if the plan is replaced or redesigned to link it with the core business issues. This is the challenge of designing reward systems that are genuinely oriented to the economics and risks of the business. It is no wonder that these executives are reluctant to extend incentives to other areas of the organization. The paradox is that they won't give up the comfortable features of their plan, *nor* design a plan that would be effective in reinforcing the desired behavior of others. This is a typical example of resistance to change.

Understanding the Purpose of Variable Pay Plans

One of the most interesting features of variable pay plans is the extent to which they vary from one company to another. Few companies do, or should, install the plans developed at another company. Each situation is different; each strategy is different; and cultures reinforce behaviors that are different. Thus each plan *should* be different and reflect the *special* requirements of the organization.

A central issue in developing such programs is determining the fundamental purpose of the plan. Is the plan intended to reward individuals for their own achievements, or is it intended to motivate individuals to collaborate in improving team or unit performance? Often I find that executives are attracted to incentive pay plans because they offer a method to reduce the fixed costs of compensation and make pay more variable. While this may serve the executives' interest in managing costs and is often a benefit of such programs, the philosophy may inherently establish a win-lose framework for the plan. Hence it is better to focus the plan on requirements for improving performance and then provide rewards for these achievements.

The plan needs to stimulate new actions by people so that the organization is more competitive and more successful. This approach will yield a true win/win arrangement, in which the corporation becomes more successful and competitive and its employees not only benefit financially, but feel more appreciated. It does depend on management making the right decisions, based on market opportunities and the firm's strategy. If this collaborative approach is the underlying philosophy, the incentive plan can become a very important reward system.

An organization may have a variety of different plans, each uniquely suited to different employee groups. For example, it is common to have the sales staff on one type of incentive plan and the senior managers on another, operational employees on one plan and support staff on another. This portfolio approach to incentive plans enables the organization to target specific reward systems to the roles and tasks of employees consistent with the overall competitive strategies of the firm.

When considering a variable pay program, it is very important to determine which group or groups to include in the plan. These are known as the *target groups*. This task segments the workforce into logical groups organized around work processes, customers, and/or line of business. The analysis and design process can then be focused on the specific performance requirements of the group.

Assessing Readiness

Incentive pay plans are not for every organization. While many managers are interested in installing variable pay programs, there may be good reasons for caution, as the following questions suggest:

- Is my organization ready?
- Will the program work for our situation?

- What are the risks we are likely to encounter?

Such concerns are often well founded, and managers would be wise to assess the firm's readiness before proceeding to develop a variable pay plan. The benefits of installing such a program must outweigh the costs and risks. It is important that the conditions are supportive, or at least neutral, before beginning such a program.

Assessing the readiness for incentive plans serves several very important purposes. First, it indicates whether or not developing an incentive plan will make any sense for the organization and the selected target groups. Second, if conditions are generally satisfactory but there are some concerns, the process can provide an insight into what needs to be done to prepare the organization for changes as well as indicating potential critical design or implementation issues. Finally, the assessment can provide an understanding of what is possible for improvements in performance. Hence, the readiness assessment is often a critical first step in the effective development of a variable compensation plan.

Seven Key Factors for Assessment

While the importance of an assessment process is clear, what is one to assess? What are the critical factors leading to a well-designed and implemented incentive program? Figure 6-1 shows seven key questions that can be used in the readiness assessment. They are discussed in detail in the next few pages.

1. To what extent does the target group control its performance?
2. Have most of the major structural or system changes been completed? Is the group relatively stable?
3. Do clear, reliable measures exist for the unit?
4. Is the current compensation adequate from an internal equity and external competitiveness standpoint?
5. Are the managers of the unit generally effective in providing the leadership necessary for the group?
6. Is the culture of the organization characterized by trust, mutual respect, and a willingness to work together for common goals?
7. Does the plan have a sponsor and a champion?

Figure 6-1. Assessing the readiness for incentives.

1. To what extent does the target group control its performance? If you are designing a variable pay program for a group of employees who have little control over the variables in their performance, the process is destined to fail or result in payouts that are not directly caused by the actions of the target group. While no individuals or group of employees has total control over their performance, it is important to assess the degree of control they do exercise. In general, the target group for the incentive plan should have a high degree of control over their performance.

2. Have most of the major structural or system changes been completed? Is the group relatively stable? We live in a time of tremendous change. Organizations are downsizing/rightsizing, reengineering or reinventing themselves, and changing the roles of managers and employees. If the target group is on the threshold of major changes or in the middle of such changes, incentive plans may not be a good idea. The primary reason is that people in times of high-stress change seek clarity about their roles, security for their futures, and an understanding of what is necessary to be successful. Further, the measures, objectives, and baselines of performance data may be unclear, which may lead to incorrect design decisions. Hence, if the group is undergoing major change, it is best to either postpone the plan design process until basic strategic and structural decisions have been made or use the process of developing the plan as a vehicle for developing consensus on the work redesign decisions.

But change should not be an excuse for forgoing useful reward systems. The organization may find that the use of a variable pay plan can enhance the change process in terms of speed or effectiveness. For example, a large newspaper organization was planning on eliminating its evening edition and use the capacity to sell higher margin business. The introduction of the variable pay plan helped the transition because managers and employees could see personal economic benefit from effective implementation of this change.

3. Do clear, reliable measures exist for the unit? Performance measures are an essential element of variable pay plans. If measures do not exist, it will be very difficult to develop a sound variable pay plan. I have often used the design process as an opportunity to develop concrete, controllable performance measures. I have found that, after the design of the incentive plan, there is often a broader consensus that the current measures used to guage a group's performance need to be modified or replaced by more relevant and meaningful ones. (This will be discussed further in Chapter 10, in which we examine how to develop performance measures.)

4. Is the current compensation adequate from an internal equity and external competitiveness standpoint? A variable pay plan should be used to address its stated purpose rather than fix some existing pay problem. The primary task of the reward strategy is to define the purpose of the various pay plans. If there are basic issues regarding the base pay system, either because of its inequities within the organization or because of its inadequacy in the external market, the variable pay program may become diverted from its original purpose. There are situations, however, in which the variable pay plan can be used to enhance the organization's competitiveness from a total compensation perspective. While this can be a benefit of the plan, market competitiveness should not be a primary objective of the plan. This needs to be understood and stated as part of the objectives of the program prior to its design.

5. Are the managers of the unit generally effective in providing the leadership necessary for the group? This is a critical issue for the implementation and ongoing management of the program. Managers who wish to be effective at managing incentives should:

- Provide an effective sense of purpose and direction based on the overall objectives of the unit and supported by the incentive plan

- Use reliable, meaningful measures to track performance

- Use ongoing, real-time, data-based feedback to the performers

- Reinforce behaviors for progress and celebrate the results

There is often an unstated assumption or hope that if the incentive plan is well designed, it can replace the task of management. Nothing could be farther from the truth. In fact, effective incentive plans require *more*, not less, management involvement. However, the essence of the manager's involvement lies in translating the performance measures into meaningful directions and actions for people; in ensuring that people be informed of how well they are doing (and in as timely a manner as possible); and in providing coaching, encouragement, and reinforcement to people for desirable behaviors. The manager is often called upon to listen to ideas for change and improvement in the work process and to take actions to address problems within or outside the group that are interfering with its ability to perform. With incentive plans, a manager's job becomes even more important and more rewarding.

6. Is the culture of the organization characterized by trust, mutual respect, and a willingness to work together for common goals? Few organizations would be able to say that they have a corporate culture highly supportive of trust, respect, and teamwork. The dimension to examine here is more one of degree than of absolutes. If the employees in the target group do not fundamentally trust what management has said or believe the measures and performance feedback, it will be difficult to install an incentive program they will look on positively. If there is general confidence in management's ability to make the right decisions and implement programs effectively, the variable pay program will probably be viewed positively. If conditions are adequate but not desirable, the process can be used to strengthen trust and confidence relationships. This can be done through a variety of strategies, including the selection of a representative team that involves employees in the design of the plan and communicates it to employees.

7. Does the plan have a sponsor and a champion? In any process of major organizational change, there need to be individuals who can play several different roles. The *sponsor* is the individual who sanctions the work, provides the resources, and creates the environment in which the plan can be developed and implemented. The sponsor is critical to the development process because, without such support, the plan will not have sufficient commitment from senior management to gain approvals. The *champion,* on the other hand, is the one with the technical skills and drive to see that the program is created. The champion can, in some situations, also perform the role of the *change agent.* The change agent is the individual who wants to see the program developed and implemented and who will do practically anything within reason to make it successful. Without the contributions of a sponsor, a champion, and a change agent, the development of a variable pay plan will probably never progress beyond the thinking stage.

Asking and answering these seven questions will provide an effective framework for assessing the conditions necessary for a successful variable pay plan. As mentioned in connection with several of the questions, the issue is one of degree, not absolutes. After examining each of these seven areas, one of three possible conclusions can be reached:

1. *Stop—Wait for better days.* In this situation, there are many reasons why the time is not appropriate for the variable pay plan. The assessment should have identified those areas that present the most critical barriers to the plan, and the choice is then to address them or take another course of action.

2. *Proceed with caution—Use the process strategically.* This is the most common situation. There are important barriers, but they can be addressed as the plan is constructed or implemented. For example, if trust is a major factor in this assessment, you can involve the opinion leaders of various constituencies in the development of a

common plan. This will either create a plan that will be effective for everyone, or keep the plan from being implemented at all. In either case, the process will indicate whether further organizational work is appropriate or not.

3. *Go for it—Design the plan.* In this case, there are important indicators supporting the development of the plan. Although one must always work to create a plan that reinforces the right conditions for performance improvement, the absence of major inhibiting factors indicates that there is real support and opportunity to realize successes with the plan.

Overview of the Design Process

One should not expect that designing a variable pay plan will be a neat, linear process. Each step, although logically leading to another, will need to be reviewed once subsequent decisions are made. It is often best to describe this process as a spiraling activity, one that backtracks at times to review and ensure a strong linkage of the plan's different elements. No decision should be complete until all decisions are complete.

There are several alternative strategies for developing a plan. First, the plan can be developed by an outsider, whether he or she is from another area of the company or is an external consultant. The advantage of this tactic is that the outsider tends to see critical issues from an objective, or nonbiased, perspective. The use of an outside expert who has experience with similar organizations can also speed up the development process. The disadvantages of this approach are that the person may need time to learn the business, may not fully understand the uniqueness of the business from an organizational or operational standpoint, and may not design the plan from the point of view of those who need to use it. If the commitment of the performers is not achieved during the design process, it will need to be addressed during the implementation and overall management of the program.

Another alternative approach is to use a management design team composed of the senior managers of the target group. This has the advantage of putting the managers in a situation in which they will be designing a reward system to support their primary accountabilities. The disadvantages are that they may not fully appreciate the work conditions and culture deep inside their organization, and that the plan may not be seen by the participants as one that is directed to achieve win/win conditions. The workforce may be skeptical of the management design team's true intent and resist changing behaviors to achieve desired results.

The third alternative is to use a cross-functional design team composed of potential participants in the plan—managers, supervisors, operational employees, nonexempt clerical staff, etc., as well as customers of the target group. The advantage of this method is that it can serve to create support and commitment to the plan among all the participants. Often these representatives have a wide variety of perspectives that will enrich the program. The primary disadvantages are the need to build a higher level of trust and skill among people who may have never worked together and the necessity of educating some people in the functions and strategic issues of the organization. Furthermore, this approach often takes more time, and the expectations of others in the organization need to be managed very carefully.

In developing such plans, several important steps need to be taken at the start. First, if a design team is used, it must be given the full and complete authority to develop a plan it believes will work for the organization. Often senior managers want to specify several limits on their considerations, such as types of measures, the need for the plan to be self-funded, the eligibility criteria, the timing or size of payouts, etc. While these limits may be important to the sponsor, they often reflect a lack of trust and confidence in the design team itself. When this happens, the team members often question the true motive for their involvement. Do senior managers want the team to create the optimal design or are they just putting up a facade of participation and involvement?

The ultimate task of the team is to design a plan that meets the needs of the organization. This often means designing a plan that management can fully support. The team needs to keep the senior managers informed at critical times during the developmental process so that the basic direction is not in conflict with the strategic requirements of the company. Senior managers will ultimately need to approve the plan. An important task of the design team is to utilize the knowledge, objectives, and experiences of both the executives and the target group.

Second, employees should be assured that they will not face layoffs if there are improvements in performance. Employees often question what is likely to happen to their annual pay increases as well as to the overtime provisions that affect them if a new variable pay plan is put into effect. Depending on the purpose of the plan, the managers will need to make the appropriate assurances. An ACA study on variable pay plans[6] indicated that 84 percent of the plans were add-ons to existing base pay plans, 10 percent reduced future pay increases, 2.4 percent reduced base pay, 2.4 percent replaced an existing incentive plan, and 1.2 percent replaced an existing recognition plan. So in most cases, the plans were in addition to existing pay plans, and therefore focused efforts on different performance dimensions of the organization.

Finally, as the design team begins its work, it will quickly find that the task is very complex. There is often a need to simplify early on, so that people can understand the plan. The risk here is that the resulting plan may be *too* simple to truly address the critical issues facing the business. It is very important that the plan be simple enough to understand, but not overly simple in the way it addresses the task of changing human behavior.

If the organization is reducing the historical pay increase levels, this should be done separately to the design of the variable pay program. This keeps the focus of variable pay on improving performance and not a mask for base pay reductions

Developing the variable pay program will involve addressing seven major tasks, as illustrated in Figure 6-2. Each is described in detail on the next pages.

Purpose of the Program	The Primary Target Group
	The Overall Purpose and Philosophy of the Program
	The Basic Approach
Performance Measures	Desired Results and Behaviors
	Performance Levels—Baseline, Goals, etc.
	Linkage to Other (nonparticipating) Groups
Payout Mechanisms and Opportunities	Formula or Mechanism that Determines Payout
	Feqeuency or Triggers for the Payout (Timing)
	Payout Levels at Target Performance (Opportunities)
	Modifiers to Performance Payouts
Eligibility	Who Will Participate
	Minimum Requirements for Participation
Funding and Return on Investments	Sources for Incentive Payouts
	Performance to Payout Ratio
	Threshold for Payments
Special Issues	Implementation Requirements
	Linkage to Employee Benefits
	Linkage to Overtime Payments
Implementation and Management	Communication to Plan Participants
	Use of Support Systems
	Development of Management Skills to Use the System

Figure 6-2. Overall incentive design decisions.

The Purpose of the Program

The purpose of the plan should be to define several critical elements. Is its chief focus going to be on individual performance or group performance? Should its emphasis be on improving business results or on recognizing performance achievements? How much of a role should the external compensation marketplace play in the design and opportunities of the plan? Do you want the plan to enhance the firm's attractiveness as a way of aiding recruitment efforts, or is its focus primarily on existing staff? Finally, how are the business challenges now facing the company linked to the reward program? The purpose statement needs to address all these issues.

The purpose statement should also include both an overall statement and a set of principles or guidelines from which the design team will design the plan. The reward strategy outlined in Chapter 4 may provide additional information for the process of articulating the plan's purpose. Two examples of plan purpose statements are shown in Figures 6-3 and 6-4.

Once the overall purpose has been determined, the next issue is to define the overall approach. Though this will be discussed in more detail when we examine payout mechanisms, the approach defines the nature of the incentive plan. For example:

- What will be the primary unit of focus? Will the plan be for a natural work group, like a department, division, or section, or will it be for cross-functional task forces or similar temporary teams?

The purpose of the Performance Sharing Program is to share with our employees the gains from our achievements in improving total quality, customer service, and increasing volume and profitability.

---

1. To *recognize, reinforce and reward employees* for improvements in performance and quality.

2. To improve the *financial performance* of the company through strengthening our competitiveness and increasing the utilization of our resources.

3. To increase the company's *flexibility and responsiveness* in meeting customer needs, supporting marketing strategies and implementing new management systems.

Figure 6-3. Example of a Plan Purpose Statement.

The purpose of the Performance Challenge incentive compensation program is to *Recognize, Reinforce,* and *Reward* employees for:

- Focusing on the customer
- Seeking ideas for improvements
- Eliminating low-value-added activities
- Increasing a sense of urgency
- Encouraging risk taking and change
- Promoting teamwork

The Primary Principles of the Performance Challenge Program:

1. Reinforce teamwork within and across Divisions.
2. Include as many employees as possible.
3. Measure both financial and critical operational results.
4. Be understandable and meaningful to the performers.
5. Provide incentive payouts as frequently as possible.
6. Reward performance in relation to its contributions to the financial and operating success of the company.

Figure 6-4. Example of a plan purpose statement.

- Will the plan provide participants with a share in the economic benefit of improved results or will it target a series of performance levels and provide a payments when certain results are achieved?
- Will the plan be designed for a temporary period of time or is it intended to exist as long as it is effective for a work group?

The answer to these questions will define the target group further and outline the basic approach. The next stages of the design process will define performance measures and other elements of the variable pay plan.

Performance Measures

Perhaps the single most important and difficult issue in developing variable pay plans is selecting meaningful performance measures.

Since the basis for the payout and the focus of the participants' attention are on measures, they need to be selected carefully. When companies start the design process with measures, they often find that they look to what is currently being measured. The inadequacy of these systems then becomes a controversial issue and may cause the design process to be slowed or stopped all together. The alternative is to start with an understanding of the customers and their wants and then establish common factors that define themes or elements necessary to the unit's success. From this analysis one can identify performance measures that have more meaning and purpose than do traditional control-oriented measures.

There are typically five types of performance measures in an incentive plan:

1. *Financial measures.*   These relate to the revenues or costs of doing business as well as the economic return on investments or value added nature of the work.

2. *Quantity measures.*   These relate to the number of tasks performed by the unit, such as production levels, number of units processed, number of calls handled, etc.

3. *Quality measures.*   These relate to performance variables that define the value of the work, such as acceptance/error free rates, customer satisfaction, meeting specifications, etc.

4. *Timeliness measures.*   These relate to meeting prescribed schedules, customer commitments, or the speed at which certain work is accomplished, such as on-time delivery, cycle time, days ahead of deadline schedule, project milestones, etc.

5. *Safety measures.*   These relate to the exercise of safe behaviors in performing work activities, such as doing something the safe way, loss-time accidents, meeting OSHA requirements, etc.

In many situations, a combination of measures describes the true results needed by the organization. While the financial performance may define the size of the monetary award available, operational measures may be used to modify the payout (i.e., either increase it or decrease it), depending on these results. Incentive plans should be limited to between three to five measures. This enables a variety of complex issues to be addressed simultaneously with a clear focus on actions. Most functions and jobs are not sufficiently simple to require a single measure, particularly when collaboration is required.

By its very nature, collaboration involves creating win/win situations from potentially conflicting situations. Therefore, a single performance measure is often inappropriate. The exception may occur when a single, common outcome is most reflective of the desired actions of the customer. This usually corresponds to a transaction-related customer relationship. Examples might include the following:

- *Residential Mortgage Company.* Increasing the volume of mortgage applications per month
- *Distribution Company.* Increasing the number of deliveries per day
- *Trucking Company.* Increasing the number of shipments delivered on time
- *Telemarketing Function.* Increasing the number of calls made per hour or handled per hour

Each of these examples reflects a single, priority function that is of primary importance to the customer or is a primary indicator of key success factors. In this case, the team collaborates to perform the actions necessary to achieve the common desired result. The behaviors or process variables are established through conducting an analysis of the factors that contribute to success.

These measures provide a mosaic of the factors that determine the success of the unit and define the balance of conflicting pressures or the trade-offs necessary to achieve an optimal level of performance. When measures are inherently in conflict, the performers need to seek an appropriate balance between the measures that address current situations and those that serve the needs of their customers. (Chapter 10 focuses exclusively on this important subject. The reader is advised to read this material if your interest lies in establishing customer-focused performance measures.)

Payout Mechanisms and Opportunities

The next major step involves translating the performance measures into a mechanism that will yield a desired payout for desired performance. This is the engine that will drive the incentive compensation plan.

The SMART criteria introduced in Chapter 3 will provide a guide to understanding various approaches for determining payouts.

Specific

For an incentive plan to work effectively, people need to understand the relationship between their efforts and the desired results. This is often referred to as the *line of sight*. While the desired relationship is a direct relationship—John does X and gets Y—this is not always feasible or appropriate given the many conflicting requirements for meeting the needs of the customers: quality versus productivity, delivery versus cost, timeliness versus accuracy, etc. While the creative work team will find avenues for achieving both (the optimal solution), there are situations in which true performance is a combination of complex factors. The measures defined earlier should direct performers to high-priority tasks and provide guidance about how they should and should not do them.

This specificity is important for determining how much money (i.e., payout opportunity) will be available from the plan. If there are many intervening variables, the amount of influence the performer has on results will be lessened. If the forces that define success are changing, the performer needs to retain a high degree of flexibility. Consequently, the payout mechanism and the opportunity for earnings need to be moderated so as to not overpay or underpay for the performance.

Meaningful

There is a conventional wisdom in the professional field of compensation that unless an incentive offers between 10 percent and 15 percent of base pay the performer will not be motivated to achieve the desired results.[7] This commonly held belief has not been substantiated by rigorous behavioral research, however. In fact, research completed by A. Dickinson[8] and her associates at Western Michigan University's, Department of Psychology indicated that a 3 percent incentive yielded the same level of performance as did rates of 13 percent, 25 percent, and 55 percent. The performance was significantly greater than for those without incentive, but there was no significant difference between alternative payout levels. This 3 percent level was further substantiated as the average payout for successful group incentive plans by the 1992 study conducted by the American Compensation Association.[9]

There are other factors of course—the clarity of the task, the performer's ability to perform it, the frequency and meaningfulness of feedback following the task—that impact performance far more than the simple opportunity for additional money. This is because reinforcement from the work environment, the task itself, one's peers, one's superiors, etc., can be more immediate and powerful than a monetary reward.

This is not to ignore the importance of a high payout opportunity. Rather, it means that *meaningful* needs to be defined by the performer, not the organization. A performer may be aware of comparable pay practices within the organization or within other organizations. A performer may translate the value-added nature of the work to the effort he or she expends. For example, when an individual salesperson makes a $1 million sale of goods or services that generates $180,000 in profits for the company and receives only a $3,000 payment in return, he or she is likely to see an imbalance in the rewards system. When a team saves the company $3 million by working significant overtime (i.e, nights and weekends) and receives a $500 special award for each member, they may see the reward as unworthy of their efforts. Here other reinforcers as well as additional dollars would be appropriate. The degree of meaningfulness of the payout can be measured by observing whether people: (1) do extra, (2) talk positively, (3) say they feel valued, (4) repeat the behavior.

Achievable

As David McClellan, former professor at Harvard University, has indicated in his research, high achievers set goals that are challenging but achievable.[10] Goals that are perceived to be too easy are not reinforcing. Goals that are seen to be too difficult to achieve are not pursued. In the latter case, the process of extinction is at work and will result in the performer trying hard initially but eventually giving up or making do, realizing that the reinforcement is not likely. Consequently, the best goals are not *stretch goals* (i.e., unachievable goals) but goals that are generally viewed as achievable with focused effort.

When a plan has a single goal associated with each measure, the performers usually work to achieve the goal by the deadline. The performer produces just enough to avoid not receiving the payout. This is characteristic of the behavioral pattern associated with negative reinforcement. The problem is that the performers may not seek to go beyond the goal in terms of actual performance, deadlines, or budgets. This is an important concern when it comes to constructing the levels of performance in an incentive plan.

When there is a target, with a minimum and maximum level, performers focus on the target or the maximum and define success in terms of an achievable, personal target. If the level is not achieved, they will experience the extinction consequence because they have not received something they wanted for something they did. The optimal method is to provide performers with a range of performance levels, so that any incremental improvement in performance can be reinforced in terms of progress from a baseline, rather than be seen as a shortfall from a target. This is inherently more reinforcing and therefore more motivating. (See Figure 6-5.)

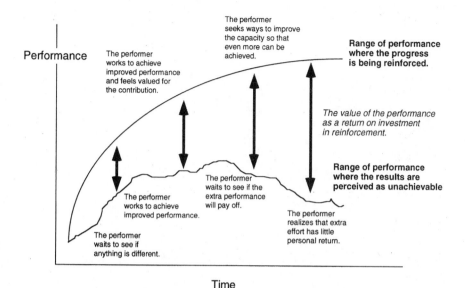

Figure 6-5. The difference between achievable and unachievable.

Reliable

The reliability of an incentive system has a direct impact on the design of the payout mechanism. First, a system that is so complicated that the performers must wait for knowing the results will have less immediate and positive impact on performance. However, a program that is so simple that it reinforces the wrong behaviors is equally inappropriate. The design process needs to achieve the right degree of sophistication.

Figure 6-6 illustrates two dimensions of this concept: the degree of sophistication and the degree of impact on performance. For an organization to achieve the highest impact on performance, it needs to find the right balance of sophistication and impact. One that is too simple will not achieve desired impact because it may set up conditions to reinforce the wrong behaviors. One that is too sophisticated will not achieve the desired impact because people will not understand how the system relates to what they need to do differently. The degree of sophistication is defined by the nature of the work, the experience of the performers with such systems, and the availability of support.

The process of designing an incentive plan involves addressing a wide array of both business and behavioral issues. The ideal plan has something in common with an automobile, a very complex and sophisticated piece of machinery. It has an onboard propulsion system, guidance and steering system, braking system, environmental control system, entertainment system, safety system, etc. Yet it can be

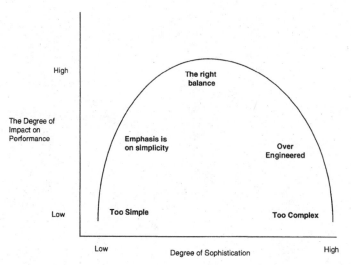

Figure 6-6. Determining the right degree of sophistication.

operated by an individual with minimal formal education and little training. Similarly, an incentive system must be no more sophisticated than the target group can comprehend, but it must not be so simplistic that it fails to address the underlying need for changes in behavior that will impact the future of the organization.

Timely

This factor relates to the frequency of the payout. Reliance on an annual payout cycle usually leads people to pay little attention to the incentive until the end date is in sight. If an effort can be put off till next month, more immediate concerns can take priority, leaving the incentive plan basically nonoperational for three-quarters of the year. Depending on the sense of urgency required and the types of behaviors and results necessary for success, the timing of the payout is a critical issue. A plan that pays out on a quarterly basis creates a strong sense of urgency to achieve the necessary results quickly. This has the advantage of creating more pressure for performance. The disadvantage is that this approach requires the performance measures to correspond to stable business cycles that may not reflect the natural rhythm of the marketplace. For example, if most sales occur in the third quarter and returns occur in the first quarter, plans that do not adjust for this buy-and-return pattern may distort the understanding of performance.

In some cases companies have moved to monthly payout schedules

Performance

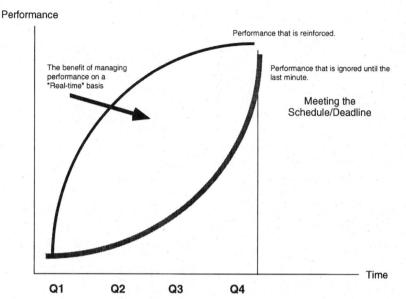

Figure 6-7. The "J" curve versus frequent reinforcement of performance.

in order to create a sense of urgency about achieving desired results. Such actions need to be considered carefully so that people do not adjust their performance in such a way as to maximize their income at the expense of the organization. In behavioral terms, such an outcome is referred to as the J curve.[11] This means that performance/behaviors proceed along at a minimal pace for a period, then pick up in intensity as a deadline approaches. The challenge is to create conditions in which results are achieved earlier without tying rewards to a schedule and sacrificing an optimal level of performance.

The conflict between schedule and quality is reflected in these comments by employees:

- *"On Monday we ship quality. On Friday we ship quantity."*—Supervisor

- *"Poor products are often put back into the line for rework or shipment toward the end of the month so the supervisors can receive their bonuses."*—Operational employee

- *"The last two weeks of the quarter are always a challenge. I wish we could smooth out our production schedules to achieve more regular delivery performance. It costs us in overtime, product quality, and just pressure. But we've always made our targets."*—Plant manager

- *"We don't usually schedule any meetings during the last quarter of the year. That's when we make up for the year's slippage."*—Functional director

Another example of a J curve was symbolized by a chair manufacturing company's "healing walls." During the month, the employees were empowered to remove any chair that they felt did not meet the customer's quality specifications. They placed the chair on a back wall of the plant for observation and repair. The wall provided a visible measure of the quality in the plant. This process operated well until near the end of the month. If actual production was below quotas, the supervisor would go through the chairs that were stacked on the back wall and select ones to be put back into production. When asked, the supervisor would say that the problem was not significant and could be repaired later in the process, or that the customer would never notice. This place was was referred to by the operators as the healing wall because that is where the chairs became "healed" during the production process.

These comments reflect this pattern of timing associated with rewards. If there is a need to increase a sense of urgency and focus people's attention on critical issues, a shorter time frame is often desired. But the payout schedule needs to reflect the natural cycles of the business so that people can respond effectively to predictable conditions.

To summarize briefly, the critical considerations regarding payout mechanisms and opportunity should include the following:

- The specificity of the performance measures
- The degree of control over the performance factors
- The marketplace practices used as reference points by the performers
- The reliability of the basis for establishing the performance levels or expectations
- The economic benefit provided to the organization from improvements in performance

These considerations will determine how much money is appropriate for the incentive plan and what type of mechanism should be used. The nature of the performance measures will often determine the most obvious payout mechanism.

Determining the Payout of an Incentive Plan

Although there are many variations, there are basically three different approaches to determining the payout of an incentive plan. These are:

1. A formula or a portion based on achievements in a single measure (profitability, ROI, productivity, etc.)

2. A set of specific objectives and targets that must be reached to achieve a payout (e.g., program implementation, performance to plan or budget, etc.)

3. A set of measures with associated payout provisions at different levels of performance (on-time delivery, yield rates, error-free rates, new product launch, etc.);

Each of these is explained in more detail below.

Formula-Derived Pool.   Most gain-sharing-type plans use this approach to determine the payouts. Simply stated, when performance exceeds a historical or baseline level, a portion of the overage is provided to the performers. For example, if the gross operating margin for a unit exceeds 20 percent, the members of the unit split 50 percent of the excess margin with the company. Other examples might include cases in which the productivity of a unit exceeds an X rate; or in which a pool is generated based on the dollar value of this productivity increase (say $Y for each unit produced over the productivity threshold); or in which Z percent of the sales/profits over a threshold is provided to the performers. The formula should be derived from a few (one or two) performance measures, reflect customer-focused achievements, and demonstrate true economic value to the corporation.

Performance Targets/Objectives.   Performance objectives or targets are useful when the nature of the work is a project, meaning that it has a fixed end point (such as implementing a new MIS system by April 1, launching a new product for the July 15 trade show, or resolving specific audit report discrepancies by January 1). Such projects have a finite dimension, and achieving them earlier or with a variety of quality levels is not essential. Most "management by objective" type programs have this character. If there are multiple levels to the performance dimensions, so much the better.

Multiple Measures.   When a variety of measures are needed to achieve the desired performance requirements, a matrix can serve a useful purpose. Figure 6-8 shows a matrix that will accommodate a variety of measures, enable the organization to weight them differently, and define an array of ten levels of performance. As shown on the performance matrix, the target level of performance is set at 100. A minimum level of performance is set at 50 and a maximum level of performance is set at 140. In most circumstances, the historical performance or baseline comparator performance is set around the 60 to 80 level, meaning that performance needs to improve in order to achieve desirable payouts. Each measure is weighted based on a total 100 percent allocation.

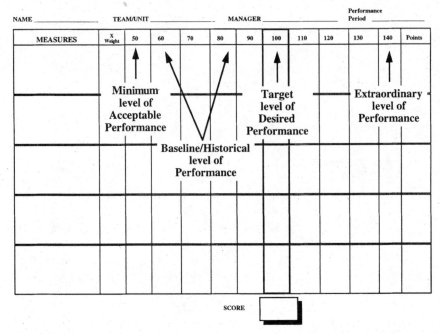

Figure 6-8. Performance matrix.

Therefore, the score can be easily calculated by indicating what level (50 to 140 points) is associated with the actual performance, multiplying it by the weight (as a percentage of 100 percent), and entering the score in the far right column. The scores for each measure are then added, and the total score indicates the performance for the period. The final score can be used as a percentage to be applied to a target payout (say 5 percent, 10 percent, or 15 percent) or can be used as a score to determine the payout, as shown in Figure 6-9.

Having an array of performance levels is very important in behavioral terms. First, the wide range of possibilities gives performers an opportunity to find an achievement level within their grasp. Some plans have failed to produce desired behavioral change because they offered only one performance threshold that the performers felt was beyond their reach. Second, being able to indicate even minor levels of improved performance enables an organization to reinforce those actions that produce improvement even when the payout is not significant. Let's say, for example, that a team's performance improves from 65 to only 75 or 80. Even though its current performance remains well below target level, there is still reason to celebrate—and an opportunity for positive reinforcement to continue the improvement.

Range of Performance		% Payout
From	To	
Below	75	0%
75	89	2%
90	99	3%
100	110	5%
111	125	7%
126	140	10%

Figure 6-9. Illustrative payout opportunity table.

Third, the matrix enables the organization to chart ongoing progress in performance. This is important in supporting the feedback necessary for behavioral change. The matrix also enables the organization to integrate a variety of measures (some of which may in fact be conflicting); to weight them properly for the immediate priorities; and to work with employees on actions necessary to achieve optimal performance levels. The matrix, though complex at first glance, has, in the author's experience, proven to be a very powerful tool in the design and management of incentive plans.

In summary, the payout mechanism and opportunities are the engine that drives the incentive program. They determine how much is to be paid out and how it is to be done. They give the performance measures special meaning. Finally, they are the primary focus of most participants' attention.

Factors Influencing the Payout Mechanisms

Once the approach has been determined, there are other critical factors that may influence the payout mechanisms and opportunities of the incentive plan. Among these are the following concerns:

1. Will the payout be paid as a percent of the individual's current base salary or as a flat dollar amount to each participant? This question is always one of great concern when the plans involve both management and nonmanagement people. If the payouts are a percentage of base salary, supervisors and upper managers will get more money because their salaries are usually higher. However, if the incentive is paid equally, then everyone will get the same amount, but it will be a lower percentage of pay for the higher-paid individuals. In this case the payout needs to be adjusted for overtime payments, as required by the Fair Labor Standards Act. Further, equal payouts may not reflect the real differences in accountabilities and the impact that specific individuals have had on the organization's performance.

2. Should there be a minimum threshold of performance before any payout is provided? Most organizations maintain some form of escape clause, meaning that if the financial performance of the company falls to a critical stage, the plan will be suspended or not paid out. However, some organizations require at least a baseline level of overall performance before the plan is paid. While this may protect certain costs of the organization, it can have a negative impact on the perceived effectiveness of the plan. If the participants feel the threshold is too high, they may disregard the opportunities of the plan and not change their behaviors.

3. Should there be modifiers to the plan's payouts? By *modifiers* I mean those performance factors of the organization that should influence the firm's ability to pay or special areas not included in the measures of the plan, such as employee safety, product quality audit, and customer satisfaction. These are modifiers as opposed to thresholds or measures, because they may increase or decrease the payout after it has been calculated. For example, a large health care organization modified its incentive payouts to all its employees based on the results of patient/physician satisfaction surveys. A cable TV system modified payouts based on specific community relation activities that enhance the system's image in the marketplace. Other companies have modified the payouts based on overall profitability, employee safety records, and absenteeism.

4. Should there be caps on the payouts? A *cap* means that there will be a maximum payout to the participants. They are used when the payout is based on a predetermined formula. Caps are appropriate when the relationship between the payout and the performance is not clear. If there is little historical data to support setting levels for the performance measures, the opportunity for performance improvements is uncertain. In other circumstances, when the organization is continuing to make capital and/or process changes to increase the productivity of the unit, caps can prevent the organization from paying too much for a given level of performance. This can be especially important when the performance level is a result of factors beyond the performers' control, such as investments by the company, a surge in market demands, engineering product changes, etc. Caps can have a negative impact on performers by restricting the payout opportunity, but there may be an appropriate justification. As with the use of the matrix, certain payout mechanisms have caps inherently built in.

5. Should a portion of the payout be held in reserve? When a plan is paid out more frequently than annually, there is often a question about whether any of it should be held back until the results of the annual performance are determined. The primary concern behind this action is that the organization might pay out incentives during a first or second quarter only to have the entire year's performance fall below standard level. In this case, the firm will have paid out funds with no annual gain in performance. The reserve fund is a common practice in many gain-sharing plans. The ACA study reported that 13 percent of the plans had such a provision and held back an average 25 percent of the payout. In practice, the amount is between 20 percent and 50 percent of the payout, and all or a portion of the reserve amount is paid out after year-end if the organization has achieved its financial objectives.[12]

The reserve method is used because the incentive plan is viewed as an annual plan with quarterly progress payouts. This assumption may be appropriate for the executive pay plan, since executives impact performance during the fiscal year, but it may not be appropriate for operational units that operate on a different basis. The fiscal year is a product of accounting practices and stockholder expectations, which may not necessarily use the same time frame as the one for serving customers. This point should be discussed by the design team.

An alternative developed by several organizations is to establish a target payout, say 10 percent of salaries, and pay 2 percent of annual pay on a quarterly basis and 2 percent for annual results. Each quarter is considered independent of the others. If a payout is made for one quarter, the next quarter does not reflect a year-to-date progress but rather performance against that period's objectives. The annual payout reflects total annual results. Using this approach, the firm can increase the sense of urgency on a quarterly basis, focus its people on the key issues, and improve its ability to meet deadlines and performance targets.

6. Should the performance levels, or baseline, be raised? The consideration behind this question is the desire to increase standards of performance as results are achieved. As an example, some of the incentive gain-sharing plans at the 3M Corporation have a single measure of performance: the value of the units produced divided by the total number of hours of all the people in the plant. The incentive is paid out when the value per hour exceeds a baseline level. The baseline is a rolling average over a 12-month period; the payout is determined on a quarterly basis.

This approach reflects the desire not to continue to pay for performance improvements that have been achieved by the firm. From the organization's perspective, this is reasonable because it has already paid for *process changes*, or improvements in performance. As the firm invests in capital equipment, engineering designs, or other process changes, the baseline of performance needs to be modified according-ly. From the employees' perspective, this adjustment may seem unfair because the improvements in the economics of the business can be realized forever while the payout is a onetime event only. The participants need to understand that changes in performance that are integrated into the operations of the unit may cause an adjustment in the payout opportunities and that continuous improvements are an essential element of doing business. An alternative may be to increase base pay or incentive opportunities as improvements in the performance of the unit are realized or as investments in technology are made.

7. Should the payout be in cash or some other form of reward?
For many organizations the answer is a quite simple—*cash.* However, in some organizations, the use of cash may have a negative impact on employee relations or public scruinty. A large teaching hospital that had experienced significant downsizing and trouble with the local community wanted to implement a team incentive program in order to stimulate the new direction of the organization. The use of cash would have caused significant difficulty. The hospital was in serious financial difficulty, and the external members of the Board were concerned about the image of an incentive plan. The plan was designed to support improvements in financial and service measures, but cash payouts could be taken in a negative light by members of their community. Therefore, instead of awarding individuals cash for performance improvements, they gave each team funds it could use to improve the quality of its working conditions or its members' professional skills. The rewards would be at the discretion of each team, with a review by the senior executive in its area. The funds were used for new office furniture, computer programs, and specialized training and conferences. One department purchased items it could use to reinforce other departments. The rewards were very meaningful to each team—more so, in fact, than if they had been in the form of cash.

Eligibility

Who should be included in the plan and why? I have waited until this point in the discussion to address the issue of eligibility because I have found that people generally tend to over-exclude or overly-include people when this concern is discussed any sooner. Although the subject can be introduced earlier in the overall communication of the plan, it is best to wait until this point in the design process to make eligibility decisions. The task here is to define the target groups that will be participating in the risks and rewards of the plan. This task should involve an analysis of performance measures and payout mechanisms to determine which groups and/or individuals make major contributions to performance. Once the individuals or groups who should participate in the plan have been identified, there are several additional issues to consider.

1. What should be the provision for people who leave the target group during the performance period? Should they be excluded from the payout, receive a prorata portion based on their time with the group, or receive a full share?

2. Should transfers within in the organization be considered differently from cases in which employees cease to be employed by the company? If you choose to exclude the latter, will the exclusion apply equally to employees who leave voluntarily and to those who get fired or laid off?

3. How should the plan deal with employees who retire, have long-term disability, or experience short-term disability?

4. How should the plan handle other interruptions in employment, such as jury duty, military service, special assignments, or participation in extended training programs outside the immediate area?

5. How long should new employees have to work with the group before they become eligible to participate in the program?

In most cases, employees are excluded from participating in the plan unless they are present during the performance period. Some firms require people to be employed when the payout is made, not at the end of the performance period. This can easily be handled when the payout is based on hours worked. In many cases, firms prorate payouts for employees who retire, experience any disability (excluding normal sick leave), or are on military service or jury duty. Whether an individual terminates employment for voluntary or involuntary reasons (except as noted above), they usually forfeit any rights to payouts in the incentive plan. Other special considerations concern employees who transfer from the unit or participate in some major project or outside activity that prohibits their full participation in the target group's performance. These will need to be considered in the context of the particular situation facing the organization and the primary objectives of the plan.

Funding Sources and Return on Investment

Incentive plans may require an increase in the costs of compensation. In many cases this may be offset by improvements in performance, as in the case of plans that are totally self-funded. Regardless of the structure of the plan, it is necessary to examine the potential costs of the plan at different payout levels as well as the associated impact of performance improvements. This is the reason for understanding funding not as a cost of implementing the plans but as an investment-on-return relationship.

The cost analysis of the plan should be calculated by applying various payout levels to the current compensation costs of the plan participants. This analysis is useful in anticipating the exposure to the company, in selling the program to the participants and/or in comparing actual ROI with planned ROI at some future point in time. Plan participants often figure their own ROI by comparing the payout opportunities with the amount of extra effort or change they will need to take. If the projection is positive, the new behaviors may be engaged. If not, the plan will not be viewed as a positive and worthwhile venture.

The same logic applies to executives who are considering whether to accept a recommended plan. They will want to understand the financial exposure of the plan as well as the return that will be realized from the performance. Baseline and historical performance are useful tools for determining the return on investment. Change in specific performance factors is important to understanding what is likely to be realized and relating these operational components to the key competitive pressures within the firm.

There are basically three different methods for determining the return on investment for incentive plans. Taken together or independently, they can show what impact the plan will have on the competitiveness of the organization.

Return on Compensation Investment (ROCI)

This method basically uses financial return for calculating the appropriateness of the funding levels. The steps are as follows:

1. Calculate the payout levels for all the participants at the minimum, current, target, and maximum levels of performance. This will result in a dollar cost of the plan.

2. Calculate the financial income/reduced costs that will be attributed to these four levels of performance. These financial measures may be built into the performance factors in the plan, or may be assessed in terms of the impact caused by operational or behavioral change. In either case you are seeking the economic benefit to be gained by the incentive plan.

3. Calculate the ROCI by dividing the costs into the potential financial benefit. In many companies, a $3 to $1 return would be a strong measure of success; that is, you spend $500,000 in incentive payouts at target level

of performance in exchange for $1,500,000 improved financial results. Whether these results achieve net income for the company is less material than whether they achieve these results for the target group.

The 1992 ACA study on group incentive plans reported that an average payout was $700 per employee per year (2.6 percent of base pay) and that the companies surveyed gained an average of $2200 per employee per year. This is a 3.14 to 1 ratio, or a 214 percent net gain after subtracting the payout from the financial gain. The greatest gains—over 400 percent—were reported in plans that had a combination of financial and operational measures.[13]

Investments in Performance Improvement (IPI)

In this method you are comparing the performance improvements with the necessary investments in compensation. In Chapter 1 I indicated that if a firm could achieve a desired level of performance without such plans, it should do so. Incentive plans create an opportunity for employees to share in the fortunes and risks of the business. Therefore, when examining the costs, one needs to examine the potential improvements in operational or other performance factors. The investment needs to be judged in relation to the importance of changes in these factors. For example, banks with a need to increase the number of transactions handled per hour might view the investment in compensation costs in relation to the economic value of this improved standard of performance. A customer services firm that wanted to improve the quality of its phone interactions with customers might judge improvement in performance in relation to increased incentive costs. A shipping company looking at the improvement in on-time deliveries might translate this performance (i.e., customer interaction scores) into increased competitiveness. Does an X level of performance improvement warrant a Y level of compensation investment? The measures need to relate the new, desired levels of performance with the payout opportunities provided to the participants.

Improving the Competitiveness of Total Compensation

Some organizations seek incentives in order to improve the competitiveness of their compensation with the outside marketplace. This is an important consideration if a priority issue for the firm is its ability to attract and retain key talent. This approach is also valuable when public scrutiny is an important factor in the design of the plan. When comparing executive compensation or compensation opportunities with others in different parts of the organization, one needs to assess the impact of the compensation levels from a total compensation viewpoint. The objective is to establish some acceptable level of pay relative to the outside marketplace or comparable external groups.

To complete the task, one needs to compare the current level of compensation to a peer group (i.e., marketplace or internal unit comparisons), pinpoint relevant risk issues, and compare the total compensation at various performance levels (current, target, maximum, etc.) to a comparable set of data. Most compensation surveys at this time unfortunately do not capture data on pay and organizational performance. This is becoming more available for executive compensation because of the 1992 Security and Exchange Commission ruling on proxy statement requirements. The conclusions need to be examined to establish whether or not the plan's payout provisions will enable the firm to achieve its desired market position or meet internal benchmark references.

Examining the return on investment, makes it possible to examine both the risks and benefits to the organization and employees of supporting a particular plan. With this support the primary challenge will be to make good on expectations for savings, performance improvements, and competitiveness of pay.

Special Issues

At this point the basic plan has been designed. There are always certain issues that need to be addressed regarding the way the plan fits within the fabric of the organization. Understanding and developing an appropriate response to these issues contributes directly to the effectiveness and credibility of the plan. Such issues can include the following considerations:

1. Should the incentive payouts be included in employee benefits? Customarily, incentive payments are included in employee benefit provisions when they amount to more than 20 percent or 25 percent of the employee's salary. Depending on the amount of money that is related to the incentive, a portion or all of the incentive may be included in some benefit plans. For example, defined benefit retirement plans may use total compensation for determining final years' average compensation (salary and incentive).

2. How should overtime be handled? The Fair Labor Standards Act requires that incentives for employees who are considered nonexempt (according to the type of plans described in this book) should be considered as part of their pay rates when calculating overtime rates of pay.

Hence, if participants are paid $300 per week and receive an incentive that is in effect $30 per week, the overtime is based on $8.25 per hours ($300 + 30 = $330 ÷ 40 hours), not $7.50 ($300 ÷ 40 hours). Hence, their payments for overtime will need to be increased by the appropriate amount. If they work 200 hours of overtime, they will receive a gross-up in overtime of $250 ($1.25 × 200 hours).

Another method is to pay the incentive as a percent of total wages (including incentives for managers), base wage plus overtime. This approach also meets the requirements of the Fair Labor Standards Act.

3. Who determines the performance levels and the payouts?

The decision making process that supports an incentive compensation plan is often a very critical issue in its credibility and ownership. When plans are developed by a design team, it is often useful to continue some form of a committee structure to review the results and performance goals for subsequent years. This retains the spirit of involvement developed during the initial periods of the plan. However, performance measures and levels should be a management prerogative. In one large manufacturing organization, this balance was achieved by management reviewing the performance requirements with a steering committee, discussing the rationale and competitive pressures. The steering committee made modifications to performance levels, but management retained the veto power over any decisions. Fortunately, they have not needed to exercise it.

If hourly or nonexempt employees are included in a standing committee to oversee incentive plans, one needs to be considerate of current case litigation and other rulings by the NLRB (National Labor Relations Board). The NLRB is now determining whether a standing, decision-making committee that includes hourly employees is, in fact, operating like a labor union, and should be treated as one by the employer.[14]

4. How should the incentive plan be integrated with other plans?

An organization's ability to compete with speed and flexibility often lies in the alignment between the various reward systems. In operational areas, employees are frequently concerned that their managers' performance measures may conflict or not support their own performance measures. In some organizations employees are concerned that the performance requirements of sales (for revenues) are not consistent with other areas (for costs).

One very innovative organization took an approach that integrated everyone into the core incentive plan of the company. Then special incentives were added onto the core plan for areas like sales, senior management, and technical contributors, so that there was an alignment of interests across all parties. Further, the performance measures were publically displayed, discussed frequently in cross-functional meetings, and developed in combination with each unit's customers. Here, the customers of each unit were involved in setting the measures, the levels of performance, and the weight given to various measures in the incentives. This enhanced the teamwork, collaboration, and focus of people on those areas that contributed most directly to the organization's overall competitiveness.

5. How should changes in competitive strategy, windfalls and cave-ins be handled? Every business is facing a dynamic marketplace. Part of the pressure behind incentive plans is to share the risks and fortunes of the organization with those who make it happen. The traditional attempts by employers to protect their employees from changes in the marketplace has lead to a widespread feeling of entitlement.

However, over the recent years, this commitment to career-long employment has been broken. The answer lies in sharing both the good times and the bad times with employees by bringing them into the business and making them partners with management. To accomplish this, employees need to understand the strategy of the business and the critical priorities that determine its competitiveness, as well as the challenges that face it. Employees will be less concerned about any changes in performance measures when they understand the full context of the business.

A *windfall* occurs when a unit is able to receive a dramatically positive achievement by doing little if anything. A *cave-in* occurs when the performance of a unit is hurt dramatically by a situation beyond its control. The important concept in handling windfalls and cave-ins is to retain the integrity of the incentive plan. If you are asking people to share in the downside risk, they should also share in the upside potential.

Vista Chemical, a specialty chemical company in Houston, Texas, faced a situation in which its incentive plan did not pay off because of a decline in its core business. The nonfinancial performance factors, such as quality management, on-time delivery, reduction in waste/increase in material usage, were all at superior levels. But due to the volume of business (i.e., Vista was gaining market share in a dramatically declining market), there was no payout. The question was, should the organization pay out anyway? Though the answer was "no," funds were made available to every unit that achieved above-target performance (all were eligible) to use in celebrating their achievements. The celebrations could not be in form of cash payments, but could be used for improving the unit's work areas, holding a celebration party, or anything that would be meaningful and reinforcing to the team members. Vista was able to achieve a dramatic return on its investment even though it was not able to make an actual payout.

6. If the plan is not for the entire organization, how do you handle those who are not eligible for the incentive plan? The way an organization responds to this concern depends on its overall objective. If the firm ultimately wants to put everyone on some form of variable compensation, the response can be to say, "Take a number. We will be getting to your department as soon as reasonably possible." This indicates that if a department performs the necessary business analysis and incentive design tasks, it can participate in an incentive plan. St. Elizabeth's Medical Center of Boston started with three pilot department plans in 1990, and went to over 16 in two years. Other firms respond by indicating that it is not appropriate for all areas, and that therefore, "If you want to work for incentives, offer to transfer into work areas that offer them." Regardless of the overall objective, the important thing is to indicate that people will receive incentives when they earn them, they are not a form of additional compensation to which people are entitled just because they work in a given department.

7. If the plan is primarily oriented toward team or large-group performance, how will individual performance be rewarded? A traditional thinking paradigm creates a dilemna between reinforcing individual versus team performance. The resolution is not in selecting one over the other, but in achieving both. Total Quality Management experts have taught us that productivity and quality are not opposite ends of a continuum, but interdependent forces of success. Here too, individual performance needs to be reinforced by the team, and team performance needs to be celebrated by the individuals. As has been and will be discussed throughout this book, effective systems of rewards create conditions where everyone at every level, employee, manager, shareholder, and customer can win simultaneously. Only the competitors lose. Therefore, if the objective is to reward the team, then provisions need to be made for reinforcing the individuals for contributing high performance to the success of their team. As discussed in Chapter 3, this can include verbal/social, tangible/symbolic, work related, and financially positive consequences. The effectiveness of their use will be dependent on the criteria discussed in Chapter 3, and will be measured by the degree to which the individuals continue to do their best.

Implementation and Management Requirements

Once the plan has been designed and developed, it is time to determine how it will be implemented and managed over time. This is one of the most critical steps of all. One can design an excellent system, but if it is not expertly implemented and managed, it will not yield the behavioral change or performance improvements hoped for.

A useful strategy prior to final approval is to test-market the plan with the ultimate customers: the managers, supervisors, and employees. This can be done best through a series of focus group discussions with employees. Prior to the test-market process, senior managers should be made aware of the plan so that any concerns or suggestions made in the focus group sessions can be reviewed by management before being implemented. In other words, don't communicate the plan to the workforce until you have senior management's support of the plan.

If there is a design team, this is an important step for two reasons. First, the task of going in front of one's peers creates a useful pressure to communicate the plan as simply and clearly as possible. Second, the discussion and reaction to the plan will tell the design team a great deal about what will be necessary to make the plan successful. This process will identify the importance of employee understanding and commitment to the performance measures, levels, and thresholds. It will reveal whether the payout mechanism is truly understandable and workable from the employees' standpoint, whether the payout opportunities are sufficient to warrant changes in behavior, and identify still-outstanding issues to do with eligibility, funding, etc.

Once the focus groups have been completed, the design team will need to analyze the results, finalize the plan, and prepare the recommendation for senior management approval. The approval process must incorporate the design team's final recommendations for the best possible plan, based on their work, the feedback from participants, and reviews from managers. Senior management will then have to decide whether this plan will be worth the investment it requires and will achieve its purpose.

Once approved, the implementation process will have three components:

1. Communicating the plan to all participants

The focus group sessions usually include only a small number of the actual plan participants. This implementation step is designed to explain the plan in the most direct and meaningful manner possible. One rule of thumb is to communicate the program in sufficiently small groups that employees have a chance to truly understand and ask questions about the plan. They should also be given a written document that conveys the idea that this plan is special and should be important to them as members of the organization. Managers should receive the document early in the process so they can support the communication effort. One company actually established a hot line for all employees to answer questions regarding the plan. It was not used very often, but its existence played an important symbolic role in building the employees' trust.

2. Establishing the necessary support systems

Feedback on performance on a continual basis is essential to facilitating behavior change. Depending on the measures, information systems may need to be created or changed to support this requirement. Information systems need to provide performers with reliable, timely, and meaningful data on how they are progressing. There will also need to be a decision-making process for assessing actual performance against the measures/objectives and determining the payout. Finally, the payout results will need to be communicated to people, followed as soon as possible thereafter by the actual incentive checks.

3. Managing the system to its full potential

To create and support an effective incentive program, the entire process of managing performance needs to come into play. Managers should become *more* involved, not less, and in a manner that builds the strengths of the organization, captures the discretionary efforts, and promotes a reinforcing environment for performance. This is the fundamental gain-making process of any incentive pay system. The key managerial skills needed in this process are the ability to:

- Translate the incentive plan measures into specific, meaningful, and targeted measures for the small work team or individual.
- Provide frequent, real-time feedback to the performers of the unit so that they know how they are progressing.
- Use all forms of consequences, but primarily positive reinforcement, to encourage and reward those behaviors that will lead to positive results.
- Work with the team to identify and resolve barriers to their performance. This can include work process issues, supplies, communication with customers, support from other areas, or any aspect of the work environment that might inhibit the team from achieving their maximum potential.

If it has an effective implementation process, an incentive plan has a strong chance of success for both the employees/participants and the organization. The employees win by receiving additional compensation as well as reinforcements for achievements in performance; the organization wins by realizing improved results and a stronger competitive position. That is the ultimate win/win outcome, and the fundamental purpose for engaging in a variable pay program.

Risks Versus Rewards

Variable pay plans are by their very nature at risk. This means that the payout may not occur. In order to have a positive impact on behavior, they should not be uncertain. The difference between risk and uncertainity lies in knowing what to do. Uncertainity occurs when one is not sure how to achieve or avoid a particular consequence. (Some refer to this as fear or resistance to change.) Risk, on the other hand, indicates that one knows what to do, though the actions may not produce the desired results.

Variable pay plans create for their participants a stake in the fortune of the business. While some refer to this as pay at risk, I view such plans as opportunity pay. If the firm can realize specific gains as a result of the combined efforts of its members, it can offer them the opportunity to share in the results. But sharing the good times means sharing the declines as well. That is part of life. No one can be insulated from the risks and fortunes of a challenging marketplace.

Summary

Variable pay plans are not for everyone. Developing, implementing, and managing them requires thoughtful and deliberate actions. They are difficult to undo once implemented. However, they offer one of the most powerful systems of rewards available today.

The key challenge is to design, implement, and manage the variable pay program in a manner that reinforces desired behaviors. Many incentive plans today either fail to reinforce desired behaviors or work against the principles of teamwork, collaboration, and flexibility. To develop a plan that successfully links results with behaviors and fosters win/win opportunities—both for the organization and for its members—requires the creation of conditions favorable to collaborative change. The SMART criteria offers useful guidelines for this goal.

Variable pay programs open a new force for change and an almost limitless reserve of strength for the organization. The process of developing variable pay plans is meaningful and rewarding, but it is only the beginning of what can be achieved by people who truly feel a part of the enterprise, share its goals, and take the initiative to do what has to be done.

Notes

1. American Productivity Center and American Compensation Association on Non-Traditional Reward and Human Resource Practices, "People, Performance, and Pay." Scottsdale, Ariz., 1986.

2. Tully, S., "Your Paycheck Gets Exciting." *Fortune*, November 1, 1993, p. 83.

3. "The Hay Report: Compensation and Benefit Strategies for 1994 and Beyond." The Hay Group, Inc., Philadelphia, Pa., 1993.

4. APC/ACA, "People, Performance, and Pay," op. cit.

5. Doyle, R. and P. Doyle, *Gain Management*. New York: AMACOM, 1992.

6. McAdams, J., and E. Hawk, *Capitilizing on Human Assets*. Scottsdale, Ariz.: American Compensation Association, 1992.

7. Lawler, E., *Strategic Pay*. San Francisco: Jossey Bass, 1990.

8. Dickinson, A. M., "Exploring New Vistas: Performance Management Research Laboratory at Western Michigan University." *Performance Management*, Vol. 9, No. 1, 1991, pp. 27–31.

9. McAdams and Hawk, op. cit.

10. McClellan, D., *The Achieving Society*. Princeton, N.J.: Van Nostrand, 1961.

11. Daniels, A., *Performance Management: Improving Quality Productivity Through Positive Reinforcement*. Tucker, Ga.: Performance Management Publications, 1989.

12. McAdams and Hawk, op. cit.

13. McAdams and Hawk, op. cit.

14. For a complete description of the NLRB decision, contact the National Labor Relations Board, NLRB Building, 1717 Pennsylvania Avenue, NW, Washington, D.C. 20570, and ask about decision 311 NLRB No. 88.

7
Creating a Stake in the Business

Now that I'm a shareholder, I don't think they should be spending our money like that. We have a better way.
—AN ANONYMOUS PRODUCTION WORKER, AFTER
RECEIVING SHARES OF STOCK AS A SPECIAL AWARD,
1993

The creative application of equity-based programs has long been the domain of executives and their consultants. The increasing rancor about executive compensation has led many in the media, in organizations, and in boards of directors to question the return on investment of these programs. Yet stock-related programs have been used widely in small start-up companies, especially in the technology and biotechnology fields. They offer relatively inexpensive ways for these companies to hire top talent because people are looking for a stake in the business.

This chapter addresses a wide range of ideas for developing innovative reward systems tied to the equity or ownership process of the organization. The principle underlying these systems is the use of rewards to create among employees and management alike a shared sense of identity, commitment, and goals for the organization. While not attempting to address current controversies about executive compensation or trying to explain the full tax and accounting implications of each option, the chapter seeks to provide ideas and stimulate creative thinking about equity-based programs.

Note: The reader should be aware that many of the provisions for stock-related programs may be changed by congressional tax legislation, rulings by the Securities and Exchange Commission (SEC), rulings by the Financial Accounting Standards Board (FASB), and loopholes found by executive compensation and legal experts. Therefore, before taking any action, one should seek the counsel of those who have expertise in these areas and are well acquainted with the particular circumstances of the company involved.

Overview of the Forces for Change

Perhaps of all the trends that are swirling around the field of compensation, "creating a stake in the business" is most common. As discussed in the previous chapter, group-oriented incentive plans such as gain-sharing and team incentives provide cash awards to people based on the performance of their team, department, division, etc. By their very design, profit-sharing plans offer employees a stake in the *profits* of a business when those profits exceed a certain level. Equity-related programs, the next logical step, offer employees a stake in the *ownership* of the business and thereby in the long-term viability of the organization.

The point of all cash compensation plans is that they emphasize current operating issues and encourage people to take actions that benefit them immediately. Long-term wealth, however, whether it be for the organization or for individuals, cannot be achieved by maximizing immediate, short-term cash. Therefore, structuring reward systems to encourage a dynamic balance between cash flow and value growth is necessary for a healthy organization.

Over the last several years, interest has grown in employee stock ownership plans (ESOPs). Many have been used as a creative vehicle to fund employee retirement plans. They have also been used to create a sense of having a stake in the ownership of the company. ESOPs have shown tremendous potential for creating closer links between the interests of employees and those of the business.[1]

Recent rulings by the SEC and FASB have provided a challenge to the use of stock-related programs, however. In the fall of 1992, the SEC changed the reporting requirements for the value of stock-related programs to a company's executives. The data must now be displayed in a format that is easy to understand and relate to a company's performance. The purpose behind this requirement is to increase the shareholder's accountability for executive compensation by making the information more understandable and more public. The information is to be reported in a company's proxy statement filed prior to its annual shareholders meeting. Shareholders as well as the media can now examine the relationship between executive pay and organizational performance and can judge for themselves whether this expenditure is achieving the desired return on investment.

In June 1993, FASB issued a controversial short-term decision on how companies should treat stock options. Their position is that stock-based awards are compensation to employees for services rendered and that their value should be recognized as an expense in the income statement. This Exposure Draft, entitled Accounting for Stock-based Compensation, would require companies to disclose this expense starting in 1994 and carry it on income statements for awards granted after December 31, 1996. The costs would be based on the fair value of the stock options on the grant date. This value would be determined either by an option pricing model such as Black-Scholes[2] or by calculating an assumed 5 percent to 10 percent annual stock price appreciation.

There are many challenges to the FASB position by businesses, accounting firms, and consulting companies. The primary concern is the impact on reducing net income and earnings per share for start-up companies or other firms that make a wide use of stock options. Further, most analysis conducted by accounting and compensation consulting firms indicate that there is no reliable way to value options, particularly in companies with little financial or stock performance track record.

In light of this ruling, organizations would be wise to articulate their compensation philosophy and strategy and examine the value of their stock-related programs as part of this process. They will then need to examine the value of such programs and the return on investment for the company. Early indications are that many companies are making these options available to fewer people than before. These regulatory requirements pose an important potential challenge to the architects of equity-oriented reward programs.

The principal objective behind the use of stock-related compensation programs is to create a true alignment of interests between shareholders and those accountable for the organization's success. Some companies, like Xerox, Kodak, Chrysler, and Honeywell, are seeking to apply these concepts to executives in direct ways. They are creating executive compensation programs that require executives to buy and own shares in the company in amounts relative to their total cash compensation. Whether the shares are purchased directly, bought through loan provisions, or granted through performance-based programs, the objective is to transform executives into true stakeholders. This means that the personal net worth of the executives will be tied in some measure to the fortunes of the company.

There are other programs that link employees to the fortunes of the company. In the late 1980s a growing number of employee stock ownership programs (ESOPs) offered workers a chance to gain a stake in the business. Some large companies, like United Airlines and Avis, became primarily owned by their employees. ESOPs became an attractive vehicle for providing employees an opportunity to benefit in their company's performance. The tax laws were very favorable. For example, a company could borrow money at below-market interest rates and use the funds to buy stock in the open market, thereby either increasing share price or at least not diluting current share value. The interest and principal payments were then tax deductible. Furthermore, dividends paid to ESOPs, while not tax deductible when paid to shareholders, were tax deductible to ESOP participants. Many firms saw ESOPs as a good way to ward off acquisition suitors because employees would need to vote on the sale of the company. For these and many other strategic and financial reasons, ESOPs became an attractive device for linking employees to the interests of the company.

Definitions of a Few Key Terms

Within this context it is important to define a few terms. These terms are highly abbreviated, and the provisions are subject to change based on the consideration of Congress and other regulatory agencies.

Stock Options: These are rights granted by a corporation to its executives and/or employees that enable them to buy shares in the company at a predetermined price at some future point in time (usually between five and ten years hence). For example, a stock option at $30 per share could be used to buy a share in the company in the future. So, if the price went to $35, the owner would realize a gain of $5 per share when the option was exercised.

Incentive Stock Option (ISO): These are stock options that meet the requirements established by Section 422 of the Internal Revenue Code. The IRS requires that ISOs be granted to an employee of the company through a plan that has been approved by the shareholders. The term cannot exceed ten years, and the option price must be equal to or greater than the fair market value of the stock on the grant date. The gain is not taxable until the stock is sold, and the gains are not deductible by the corporation. If the individual holds the stock option for at least two years from the date of the grant or one year from the transfer of the option to stock, any appreciation is taxed at the capital gains rate. This is a particularly attractive feature when the individual's personal tax rates are higher than the current capital gains rate (currently at 28 percent). Finally, ISOs need to be exercised in the order in which they are granted.

Non-Qualified Stock Options (NQSO): These stock options do not qualify for the tax-favored treatment (capital gains) the way ISOs do. They offer more flexibility, however. The option price can be set equal to, above, or below the fair market price. The option becomes taxable when the individual exercises the option and receives the stock, regardless of when the individual sells the stock. There may be an additional taxable gain if the stock price is held and then sold at a higher price. The gain between the option price and the exercise price (sometimes called the option spread) is taxable at ordinary income tax rates. Finally, NQSOs may be exercised in any order the individual wants. This allows him or her to maximize or minimize the gain on the exercise price.

Stock Appreciation Rights (SAR): These are compensation provisions that are similar to stock options except that they do not require a person to take ownership of stock. Instead, he or she is paid the gain between the exercise price and the market price at the time of exercise. For example, if a person has 1000 SARs and the stock price increases by $5 share, he or she is awarded $5000 in cash (or in equivalent shares of stock). The company charges this as a compensation expense, and the individual is taxed at ordinary income tax rates. SARs are usually granted as a companion to stock options in order to pay the tax liability of the option gain.

Phantom Stock: This is used when a company's stock is not available (as is the case with privately held companies) or when an attractive alternative becomes possible (as, for example, when a company wants to establish an equity simulator program for a division or subsidiary). Phantom stock operates like SARs, but the focus is on the value growth as determined by a formula, such as a multiple of earnings, book value of the unit, or an economic value-added model. The individual receives symbolic shares, which are valued at the date of grant and revalued at some future point in time. The value of the gain on the shares determines the award.

Performance Share Plan: This is a program that provides stock (or stock options) to an individual for achieving specified performance goals, usually for a multiyear period (three to five to seven years). The performance determines the number of units one earns, but the stock price of the company at the end of the period determines the value of each unit at payout. When the payout is made in cash, such programs are usually called *performance unit plans.*

Reload Options: These are new rights which, sometimes in combination with actual shares, are granted for the exercise of the participant's current stock options based on performance. For example, if an executive team is able to realize the lapse of a restriction on a series of options because it has achieved certain performance goals, the company can replace the options exercised with new options at the now fair market price of the stock. This enables the participants to realize all the future upside potential inherent in the original option grant and ensures that the participant continues to have options available. This program is sometimes called *accelerated ownership* or *restoration options.*

Discounted Stock Options: These are rights that place the option price at a rate lower than the price of the stock at the time the option is granted. For example, if the stock is trading at $30 per share, a discounted option may be at $28 per share. Thus, when the person exercises and sells the stock at $35 per share, the gain is $7. The company expenses the per-share difference and the individual realizes the gain at the $7 per share. This is available for nonqualified stock options only.

Restricted Provisions: These are requirements in stock programs that make certain rights to ownership contingent on one of a variety of factors. Some companies use continued employment with the company as the contingency for being able to exercise the options. This is usually for a three- to five-year period. Other firms use financial performance as the contingency factor—the growth of the company's stock, achievement of a certain amount of financial growth, improvement of the firm's profitability, return on asset/equity ratios, etc.

Underwater: The value of a stock option is created when the actual market price of the stock is greater than the exercise price available with the option. If the exercise price is lower than the market price, the option is considered *underwater* and has limited or no value to the participant.

Case Study of a Management Stock Bonus Plan

The ACME Drilling company (an actual company, but a fictitious name) has a long-term executive incentive program. The purpose of the program is to provide senior managers with ownership in the company consistent with their performance. The plan extends down to employees at the department management level. The plan is intended to create a sense of common interest among the executives, managers, and the shareholders. The stock options are non-qualified stock options and have a restriction that requires them to vest over a five-year period, or 20 percent per year from the date of grant. When managers cease to be employed by the company, they lose all rights to those shares not vested and must exercise any remaining options (i.e., trade them in for stock). There is a simultaneous purchase and sale of the options that enables managers to exercise the options with the sale of other options at the same time. This enables executives to acquire shares from the proceeds of exercising and selling options or pay taxes on the gain.

ACME is a publicly traded company, and stock performance has been on par with the general stock market and the industry. This

performance has not made any executive wealthy, but the
stock ownership plan is an important part of the total executive
compensation package.

Each year, after the close of the fiscal year and the awarding of the
executive/management bonuses, ACME executives engage in an
allocation process for the stock program. The compensation committee
of the board of directors and the chief executive determine the amount of
stock options that will be awarded to ACME's managers through
a formula based on earnings per share targets. Of the total number of
options available, 40 percent goes to the chief executive. The remaining
60 percent is spread among the senior executives and lower-level
managers. The chief executive allocates 30 percent to the senior
executives based on her judgment of their individual performance.

The remaining 30 percent shares are allocated on the basis of the
perceived performance of the managers as recommended by each
functional executive. Once all the recommendations have been
submitted, the CEO, the vice president for human resources, and the
chief financial officer meet to discuss each recommendation and
make final decisions. When a final allocation is made, the CEO sends a
personalized letter to each recipient telling him or her the amount of
the award and the exercise price.

The receipt of the options letter is always an important event. In
approximately 90 percent of the cases the allocation awarded is similar
to the previous year's. Those who received 200 shares last year will
probably get between 175 and 225 shares this year, for example,
depending on individual performance and the performance of the
company. Approximately 70 percent of the shares that become vested
are exercised each year—that is, the managers exercise the options
and sell a large portion of their stock for cash. This program has become
a significant element in the total compensation package of the
managers, and receiving the stock options has become an important sign
of recognition to ACME's managers, who regard it as an indication of
their perceived value.

What's Wrong with This Picture?

The original intent of the ACME stock ownership plan was to align the
interests of the executives and managers with those of the shareholders.
The underlying idea was that executives would take actions and make
decisions consistent with building long-term asset value for all stakeholders. The program was also intended to recognize individual performance
more cost-effectively than cash payments would. The idea was to emphasize the long-term interests of the company and balance this with the
immediate profitability pressures of the management bonus program.

The problem is that ACME's stock option plan is not working as
intended. Let's examine the various features of the program in relation
to the SMART criteria presented in Chapter 3 to see why.

Specific

To have an impact on behavior, rewards must be clearly linked to desired behaviors or results. ACME's plan has several limitations in this regard. First, the number of shares available and the value of these shares (i.e., stock price) are based on the *company's* performance. If the participants had a clear line of sight between their actions and the company's performance, this would be all right. But in most cases this perspective exists only for the CEO (which is probably why CEOs and their close advisors generally tend to favor this type of program). In ACME's case, most of the managers tend to treat their options as a statement of their perceived worth in the CEO's eyes, not as a reflection of their impact on the company's performance or as a way of sharing in the achievements of the firm. Further, since the pool is fixed, when some managers get more shares, others automatically get less. Hence, if any behaviors are being reinforced, they are those related to serving top management, not those related to serving customers, implementing the firm's strategy, or working collaboratively.

Meaningful

The value of the stock option rewards is determined by a combination of factors. First, the earnings of the company must be above a certain threshold before any options are available. Since this is generally predicated on minimal targets, there is little perceived risk. The amount of options may be increased on the basis of company performance, but most executives seldom understand or relate to this measurement formula.

Second, the amount of the shares a manager earns is based on his or her individual performance. While different executives have different performance expectations, this factor is easy for some and very difficult for others. Success is gauged more on who you know than what you've done.

Third, the long-term value of the options lies in achieving growth in the price of the stock. Since the stock is publicly traded and heavily held by institutions, there is little direct relation between an individual's performance and the share price.

Finally, because most of the managers sell the shares soon after the lapse of the vesting schedule, it is clear that the option program is treated as just another means of cash compensation. The time restriction transforms the program into a deferred-compensation program. Award opportunities are meaningful only when they influence managers to make decisions or take actions that benefit the long-term growth of the organization's value. The real meaning of ACME's program is as a measure of perceived esteem, not true performance.

Achievable

If the purpose of the plan is to align managers' interests with those of the shareholders as well as to maintain a competitive compensation package, the plan is not succeeding. Most of the managers are liquidating their stock options as soon as they become available. They are exercising the only aspect of the stock options over which they have control: when to exercise and sell the stock. The number of shares they receive is not directly related to their personal or collective achievements, but to how they are perceived by the CEO. The value of the shares they receive is determined by the stock market. Finally, as currently constructed, the plan operates like a merit increase plan, a zero-sum game; if one manager receives more than a strictly proportional amount, another manager must receive less. Competition, not collaboration, is built into the structure of the plan.

Reliable

The purpose of the plan is to align management's self-interests with those of the firm's shareholders. In ACME's case, the basis on which the stock is awarded is unclear and at the discretion of the senior executives. The value of the shares is determined more by the marketplace than by the performance of the individual, unit, or team. The managers have little or no ability to take corrective actions when the market price changes. Finally, there is almost no alignment between what is earned and what is received. The value of the options and subsequent stock ownership or option gain may be very important to the individual, but are not having any direct effect on his or her consideration of what is best for the shareholders.

Timely

Most stock option plans have a restriction to prevent executives from cashing them in to realize immediate gain. In theory, this provision is designed to orient the plan to long-term decisions, investment, and growth in shareholder equity, as opposed to immediate profits and cash flow. However, as practiced at ACME and similar organizations, executives take this action as soon as the restriction lapses. If the plan is truly intended to reinforce effective long-term decisions, why is the restriction feature necessary? For most managers, the real meaning of the options lies in comparing the number of shares awarded in previous years with the current year's awards to determine the relative improvement or decline in their perception by the senior executives.

ACME is clearly not realizing much value from its stock option plan. While the program is probably very reinforcing to the executives deciding on the allocation, the performers themselves tend to feel it is more a reflection of their personal standing among the executives than of their achievement of some desired level of performance. In essence, equity-related programs are beneficial to most participants but are highly uncertain and future-oriented. They have little direct impact on short-term actions. Few executives will willingly give up the equity program, but few of them feel it truly represents the strategy or values of the company. If ACME's chief executive were asked to justify the return on investment for this program, she would have great difficulty doing so.

We can conclude that ACME's senior executives need to redesign their plan to make it more effective in directing and reinforcing desired performance. But how? The answer to this question can be quite complex because stock-related programs are usually a very sensitive issue for executives and shareholders alike. No single design can be constructed to yield the desired behaviors in all cases. However, there are some identifiable conditions that can be used to indicate the direction to take in designing such plans. To that end, the following pages will provide a series of case studies in which stock-related programs have been used by different firms to address complex business and human issues.

The Case of the New CEO

The ABC Company is a small, privately held, and generally profitable company (an actual company, but a fictitious name). It has a variety of business divisions with products that serve a range of markets from aerospace to telecommunications to construction. The company has existed for quite some time and had the same chief executive officer for the 12 years. Then the CEO died suddenly, and the board decided to recruit someone from the outside.

The desired candidate had been a very successful executive at a very large industrial company. All the terms of his employment contract had been agreed upon except the provision for stock in the company. In order for the board to determine the right mix of compensation, it needed to answer a fundamental question: Is the new CEO a hired gun or an adopted son?

The answer to this question would determine how the stock arrangement should be structured. If a CEO is a *hired gun*, he or she is brought in to make improvements in the performance of the company or to take it to a new position of leadership within its markets. Then, when these objectives are accomplished, the CEO moves on to another company. The compensation plan emphasizes cash—large amounts of cash for significant improvements in the company's performance.

An *adopted son (or daughter)*, on the other hand, shares the fortunes of the other shareholders or, in this case, the values of the family that owns the company. At ABC, the CEO would be expected to make decisions that would support the family's short- and long-term interests. This would entail balancing the need to provide family members with adequate dividends from the company with the need to address the investment interests of the company. The CEO's own interests would have to be long-term in building personal wealth through building growth in the asset value and profitability of the company.

To this end, the board chose the adopted son role for the chief executive. Thus, the stock-related program involved providing shares to the executive over a five-year period based on the performance of the company. The performance was judged on the basis of the growth of the share price, which was determined primarily through a formula of book value, cash flow, and profitability. If performance exceeded expectations, more shares would be awarded to the executive. If performance fell short of the plan, the number of shares would be reduced. Further, a stock appreciation rights (SAR) program was developed as a companion to the stock plan to cover the tax liability of the shares. The objective was to encourage the executive to own stock that was five times his annual total compensation after the first five years of employment. Depending on performance, this plan would be renewed and increased after the five-year period of this plan.

The Case of the New Products

Small Company (an actual company, but a fictitious name) desperately needed to introduce new products into its current line in order to retain its market leadership. Many new, primarily foreign, competitors had entered its markets with products that were similar to Small's. While it retained a strong market reputation, the products of new competitors had attracted the attention of many of Small's key customers.

Small had been working on developing enhancements to its new products and other breakthrough technologies for several years. It had organized special product teams that included both engineering and manufacturing representatives to shift from a hands-off process to a design-for-manufacturing one. Despite this new structure, the teams still tended to work in functional subgroups with little true integration of the process.

While the concepts and prototypes were very strong and offered significant potential revenues, Small had been unable to get these products commercialized. They seemed to be caught in endless redesign cycles, and manufacturing appeared unwilling or unable to address the production requirements. The marketing function was strongly interested in utilizing the advanced capabilities of these products, but the beta tests and other trials were slow and difficult to establish. At the same time, Small's engineers were continuing to create even greater enhancements to the products, giving the company the potential for even greater market leadership. The problem was that the products had yet to enter the market and be truly tested by customer reception.

The solution was to develop a phantom share plan for each of the product teams. The program provided an opportunity for the participants to accumulate "shares" in their product. The value of these shares was to be based on the earnings they generated for the corporation. The payout would be a function of the number of shares an individual received and of the economic value of those shares.

Small established a pool of shares that would be based on the product team's meeting or exceeding its product development milestones and project budget. The team could exceed its dates or budgets if it believed such actions would enhance the economic contribution of the new products once they were released to the market. The number of shares might be lower but the value could be higher. The shares awarded at the critical design stages provided a symbolic piece of the action of the new products. Each member received a certificate with his or her number of shares and the product's name prominently displayed.

Once the new products were released, the value of the shares was established on the basis of the projected revenues and return on investment. The total potential income at target level of performance was between 50 percent and 200 percent of a team member's current total compensation, depending on the number of shares received. Over the three years following the product release, the value of the shares was recalibrated every six months according to the actual results. At that time, the product team members could cash in their shares according to a three-year vesting schedule (one-third was available each year). The team members could retain the shares in the expectation that the share value would increase over the period. If they terminated employment, they would forfeit all rights to future earnings from the shares.

The results were dramatic. There was an increase in the emphasis on bringing new products to market and on making the products excel in their performance with customers. During the early stages of the products' life cycle, the team members worked with marketing, sales, and customers to gain maximum value from the products. The share price of most of the products exceeded expectations, and the company was able to grow its market share despite the efforts of major competitors. The program provided a variety of both immediate psychic and symbolic rewards and a real tangible value as the earnings from the products were realized by the company and the team members.

The Case of the Executive Team

Pratt Industries is a large, diversified office equipment corporation (an actual company, but a fictitious name). The company has successfully rebounded from a grueling battle for survival with its competitors. In the course of the struggle, the company implemented numerous cost-reduction efforts, sold off divisions that were not related to its core business, and reinvested in technology enhancements to its major product lines. The company hired a new chief executive officer, and she brought in or promoted several new executives who infused new leadership spirit into the organization.

Pratt implemented a new organizing concept around primary customer/markets and focused its people and investments to achieve and retain a leadership position in these markets. Some of the markets were geographic, while others were industry-oriented. Pratt also focused several of its primary service and technology functions to be in support of the market divisions, with minimal corporate staff except where investments required cross-divisional support.

The challenge facing Pratt's CEO was both to focus the efforts of the senior executives on the performance of their divisions and to motivate them to optimize those areas where synergistic opportunities could be realized. For example, some of the major accounts crossed geographic and industry boundaries. The need was to maximize both divisional and company performance.

The solution was to create a stock-based incentive program in which the number of shares was used as the reinforcer, and the basis for the award was a combination of divisional and total company performance. Based on the achievement of a range of company financial performance and divisional performance levels, the company would give to each executive a number of restricted shares of stock. This was determined by using a matrix grid. (See Figure 7-1.)

The vertical axis of the grid provided a range of performance for the division. This performance determined the number of units available to the executive from that division. The value of those units was based on the performance of the company, as shown in the horizontal axis in Figure 7-1. For example, if the divisional performance and company target performance was achieved, the executive would receive 1000 units

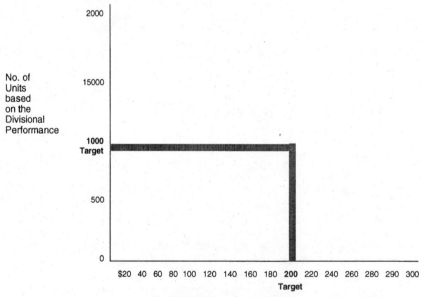

The Value of the shares is based on Company performance

Figure 7-1.   Pratt's senior executive equity-building plan.

at a value of $200 each. This would result in a stock fund of $200,000 for the executive and would be used to purchase stock in the company. The stock awards would be restricted for a three-year period. The purchase price was at the date of grant, but the shares would not become owned by the executive until the restriction had lapsed. One-third of the shares would be fully vested each year after the grant date.

There were two reasons for the restriction. First, the company wanted to create a significant share of the executive's net worth to assure mutual interests with major shareholders. It was felt that providing shares annually might not create large enough stake. The amount and value of these shares was based on performance and contributions. Second, the company wanted to retain its top executives or make it very expensive for a competitor to attract them away from the firm.

The impact of this program was both dramatic and subtle. The focus on performance of each division was of critical importance to the executives. However, they sought ways to maximize the performance of the entire company, making necessary trade-off decisions in order to increase the company's performance and hence the value of the units. Finally, as the program progressed over the years, the executives easily took on the perspective of the shareholders, looking for balancing annual operating results with long-term growth of the firm's shareholder value.

The Case of the Company in Transition

Transition Technologies, Inc. (TTI) (a fictitious name of an actual company) had passed through the initial start-up phase and was gaining a reputation for highly customized, expertly crafted factory automation-control products. The firm had begun as a spin-off from a larger technology company, with several key engineering and marketing people involved in the original venture. The firm was still owned in principle by a venture capital firm, although it had successfully introduced an initial public offering (IPO) to the market two years before.

The company was looking to grow and develop into a larger company while retaining its entrepreneurial qualities for involvement, sharing risks, and fast action. The firm needed a way of attracting talented new managers to bring leadership into the firm, highly trained technical professionals to strengthen its technical prowess, and employees (or associates as they were known) who would willingly participate in ways to improve the company. However, cash flow fluctuated greatly and was needed to build and support the operations of the company. The company could not afford to pay the big salaries of the large companies.

The solution came in the form of a stock-related incentive plan to provide an attractive program for recruiting the necessary talent, create the incentives for staff to assist in growing the company, and build a shared fate philosophy in the future of the company.

TTI considered many options. First, it looked at the idea of creating an employee stock purchase plan. While this would not have had a negative impact on the firm's cash flow, it was believed that the plan would have few participants. Although the firm could discount the share price, many employees felt that the personal capital required to create the desired stake would be greater than most associates could afford. Second, the firm explored establishing an employee stock ownership plan (ESOP). As described earlier, this kind of plan has many attractive features for tax optimization and building retirement accounts. But TTI felt that an ESOP would have minimal effect on the actions of its people, and since the population was relatively young, retirement accounts held little attraction. Finally, the firm decided to provide stock options widely within the company based on two factors: overall company performance and individual or team contributions. Company performance would be judged on the basis of growth of revenues and profit before tax (for a growing company that was increasing its profitability).

On an annual basis, the company would establish six-month and annual performance objectives. If these targets were achieved, a pool of stock options would be made available for distribution. If the performance fell short, no shares would be made available for the performance period, although they could be made up on an bi-annual basis (i.e., every two years). It was hoped that this plan would encourage not only a short-term emphasis on performance but also a view on the part of employees that short-term gains could be invested to achieve long-term (two-year and beyond) results. If the company exceeded the targets, the pool would be increased on the basis of a predetermined formula.

For distribution, each department was awarded a number of options that could be increased or decreased by 25 percent based on their performance. Once the number of options was determined, they were awarded by the divisional management for the associates, by the senior management for the middle managers, and by the CEO and board for the senior managers. The number of options eligible to any division was based on the percentage of payroll reflected in the total wages and salaries of the unit. The payout was usually in accordance with an employee's total compensation or for some extraordinary individual or team performance.

The shares were awarded on an semiannual basis, and there was a big celebration when the number of available shares was determined. Further, because the stock was publicly traded, the company offered a simultaneous purchase and sale provision for the plan, so that employees could exercise the number of shares they needed to buy the options awarded.

Senior managers closely monitored the number of shares sold by employees as a measure of the plan's reinforcement value. It was felt that if associates or managers sold the stock options when they became available, the purpose of the plan—i.e., creating a sense of common fate—would not be achieved and the plan would then have to be adjusted. The impact of the potential dilution of the shares was perceived as an issue by some of the major shareholders. However, the direct performance connection of the plan softened their concerns. If the plan were to be successful, the gain in the economic value of the company would more than offset the potential dilution of share price for the new shares being issued through options. The plan offered a way to create a real sense of ownership in the company for employees (a sense of ownership, moreover, that they themselves had earned).

The greatest future risk of this plan will be with the FASB rulings on how firms must account for the expenses related to stock options. At TTI they will wait and see, but today they are enjoying the extra advantage of a turned-on workforce.

The Lessons to Be Learned from Using Equity

The above discussion and illustrative case studies provide an opportunity for learning how to use stock-related programs as part of a total reward system. Peter Drucker, a noted author and professor of management, indicates that in many companies the use of stock options and other equity-related award programs encourages executives to be more concerned about the closing price of the stock than the right decisions that create value for shareholders and other stakeholders.[3] In many cases the root cause of this lies in the lack of a line of sight between the value of the reward and the actions necessary to achieve it. Another potential problem lies in assuming that what is meaningful to top executives is meaningful to all employees. While few employees will deny a stock option award, they indicate the value of the option when the restrictions on its use are removed. People often "vote with their feet."

The Questions to Be Asked

To thoroughly examine the implications about the use of equity-based programs, we need to address a number of fundamental questions. The degree to which these factors are relevant to the reader will determine the utility of the discussion.

1. What do equity-based plans accomplish? In theory, equity-based plans link the self-interest of the participant with that of shareholders, with the expectation that this will lead to a proper balance between short-term earnings and long-term investment in the value of the company. In reality, few plans accomplish this goal until executives have a significant portion of their net worth invested in the stock of the organization.

A second purpose of equity-based pay plans is to create a sense of identity with the company. When employees have some meaningful level of shares or options, through actual ownership or through employee stock option or employee stock purchase plans, they frequently watch the price of the stock. They read articles about what senior management and investment analysts are saying about the organization. This can translate into actions aimed at enhancing revenues, reducing costs, or protecting the firm's assets.

A third purpose of such programs is to increase the competitiveness of the employee's pay package. For some employees—particularly senior executives and individuals joining small companies from larger ones—participation in equity-related programs is an important element of their desired compensation package. Hence, if stock options are not offered, the firm may be at a competitive disadvantage.

Finally, and perhaps most important, equity-based plans are designed to be a statement to employees that they are part of an "exclusive club" within the organization. This is particularly important for those individuals who feel that this is an important part of their role and identity within an organization. Hence, used selectively, such plans can create a valuable sense of "membership" within an organization from a total organizational or division perspective.

Pepsi is an example of a company seeking to develop employee loyalty through stock options. In the early 1990s Pepsi developed a program to provide stock options to most of its employees. The program was called Share Power, and its purpose was to encourage among employees a concern about and commitment to the prosperity of the company. Pepsi was not looking for any specific improvements in performance. The company just wanted to encourage everyone to do some small part to help the company increase its competitiveness in a complex marketplace.

Through this program, over 100,000 employees were granted stock options equal to 10 percent of the previous year's compensation. The senior managers believe that through the growth in the stock price alone, they will be able to provide employees an increase in their total income of $200 million each year with *no* out-of-pocket expense to Pepsi. As in many areas of life, time will tell whether this program will have the long-term benefits its architects desire.

2. Are equity-based plans meaningful to the performer?   To create an effective program of rewards, one needs to use the right tools to reinforce the behaviors that are desired. To be positive reinforcements, they need to be seen as meaningful or important to the performers. Further, the performers need to see them as being related directly to their performance. The degree to which the behaviors do not change, indicates the extent to which the design or use of these rewards is not effective.

Some companies with extensive experience of using stock options, such as Digital Equipment Corporation, have found that many of their options are being exercised and sold when the restrictions lapse. Although this is usually counter to the wishes of the original plan designers, the reasons are quite sensible. As discussed earlier, the value of the option is in the gain in share price. This is often determined by market forces quite outside the control of employees. The only action over which participants *can* exercise control over is when to exercise the options. Further, given the tax impact of most ISOs and NQSOs, there is little reason to exercise the option and hold the shares for a future gain unless the options are about to expire. Finally, since exercising options requires cash, participants have to use other funds or immediately dispose of a portion of the shares, thereby reducing the number of shares they hold. The pressure to do so may be even more severe when the gain implies a hefty tax liability, wherein still more shares will most likely have to be liquidated.

3. How do you link equity plans with performance? If the objective is to generate alignment with shareholder interests, there are many effective tools at one's disposal. Perhaps the most important requirements are being tested by companies like Chrysler and Kodak. These companies are requiring executives to own stock in relation to their total compensation. In this way the personal net worth of these executives is linked to the growth in shareholder value expressed as share price.

In the case studies described above, equity was used to create upside opportunity to performance that was not possible with cash programs. For example, the product teams that had phantom shares linked performance to equity in two ways. First, the team members received shares as they achieved project timing and budget objectives. The shares were at one point worth nothing. But the potential for upside gain was tremendous if the product was able to generate significant earnings for the company. Hence, the team members saw a more direct link between their performance—the efforts, decisions, and contributions they made to the product development process—than through merit pay increases or a variable cash plan.

If the objective is to create identity with the organization or a feeling of being part of an exclusive club, then a targeted or narrowly focused program may be appropriate. As in several of the case studies and in Pepsi's case in particular, the option plan was merely a vehicle for creating a shared memory of success and appreciation for the company. As an alternative, one could use actual stock for an incentive award instead of options or actual stock instead of cash for a gain-sharing program. This would require both a charge to earnings and a taxable event for the individual and might represent some dilution of the stock price. This approach would also require executives to ensure that performance achievements were truly warranted, which in itself is a healthy pressure. The actual stock would have direct meaning to the participants, and would be seen as valuable if the performers valued having a sense of the ownership in the business.

The linkage with performance needs to be carefully considered. The most important element will be what the payout determinants are—i.e., how employees receive the actual shares—and the next important element will be what determines the value of the shares.

4. How much is enough? What should the element of risk be?
Risk is a complex word. Many executives are attracted to it because it implies that employees stand to lose something if things don't go well. However, since most of the equity-based plans are in addition to attractive cash compensation programs, and since employees seldom need to invest in the company with their own capital themselves, their risk is limited to not realizing a gain that they thought or expected they would receive. It is not loss, but rather *not getting something they never had* that they risk. This being the case, the plan necessarily loses some of its ability to influence behavior. People need to see the grant as a reflection of some meaningful accomplishment. At the same time, the payout needs to be achievable.

5. What are the advantages and risks of equity-based pay plans?
Assuming that what one is seeking is an improvement in performance not an affirmation of self-esteem or a general feeling of identity with the firm, equity-related plans offer some unique opportunities. First, they offer a true stake in the business, with a potentially higher upside than cash-based plans. Second, by tying personal ownership to the economic value of the enterprise, they encourage participants to consider what actions of theirs will build value in addition to creating immediate results. Third, by tying the value of the shares to collective efforts they stimulate collaboration and coordination companywide. Fourth, they can offer substantial improvement in the economic well-being of employees with little or no cost to the business. As in Pepsi's case, market forces, not the company's reserves, will determine the upside opportunity. Finally, equity-related plans can have a powerful symbolic value to participants and encourage them to take actions that benefit the whole organization.

Anything good has serious risks. First, although FASB has provided some reprieve till 1997 on the requirement to charge options to corporate earnings, there appear to be a number of factors that will make the long-term use of these programs complicated. Tax laws are undergoing change. FASB is continuing to review the various provisions of equity-programs. Times are uncertain, and design decisions that look favorable now may turn out to be very expensive later.

Second, programs that use actual stock risk increasing shareholders' concerns about a dilution or reduction in the share price because of a too-liberal use of such vehicles. Third, as they are practiced by many companies, these plans offer little real return on investment for either the individual or the company. The process of determining the amount of the award is frequently done behind closed doors. The process that values the shares is outside the influence of most performers, and may therefore be highly frustrating, as when stock options are underwater. Hence, as currently practiced, many of these plans can be unreliable as a reward system.

Fourth, if one uses cash-oriented plans, like SARs, phantom stock, etc., there is a significant potential for cash awards. The costs of these programs can be quite high. When such programs are used only for selected groups, like product teams, key contributors, etc., they can lead to charges of unfair practice and limited access to opportunity within an organization. Although such programs may offer very powerful incentives for participants, they can cause conflict with nonparticipants. Such situations, if not managed carefully, can result in a general unwillingness to coordinate efforts across all areas of the organization. The question is not how to avoid problems, but how to choose the problems one wants to have.

Summary

Equity-related programs offer both an exciting and a risky opportunity for rewards. They create a chance to recognize individual performance in relation to team and corporate performance. Utilizing equity-type plans as symbolic rewards and a real stake in the business can have a truly positive impact on human behavior. In many cases expert counsel is needed, but in all cases, expert management is essential. For some executives the problem with making all employees feel like owners of the business is that they will start acting like that.

Notes

1. "ESOPs: Are They Good For You?" *BusinessWeek*, May 15, 1989, p. 116.
2. Black, F. and M. Scholes, "The Pricing of Option and Corporate Liabilities," *Journal of Political Economy*, 81: May–June, 1973, p. 637.
3. Drucker, P. F., *The Frontiers of Management*. New York: Harper & Row, 1986.

8

Making Special Recognition Special

In organizations where winning is recognized often, winning becomes a habit.
—AN ANONYMOUS SAGE

For several weeks St. Elizabeth's Medical Center in Boston had been experiencing record-setting admissions. People were working under extreme stress, and many were putting in extensive overtime. Nearly every bed was filled. The nursing staff had almost more patients than they could handle. The laboratory group was conducting more tests in less time. The housekeeping staff was providing record turnaround levels for rooms and clinical service areas. The admitting and billing offices, medical records department, and patient accounting office were processing huge volumes of information. Each employee was aware of what was happening and was doing what ever he or she could to keep all this extra work invisible to patients and physicians.

The hospital's quality council believed that people needed to be recognized for their extra efforts. The council members explored several options, and finally decided that they would deliver a batch of cookies to each unit, take a few moments to discuss the situation, and thank people for their contributions. They decided not to wait till the volume had declined, but to take action while it was still at its peak. Ms. Marge Ransom, vice president of human resources, and Ms. Nanette Smith, manager of compensation, organized the event. They solicited the executive managers to join them in the "cookie rounds" for all departments and all shifts.

The impact of the process was overwhelmingly positive. Senior managers personally acknowledged the work efforts of the staff, extended their appreciation for the quality of the work, got people discussing how others were helping them, and delivered cookies with sincere appreciation and humor. The department managers, many of whom had been skeptical at first, appreciated this gesture. The employees enjoyed the celebration and had a brief moment of laughter at a time of great stress. The celebrations took less than ten minutes in each department but served to energize the employees to sustain their efforts. This special recognition action will long be remembered at St. Elizabeth's.

There are powerful lessons in this story about how we can create a culture that brings out the best in people. Compensation plans, by their very nature, are delayed in their ability to recognize and reinforce desired behaviors. Consequently, their impact on behavior may not be as great as an immediate comment or display of appreciation for an individual's performance. In this chapter, we will examine what managers and teammates can do to reinforce desired behaviors in a timely and effective manner. Our focus will be on how to make special recognition something that is truly meaningful to the performers. We will review the primary purpose behind special recognition efforts, examine a variety of recognition programs, and conclude with a summary of the guiding principles that make them successful in supporting collaboration as a way of life within an organization.

Review of the Principles of Reinforcement

In Chapter 3 we examined the fundamentals of effective reward systems and examined the four forms of consequences: positive reinforcement, negative reinforcement, punishment, and extinction.

The first two types of consequences *increase* the frequency of a behavior, while the second two *decrease* the frequency of a behavior. Negative reinforcement works on the "Do this or else" principle; either actually or by implication, performers are threatened with unpleasant consequences if they don't do something. Positive reinforcement works on the reward principle, performers receive something they value—i.e., they experience pleasant consequences—for something they do. If the reinforcer is effective, it will increase the probability of the desired behavior. In Chapter 3 we examined four basic types of reinforcers:

- *Verbal/Social.* Something is said or done that makes a group or individual feel valued or successful for some action. (Examples might include a "Thank you" or "I really appreciate that," a letter or note commenting on how well something was done, a pizza party, etc.);

- *Tangible/Symbolic.* Something is given in recognition of an achievement or contribution. (Examples might include a hat, pin, or sculptured piece reflecting a company logo, tickets to a movie/theater, a vacation trip, etc.).

- *Work-Related.* Something related to the tasks, responsibilities, or quality of work life is given in appreciation for some achievement. (Examples might include a promotion, greater authority, seeing ideas implemented, special office/work equipment, participation in educational programs, special assignments, etc.).

- *Financial.* Something of immediate or long-term financial value is given in appreciation of something the performer achieved. (Examples might include cash incentives, spot awards, stock options, stock grants, etc.).

When organizations develop special recognition programs, they immediately consider the use of tangible or financial reinforcers. They often use these as a substitute for more personal, verbal/social forms of reinforcement. The risk in relying on items or financial rewards as recognition is that we may create a transaction-oriented economy within the firm. Instead of enhancing value, self-worth, and self-confidence, we set up the expectation that each desired action will beget a tangible reward.

In Chapter 3 we discussed the conditions that make reinforcers effective in stimulating the same or related behaviors in the future. These criteria were:

- *Specific.* Performers must know what they did to earn their reward, and therefore what they need to continue doing—i.e., there is a clear line of sight between the performance and the reinforcer. Performance measurement and feedback are essential for consequences to be effective in shaping desired behaviors.

- *Personalized.* Rewards have to be meaningful to the performer. In order for a reinforcer to have the desired impact, it must be something the performer values. The method of delivery and the source of the reward is often as important as the item, comment, or activity.

- *Contingent.* Rewards need to be earned so that the performers feel they have truly achieved some action or result. Further, for a reinforcer to be effective, the desired behavior/performance needs to be within the performer's ability and control (or influence).

- *Sincere.* Rewards have to be given in a manner that is honest, sincere, and from the heart. Employees can easily see through actions that are calculated, manipulative, or simply intended to meet some requirement.

- *Immediate.* Rewards must be provided as soon following achievements or contributions as possible. Waiting for approvals, deadlines, or completion of an end result often dramatically reduces the impact of the reinforcer. Timeliness can also underscore the specific and meaningful aspects of the reward for the performer.

If the objective is to develop a program of recognition, the focus should be more on anchoring the memory of an achievement than on funding purchases. How items are delivered is more important than what is delivered. An important principle to remember is that the value received is not always the same as the value given. The task is better viewed as one of providing *reinforcement* for desired actions. If you want people to take certain actions, they need to know when they do it and feel valued for doing it. There are many consequences at play within the work environment. The challenge is to find and deliver those positive reinforcers that enhance the probability and frequency of desired actions. You are in competition with many other consequences affecting the individual; you need to make your efforts more meaningful than all the others. In this way, the organization can make special recognition truly special.

Types of Special Recognition Programs

There are many types of recognition programs in use by today's organizations. Few are noted for their ability to convey special recognition. Most operate instead on a utilitarian principle; few work to improve or sustain high performance. The reasons will become clear as we examine them more closely using the SMART criteria.

Within this context, there are three basic types of recognition programs (see Figure 8-1). Each is discussed in more detail below.

- *Employee Recognition Programs.* These programs are designed to notice and reinforce the contributions made by individuals or teams in the performance of their jobs. Examples include employee-of-the-month programs, spot bonus plans, and programs recognizing technical contributions that have led to patents, copyrights, or new business ventures.

- *Team Celebration Programs.* These events are designed to recognize the performance of a team or work unit. Examples include

(1) Employee Recognition Programs
■ Employee of the Month Clubs
■ Spot Bonus Programs
■ Technical Contributor Programs
(2) Team Celebrations
■ Special Dinners
■ Spot Celebrations
(3) Suggestion/New Idea Programs
■ Special Suggestion Programs
■ Quality Improvement Teams

Figure 8-1. Types of special recognition programs.

special sales meetings at which individuals and teams are recognized for their sales results, weekly plant/company meetings at which people are recognized for the production or productivity achievements, and annual recognition dinners for employees. In short, these programs are intended to celebrate the contributions of teams, units, or individuals toward the achievement of company goals.

■ *Suggestion/New Idea Programs.*   These programs are intended to recognize individuals or teams who have generated solutions to problems or contributed ideas that have improved the performance of the overall unit. Frequently they involve cash rewards based on the value of the idea—say 10 percent of the money an employee's suggestion saved the company during the first year of its implementation. In organizations implementing total quality management efforts, special cross-functional teams are often used to form the new generation of suggestion/idea units addressing performance issues within the firm.

Each of these types of programs attempts to provide individuals with a recognition of their contribution that is beyond their daily work. Such programs may use a variety of reinforcers—verbal, tangible, work-related or financial—and span a wide variety of time frames and organizational levels. The dimension that differentiates one from another is the nature of the behaviors being reinforced. Each of these plans is discussed in more depth on the following pages.

Employee Recognition Programs

Employee recognition programs have a long history in American industry, and a great variety of programs have been created for special applications. Perhaps one of the most widely used programs of special recognition is the employee-of-the-month plan. Other employee recognition programs involve the use of spot awards or the giving of cash bonuses when a particular project has been completed or a major goal has been accomplished. Sales contests are often used as a way of rewarding individuals for the highest new sales, the fastest growth in new business, or the most effective promotion of new products or services. Employee recognition programs have also been used in the scientific and research community to recognize individuals who have submitted articles for publication, applied or been accepted for patents/copyrights, or made a major contribution in their field. To fully understand how these programs can impact human performance, we should examine a variety of different applications.

Case Study of an Employee-of-the-Month Club

People's Bank has an employee-of-the-month club (a real company, but a fictitious name). Each month the supervisors recommend to their senior managers an employee they feel is deserving of being selected as the employee of the month. The senior managers go through the names and select the one individual who has clearly demonstrated superior performance. This individual is awarded a $100 check presented by the division executive or the employee's supervisor. The individual's picture is also published in the employee newspaper and displayed in a large frame in the employee cafeteria.

Over the last few years, in keeping with the spirit of empowerment, senior management has delegated this selection process to a special committee of employees who were past winners. The supervisors make their recommendations to this group, and the selection is made by the employee committee.

The original purpose of this program was to recognize individuals who had clearly distinguished themselves from their peers. Although there has been a concerted effort to spread the awards around, certain individuals have been nominated again and again. At the end of the year, those employees who have won the monthly awards are eligible to receive an employee-of-the-year award. This award includes a special article on the individual and his or her family in the newspaper and a check for $1000. The program is open to all employees below senior management, although the program is most often won by high-level nonexempt people and midlevel professionals. The executives clearly enjoy handing out the awards.

A recent interview with an individual who has won several times revealed a mixed reaction to the process. First, the award winner didn't really know why she had been selected for the award, though she had been frequently praised for her creativity in getting things through the system and serving customers as quickly as possible regardless of the costs. But she felt that having her picture in the cafeteria and newspaper was very embarrassing, and, while the money was nice, it was gone quickly. She enjoyed meeting the senior managers, but wished they would pronounce her name correctly. On balance, she felt that the program operated more as a way to make the executives look and feel good than to truly recognize individuals.

In one recent case cited, an individual who has frequently been nominated for the award by senior managers is really not well regarded by his peers. It seems that whenever a senior manager calls for a special request, this employee goes into action. He drives through all procedures, interrupts any priorities, and gets the answer sought by the executive in record time. However, when work is at a normal level, he does little to support the group. When he was nominated and eventually selected for a certain month, the peer group knew the system of recognition was flawed. They did not want to be selected because it was clearly not based on fact, but on the notions of the senior managers.

What's Wrong with This Picture?

If we examine this system in relation to the SMART criteria, we can easily discover several major weaknesses in it.

Specific

The criteria for selection is usually very unclear to both the performers and the selectors. People have little understanding of what they need to do, and executives have little data on which to base their selection. In fact, as shown above, some employees may be disrupting the work of others in order to receive the attention of the executives. Consequently, employees do not feel the selection reflects their performance and the executives are clearly reinforcing actions that benefit them rather than the people the program was intended to benefit.

Meaningful

While few people turn down the award, many do not feel it is a meaningful reflection of their contribution. The issue may not only be the amount, but the method of delivery. One of the most important aspects of reinforcement is how it is delivered. Hence, whether a check is delivered by a supervisor or handed out by a senior executive may or may not matter to the employee. The test for the value of the process is to examine what employees talk about after receiving the award. If he or she feels proud of the ceremony, it is likely to have been a memorable event. If he or she barely mentions it, the process is likely to have had little personal value. Finally, some of the employees selected are actually embarrassed by being selected, while others do not want to be associated with those who have been selected. The overall meaning of the awards may actually be more negative than positive.

Achievable

Perhaps of all the success criteria, employee-of-the-month clubs fail to meet this one. The People's Bank has over 1800 people, yet only 12 people can be selected each year. That leaves 1788 people without recognition by the process. Hence, the program is basically out of the reach of most employees and has no impact on their performance.

Reliable

When a system has unclear measures and undefined decision criteria, it is simply not reliable. The supervisors in this system use few shared criteria to nominate employees. The criteria used by the executives or the employee selection committee are just as inconsistent. Although it is relatively simple to administer, it is so simplistic in its approach as to have no value.

Timely

Monthly performance recognition of this nature is not likely to have much influence on the employees. It is not linked to any particular achievement of performance. This program is tied more to a calendar than to actual performance. The annual award selection therefore has little immediate impact on performance.

In terms of costs, People's Bank is spending approximately $2200 per year for the program. It is clear that there is little true performance being reinforced by this program. The only groups that appear to be receiving positive reinforcement from this program are the executives who hand out the checks. They see the employee smile and say "thank you." They can feel they are promoting excellence by recognizing top performers. They can take the time from their busy schedule to be nice to some employee. The performers will play the game because the negative consequences for not doing so may be career-limiting.

My recommendation about employee-of-the-month clubs is: *eliminate them*. Company time and resources would be better spent in trying to understand what people are really doing in their jobs. Further, programs of this nature tend to give managers a false sense of confidence that they are reinforcing desired performance. The reality in most organizations is that these programs are at best a waste of time and money, and at worst a counterproductive force.

What's the alternative? Let's examine another situation.

The Case of the Top Gun Club

Allied Systems (this is an actual company and the real name) is a transportation company that delivers automobiles from factories and train depots to dealer showrooms. When ever a nick, scratch, or break is encountered enroute, the cost is significant, both in terms of repair and in terms of the inventory that is not immediately available to the customer. Although Allied's performance was for a long time comparable to the industry's generally, it was not giving the company an advantage in this intensely competitive marketplace.

Allied decided to develop and implement a program to recognize those drivers who were able to deliver autos with minimal defects. They entitled the program the Top Gun Club (a name that came from one of the drivers). When Allied analyzed its driver's defect records (lists indicating the number of times there was a difference between the pickup inspection and the delivery inspection), about 10 percent of their drivers could boast a 99 percent damage-free record for 12 consecutive months. The challenge was to bring 90 percent of the drivers to the same level as the top 10 percent.

When a driver was able to achieve this 99 percent damage-free performance for a month, his name was listed as a member of the Top Gun Club. At the time of initiation, he or she receives a special hat with the Top Gun logo. As drivers sustained this status for longer periods of time—quarterly, annually, etc.—they would receive Top Gun patches, license plates, and other symbolic trophies for being in the club. Over a 3-year process, the damage-free standard rose from 99 percent to 99.7 percent and the percentage of drivers in the club grew from 10 percent to over 60 percent.

Bernard DeWulf, Allied's chief executive officer says, "One thing we've learned is that programs don't have to be expensive. What this has done is develop a culture in the company where people want to perform properly.... We provide the vehicle for better performance and recognize that performance. The pride aspect is really what works the most."

Allied's program had several very important features. First, the measures were specific and could be reliably measured by the performers themselves. Thus feedback could be almost instantaneous. Second, by setting a performance level that some people had already achieved, the managers were communicating that the requirements were achievable, a fact underscored by their gradually raising the standard as more and more people achieved the level. Third, there was no zero-sum game; no one won at the expense of someone else. In fact, it was in everyone's interest to get as many people over the threshold as possible. Increased performance increased the competitiveness of the company and this enhanced everyone's job security and feeling of being a winner. Fourth, performance was summarized on a monthly basis but measured daily. Awards were announced monthly by publishing the list, and people were reinforced for keeping their name on the list for long periods of time. Finally, the rewards were meaningful for the status they conferred rather than for their financial value.

Allied Systems had initially tried using tangible rewards like VCRs, radios, etc., but they had had little impact on performance. The club concept was used because many of the performers already belonged to clubs and similar groups in their off-work time. By understanding the natural reinforcers in the work setting, by observing what people did when they had choices, Allied Systems was able to identify reinforcers with high value to the performers. By making membership in the club a measure of status and using tangible symbols and celebrations, Allied was further able to create a high value ratio for the reinforcers. The essence of this program was fundamentally a win/win for all parties.

Spot Bonus Programs

Spot bonus programs are a way to provide cash awards to individuals (or teams) for accomplishing some major milestone or level of performance. These programs work in a variety of ways. First, some spot bonuses are provided to individuals or teams when they accomplish an important project milestone or achieve some major result, such as acquiring a new, major client. These are usually given at the time when the result or achievement occurs. The payouts may range from $1000 to several times that amount, depending on the impact of the achievement. In some organizations the decision process involves a review by several levels of management, even though some of them are clearly associated with the achievement.

A second type of spot bonus program is much smaller in scale and is usually undertaken by a manager or supervisor with little upper-management approval. These awards are given on the spot and are usually for important tasks, such as completing a crucial project, negotiating a successful deal, or covering for a coworker. The amounts tend to be less than $500; they usually in range from $50 to $100. While the award may be in cash, it is sometimes given in the form of dinner or show certificates worth an equivalent amount of money.

The third type of spot bonus goes to the other extreme and usually reflects a major accomplishment by an individual or team. Such awards are limited to very few company employees and are given only after much review and assessment by senior managers. Examples of the kinds of major achievements warranting this type of spot bonus might include getting a plant up and running under budget and ahead of schedule or developing a new process or technology with significant impact on the company's competitiveness. The dollar size for these awards can range from $5000 to $20,000. IBM has been known to award sums up to $100,000. Needless to say, such awards are very infrequent and limited to a very few people. Their power, however, lies in their size and the notoriety that often goes along with the cash. Hence, they can be very meaningful to the recipient. Because of the small number of individuals who are truly eligible, however, they provide little motivation to most employees except those in highly technical or strategic roles within the organization. It is also an irony that some recognition recipients are told not to tell anyone outside their immediate family about the award. These are often not awards to celebrate, but to be embarrassed or secretive about in the presence of one's peers.

Spot bonuses of the first type also have their limitations. Their effectiveness depends on specifying the achievements that qualify employees for them, but, since companies tend to present these awards to special teams (like new product development or project management units), they offer little opportunity for those whose primary focus is normal, everyday jobs. Such awards are effective reinforcers only for those involved in a special undertaking of the corporation. They are usually provided in conjunction with some ceremony, which gives them the potential for having a significant immediate impact on the recipients. Their potential impact on other employees lies in the hope and expectation of achieving the award if they achieve certain levels of performance. *The performance requirements need to be very clear,* however. This clarity can come from communicating the requirements or by applying selection criteria that are consistent and well understood by everyone concerned. In this way, such programs can be effective reinforcers for participants working to achieve a special level of performance.

Perhaps the most frequently used and abused program of spot bonuses of the second type, in which "spot awards" of relatively small sums are given out by managers. Such awards derive their potential impact from the timing of the cash presentation and the relationship it has with the desired behaviors. For example, a division of a large multinational presented crisp, new $50 bills when units achieved specific on-time performance standards and sustained their level of performance for an entire quarter. A $50 bill was given when they first achieved it, and again when the team continued the practice for an entire three-month period (not necessarily related to the company's fiscal quarters). The power of these rewards was their timeliness.

This kind of program can be abused, however, unless the company is absolutely clear about what the individual or team has accomplished. Recipients have been known to falsify records, take inappropriate shortcuts, and fail to support other teams in order to receive their prizes. Also, supervisors have been known to use such programs for manipulating others to perform a task that may be inappropriate or unsafe. Objective data and actual observations, are critical to prevent these systems from being misused.

Nonetheless, depending on your leverage factor—Specific, Meaningful, Achievable, Reliable, or Timely—spot awards can be effective in supplementing an array of practices to reinforce behaviors that achieve desired results.

Technical Contributor Programs

The research and scientific community has long been a user of award programs that focus on the achievements of individual technical contributors. The primary focus of these programs is usually to recognize the contributions of the men and women who perform research and development activities within the organization. Their work often involves rigorous scientific procedure, trial and error, the building of long-term models, and the analysis of data over long periods of time. The frame of reference for performance evaluation in their case often includes incremental progress on research studies and slow feedback through peer reviews. When they apply for patent rights, publish a paper, make a presentation at a recognized symposium, or perform similar externally validating activities, technical professionals receive some degree of recognition. Companies wanting to encourage such long-term investments often create special programs to further reward these individuals for their contributions.

There are often a wide range of awards available. First, an individual may receive $500 or so for filing a patent application, having a major paper accepted, or making a presentation at a respected conference. Second, he or she may receive $1000 to $10,000 for acquiring a major patent, publishing a book, or receiving an award from peers in the scientific community. For example, a midsize investment banking firm awarded one of its members $5000 for publishing a book on understanding the dynamics of the stock market. The individual received full royalty rights for the book, and the firm's reputation was enhanced by the employee's contributions and continued employment. Firms have awarded as much as $10,000 to $100,000 to an individual for making a major scientific or technological breakthrough for the company. In these situations, the individual receives more than cash; there is usually a major celebration to honor the recipient. The value of such an award is frequently gauged by the economic potential contribution of the achievement.

However, there can often be a major conflict concerning who owns the patent rights and who is eligible to receive the royalty payments, if any. An important software development company encountered a problem of this kind with a particular individual. As she saw it, her efforts, talents, and personal sacrifice were responsible for a major technical breakthrough that had made a significant contribution to the company. As a direct result of her work, the firm had been able to develop application programs that were highly competitive and yielded it much revenue. From the firm's perspective, the employee had not only been well compensated for her performance but had been well provided with the firm's resources to achieve her breakthrough; furthermore, it was the company and not the employee that had commercialized the new technology.

What was the appropriate response? If the company were not to recognize this individual's major contributions, others like her would receive a clear message that such achievements would not be properly valued. They might, as a result, seek employment or other opportunities elsewhere. For the company, the invention was only part of what determined its commercial success. The product needed to be developed, manufactured, marketed, and sold to paying customers, and there needed to be an accounting for expense and revenues, for taxes and account receivables. Taken together, all these actions contributed substantially to the success of the invention.

In this case the company provided the inventor with a portion of the revenues over a five-year period of time; half was provided in actual cash and half was provided in restricted stock. The stock was vested over a five-year period of time contingent upon her continued employment with the firm. The value of the stock was in part a measure of the commercial success of the invention. Hence, some of the award was immediate, some was long-term; some was personalized, and some was restricted. In each case, her contribution was well recognized by her peers and by the senior mangers of the firm. Their hope and intention was to encourage this young creative inventor and others like her to continue to make contributions to the firm.

Why Is It Important to Recognize the Individual?

According to the teachings of many quality management gurus, the individual has little special value to the world of work. They often contend that performance is primarily driven by a combination of work efforts, and that it is through a team concept that organizations truly flourish. It is easy to understand where this belief comes from when one realizes that many TQM principles first took root and flourished in the Japanese workplace environment—an environment which for many centuries had traditionally discouraged and downplayed individual efforts.

However, in the American business culture, where the rights of the individual are held in high esteem, we see a conflict. When employees see a great reliance on teams within an organization, they fear that their own particular uniqueness, their own particular contribution will not be noticed. Even though most organizations provide little direct reinforcement, the root fear is that people will lose what little reinforcement they currently receive. If we recall the impact of the extinction consequence (i.e., individuals stop doing something for which they do not receive the reinforcement they wanted or expected), performance will decline. Therefore, whatever method of management we install in American organizations, we need to account for the contributions of the individual.

In point of fact, one cannot reinforce a team; one can *only* reinforce individuals. A team that is exceptionally productive provides its members with a high degree of positive, personal, immediate, and meaningful reinforcement. A team that relies primarily on negative reinforcement (i.e., the fear that you will experience unpleasant consequences if you don't behave in a certain way) may be productive in the short term, but soon loses its members' commitment. To be truly effective, reward systems need to be applied in creative ways to recognize, reinforce, and reward the contributions of the individual according to the level of effort, commitment, and talent each displays.[1] Furthermore, high performance teams reinforce their members for those behaviors that contribute to the success of the team or business. So, the question is not to reward the team vs. the individual, or vice-versa, but to do *both*.

Team Celebrations

At a recent special recognition dinner hosted by a large medical products firm, attendees were heard saying:

"I wonder when this will be over."

"I wonder when he will stop talking."

"She doesn't really understand what we did. Notice how she got the facts mixed up. She even mispronounced the project leader's name."

"I wonder where they got this food from?"

"This is the seventh dinner we've been to, in the same hotel, this year."

"We have a lot left to do to live up to what they say we've accomplished."

"I wonder when this whole charade will be over."

Recognition dinners and similar team celebrations do not necessarily mean that the people being recognized really feel valued for their accomplishments. While the objective is usually well intentioned, the delivery often leaves much to be desired.

To illustrate, let's examine a true story. Joan, a highly skilled technician at a medical electronics firm, had had perfect attendance for 12 years and was regarded by her coworkers as a strong contributor. As one of those being honored at the company's annual awards dinner, Joan was asked to sit at the head table with the firm's top executives. She was driven to and from the event in the company limo. During the ceremony, she was presented with a large lucite sculpture of the company's logo. What were the results? The next day she called in sick.

While there are is no single right way to conduct team celebrations, there are some core principles that can make such occasions both meaningful and positive for the participants. Once again, our criteria are the five SMART checkpoints.

Specific

People on the team need to know exactly what achievements they are celebrating. Data kept by the team and communicated to its members can play the most valuable role in this effort, while recognition by others who are important to the team can be useful too. "Getting the news out" can be accomplished in several ways:

- Display the data during team celebrations.

- Have the group discuss *how* their results were achieved (i.e, relive the plays, actions, and special contributions that made the achievements real).

- If someone in authority is invited to speak, let the person spend more time *listening* to what people did than *telling* them what the team accomplished.

- Let the team hear the impact of their accomplishments, such as why it was important to the larger organization and/or to their customers.

Meaningful

The primary purpose of the team celebration is to anchor the emotional memory of achievement. It is an opportunity for people to feel valued for what they have done, regardless of whether it was large or small.

Thus, the more specific the individuals' actions that are reinforced during the celebration, the more each individual will be able to relate to the accomplishment. Specific reinforcement makes the celebration meaningful. It is very important that these times are not used to single out a few individuals while others watch and remain unnoticed and unvalued. Further, big glitz and major expense may not be necessary. While fancy celebrations are sometimes called for, they can also prove to be no more than an expensive way to anchor the memory. One needs to judge the desired return on investment to all concerned, given the achievements being celebrated, the people involved, and the impact intended.

Achievable

Team celebrations by their very nature reflect accomplishment milestones. Unfortunately, many organizations put on such events only at holiday time, and do not relate achievements to them. Aubrey Daniels offers an important insight: "The key to deriving bottom-line benefits from a festivity is knowing that its purpose is not only to eat, drink, and be merry, but to relive an accomplishment in a memorable fashion."[2] Team celebrations have greater impact when they are related to the achievement of a specific goal, milestone, or performance factor worth noting.

Reliable

Many celebrations are well intentioned, but fail to create the desired impact on participants. This occurs most frequently because the customer, or person for whom the celebration is given, shifts from being the team to being the sponsor, the executive, or someone external to the team. Such nonparticipants tend to get recognized in cases where an executive makes a longwinded speech to the team with little real data, interest, or concern about the employees present. Celebrations can also lose their meaning when they begin to resemble each other, become routine, and show a lack of thought and attention on the part of the company. (Some firms opt for pizza parties over and over and over again, for instance.) The use of surprises, special foods, or activities that have particular meaning to the members can give celebrations the impact they are intended to have. The "cookie rounds" at St. Elizabeths Medical Center are a good example.

Timely

Celebrations need to occur as close to the achievement of the goal or result as possible. Those that are put off until the end of the year, the end of the quarter, the next holiday, or "sometime when everyone is available," will have far less impact on participants. For events that are major, minicelebrations can occur that lead up to the gala event. These can center on special activities to plan and prepare for the "big event" or involve people in the planning of the event in fun and meaningful ways.

In summary, the value of the event cannot be measured in terms of its costs. Participants gauge its value in human emotional terms. A good assessment of the celebration's success is to find out whether people feel they would work as hard and as well again in order to experience a similar celebration.

Examples of Effective Team Celebrations

There are many examples of effective team celebrations. A few are noted below:

- A team of employees at a division of Honeywell Corporation staged a theatrical presentation about how they achieved improvements in their work-flow process. Their skit was called "Murphy's Law" and depicted the before and after flow of their work. Each team member represented a certain task within the system, and contributed to a very humorous and instructive presentation. The skit taught them as much as it did their audience, and everyone enjoyed it.

- A new product team from Ciba-Corning Diagnostics developed a video on the history of the development of one of their major products. They interviewed people as the new product was being created, filmed the special events and milestones, and showed the new product performing its function at the customer's site. The video created an opportunity to relive how the battle was won and how each person played an essential part in developing this important new product.

- A division of the Norton Company brought all the employees together for an ice cream sundae social, served by the managers and supervisors when the division accomplished a major breakthrough in their on-time delivery. Charts and graphs of each unit were on display in the cafeteria, and people were asked to tell how they made improvements in their work process that lead to improved delivery performance. It was both a meaningful experience and an opportunity to press for even greater delivery performance.

- A division of Analog Devices conducts a weekly meeting with all employees to review two critical variables in the business of the division: new orders and shipments. The division general manager stands in front of two thermometer-type charts and discusses the week's key events. He tells the group the results, and then selects a member from a department that did a special activity during the week. The activities mentioned include handling a high volume, overcoming a problem, helping another department, or demonstrating significant performance improvements. The representative of the department then colors in one of the two charts for the week's performance. Two departments are singled out each week. The entire process takes less than 20 minutes, and people often talk about the meeting all week long.

Team celebrations offer an important opportunity for organizations to recognize the performance and achievements of many people. To take full advantage of the opportunity, the celebration needs to be founded on the principles discussed above and tailored to the person or persons being honored. A Quality Manager at a large chemical company often says, "Reliving an experience is often more meaningful than living an experience."

Suggestion Systems

One of the oldest forms of employee involvement is the suggestion system. Started in the early 1900s, suggestion systems sought to encourage employees to contribute ideas that would improve productivity, working conditions, or the quality of a firm's products. The concept was simple: place little red boxes throughout the plant facility and encourage people to write down their suggestions and put them in the box for consideration by management.

Needless to say, the results of such practices were less than overwhelming. Then management began offering to share as much as 10 percent of its first year's savings from a good idea with the employee who contributed it. There has been a significant increase in the number of suggestions, but many of them have proven impractical. In some cases, ideas have actually been stolen from employees and awards have been given to the wrong person. Periodically, the major media publish stories about an employee who receives a very large sum of money for a major suggestion, but, like winning the lottery, it happens too infrequently to have much impact as a reinforcer.

In the 1970s American companies imported an idea from Japan called *quality circles*. These were meetings at which employees were trained and then encouraged to develop ideas that would improve the business. Employees tolerated the process; after all, it was better than working at a hot or noisy machine. From time to time good ideas arose from these quality circles, but they usually meant more work for the supervisors and engineers who then had to do the documentation and justification for the change. The reward, if not the 10 percent, was usually a "thank you" from the plant manager, along with a comment that the idea was either too expensive or would involve too much effort to be implemented.

With the current interest in total quality management, employee empowerment, and the self-managed workforce, firms are once again very interested in the suggestion system. In 1986 the Modern Management Co., Ltd., conducted a study that compared the suggestion systems in American firms with those in Japanese firms.[3] The executive director of Modern Management, Hiroshi Yamada, reported some very interesting findings. The primary points are shown in Figure 8-2.

To summarize the study's key points, Japanese companies yield a significantly greater number of suggestions from their employees than do American companies. The participation rate is higher, the number of suggestions per employee is higher, the percentage of suggestions implemented is higher, and the overall savings are 13.5 times greater. While American firms are able to achieve a higher saving for a given suggestion ($5554 versus $141), the suggestions implemented are so few as to have little real impact on the firms.

In behavioral terms, one can see that the act of making suggestions is more reinforced in Japanese firms than in the United States. In fact,

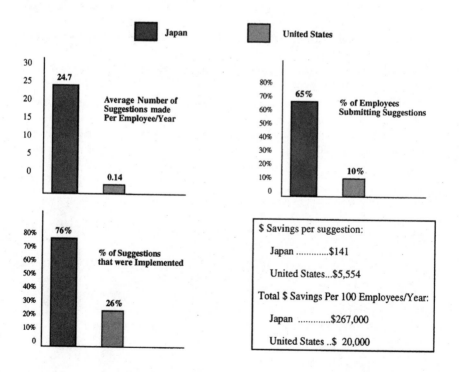

Japanese employees receive significant social recognition for any suggestion, regardless of how small or insignificant it appears on the surface. Japanese managers are rewarded (nonfinancially) when their people are able to find solutions to problems in the product, work process, or equipment. They are also accountable for the speed at which they get back to the employee with a response to their ideas. American managers are seldom recognized for such suggestions, nor do they recognize their employees for such actions. In most American firms, more suggestions just mean more work for the supervisor and the engineering departments. The reverse is true in Japanese firms.

In the United States we expect that special suggestion programs will drive out the desired ideas. In reality, the most value comes when the process is a normal part of doing business.

Case Study of an Employee Suggestion System

Dow Chemical Canada, located in Fort Saskatchewan, Alberta, recently changed the method by which it solicits and handles employee suggestions. After comparing Japanese and American styles of managing suggestions, they realized that more would be gained by increasing the sheer amount of ideas than by simply looking for the "big win." Hence, they developed a simple but highly effective approach. The first element of their suggestion system was to explain the importance of new ideas to their workforce. They placed the presentation in the context of competitive challenges and the need to make certain changes to improve the quality, speed, and use of resources within the plant. Then a simple form was introduced. The form was provided to each work center, and was the subject of weekly meetings between employees and supervisors.

The form had a simple point system. The suggestion would receive one point if an opportunity for improvement was identified. The suggestion would receive another point if there was supporting data related to the frequency, severity, cost, or extent of the problem. (The nature of the data was determined by the nature of the problem. Supervisors did not want to make this element too rigorous lest they discourage any new ideas.) The suggestion would receive two more points if specific actions were identified to address the problem. Or, if a problem had been handled in an innovative way, the person whose suggestion it was would note the actions taken. Supervisors and employees would examine the impact and note any significant change. Finally, after the implementation had been in place for some period, the suggestion would receive another point if the results were documented. The suggested savings were also noted as a way of reflecting the positive impact of the suggestion on the work group or company.

The point system was designed to do several things. First, it provided a way to track the number of suggestions and the progress of those

suggestions within the work center. Charts were displayed for
the different work areas showing the number of points racked up by that
department on a weekly basis. Second, every step along the
suggestion's path was reinforced. No suggestion was too small, no
amount of involvement was too restricted for inclusion. Third, the focus
was not on the individual or team developing a suggestion, but on the
whole suggestion-generating process. People from across the entire plant
were involved in suggestions, and everyone was encouraged to
generate, support, and find creative ways to implement the changes.

Supervisors conducted the actual scoring of suggestions and created
charts for their work areas. The suggestions were discussed in
weekly work center staff meetings and in the manager/supervisor
meetings within the plant. Everyone was involved, and actions
supporting this process were continuously reinforced.

The results are quite impressive. Some of them were as follows:

- 75 percent of the employees were involved in making suggestions
- 77 percent of the suggestions were implemented
- The average saving per suggestion was approximately $150
- The cumulative savings were over $30,000 per month in the first year

The reinforcement came in a variety of forms. When people handed a
suggestion to a supervisor, the supervisor took time *at that moment* to read
it and comment positively on it. He or she scored the items and provided
a weekly feedback on the work centers' total points. As ideas were
implemented and savings were documented, the supervisor noted this for
each department as well. People received special recognition for their
ideas in weekly staff meetings as well as in plantwide meetings. People
saw their ideas being implemented quickly, or, if they were not approved,
had the reasons explained to them within a week. Positive comments by
various departments were written on the suggestion forms and given back
to the employees. Finally, to get the program started with a bang,
supervisors gave 50¢ per point. The awards were minor in relation to the
impact of the suggestions, but the power of the reinforcement
encouraged the desired behaviors.

What's Right with this Picture?

Analyzing this program using the SMART criteria, we can quickly
understand why this suggestion process was so successful.

Specific

Employees knew why suggestions were important and they were reinforced for any sets of behaviors leading to identifying, researching,
solving, and providing follow-up to suggestions.

Meaningful

Although the employees received financial rewards (50¢ per point), they were minor in comparison to the personal recognition and appreciation they received. Their ideas were discussed in open forums, in staff meetings, in plantwide meetings, and through various other communications. Sometimes their names were associated with the idea, and sometimes an original idea was built on by many others and took a new form. People knew that their ideas were being valued, and this was the part that was meaningful.

Achievable

There was little effort needed to realize recognition from this process. As ideas were being generated, employees began to set their own limits as to what was a reasonable suggestion. More reinforcement was given to those with ideas that would have a substantial impact on the company.

Reliable

The process was managed by the supervisors and work teams. They valued the suggestions, charted the points, and implemented the ideas. Occasionally, the plant manager and other members of upper management reviewed the results in the departments, but they were looking more for the positive impact of ideas than seeking to find cheaters. Cheating is a problem only when there is more reinforcement for fabricating the information than for getting it right.

Timely

This is perhaps the most important element of this program. The feedback was immediate. The supervisor reviewed the suggestion on the spot. There were weekly reviews about point levels and specific suggestions that were in process. Employees were reinforced as they contributed their ideas to the overall effort of building Dow Chemical into a more competitive organization.

The process became a way of doing business. It moved from being a program to becoming a process. Initially, suggestions included generic complaints and meaningless ideas. There were scored and valued, but ideas that made more sense to the business got a lot of public attention. Hence, the action of making more and better suggestions, seeing to their implementation, and measuring their cost savings was encouraged. The suggestion process continued because people found very creative ways to address the complex challenges of the firm.

Employees were reinforced when they made suggestions and when they saw their ideas, sometimes enhanced by others, becoming a reality. It didn't take long to do this, but it did take a recognition that there is a better way than a suggestion box. For Dow Chemical Canada, the suggestion process has become part of their culture and their way of doing business.

The Guiding Principles for Making Recognition Special

This chapter has provided an overview of many techniques to reward and reinforce individuals and teams for their performance. Special recognition techniques have certain advantages over the base and variable pay plans. They can be more timely, more personalized, and more contingent on the process of achieving specific results. As stated earlier, there is no single right way to recognize contributions. But not *any* way is right either. We can draw some very important and powerful conclusions at this point about how to create, develop, and manage such special recognition programs.

Focus on the Customer

Special recognition programs are targeted to reinforce individuals for doing something the organization needs. In most cases these are actions that are outside the scope of employees' normal, daily activities, or represent a major achievement within such activities. Whether the group involved includes technical researchers, teams of engineers and marketeers, operational employees, support staff, sales staff, or managers, the group to be targeted for the special reward program must be clearly identified. It is imperative to know *who* you want to do what.

Make the Reward/Recognition Contingent on What You Want People to Do

Some programs are used to recognize people generating new ideas, regardless of their size or impact. Others are used to recognize a team that has developed some new applications of existing technology. Still others are used to recognize individuals who have made important contributions to get work performed by others. By segmenting the marketplace (i.e., the organization), the program can be designed around what action or behavior best reflects what is desired.

If It's Worth Doing, It's Worth Measuring

Measurement is essential if rewards are to have any meaning and credibility. Whether or not the measurement process is used to determine the criteria for selecting teams or individuals, it is essential to use it in applying the criteria. Measurement helps make the basis on which the reward is given more specific, and thereby more clearly in the performer's line of sight. Finally, measurement reveals whether the performer has actually accomplished what you wanted. It is an essential element of the process of reinforcement and feedback. It defines the difference between an "ata-boy" or "ata-girl" and true positive reinforcement.

Make It Personal and Meaningful to the Performer

While money may be the universal reinforcer, it is not universally applicable. When one is starting out with a new form of recognition, it is often best *not* to start with money. It is always relatively easy to progress to using money, but it is very difficult to go back without making employees feel that something had been taken away, even though the substitute award may be of the same financial value. Further, if you want to see what is meaningful to an individual, note what they do when they have choices. Look for those things that people do in their own time, that create naturally reinforcing conditions, and you will find the kind of rewards they see as positive and meaningful. (See Figure 8-3.)

---

1. Focus on the customer.

2. Make the reward/recognition contingent on what you want them to do.

3. If it's worth doing, it's worth measuring.

4. Make it personal and meaningful to the performer.

5. Make it timely.

6. Make sure everyone can win.

7. Remember, you are competing with other consequences.

8. Reinforce the reinforcers.

Figure 8-3. Guiding principles for special recognition.

Make It Timely

Perhaps the reason that special recognition has more impact on performance than do compensation systems is its immediacy. Pay systems have an inherent limitation to them. The recipient has to wait till the annual performance review, the final accounting of the firm's numbers, or changes of the marketplace. Base pay is often in the future, and variable pay is usually uncertain. But special recognition can be given *at the time* when the desired event or behavior occurs. If an employee achieves a desired result, it can be recognized immediately and with certainty. This requires a measurement process that is clear and very easy to handle. Above all, it requires that supervisors, managers, or others be aware and attentive to rewarding the desired actions.

Make Sure Everyone Can Win

As illustrated by the Allied Systems case history, everyone can win. Allied did not establish a ranking process or set up any other form of destructive competition in order to achieve a desired result with its drivers. People work hard when they know they will be reinforced for it. Competition inherently creates winners and losers. Special recognition, when it operates at its maximum potential, has only winners. If people do not accomplish something desired, they are not recognized; those who do, *are* recognized. Since everyone has the same opportunity, there is a level playing field. The best situation is one in which everyone can get over the goal line by winning their own individual race.

Remember, You Are Competing with Other Consequences

The workplace has numerous conflicting consequences. People are affected by many personal situations that require or attract their attention. The performers' peers have a major impact on their performance. Management does not always understand, realize, or address the other factors influencing what employees do. Hence, it is important to realize that recognition systems are in competition with other consequences that have an impact on the individual. In order to win more often and encourage employees to feel valued and rewarded for achieving the results needed by the organization, a company's recognition systems need to be more attractive to its employees than other positive consequences in their environment.

Reinforce the Reinforcers

Many special recognition systems are meant for employees, not supervisors or managers, on the principle that supervisors and managers are recognized as a normal part of their job. But as most individuals in first-line and middle management positions will indicate, they are often the most left-out, ignored, and underdeveloped resource within the organization. This is especially unfortunate, because a special recognition system will not work without managers and supervisors who are reinforced and skilled at driving it. If an organization wants its managers to reinforce its supervisors, and its supervisors to reinforce the staff below them, its managers and supervisors must be reinforced themselves. Otherwise, the system will just be seen as yet another burden that top management is "laying on" the organization.

Many organizations have established reward and recognition committees, task forces, or special councils that flounder around searching for some way to help increase the amount or effectiveness of recognition practices. In this author's opinion, their task can be made much easier by simply finding ways to increase the rate and effectiveness of reinforcement within the organization. *Recognition* as a word simply does not fully convey the nature of the effort required to support the changes needed in today's organizations. Recognition is really about multiple rewards and meaningful reinforcement.

Summary

This chapter has explored multiple facets of the recognition process. It has attempted to expose the fallacies inherent in some current practices and provide an understanding as to why these approaches do not work. Further, it has attempted to show what can be done when one takes a behavior-based approach and understands that the nature of the task is to reinforce desired behaviors.

By understanding recognition as a function of reinforcement, we can make special recognition truly effective. When it *is* effective—keyed to what is positive and meaningful to the individual—the results will be clear and impressive. Recognition and reinforcement are an essential part of the process of change within an organization. Change, especially change involving increased collaboration, means that people need to do some things differently. Special recognition and reinforcement practices can create the context in which these new behaviors flourish. They become the process *between* the pay checks, whether base or variable. By taking this approach, we can create a different sort of organization and foster a process that is more clearly able to achieve a win/win for all members concerned.

Notes

1. Wilson, T., "Why Self-Managed Teams Work," *Industrial Management,* February, 1993, Special Supplement.
2. Daniels, A., "Parties—With a Purpose," *SKY Magazine,* December, 1992.
3. Snyder, G., "May I Make a Suggestion?: Dow Chemical Canada Says 'Yes'," *Performance Management,* Vol. 8, No. 2, pp. 10–15.

9

Replacing the Performance Appraisal

Definition of a performance appraisal:
One of those special human encounters where
the manager gets no sleep the night before,
and the employee gets no sleep the night after.
—THOMAS B. WILSON

Throughout this book we have explored many ways to establish pay and recognition systems so that they reinforce collaboration, teamwork, and a focus on the priorities of the business. There is perhaps no aspect of management that has stimulated more articles, speeches, or controversy than the performance appraisal. The issues stem from a variety of conflicting pressures:

- The quality management gurus (e.g., Deming, Joiner, and Juran) strongly argue that appraisals should be eliminated because they inaccurately portray individual performance as a major influence on results and inadequately address systems-based issues.

- Managers want the ability to recognize and reward superior performers (as with pay for performance).

Figure 9-1. The primary elements of the total reward system.

- Employees want honest and timely feedback, specific development, and an opportunity to receive coaching and assistance on how to improve.
- Compensation managers want a system to ensure that compensation dollars are allocated according to performance levels and salary budgets.
- Human resource executives want the ability to identify top performers, plan for their development and succession, and reward them adequately.

While these needs are not inherently contradictory, they place conflicting pressures on the performance appraisal process that it is ill-equipped to resolve. The result is that virtually everyone is dissatisfied with the performance appraisals.

In the earlier chapters of this book we examined three core elements of the total reward system. (See Figure 9-1.) The first was base pay, the second was variable pay (e.g., incentives and equity-related programs), and the third was performance management. This third element involves both special recognition and the management of performance. In this chapter we will examine the performance management process, and develop alternative models to the traditional process. I believe that managers can and should earn the right not to do performance appraisals when they manage performance on a real-time basis. The focus on performance appraisals will then shift from feedback and rewards to review and reinforcement—from appraisal to the management of the performance.

Background

A 1992 survey by Bretz, Milkovich, and Read indicated that approximately 95 percent of the *Fortune* 100 companies currently use performance appraisals.[1] The primary objectives of this process are to:

- Provide employees with feedback on how to improve performance
- Provide a basis for allocating pay increases and incentive awards
- Focus training and development activities
- Identify candidates for promotion
- Create an opportunity for employees to receive recognition
- Assure adequate documentation of performance that satisfies the requirements of the 1964 Civil Rights Act and Equal Employment Opportunity Commission guidelines
- Improve communication between the manager and employees
- Establish performance goals and standards for the next performance period

A study of managers and employees in 268 divisions of large manufacturing and service companies by Longenecker and Goff reported that over 80 percent of performance appraisal systems are ineffective.[2] Another study by Yankelovich in the late 1980s indicated that neither managers nor employees see a relationship between their pay increases and performance. In this study, fewer than 30 percent of the organizations reported a positive pay/performance relationship. If the objectives are important and the process is viewed as ineffective, why are so many companies continuing with the same process?

W. Edwards Deming has made the strongest case against performance appraisals.[3] The eleventh and twelfth of his 14 points addresses many of the issues involved in appraisal systems. He refers to performance appraisals as the "deadly disease" and a "plague and affliction to be purged from the earth." To summarize briefly, the reasons why Deming is so strongly against appraisals are as follows:

1. The performance appraisal process usually concentrates on the individual's performance, while work is always a function of the systems and processes in the organization.

2. Most of a group's results are accomplished by its collective actions, yet the appraisal usually focuses on individual performance independent of group performance considerations. Performance appraisals seldom examine the combined contributions of individuals.

3. Appraisals tend to examine performance over a relatively long period of time: one year. They assume that performance is consistent and within the control of the performer. However, systems, processes, and environmental forces are in constant motion and are often beyond the individual's awareness or control.

4. The setting of specific goals or standards for performance evaluation encourages performers to achieve these levels only and only

up to certain levels. This limits both the focus of the performer and his or her potential achievements.

5. Performance appraisals ultimately set up a win-lose situation, especially where the ratings or raises must follow a prescribed distribution. The result is a discouraged worker who sincerely wants to do a good job.

Longenecker and Goff's study of performance appraisal systems gives additional reasons for why they fail to accomplish their objectives:[4]

- Managers lack sufficient information to judge performance accurately.
- The goals and standards are unclear and subjective.
- They make employees defensive.
- The process is not taken seriously.
- Managers do not prepare adequately.

Despite these continual warnings about appraisals, they go on being done. In fact, according to a 1992 survey of performance management practices in companies with total quality management, sponsored by the General Accounting Office, 68 percent of the companies studied saw little conflict between their TQM efforts and existing performance appraisals.[5] These firms sought to utilize the appraisal process as an opportunity to examine individual employees' performance and contribution to the quality goals.

The practices studied in this survey contrasted with the practices of an increasing number of organizations spotlighted in the major media.[6] Companies as diverse at Kodak, Xerox, General Motors, and Procter & Gamble are experimenting with alternatives to traditional performance appraisals. They are attempting to institute pass/fail systems rather than individual performance ratings or they do not include any ratings at all. They are seeking to implement peer review systems instead of manager-driven performance evaluations. They are using these review periods as a means to counsel employees on their careers and promotional opportunities and seeking ways to keep top performers from falling through the cracks. They are minimizing the relationship between an individual's performance and his or her pay raises.

It is clear from these surveys, teachings, and organizational experiments, that some organizations are seeking a different approach to accomplishing the objectives of the performance appraisal. As we begin to explore alternative methods, we will focus on understanding current practices and requirements from a legal, managerial, and performer perspective.

How Appraisals Really Work: A Case Study

As the job anniversary approached for Charlene Wilde, her manager, J. Charles Marsh, began preparation for her performance appraisal. He knew that the appraisal needed to be submitted to the personnel department by Friday or Charlene's merit pay increase would be delayed.

To begin the process, Charles pulled together a variety of data. First, he retrieved Charlene's annual performance goals and her last year's performance review. Second, he obtained the new performance management review form and the employee self-evaluation form from personnel. He gave the self-evaluation form to Charlene to complete prior to their meeting. Third, he scheduled a meeting with her for about two hours Thursday morning in his office. Finally, he combed through his department's performance records for any information about Charlene's specific performance results.

Charlene had worked for Charles for approximately two years since his transfer to the marketing department. Charlene was a product manager for one of the firm's major lines of business. She had been in the department for approximately three years, and had shown significant potential. She and Charles had a good relationship, with strong mutual respect for each other's talents—his in marketing and hers in technical product knowledge and work commitment. The previous appraisal had identified several areas that needed improvements, and these would be considered during the appraisal discussion.

For two hours on Tuesday evening Charles prepared the performance review. He liked the narrative part of the form, and was able to describe his assessment of her achievements. He was also able to identify priority areas that "need improvement," and summarize her overall strengths and potentials. On Wednesday Charlene gave Charles her self-evaluation highlighting her quantitative results. She did not refer to the chaos she had created in the engineering group, the conflicts she had caused in manufacturing, or the problems she had had with other product managers and several regional sales managers. Charlene was very results-oriented, and always made her specific product financial and market share targets. Neither the form nor the financial systems enabled Charles to back up his concerns about her relationships with other departments.

The performance evaluation discussion began as normal with general conversation about work, special projects, and the company. When they settled into the specific discussion on Charlene's performance, Charles reviewed each of the objectives and the results accomplished. The data on the financial targets were very clear, and Charlene had met all the objectives. Performance on the more process-oriented objectives was substantiated with letters, comments, and critical incident reports collected by Charles during the year.

Charlene was very surprised by much of the qualitative data and challenged many of the conclusions. She was clearly expecting a "distinguished" performance rating and a very high pay increase. Charles rated her as a "strong performer" (a 4 on the company's 5-point scale). He concluded that while she had reached all her primary goals, she had caused numerous problems that Charles had had to address in other areas of the company. Her singleminded focus on results was preventing her from gaining support and commitment from other areas of the organization. She thought she was doing what he wanted, but he felt he had too often had to clean up after her encounters with others in the organization.

Following the performance appraisal, Charles completed the forms, obtained her signature, and turned it into personnel. Once it was received and approved, he was given the okay to process her merit pay increase. He told her the amount of pay increase early the next week and she was clearly disappointed. The overall company limits to increases in base pay (between 0 percent and 7 percent, with an average of 4 percent) was less than in previous years. He explained the policies to her, showed her the salary increase grid, and stated that she had received an above-average rating compared to others in his department. Although this was reassuring, Charlene felt that Charles did not fully appreciate her achievements.

This case study describes a traditional performance appraisals experience. There are several core elements to the process that need clarification for us to truly understand its operation (see Figure 9-2).

Elements of Traditional Appraisals

- *Goal Setting.* This usually means management-by-objectives for professional/managerial positions and performance standards for operational, clerical positions. Both are usually based on individual performance; people with the same job usually have similar goals.

- *Measures.* These are the tasks or levels of performance used to gauge whether or not a person has achieved his or her goals. They may include primary milestones or the results of periodic reviews of performance.

- *Feedback.* This is a summary of how an individual has performed against the goals or standards. It is usually provided at the end of the performance period.

- *Performance Rating.* Based on the feedback, the supervisor makes a judgment on an overall rating of performance. In most cases this

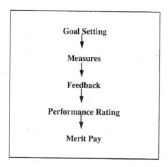

Figure 9-2. Elements of traditional performance appraisals.

is based on a 1-to-3 or 1-to-5 point scale, with dimensions like "needs improvement/marginal" (Level 1), "below standard" (Level 2), "competent" (Level 3), "commendable/superior" (Level 4), to "distinguished/outstanding" (Level 5). The rating may be in absolute terms—such as how the person did in relation to desired performance—or in relative terms—such as how the person did in relation to others. Many organizations seek to limit the number of people at each rating so that managers are forced to distribute ratings according to an expected normal distribution performance curve.

- *Merit Pay.* This is the pay-for-performance component of the performance appraisal process. In many organizations the amount of the pay increase is based on the performance rating and the salary range or market price for the position. (This was described in some detail in Chapter 5).

Thus the traditional performance appraisal process has a strong pay-for-performance component. Or does it?

What's Wrong with This Picture?

The above discussion and case study outline the general pattern of performance appraisals within organizations. Although many organizations are changing certain elements of the process, the essential function remains the same. Managers render a judgment on the employees. Let's examine the traditional performance appraisal process according to the SMART criteria for an effective reward system.

Specific

The process of goal setting and performance standards is supposed to provide the performer with a clear set of criteria on which the performance evaluation is based. However, as reported by numerous studies, most employees believe the criteria to be vague and subjective. Much of the traditional training for managers in performance appraisals focuses on goal setting and feedback discussions. It is hoped that goal setting will provide the necessary ingredient to achieve superior performance.

However, the efficacy of appraisal systems continues to be regarded as neutral at best in terms of managing performance. The reasons most often cited relate to inadequate goal setting or failure to align consequences with achievement of goals. As shown earlier, annual merit pay increases are basically inadequate as a means of driving desired performance—except close to the deadline, or "judgment day." As reflected in the case study involving Charlene and Charles, the traditional process is notable for the lack of specific measures or feedback that are known to the performer, meaningful to the organization, and related to the consequences that impact desired actions.

Meaningful

For performance appraisals to have any meaning to the performer, they need to have an impact on behaviors. The most obvious concern is that even when goals are set, they are seldom monitored during the year, so that whether or not they are achieved has few consequences until the end of the performance period. Thus, the appraisal process is basically not in operation during three-quarters or more of the year.

Achievable

Once again, it is difficult to relate this factor to a process that basically uses general or after-the-fact performance parameters. The goals set often have a single level of achievement only. Potentially, there are negative consequences if they are not achieved, and limited-to-no positive consequences if they are exceeded. Hence, the pressure to perform is more of a negative reinforcement (See Chapter 3) than an opportunity to provide positive reinforcement. As a result, performers seek evidence to demonstrate that the desired level has been achieved to rebut any potential criticism from supervisors. The process is neither collaborative nor reinforcing.

Reliable

The measure of reliability depends on the purpose of the program. In the case study above, the performance appraisal process was intended to provide the employee with feedback, coaching, and recognition for achievements. Since the manager sought to examine both the results and the process and the performer was focused on achieving the results, the process became more of a negotiation than a feedback, review, and coaching session. Further, because the manager had to *force distribute* the merit increases, he was not able to provide the rewards desired. Though well-intentioned, the process as it is currently configured does not serve its desired purpose.

Timely

The goals are set for an annual performance period. The review is provided near the employee's anniversary date. Although performance is supposed to be reviewed more frequently, it seldom is. The manager may collect data on critical incidents, but these are often kept in a file until the review discussion. Like wasted fruit, this fresh performance data ripens and rots before it can be used.

In summary, the traditional performance appraisal process fails to meet the SMART criteria. In many organizations, appraisals are used to ensure that there is sufficient documentation to discharge or conduct downsizing/layoffs, and to comply with legal requirements. In some organizations, appraisals are used to ensure that the merit increase dollars are allocated to those who are regarded as top performers. In other organizations, appraisals are intended to be coaching sessions so that performance and motivation can be maximized. However, since they only occur once a year, they have little positive impact over the performance period. Therefore, as we have found with other methods of rewarding performance, our question is not, why do appraisals not work, but, why did we ever think they would?

Now let's try to pinpoint the issues related to performance appraisals. The remaining sections of this chapter will build a case for the best options available for addressing these issues.

The Reasons for the Limitations of Appraisals

The performance appraisal process faces a variety of challenges. First, individuals both want and need feedback on their performance. While the quality experts make strong, legitimate points regarding the impact of individual feedback on team performance, how can individuals receive the recognition they need when all the emphasis is placed on teams or systems? The challenge is to create conditions in which individuals receive more immediate and meaningful feedback on performance in relation to their contribution to a team's achievements.

Second, the Civil Rights Act of 1964 (Title VII), as well as legislation and court rulings since then, have identified performance appraisals as a basis for many selection-type decisions (i.e., promotions, merit increases, etc.) and therefore must comply with antidiscriminatory requirements. This is to protect individuals from poor management practices. However, the requirements often lead to intensive documentation procedures that do more to reinforce bureaucracy than to encourage collaboration. Can appraisals be used to enhance the feedback and reinforcement of desired behaviors and still comply with legal standards?

Third, goal setting has long been a major component of the performance appraisal process. In times of dynamic change, during which interdependencies and relationships change with little notice, how can single-focus goals retain their currency? Further, goals tend to focus on end results. How can they be related to the emphasis on process espoused by quality management experts?

Fourth, many organizations feel that a forced distribution of performance evaluations will cause managers to make tough decisions about the allocation of rewards. Without such requirements, it is believed, managers will be able to avoid the conflicts required in making winners and losers out of their people. The result is that managers water down their performance decisions. Employees often feel that their evaluations are vague and biased. They may not hear the negative performance feedback, and managers continue to resist decisions to allocate rewards. As discussed in Chapter 3, when people work under negative reinforcement conditions, they return to old habits as soon as the threat is diminished. The advent of forced allocation of evaluations is not producing a better management of performance.

Fifth, the point of many performance appraisal systems is to focus on the results achieved by the performer. But the focus of many managers is on *how* the results were achieved. As shown in our case study, the performer often wants to discuss results without regard to the process or efforts taken in reaching them. Or, when the results are poor, the performer wants to discuss the effort expended and claim that the results were outside his or her control. Traditional thinking relates behavioral measures to the traits of the performer. The manager is often faced with a choice between examining the results or examining the behaviors that achieved the outcomes. This presents a dilemma for both measurement and feedback. Are there better alternatives?

Finally, performance in the appraisal process is generally judged at the end of the performance period. The central question is, did the performer do what he or she committed to do? Feedback is given in relation to these end-of-period results. Measurement is focused on providing sufficient information so that the resulting evaluation of performance can be done with some degree of reliability. If we examine the power of continuous feedback and frequent reinforcement, we realize that we can maximize the discretionary and motivated effort of the performer. How can feedback be viewed as an essential element of the performance management process rather than as a justification for performance evaluation?

These questions remain unanswered largely because of the traditional way we have posed them. We see goal setting as an activity that focuses attention on an end point. We use feedback as a way to justify an evaluation of performance. We force managers to allocate evaluations so that all performers will not be rated high. We have difficulty evaluating the performance of the individual versus the performance of the team. We even force managers to do performance appraisals by holding back the merit increase of their employees. These and other unresolved dilemmas have often resulted in the performer receiving little feedback or misinterpreted feedback on his or her performance. The manager, seeking to do the right thing, has to make trade-off decisions between what is best for the individual and what is best for the organization. The win/win process of collaboration is short circuited because of what we expect and require the performance appraisal process to do. In this way, we have created a system that serves neither the performer nor the organization—and the manager is caught in the middle.

The Fundamental Requirements for Performance Management

Having examined the issues related to the performance appraisal process, we can see several emerging themes. Considered from a different perspective, these themes provide an outline of the requirements for an effective performance management process, which this chapter will examine in the light of the relevant available research. This will give us a conceptual foundation for developing a process that will achieve the primary objectives and support not only the other reward systems but also collaboration within the organization.

Goals Setting

Much has been written about goal setting. One of the best discussions of the impact of goal setting has been contributed by G. Latham and K.

Wexley.[7] Their research has shown how goal setting has been associated with improved performance in both laboratory and real-world settings. Goal setting is basically an *antecedent*—that is, goals are designed to initiate a behavior. However, the force that causes the behavioral change to continue and be sustained is the consequences. Within this context, positive reinforcement is the only consequence that is able to achieve lasting desired behavioral change. Therefore, for goal setting to be effective it needs to be paired with positive reinforcement. This pairing provides a powerful combination for impacting human performance. Managers should not be mislead into thinking that goal setting is the root cause of the weakness in appraisals. Antecedents like goal setting help people know what to do, but the consequences provide the reasons for doing it. The task in the performance planning process is to provide goals that are both positive and meaningful to the performer and clearly aligned with the strategies of the organization, and supported by specific consequences.

Measures

In most organizational cultures, measurement is associated with two experiences: An individual performs a desired action but gets little or no feedback (i.e., the process we call extinction), or the information about performance is used to tell the performer that he or she is not doing enough (i.e., the process we term negative reinforcement). When using measurement to punish, we create "stealth" employees—a person that is able to avoid all performance detection systems of the organization. In neither case is the process regarded as a positive one. In the desired model of performance management, measurement creates opportunities for meaningful positive reinforcement. Measures provide the basis for that information that acts as feedback to the performers. They indicate how employees are progressing and what they need to do to achieve more or to enhance the quality of what they are already achieving.

A good illustration of this process in action is the use of phone monitoring by the customer service department of a large Blue Cross and Blue Shield organization. Conventional wisdom would suggest that employees would resist such a practice as a "big brother" tactic. However, most of the employees in this organization actively seek to be listened to in order to be scored by their supervisor or teammates against established criteria. The employees themselves were involved in developing the measures and the team's overall daily score is charted in the work area for everyone to see. Periodically, individual employees replace the supervisor as monitor. Each person keeps his or her own score log and, as if it were a sports activity, they enjoy improving their daily scores.

- Checklists
- Factor Scales
- Behaviorally Anchored Rating Scales
- Critical Incident Reports
- Management-by-Objectives
- Performance Matrix

Figure 9-3. Techniques for performance measurement.

There are several techniques that can be utilized to enhance the quality of feedback. These include checklists, factor scales, behaviorally anchored rating scales, critical incident reports, management by objectives, and the performance matrix. (See Figure 9-3.) Each of these is discussed in more detail below.

Checklists. These are statements used to indicate the completion of tasks. Checklists are applied most effectively to jobs that involve relatively routine tasks, such as housekeeping, safety procedures, assembly operations, etc. Some organizations have made creative applications of checklists in examining training tasks, behaviors to support teamwork, and implementing projects or programs. Checklist items can also be weighted so that a score can be determined for accomplishing the prescribed tasks.

Factor Scales. These are measures that combine a list of specific dimensions with a common scale (e.g., low to high, never to always, etc.). These scaling techniques require a specific list of dimensions related to the particular task. The scale rates the dimensions in terms of frequency, severity, degree of accuracy, etc. The ultimate addition of the ratings produces a score that can be used for charting data or comparing scores across other factors or organizational units.

Behaviorally Anchored Rating Scales (BARS). These were created in the early 1960s and have been adapted and applied to a wide variety of situations.[8] BARS describe in specific, behavioral, or observable terms an action along a continuum for each dimension selected. The rater selects the description on the scale that corresponds most accurately to the action taken. The descriptions work by providing concrete specifications for the measures, but they require extensive development to ensure that they are valid and accurate representations of each dimension measured.

Critical Incident Reports. This method involves describing in detail situations that are viewed as critical to the performance. The task requires recording as accurately and specifically as possible the situation and activities related to an event: the circumstances that preceded the incident, the setting, the specific action taken by the performer, and the impact of these actions. When this information is provided to the performer immediately after an incident, it can provide a valuable record of the event and serve as an important learning tool. Over the course of a performance period, such reports can provide a rich source of information for reviewing performance. To be effective, the method requires skillful descriptions of events and significant commitment to keep the procedure in operation.

Management by objectives (MBO). This process, made popular by George Odiorne[9] and Peter Drucker,[10] involves the development of specific goals or objectives for the performance period. The performance is evaluated in terms of the extent to which these goals were accomplished. Organizations have integrated this process into strategic and business planning, and it has often been an important element of the planning process for professional and managerial positions. Odiorne believed that the goals should be developed collaboratively between the manager and employee, that they should relate directly to the employee's accountabilities, and that they should be used as dynamic guidelines for taking action. Latham and Wexley[11] reported significant improvements through the use of goal setting. But, as shown earlier, the effectiveness of this process depends on pairing it with desired consequences.

Performance Matrix. This process combines BARS with MBOs. The matrix uses a set of specific measures, weights them, and indicates a series of performance levels along a scale. The scale provides a performance continuum, such as minimum threshold, baseline or historical, target and distinguished/outstanding performance. Instead of having a single goal level, there is a range. This enables the performer to be recognized for any incremental improvement in performance and increases the opportunities for reinforcement. The matrix can produce an ultimate score that can be charted or used for a variety of actions. (The matrix was shown in Figure 6-8 in the chapter on variable compensation.)

These alternative methods of measurement are only a partial list. They represent different approaches and an opportunity to expand, create, or adapt them to different situations. To summarize briefly, the purpose of measurement is to identify the information needed to monitor performance in the key result areas. This is the basis for feedback, the next important element of the performance management process.

Feedback

The purpose of feedback is to provide the performer with the information necessary to know how he or she is doing. The more specific and timely the information, the better. In fact, information that is collected and displayed by the performer is often much more effective than that generated elsewhere in the organization. The power of statistical process control (SPC) charts as a quality management technique is the immediacy of the feedback it provides to the performers on their actions.

F. Balcazar, B. Hopkins, and Y. Suarez have conducted some very interesting research on the impact of feedback.[12] After examining more than 126 different research-based applications of feedback to determine the factors that enhance the effectiveness on human behavior, they concluded that feedback alone does not uniformly improve performance. Rather, when feedback is combined with goal setting and consequences, it has a clear and consistent impact on behaviors. Their research led to several other important findings regarding effective feedback:

1. Feedback functions to improve performance when it is related to some meaningful and primary consequence for the performer.

2. Feedback that is quantitative has more value to the performer than narrative, observation, or subjective assessments.

3. Feedback that is displayed in graphic form has the highest positive impact on performance.

4. Public feedback has an impact on performance equal to feedback provided privately. This is not to indicate that negative personal feedback should be made public. Other studies have shown this to be highly punishing. One useful guideline is to use public displays for group results and private meetings for individual feedback.

5. The frequency of feedback is a critical dimension of its effectiveness. Feedback that is daily, weekly, or biweekly has the most value to the performer.

6. Feedback that is self-generated does not have a consistent impact on performance. Rather, feedback that is provided by a supervisor or in collaboration with others has a higher impact. While current research has not definitively ascertained the impact of feedback by peers, customers, or subordinates, it is clear that self-assessments have little value as a source of meaningful feedback.

7. When pay is made available for improved work, it is not effective until the feedback indicates that progress is being made toward earning the additional pay. Simply saying that there is a relationship between pay and performance does little to impact behaviors. Behaviors do change when people see a clear opportunity to earn additional pay as a result of feedback data.

This research clearly demonstrates that feedback alone is not an effective tool for managing performance. Goal setting provides the direction; feedback provides the sense of progress; and consequences provide the reason for action. Hence, feedback in an essential element of the desired performance management process—but only an element.

Performance Rating

In traditional performance appraisals, the process concludes with the rating of the individual. We need to examine the utility of this element from three perspectives: the reliability of the rater, the legal requirements, and the needs of the performer. In this way we can gain some insight into how to make this process more effective.

Rater Reliability. Since the early 1920s behavioral scientists have attempted to understand and increase the ability of raters to evaluate performance. As R. M. Hogarth has stated, "the literature paints a depressing picture of human judgmental ability."[13] The research indicates the following primary problems with our ability to reliably judge the performance of others:

1. *There is insufficient data on which to judge the performer's actions.* Judgment about a performer's actions is usually derived from comments, results, and contextual data. There is not enough valid data on which to make sound judgments. This will continue to be a problem as organizations continue to increase the span of control for individual managers and involve them in more activities outside their immediate work groups.

2. *The "halo/horns" effect is alive and well.* The research indicates countless studies in which raters see and hear only the data that reinforces their preconceived notions about an individual. W. H. Cooper cited research in which raters subtracted and added information about performers independent of the true data.[14] (This is referred to as *"cognitive distortion."*)

3. *The rating scales are often vague and lack sufficient concreteness to be valid tools for measurement.* Behavioral scientists have sought to develop valid instruments for providing more specific measures, but few have found their way into the business environment. Hence, the rating scales are unclear and vague. Further, most specific measurement systems that have been developed do not take into consideration a variety of systemic and environmental factors to understand why certain actions were or were not taken.

4. *Raters often act in an overconfident manner and are not motivated to gather the data, analyze it carefully, and reach sound conclusions.*

Raters often ignore data about performance and are often reinforced for taking quick, decisive action. Working through extensive
amounts of performance data is simply not common practice
among successful managers.

These findings are corroborated by the manager/employee survey
conducted by Longenecker.[15] Employees often feel that managers do
not use clear, well-prepared, and complete information when making
judgments about their performance. One can easily see why Deming
and other quality gurus have been deeply skeptical about the performance appraisal process.

The Legal Requirements.   In 1964 Congress passed the Civil Rights
Act and with it, Title VII which specifically states that employers cannot discriminate in employment decisions on the basis of race, color,
religion, sex, or national origin. (Congress went on to add age discrimination in separate legislation.) Further, a series of court cases have
clearly linked the process of performance appraisals with discriminato-
ry decisions and have stipulated requirements for their conduct [e.g.,
Bito v Zia Company (1974), *Griggs v Duke Power* (1971), *Wade v Mississippi
Cooperative Extension Service* (1974), *Albermarle Paper Company v Moody*
(1975), etc.].

In 1978 Congress passed the Civil Service Reform Act (CSRA) to
address the need for a performance appraisal process for most federal
agencies.[16] The CSRA was important because it outlined the government's attempts to define the requirements for a performance appraisal
process with the expectation that this would form the standard against
which other systems would be judged. The CSRA requires the following conditions for performance appraisals:

1. Each agency shall adopt one or more appraisal systems. In other
   words, each organization needs to have a formal performance
   appraisal system.

2. The performance measures must relate directly to the job requirements of the position (i.e., not be trait-oriented).

3. Employees are encouraged to participate in establishing the performance standards.

4. Performance evaluations need to be based solely on the job criteria.

5. Appraisals are to be conducted at least once a year.

6. The results of the evaluation must serve as the basis for making
   decisions regarding training, paying, promoting, layoff/downsiz-
   ing, and terminating employees.

These practices, which can be assessed in terms of their effectiveness, are directed at protecting individuals from ineffective management practices. The overall objective is to provide employees with a process that helps them understand the requirements of their role, gives them feedback on their performance, and rewards them for their achievements. These principles are consistent with best practices in performance management systems. The challenge lies in creating a process that is meaningful to the performer within the context of today's newly competitive workplace.

The Needs of the Performer. Throughout the analysis of performance appraisal systems, we have focused on the elements of the system and the practices of managers and supervisors. Within an organization there is no system more directly related to the needs of employees than the performance management process. Employees are the customers of this system. Although no extensive research has been conducted on the needs of this customer group, it is important to understand which needs we are attempting to meet with the design of the system. If the system meets these needs and serves to support the actions required by the organization, we can achieve a win-win situation: collaboration. These are some of the possible needs of the employee-customers of this process:

1. *A clear sense of direction.* Employees want and need to understand what they should do to help the organization become more successful. Everyone has a role within an organization, and everyone needs to see this role within a context of the firm's competitive strategy and key success factors.

2. *An opportunity to participate in the goals and standards for performance.* Employees want to be involved in ways that help them understand what is expected of them and why. Their involvement is necessary to enhance their understanding and commitment.

3. *Timely, honest, and meaningful feedback on their performance.* Employees want to know how they are doing *as they are doing their work.* Waiting until some annual event is not an effective way to help them sustain or improve their performance.

4. *Immediate, meaningful, and sincere reinforcement for their efforts.* Employees want to be valued by the organization for their accomplishments and their efforts to help the organization become more successful.

5. *Coaching and assistance on ways to learn more and improve how one performs the job.* Employees want to continue to develop their skills and abilities; they value sincere assistance that is provided on the job. This involves hearing about problems in their performance that are presented in a direct, helpful, and sincere manner.

6. *Be treated with fairness, sincerity, and respect.* Employees want to be treated as adults and have others assume that they are committed to the organization's success.

7. *Have an opportunity to understand and possibly influence decisions that affect them.* Employees understand that they are not in control of their careers. However, they want to be involved in some measure about decisions that affect them, their careers, and their actions on the job. This involvement again enhances their understanding and commitment. No one likes to be told to do something without understanding why or being able to shape it in any way.

These seven needs of the employee-customer need to be integrated into the desired performance management process. By understanding and relating to these needs, we can establish a system for managing performance that is truly appreciative of the employee-customer and consistent with the requirements of the organization. In this manner, we can build a true process of collaboration into the functions of the business.

Merit Pay

There are few issues in performance management systems that generate more controversy than merit pay. There are four main concerns:

1. Giving pay increases to individuals when their performance is really a function of the team's results or the workplace systems.

2. Giving more pay to some people and less to others on the same team, thereby undermining the cohesion and equity of the team.

3. Making pay increase decisions with little reliable data from someone, like a manager, who has little firsthand, objective information on the individual's performance.

4. Having sufficient funds to reward the eagles of the group very well, and restricting the pay increases of those individuals whose performance was not adequate.

The central question is should merit pay increases be included in the performance management (PM) process? The answer depends on what you want the PM process to do. If the purpose of the performance management process is to focus activities, facilitate feedback, and encourage developmental actions, pay should probably not be part of the process. Instead, individuals should have their pay adjusted based on external market conditions, overall team performance, or personal achievements that are developmental in nature. If the purpose is to recognize and reward individual performance, then pay should be linked to the assessment of individual performance.

The other issue involved in merit pay is the timing for pay adjustments. If the focus is on developmental dimensions, then pay increases should occur when the individual demonstrates these new capabilities for a sustained time period. If pay is tied to performance of the individual or the team, then adjustments should occur in relation to the performance period. If pay is tied to market adjustments or overall group performance, then adjustments should be tied to the implementation of these changes in pay rates. Hence, pay adjustments that are tied to one's hiring anniversary date make little sense in today's performance oriented business climate. Other ideas for determining pay adjustments were discussed in Chapter 5.

Developing a New Approach to Performance Management

The answer to resolving these issues does not lie in producing a new form. Nor is the answer to be found in more training for managers or more policies or control procedures to increase the frequency or firmness with which certain actions are taken. The problem with performance appraisals is that we already ask them to do too much. Instead of linking yet more human resource management programs—(such as succession planning, training needs analysis, and incentive compensation) to existing appraisal systems, we should make a fundamental

---

1. Recognize that there is a problem.
2. Reformulate the purpose of the performance management process.
3. Use objectives to focus activities, use goals to reinforce progress.
4. Measure both results and behaviors.
5. Provide continuous, real-time feedback.
6. Make reinforcement a part of every day.
7. Use performance reviews to celebrate and to learn.
8. Make review meetings as frequent as necessary.
9. Reward results and reinforce behaviors.
10. Earn the right not to do annual performance appraisals.

Figure 9-4. Guidelines for a new approach to performance management.

shift in the *direction* of appraisal systems. These ideas are discussed more fully below (see Figure 9-4).

1. *Recognize that there is a problem.* In most organizations few people feel that the performance appraisal system is working to their benefit. The reasons are as varied as their organizational settings. The first task is to examine the purpose of the program and assess the extent to which it is working consistently with the purpose. The costs of these current practices are often more dramatic and important than will be identified on a profit and loss statement. The organization needs to recognize when and where there is a problem with the existing system, examine the negative impact of continuing with these practices, and commit to taking a different course.

2. *Reformulate the purpose of the performance management process.* Earlier in this chapter we identified a variety of objectives and applications for traditional performance appraisal programs. In many organizations the more important the applications, the greater the justification for making managers follow the procedures. Instead of adding more to the process, the organization should add less. I would recommend that the organization refocus the performance appraisal process away from all the varied attempts to justify its existence and concentrate instead on the process of managing performance. This means that the process should facilitate the conditions necessary to maximize the performance of each individual—manager and employee alike. Hence, what I refer to as performance management is not simply adding merit increase provisions to an annual performance appraisal, but rather addressing the heart of the requirements for managing performance.

3. *Use objectives to focus activities, use goals to reinforce progress.* In the traditional performance appraisal process, goal setting is seen as a means to set standards against which performance will be judged. Under these conditions the employee seeks to minimize the level of difficulty or make the tasks so specific and controllable that achievement cannot be questioned. These conditions are sought in order to diminish the probability that negative consequences will result. The manager, on the other hand, will either yield to the needs of the employee or set stretch goals so that performance rewards can be justified. This creates a situation with an inherent conflict.

In the approach discussed here, goal setting is the third step in the process of performance planning. The first task is to define overall objectives for the role, tasks, functions, or mission of the unit. These objectives should define the long-term nature of the tasks and identify the priorities for focusing efforts. They should align with the mission and strategy of the unit, and provide a basis for tracking how well the team is progressing toward fulfilling this mission or strategy. They provide the framework and context for planning specific performance.

Once objectives have been determined, the next task is to determine how progress will be measured. Measures should meet the criteria discussed in Chapter 6, PROACT:

Positive

Reliable

Observable

Action-Oriented

Controllable

Timely

Measures are used to track the progress and provide opportunities for the performer to know how he or she is progressing. Ideally, these measures will provide the data necessary so that the performer can measure his or her own progress.

The performance planning process then uses goals to identify meaningful milestones. These are points along a continuum that define how well performance is being achieved. They pinpoint the specific levels of performance and identify a range of levels. They are not focused on a single level. Therefore, if the performer breaks through one goal, he or she can achieve another, and another, and another. The performer is reinforced for the attainment of each level and always knows that there is more to do. Goals create opportunities for positive reinforcement and demonstrate achievement by achievement that it is possible to attain superordinate objectives.

4. *Measure both results and behaviors.*   As shown earlier in the case study of Charlene, a single-minded focus on results can lead to ignoring another important component: how one got there. In Chapter 4 we discussed the importance of measuring both results and process. In terms of performance planning, we are using the terms *process* and *behaviors* in a similar way because behaviors are what one uses to implement a process. Both differ from procedures or prescribed rules.

Managers are frequently reluctant to focus on process because it appears too difficult to measure and usually pits one person's opinion against another's. The performance planning process should reflect the key results needed (i.e., objectives, measures, and goals) and the important process variables that define true success. Many of these process measures will reflect the values of the organization and the way goals need to be accomplished.

5. *Provide continuous, real-time feedback.*   Feedback that is held until the appraisal discussion is worthless, if not counterproductive in building a high-performance relationship. Feedback is data that tells the performers how they are progressing. Feedback may include

observations about how certain actions were taken, but more importantly it is *data*. Tables and charts that are kept in top drawers of desks are a waste. To be meaningful, they need to be provided to the performer as soon as they are available, and in some cases should actually be collected, analyzed, and displayed by the performers themselves.

Charts and graphs do not need to be pretty. They need to be personalized, and reflect themes or images that are important to the performers. For example, a manufacturing company that was implementing a series of materials requirements planning (MRP) programs used a graph that displayed stages of development of the program and different departments. They used images of race cars, ships, and airplanes for each of the departments. These images were moved across the chart as each department completed different elements of the program. In another setting, a finance department of a large technology company used a table to display play-money bills stacked on top of each other to reflect the account receivables that were collected. This was a three-dimensional chart. The use of images and symbols that can actually be moved provides a different view of feedback, one that can be more meaningful and important to the performers.

Feedback can be used to help the performer know whether or not certain actions are producing desired results. Feedback that is owned by the manager, held and given in some feedback discussion, inhibits a collaborative relationship. A manager's accountabilities are to provide the performers with as frequent feedback on performance as possible so that they, the performers, can take action. The manager and the performers can work collaboratively to identify the barriers to progress, implement new ideas, and ensure that the data is correct and accurate. This builds teamwork within the vertical structures of an organization. It is also more fun and rewarding.

6. *Make reinforcement a part of every day.* Measurement and feedback are essential elements in making reinforcement effective. Reinforcement that is not part of key result areas becomes just "ata boy/ata girl" and is usually worthless to the performer. The manager may feel that he or she is doing the right thing, while the performers view it is as insincere. Reinforcement can come in many shapes and sizes. (See Chapter 3, "The Fundamentals of Rewards.")

The task of performance management is to create practices and habits that build reinforcement into everyday activities.[17] This is the action-oriented part of managing people. But, it should not be limited to managers. Coworkers and customers, suppliers and subordinates, top managers and others can create a reinforcement-enriched environment. People will know how they are doing. Reinforcement that is specific, personalized, contingent, sincere, and timely (see Chapter 3) will give performers the reason to excel. This kind of reinforcement is not limited to some coaching session or appraisal discussion, but rather becomes a part of daily practice. Creating these conditions is a major, if not *the* major responsibility of managers.

7. *Use performance reviews to celebrate and to learn.* Annual performance appraisal discussions are in most part worthless. The element in them that performers look forward to is the review of achievements, the celebrations of accomplishments, and the time to reflect and learn what worked, what didn't, and why. Hence, in this method of performance management, we replace the annual appraisal interview with a *review* of the feedback data and an *analysis* of what worked and what didn't. The development process comes through when one seeks to uncover insights and explore new ways of attacking similar problems. It is meaningful to the performer because it engages both the manager and employee (and sometimes fellow employees) in a discussion of how the game has been played. The purpose is not feedback, coaching, or development. It is the mutual search for the truth, for ways in which things can be done differently, and for reinforcement of actions that have worked. There is no need to provide feedback during these meetings; the data should already be present. There is no need to evaluate performance; the discussion is about reviewing the results and process. The manager may have additional insights or experiences that are of value. The employee may have additional data to help explain why things worked out as they did. Together, they seek to learn from past experiences so that actions that worked can be reinforced and actions that didn't can be changed. Then, the documentation can be used as a record of the discussion to enhance the learning of both parties.

8. *Make the review meetings as frequent as necessary.* The review meeting discussed above is different from the annual performance review because there is no need to wait until the end of the performance period to have it. In fact, if you wait, you are placing the achievement of desired performance at risk. If these discussions are indeed valuable to both the performer and the manager, why wait until the game is over before you have them? In sports, the coach meets often with the team to discuss the game's tactical strategies and specific plays. The discussions are intended to improve the chances for winning. Annual performance appraisal discussions have given managers a false sense of security that they are managing performance. At the end of the year, the game is over and any value that might be gained from these discussions will have to wait until next year's game to be applied. The managers of a large electric utility, for example, after being trained in the process outlined above, were asked to provide these reviews on at least a quarterly basis. Their response was "Can we do them more frequently? Say, every month? Also, can we

involve the entire team in the discussion of our overall results or must it be done one-on-one?"

Using this approach, the team can engage in the review of results and process, and individual discussions can be provided to those who need it or find it valuable. Often data is enriched when several people are adding their perspectives. Private discussions can be provided to those individuals who want and need a personal discussion of their accomplishments or performance issues. The manager can also provide specific reviews with individuals who need special attention to improve their performance. This is a very different model of performance reviews from the traditional appraisal program.

There may be a need to conduct an annual review. This should correspond to the cycle of the business and be a review of a longer time period than that covered in the periodic sessions. The purpose may be the same and the documentation requirements may be similar. The key will be to not turn this into a negotiation or a judgment-oriented session, but to conduct a meeting that anchors primary learning experiences and builds plans for the upcoming performance period.

9. *Reward results and reinforce behaviors.* Traditional performance appraisals often put too many factors in the program and do not perform any of them well. This process focuses simply on the results and behaviors needed to accomplish overall objectives. It uses measures, goals, feedback, reinforcement, and reviews to provide real-time information and reinforcement of performance. What about rewards? In Chapters 5, 6, and 7, we discussed alternative reward methods. Depending on the reward strategy (Chapter 4) it chooses, an organization can and should employ those programs and systems that are consistent with its management requirements.

Should pay be linked to the performance reviews? Probably not. The answer depends on the nature of the reward system the organization is employing. The performance reviews discussed above should occur as frequently as necessary to learn and stimulate new, high-level efforts. When they are linked to pay, they tend to change the focus to justifying a desired pay increase.

Won't people want to know about their pay? The answer is yes and no. Initially they will, but soon the focus will be on the work, not the reward. At some point, they will not want to know a lot about their pay adjustments. Since we are providing people with a wide variety of rewards—merit pay, incentives, special recognition, celebrations, etc.—increases to base pay should not be the sole focus of their attention.

Managers often believe that pay is the problem when the root cause is really the lack of reinforcement performers are receiving. If pay is an issue, the manager should explore the reasons for the pay issue and determine whether or not it can be handled by the current pay and other reward systems.

10. *Earn the right not to do annual performance appraisals.* As demonstrated earlier in this chapter, traditional performance appraisals are not highly regarded by either managers or employees. But if we just eliminate appraisals, as many of the quality management experts suggest, employees are likely experience extinction— that is, they may continue to perform as expected for a while, but will generally slack off in their efforts if their sense of feedback and involvement in the organization is not encouraged and reinforced. Therefore, appraisals need to be *replaced* with something more meaningful to both the performer and the manager: the performance management process. In order for managers to move away from traditional appraisals, they need to implement and practice the provisions of the desired performance management process. When they implement the changes discussed here, managers earn the right to take a different approach.

Indicators of Successful Performance Management

This right to stop doing annual appraisals must not be just handed to managers; they must earn it. Given the importance of these tasks from a legal and human resources perspective, people need feedback. Therefore, a manager can stop doing performance appraisals when he or she manages performance on a real-time basis. How is an organization to know that this is happening? There are several important indicators that true performance management is taking place. These are as follows:

1. All measures are understood by the employees and they can describe the importance of their activities to the business.

2. There is a tracking system for monitoring performance in the areas identified.

3. The performance measures and progress are displayed in a public area.

4. The data on the performance charts is current.

5. The team leaders/managers are actively engaged in coaching staff members or providing assistance to improve performance.

6. There are periodic celebrations of achievements as they are realized. These celebrations are regarded as positive and valuable to the staff members.

7. The data indicates that performance is improving.

Case Study Illustration

Technology Enterprises, Inc. (a fictitious name but a real company) has adopted a different approach to performance appraisals. The purpose of their program is to facilitate the feedback and reinforcement of performance on a real-time basis, and to particularly emphasize the contributions of individuals to their teams.

In terms of process, each team establishes, in concert with group managers, their performance measures on an annual basis. These measures may be modified on a semi-annual basis, but most target annual goals. Some measures concentrate on results like delivery performance, product/service quality, and costs, and others focus on special developmental projects to improve the performance of the team or the group. The team then discusses how they will achieve maximum results with their members and assign accountabilities to individuals and subunits. Each measure has a continuum of performance levels and the team utilizes a Performance Matrix discussed earlier. Furthermore, TE, Inc. has developed a Personal Performance Checklist of the critical behaviors necessary to support a team's performance.

Monitoring results and providing feedback is very important to the team's success. The team monitors certain measures on a daily and weekly basis, and others are analyzed on a monthly basis. The team has charts displayed in their work areas, and they are frequently the subject of great discussions. The team examines the performance of the team, analyzes any barriers to their success, and scrutinizes the contributions and commitments made by each individual. Periodically, the group manager attends the review meetings to listen to their progress, reinforce their efforts, address their concerns, and determine what assistance the team may need to achieve its maximum potential.

Every two to three months the team members complete the Personal Performance Checklist. The process is relatively simple. The individual, in collaboration with the group manager, selects five people to conduct an assessment of the individual's contribution. Usually these people are other teammates, but they may be customers or other members of the division. The individual completes a self-evaluation and the group manager completes one on each person. The group manager then collects the checklist and summarizes the results. He or she then discusses the results of the feedback with the individual and plans appropriate actions to either improve performance or change the perceptions of others. In some of the more developed teams, individuals use these groups to discuss strategies for improving one's effectiveness with the team. Some teams chart the overall scores of their members as a measure of their team's effectiveness.

The teams and group managers use the overall performance data in two very important ways. First, they track how things are going and identify barriers to their continued growth and improvements. Second, they use the data to celebrate victories. Based on performance the team has access to a fund for recognizing their own performance and those of other individuals or teams throughout the division. The quarterly and semi-annual reviews are often marked with some crazy event (e.g., an ice cream party or family trips to a theme park); the monthly and quarterly individual reviews are seen as an important part of the process of reinforcement and development.

Increases in pay are determined through a variety of vehicles. First, the size of the merit pool is determined by the semi-annual and annual results of the division. This determines the average size of the awards available for pay increases. Second, the performance of the teams determines the pay opportunity for each individual. In high performance teams, individuals may have a 2 percent to 4 percent higher pay increase opportunity than the normal increases. Individuals on poor performing teams may face little if any pay increase opportunities. The individual award is determined by the group manager based on several inputs. He or she solicits inputs from the team on the performance ratings of each individual, examines the performance levels and growth of the individual on the Personal Performance Checklist, and the manager considers the internal relationships of pay. Based on these factors, the pay increase is determined. But, since this is only on annual event, the performance trends are usually well known to the individual, and there are numerous opportunities for individuals to be recognized for their performance. There is often little importance attached to pay adjustments. In other divisions of the company, they have adopted pay-for-competencies-employed type programs and pay adjustments are based on the increase in applied skills.

Summary: Step to the Music

Henry David Thoreau suggested that there is an alternative to traditional patterns of living. He said: "If a man does not keep pace with his companions, perhaps it is because he hears a different drummer. Let him step to the music which he hears, however measured or far away." After reviewing traditional performance appraisals, I have presented a way to unbundle, refocus, and renew the process so that it can have a consistently positive impact on performance. This is clearly a path less traveled, but it builds on proven principles of human behavior.

The Performance Management process presents the third primary element of the total reward system. It is the process that impacts performance between the paychecks. It is more real-time to managers and employees, and provides the basis on which results are measured. It is the gain-making component of a comprehensive approach to gain-sharing. It is the bonding agent in programs that direct rewards to true performance. Finally, it is what managers do and what self-managed work teams engage in that enhances their positive impact on others. In this way, performance management offers the fundamental process through which an organization can realize true collaboration.

Notes

1. Milkovick, G. and C. Milkovich, "Strengthening the Pay-Performance Relationship: The Research," *Compensation and Benefits Review*, November-December, 1992, p. 53.

2. Longenecker, C. and S. Goff, "Why Performance Appraisals Still Fail," *Journal of Compensation and Benefits*, November-December, 1990, p. 36.

3. Deming, W. E., *Out of the Crisis*, Cambridge, Mass.: MIT Press, 1986.

4. Longenecker and Goff, op. cit.

5. Wyatt Company, "Compensation and Performance Management Practices in Companies with Total Quality Management," A study conducted for the U.S. General Accounting Office. Washington, D.C.: U.S. General Accounting Office, 1991.

6. Garbor, A., "Take This Job and Love It," *New York Times*, January 26, 1992.

7. Latham, G. and K. Wexley, *Increasing Productivity Through Performance Appraisal*. Reading, Mass.: Addison-Wesley, 1981.

8. Bernardin, H. J., and P. C. Smith, "A Clarification of Some Issues Regarding The Develpment and Use of Behaviorally Anchored Rating Scales," *Journal of Applied Psychology*, Vol. 66, 1981, p. 458.

9. Odiorne, G., *Management by Objectives: A System of Managerial Leadership*, Belmont, Calif.: Fearon Pitman, 1965.

10. Drucker, P. F., *The Frontiers of Management*. New York: Harper & Row, 1986.

11. Latham and Wexley, op. cit,

12. Balcazar, F., B. Hopkins, Y. Suarez, "A Critical, Objective Review of Performance Feedback," *Journal of Organizational Behavior Management*, Vol. 7, Fall 1985/Winter 1986.

13. Hogarth, R. M., "Beyond Discrete Biases," *Psychological Bulletin*, Vol. 90, 1981, p. 197.

14. Cooper, W. H., "Conceptual Similarity as a Source of Illusory Halo in Job Performance Ratings," *Journal of Applied Psychology*, Vol. 66, 1981, p. 302.

15. Longenecker and Goff, op. cit.

16. Civil Service Reform Act, Public Law 95–454, 1978, 92 STAT.

17. Daniels, A., *Bringing Out the Best in People: How to Apply the Astonishing Power of Positive Reinforcement*, New York: McGraw-Hill, 1994.

10

Measuring Customer-Focused Performance

If you can dream it, you can create it.
> —WALT DISNEY
> *The Man Behind the Mask*

You see things; and you say, "Why?" But I
dream things that never were; and I say,
"Why not?"
> —GEORGE BERNARD SHAW
> *Back to Methuselah, 1921*

In the previous chapters we explored a variety of reward systems, the problems with current practices, and innovative ideas or approaches for developing new ones. In each discussion we focused the reward system on specific performance measures that would reflect desired behaviors. The actions of people produce results. Performance is a function of behaviors. Hence, behaviors and measures are a critical link to an effective reward system.

Further, the performance of an organization often defines its competitiveness in the marketplace. Because customers usually have choices, this performance needs to be defined in terms of the customer's needs. If an organization is able to focus its measures on the needs of the customers and if its people are able to act accordingly, that organization will clearly have a competitive advantage.

This chapter will examine ways of developing performance measures so that they focus on the needs of the customer. The emphasis on the customer is important because many performance measures used by companies focus more on the need for internal control. For example, the number of units a team produces in a day is a control-oriented measure, while the time it takes for a customer to receive an order is a customer-focused measure. With a customer focus, the measures can be used as the foundation for an effective rewards and reinforcement system.

Traditional Approaches to Performance Measures

The idea behind traditional approaches to compensation management is to use the measures imbedded in the compensation plan to implement the strategic aims of the company. While this is theoretically appropriate, many managers wind up using this process to exert greater control over their workforce. For example, measures such as expense to budget, error rates, number of units per time period, customer complaints, scrap rates, return on investments, absenteeism, and government or safety compliance lead managers to seek problems in current performance. Managers focus on ways to create greater control over the workforce, rather than seeking actions that will enhance the value to customers. As a result:

1. Performance measures are used to identify problems and highlight the points at which performers are not meeting standards.
2. Performers are required to complete reports to senior management, but get little or no feedback from them.

Not surprisingly, performance measures have acquired a bad reputation. The news that an external consulting firm has been hired to develop performance measures for a particular work unit, for example, is likely to elicit a general reaction of fear and concern among the performer's involved. Will this effort identify what the individuals are not doing right and/or will it simply require more work to collect and provide data to senior management? Will it lead to layoffs and/or some other punitive action in which the data will be used against the performers?

Dr. Edwards Deming stipulates as his eleventh point: "Eliminate work standards (quotas) on the factory floor. Substitute leadership. Eliminate management by objectives. Eliminate management by numbers, numerical goals. Substitute leadership."[1] His reasons are very clear. Management has come to use measurement systems as a means to control and punish workers. Employees' normal response is to avoid being measured, to seek ways to do just enough to get by, and to negotiate with their supervisors. These are low-value-added activities, because they emphasize the relationship between the supervisor and the performer rather than focus on the customer. Leadership, in the model presented in this book, is to provide clarity of direction and positive reinforcement for people taking desired actions. As Deming points out, the emphasis must shift from setting standards to using measures to monitor and manage work activities.

Many executives are concerned about providing too much information to their employees. They hold certain beliefs about employees' response to data. These include the following:

1. *Employees won't understand or care about the information.* They won't have the sophistication to comprehend the data or use it effectively. They won't even be interested in it, so it will be a waste of time.

2. *Employees will use the information against management.* Once they figure out how much profit is really being generated by their performance, they will want more of it. They will seek more expenditures on the workplace or more compensation for themselves.

3. *Employees will give the information to the competition.* If employees really understand the competitive strategy of the business, they will somehow leak it to a competitor, who will then use the information against the company.

There is a kernel of truth in these assumptions. Employees *won't* understand the data or care about it unless the information is presented in terms to which they can relate. This makes it the executives' responsibility to translate corporate measures of economic returns, market share, and product positioning into terms that employee *can* understand. An initial process of education is required before employees can fully relate to the numbers that executives deal with on a daily basis.

A manufacturer of industrial shelving products, for example, provided a series of infomercials for its workforce on understanding product costs, gross margin, customer returns, and production forecasts as part of their biweekly business updates. It took approximately three months before management could use a common set of concepts and language to discuss the ongoing state of the business. The process was based on the need to create economic literacy in the workforce. This information was part of the feedback process in support of the company's gain-sharing program and has become a very important element in building the desired partnerships within the workplace.

When employees have experienced an environment based on negative reinforcement for many years, they do not necessarily react warmly to information about large profit margins. They may feel that they were deprived for years in order that some executives could enjoy lavish lifestyles. In many cases, they are correct, and their response is perfectly understandable. Thus, when financial information is presented about large profit margins, they need to understand how these funds are being used to support other areas of the business. This can set in motion various challenges to management decisions (such as justification why funds from a "cash cow" are transferred to an "invest-and-grow" segment of the business). The point here is not that strategic decisions should be opened to the workforce, but that employees should be helped to understand the rationale on which strategic decisions are based.

Management's concern that the information may fall into the hands of competitors is usually unfounded. More competitive information is lost by way of executives and senior technical contributors who are hired by competitors than by way of disgruntled members of the workforce. In most cases little useful competitive information is provided through such sources. Further, the success of a competitive strategy lies more in the execution of a company's own efforts than in knowing about a competitor's plans. The information provided to employees through performance measures is seldom of interest to competitors except in terms of benchmarking performance levels.

For all these reasons, the focus of performance measures needs to shift from one of control to one of providing sufficient information in a timely and understandable manner so that performers can begin to take the decisive actions needed.

Developing a New Purpose for Measures

Performance measures, in their most fundamental state, translate the strategic requirements of a business into actions that people can take. In this context they serve several important purposes:

1. *Measures provide the focus for taking action.* When performance measures are effective, people know what to do. They bring the vision into focus. They bring the strategy into everyday consciousness. They identify the critical priorities of the business. They define what is expected and what will be inspected. They become the basis on which

people take, or do not take, certain actions. Further, they define whether success is achieved by internally based action or is dependent on events that occur outside the target group. They describe results in terms of short-term actions or long-term development efforts. Overall, they provide the clarity of direction people need to engage in the desired work of the organization.

2. *Measures provide the basis for monitoring work activities.* Measures provide the information necessary to provide feedback to the performer. They enable the performers to know whether or not they are taking the correct actions. Further, they provide a basis for establishing desired performance levels. Measures need reference points, such as historical or baseline performance, competitors benchmarks, or corporate objectives. These reference points provide meaningful milestones or calibrations for monitoring activities. The desired end point is reached when the performers themselves track, monitor, and display their own performance data, making it more immediately useful, usually more reliable, and surely more meaningful to them.

3. *Measures create opportunities to provide positive reinforcement.* Measures that are used to threaten people will yield actions in which people avoid or manipulate data. They may indicate that certain performance levels are impossible to reach or that certain activities cannot be measured reliably. When measures are used for positive reinforcement, people are more likely to appreciate them, because they associate them with gaining something they want or value. These gains may be external, such as praise from supervisors, peers, or customers, or internal, such as the inner satisfaction of seeing a process take shape in some desired fashion.

This process is clearly reflected in our use of measures for personal, nonwork-related activities. Most sports activities, for example, like golf, bowling, baseball, and tennis, have scoring systems built in; the measurement system defines the game. For other activities, like cooking, sewing, painting, jogging, hiking, fishing, and skiing, we tend to a different kind of measure, defining success in terms of excelling our "personal best" level of performance. When measures are used to achieve reinforcement, they become a natural order of things within the activity and are desired by the performer.

Measurement systems are an integral part of any purposeful human activity. They need to be utilized in ways that create a rewarding environment to encourage performers to go on striving to do their very best. In the work environment, the focus of measures needs to be on meeting the needs of the customer.

Developing Measures with the Customer's Needs in Mind

As discussed above, most traditional approaches to measures center on finding the right mechanisms to direct and control the work. Without a focus on the customer, this search for the right measures can be a confusing, conflict-ridden, and complicated process.

There is an alternative approach. The model shown in Figure 10-1 describes a four-step process that begins with understanding the customer and ends with understanding what people need to do within the unit or target group. Focusing the measurement process on the customers and what they want will greatly increase its chances of success.

The first step involves developing a customer profile:

- Who are your customers?
- What do they want?

All groups have customers. The customers may be internal or external to the organization. This analysis should reflect a horizontal line of sight in the organization. Senior management or shareholders are beneficiaries of the effort; they receive something of value in return for

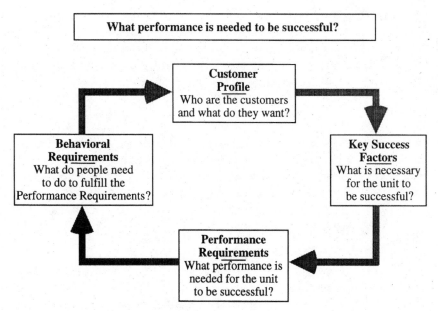

Figure 10-1. Performance measures.

providing sponsorship and capital investments. But senior managers should not be customers. (This is not to say that profitability or economic value added are not important, because they are a measure of success for the entire company and should be a concern for all.)

After identifying the customers, it is possible to identify or describe what the customers want. What exactly does the customer need from the unit's products or services? The requirements may include factors related to quality, delivery performance, reliability, low price, functionality, responsiveness, special design, etc. A useful task in developing measures is to verify these requirements with customers or those with direct knowledge of customer needs.

The second step is to summarize the needs of the customers in terms of the key success factors (KSFs) of the unit. Most target groups have multiple customers. KSFs help define the primary factors by assessing the risks and interdependencies in the customer-supplier relationships. Key success factors reflect the priority areas that will determine whether the unit is successful. They are based on an understanding of the customers' wants as well as on the group's *core competencies*—the work the target group does particularly well. KSFs are the link between these competencies, customer needs, and the viability of the group.

The third step involves identifying the indicators that show whether or not the group is fulfilling the key success factors. These indicators, called *performance requirements,* should clearly relate back to the customer's needs and provide the information necessary for the target group to know whether or not it is successful.

The fourth step involves identifying what behaviors on the part of the target group are necessary to fulfill the performance requirements. These behaviors (which may include starting or increasing certain actions and/or decreasing or eliminating certain others) should be identified as specifically as possible so that the target group fully understands what it needs to do to be successful in serving the needs of the customers.

These four steps, as illustrated in the business analysis formats shown in Figures 10-2 and 10-3, usually provide all the information necessary for selecting performance measures. The critical considerations in selecting the right measures include assessing both the environment and the opportunities for performance improvements. When clear, independent measures cannot be identified, it is an indication that the group may be too interdependent on others to achieve specific results. In other words, the performance of the unit depends more on factors in its environment than on the actions taken by people within it. It can also happen that the measures are appropriate but the unit does not have the ability to track or perform the necessary actions. In either case, there is clearly a need to develop a deeper understanding of the performance requirements of the unit.

CUSTOMER PROFILE

Nursing   Right product at the right time, at the right place

Managers   Delivery of products as ordered

Purchasing   Inventory information is timely and accurate

Senior Management   High level of service at minimal cost

KEY SUCCESS FACTORS

Unit supplies are filled to meet demand

Inventory levels are minimal to maximize turns and cash flow

Actual inventory supplies match general ledger

Nursing and managers feel they receive responsive service

PERFORMANCE REQUIREMENTS

Fill rates equal 95%

Inventory turns equal 14 times per year

Inventory levels are ± 2% of general ledger

Nursing units are satisfied with level of supplies and responsiveness

Turnover rates are kept to a minimum

BEHAVIORAL REQUIREMENTS

Being present and punctual

Being responsive to call for assistance or complaints

Coordinating with other locations in getting needed supplies

Handling of materials in a safe manner

Being courteous and friendly to customers

Accurate and timely handling of information

Figure 10-2. Example of the business analysis for the materials management department at ABC hospital.

The Why's and How's of Taking Action

Once the unit has defined the requirements for performance, it is important to know exactly how to achieve them. The purpose of this process, which is illustrated in Figure 10-4, is to link the desired

CUSTOMER PROFILE

Patients	Caring, respectful, timely service
Nursing	Patients delivered to the right place at the right time
	Being kept informed
Billing Office	Complete and accurate patient information
Physician's Office	Timely scheduling
	Billing information is complete and accurate
	Know patients are treated well

KEY SUCCESS FACTORS

Complete and accurate patient information

Patients feel well cared for

Nursing and physicians feel well informed

Minimal time to admit patients

Physicians feel they have ready access

PERFORMANCE REQUIREMENTS

90% of patients admitted in 25 minutes

90% accurate rate on billing information

Nursing and MDs satisfied with assignments

Patients feel informed and well cared for

95% of pretests and procedures completed

BEHAVIORAL REQUIREMENTS

Collect and compile information from patients

Display sense of caring and consideration to patient, physicians, and nursing

Inform nursing of problem in a timely manner

Figure 10-3. Example of the business analysis for the admitting department at XYZ Hospital.

results to a hierarchy of value-creation activities. The answers to the core question—How can this desired result be achieved?—form a basic hierarchy of results or actions that will define the overall process necessary to achieve the desired ends. Once this first level of results is defined, the same question—How can this be achieved?—should be asked about each subordinate result, and the process should be continued until each of the desired actions, behaviors, or tasks has been sufficiently defined. Figure 10-4 uses this process to define some of the tasks mecessary to achieve on-time delivery.

The process can be verified by selecting a task or result and asking, *Why* should this be done? The answer should lead one to the next level up the hierarchy. If intervening variables are discovered when one asks why, they should either be added to the next level up or take their place as an additional layer in the action-planning hierarchy.

This process is similar to a Pareto analysis, root-cause analysis, or cause-effect diagram. The focus, however, is on the *hierarchy* of actions necessary to accomplish a desired end. By asking how and why, one can outline the tasks needed to achieve the required results and then pinpoint the measures needed to monitor the performers' progress in achieving them.

When to Use Results and When to Use Behaviors

In some cases it is more important to focus on the actions that contribute to the desired results than it is to focus on the results themselves. While one may jump immediately to establishing measures based on the performance requirements (Step 3 in Figure 10-1), one should consider whether the target group might be better served by examining the behavioral or process elements (Step 4 in Figure 10-1).

One should select *results* when the following conditions exist:

- The current results are at a relatively high level, and the desire is to encourage incremental improvements.

- The results are clearly improving, and the desire is to reinforce this progress.

- The performers are highly skilled and competent to perform the tasks necessary to achieve the desired results.

- There is a high correlation between the actions people take and the results they achieve, reflecting the target group's degree of control over the performance factors.

On the other hand, one should select *behaviors* or *process* when the following conditions exist:

- The current performance is a long way from the goals.

- New skills and behaviors are needed to achieve desired results.

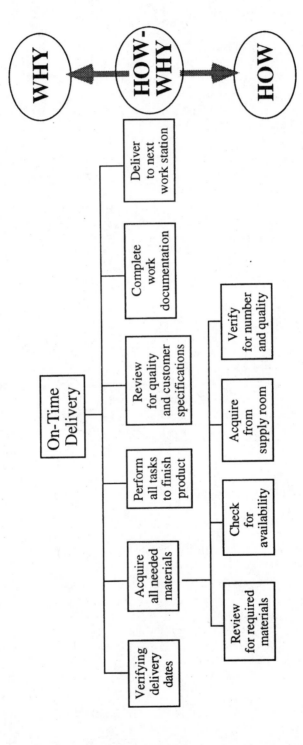

Figure 10-4. Selecting the measures: the measurement hierarchy.

- The results are very delayed, or there is a long interval between what people do and the opportunity to measure the results.

- There are many intervening variables or forces outside the influence of the performers that impact the results.

If these are the conditions, the measures should focus more on the specific actions people take or on the progress they make in the key result areas.

What It Takes to Make a Measure Reinforceable

Within this context, the measures can be selected and developed to focus the efforts of the target group's members. The traditional paradigm regarding measures often makes them impersonal and negatively reinforcing. For example, traditional concepts dictate that measures should be:

- Objective

- Outcome oriented

- Time-bounded

- Able to define the level desired

- Able to reflect a stretch in performance

Consider these criteria. When measures are outcome- or result-oriented, they usually encourage people to focus on *what* was done, not *how* it was done. In cases in which there is a clear relationship between action and result, this focus may be appropriate. However, many of the total quality management principles stress the importance of understanding *how* one achieves desired results, in order to enhance the process.

When measures identify a time deadline and only indicate a single pass/fail level of achievement, they may be perceived as carrying an implied threat. The inclusion of a stretch element may actually indicate that the probability of achievement is remote. In each of these cases, the measure defines what the performers are *not* doing, rather than what they are doing well and can further improve.

Measures that reinforce desired performance should fit the following criteria:

1. *Positive.* Measures should be expressed in terms that are viewed as positive by the team members and that create opportunities for providing positive reinforcement in and of themselves. If the data is being charted, for example, progress can be shown by a line or

bar moving up. The terminology used should underscore progress. Instead of measuring late shipments, a chart can measure on-time delivery; instead of measuring error rates, it can measure error-free rates or 100 percent accepted rates; instead of measuring amount of cost reduction, it can measure amount of savings achieved.

2. *Reliable.* The measures and methods of capturing the data should be consistently accurate and verifiable. These criteria reflect both the nature of the data-collecting process and the administrative feasibility of providing the information. Further, administrative systems should be viewed as supporting elements, rather than as restrictions and demands to which the measures must comply.

3. *Objective.* Measures should reflect the work that is actually performed. Judgments by a single individual can be distorted. An assessment based on perception data collected from a large number of people who have used specific measures has considerably more credibility and objectivity. The measures need to reflect what is actually done, quantitatively or qualitatively.

4. *Action-Oriented.* Measures need to reflect the aspects of work that the performer can do something about to achieve desired progress. If people can actually achieve the result by doing nothing, you do not have a good measure. For example, reducing waste can be accomplished by doing no work. The goal should be to find how to use 100 percent of the materials.

5. *Controllable.* Measures need to describe work or tasks that are within the influence of the performer. Although very little is actually within a performer's total control, the point is to select measures that are to a high degree within his or her ability to impact. The reason is simply that the organization is preparing to pay additional compensation or rewards for achieving desired performance. It should know that what it is paying for is truly achieved by the performer. This assures that the return on investment can be determined accurately.

6. *Timely.* Measures and feedback should reflect those actions that can be determined on a timely basis, depending on the overall time frame of the business cycle—monthly, quarterly, or annual, or longer. The measures should tell performers if they are not being successful in sufficient time to allow them to respond. Although there is little hard scientific evidence, the author's experience indicates that the performance data should be reviewed at least three to five times before an incentive payout calculation is determined. In order words, if you have a quarterly incentive plan, the data should be provided to the performers at least monthly, if not weekly or biweekly.

These six criteria provide an acronym of *PROACT,* a shortened form of the critical word *proactive.*

The Types of Measures That Make a Difference

When measures focus on the customer, they tend to fall into a two categories: those that define the *economic variables* of the organization and those that define the *values* of the organization. By economic variables I mean those actions which utilize the resources of the organization to create value for the customer. They are the value-added drivers of the business, because they represent a methodology that utilizes the resources and competencies of the organization. Some of these measures may include the following:

Revenues	Costs
Resource yields (ROI, ROA, etc.)	Timeliness (cycle time, delivery, etc.)
Accuracy	Reliability
Service	Customer satisfaction
	Market position

By their very nature these measures are indicators of how well the organization uses its resources to meet the needs of its customers.

The second category of measures relates to the values and culture of the organization. These measures define the methods by which the organization fulfills its mission, how it becomes a special place, and the principles that underlie the nature of the work it performs. For example, value-oriented measures may include the following:

Competencies/capabilities	Development of talent/skills
Empowerment/commitment	Integration
Improvement	Responsiveness
Involvement	Teamwork
	Safety

By their very nature these measures are indicators of the behaviors reinforced within the firm. They are important when the organization needs to examine the process by which it accomplishes its economic-based objectives.

Within this context, measures tend to be oriented to one or a combination of three areas. First, they are oriented to *resource utilization*— they assesses the degree to which the tasks performed are completed using various levels of input (in terms of materials, effort, skills, dollars, etc.). The key strategy is to perform the tasks at the required level of performance using minimal resources. This creates the basic value added model of performance.

Value-added measures are becoming increasingly popular. They are essentially a method of establishing the difference between the worth of the inputs and the worth of the outputs. This fundamentally measures the economic value of the transformation process. In its most simple form, one would determine the cost of materials, labor, equipment, etc., and the market value of the final product to determine the current value added. Then, incentives or other awards would be based on increasing this difference. In more sophisticated forms, economic value added (EVA) has been used for establishing executive compensation. In this application EVA is determined by measuring the difference between net operating profit after tax and the weighted cost of capital employed by the firm. The capital is defined by the total debt and equity of the firm, and cost of capital is determined by cost of debt (i.e., effective interest rates) and the cost of equity. O'Byrne reports that this type of measure is used to determine executive compensation at Coca-Cola, ATT, CSX, and Wal-Mart, to name a few.[2]

The second area is *time to market*. Every task requires some time to complete. As Jack Welch of General Electric has indicated in numerous speeches and writings, speed is a key competitive advantage. The more time it takes to perform a task, the more additional resources it usually requires. And for most firms, meeting the time commitments of the customer is essential to achieving a competitive advantage.[3] Many organizations are attempting to use cycle time as a primary focus for change and continuous improvement.

The third area is *customer satisfaction*. Unless it meets the needs of the customer, the process has failed. A *customer* is simply defined as one who uses and depends on a unit's products or services. The degree to which a group meets or exceeds the expectations of its customers—whether they be inside or outside the organization—is the degree to which it will be able to retain them. Meeting or exceeding customers' needs is key to continual survival and prosperity.

Examples of Measures and What They Do

Measures come in many shapes and sizes. In Figure 10-5 you will find a list of measures that focus on a variety of end results. The list is designed to stimulate ideas and enable the reader to identify measures that may help him or her to accomplish a desired end. Organized around a variety of functional areas within an organization, the list presents only a few of the many different measures organizations can

Function	Measures	Contributes to
Sales		
	Revenues	Customer satisfaction
	Account penetration	Customer satisfaction
	Product mix	Customer satisfaction
	Accuracy of sales forecast	Resource utilization
	Customer returns	Customer satisfaction
Operations		
	Delivery schedule	Time to market
	Productivity	Resource utilization
	Scrap/waste rates	Resource utilization
	Error-accuracy rates	Resource utilization
	Units per hour	Resource utilization
	Costs per unit	Resource utilization
	Cycle time	Time to market
	Rework	Resource utilization
	Work in process inventory	Resource utilization
	Equipment uptime	Resource utilization
Distribution		
	Delivery schedule	Time to market
	Shipping costs	Resource utilization
	Cycle time	Time to market
	Shipping accuracy	Resource utilization
	Inventory turnover	Resource utilization
Engineering		
	Product/process costs	Resource utilization
	New product introduction	Customer satisfaction
	Work in process inventory	Resource utilization
Finance		
	Report/task timeliness	Resource utilization
	Report/task accuracy	Resource utilization
	Outstanding receivables	Customer satisfaction
Purchasing		
	Material costs	Resource utilization
	Material quality (incoming)	Resource utilization
	Inventory turns	Resource utilization
	Material availability	Time to market
	Material receipt schedule	Time to market
	Accuracy of inventory records	Resource utilization
	Inventory fill rates	Resource utilization

Figure 10-5. Representative list of performance measures and their impact.

Function	Measures	Contributes to
Quality Assurance		
	Product test accuracy	Resource utilization
	Product error rates	Resource utilization
	Awareness of quality	Customer satisfaction
Human Resources		
	Costs to hire	Resource utilization
	Time to hire	Resource utilization
	Succession availability	Resource utilization
	Project completion	Customer satisfaction
	Competitiveness of pay	Resource utilization

Figure 10-5. (*Continued*) Representative list of performance measures and their impact.

use to drive performance. Each needs to be examined in terms of the actions necessary to achieve the desired results.

Alignment Increases Their Strength

The issue facing many managers and employees is not the lack of measures but the lack of their alignment and integration. Organizations that have a history of strong command and control structures often have many measures. They are often conflicting and seldom relate clearly to the competitive strategy of the business.

ATT places a significant emphasis on aligning measures to the competitive strategy of their business divisions. They call them "The Golden Threads" of the business. The hierarchy of measures model discussed earlier, the how's and why's, enhance the ability of a firm to trace measures through the organization. This is significant because when measures are clearly aligned with the key factors to a firm's success, they gain strength and importance to the people whose actions determine the performance.

One of the more useful tools in achieving an alignment is the Balance Scorecard. R. Kaplan and D. Norton[4] describe a process to integrate a variety of measures into a management framework. While each organization develops a variety of measures, they tend to fall into the areas of finance, internal business, innovation and learning, and the customer. Specific measures are developed in each of these areas, and monitored on a regular basis. This Balance Scorecard approach expands the focus of executives from simple profitability, gross margin, and return on investment indicators of performance to a broader, more holistic perspective of the organization.

Furthermore, a focus board offers a visual display of the alignment of measures.[5] Essentially a focus board is a display of four to seven critical dimensions of performance for a business unit, such as a plant, a division, or a company. These dimensions are listed across a large board. Under each dimension are the goals, measures, projects, or other reactions that support performance improvements. Further, some organizations use these boards to display progress and results. They may show charts, photographs of key players, comments from customers, etc. Hence, these boards create a visual display of the primary drivers of the business and create opportunities to reinforce the progress and the performers.

Once again, the value of performance measures is determined by their alignment with critical competitive strategies and their meaningfulness and association with positive reinforcement for the organization's members.

What Makes Performance Measures Meaningful?

Executives and managers are often very preoccupied with performance measures. There is a belief that if one gets the performance measures right, the right actions will follow. Organizations often spend thousands, if not millions, of dollars on developing performance measurement systems. Measures are used to provide managers with the information necessary to take action. Often this action is viewed as punitive by employees. When new systems are effective, people will start to respond to the new information in desired ways. When desired performance is not realized, managers tend to increase the pressure in various ways (by yelling louder, for instance).

As discussed in Chapter 3, antecedents precede a behavior or action. They are important because they provide the performer with the information to know what to do. If they are effective, antecedents get a set of behaviors started. Measurement systems help the organization provide feedback to the performers. Consequences determine whether the individual will continue to practice new behaviors. Goals are essential to achieving desired end results, but they are only the first part of the process.

We can understand the role of measurement and feedback systems when we view them from the perspective of the performer. If a team is made aware that late shipments are a serious problem for the customer, measuring on-time performance will not cause resentment. Measures used to enhance workers' understanding of quality—in relation, for example, to the completion of a report, the production of a component, or the handling of a sales call—empower those workers to focus their skills on achieving the quality desired. Measures provide meaningful and immediate feedback to the performer so that necessary actions can be taken. Without such information, the quality of the product or service produced may be inconsistent.

From a manager's perspective, measures can become a vehicle for communicating what is important about the operation of a given unit. Whether linked to the strategic plans that guide an organization, to product development schedules, to productivity levels, or to costs, measures provide an important means of communicating with the workforce.

If performance is not at the desired level, a manager can take action to improve the antecedents or pinpoint the problems or barriers to performance. These corrective steps will work if the performers associate these tasks with achieving more desired consequences. They will fail to work if, after providing the additional reports or collecting more data, the performers hear nothing about the results. Without any response as to whether the information was of any value, was correct or incorrect, or was even read by anyone, performers will see the measurement system as just adding unnecessary work. This condition—what we call the extinction process—can be swiftly followed by the process of negative reinforcement.

Negative reinforcement occurs when individuals perform the necessary tasks for no other reasons than to avoid unpleasant consequences. If performers are receiving little value from providing the information required by the measurement system, they will either stop doing it or do just enough to get by. Their reports will be received when due, the product specifications will be met (but not exceeded), and all innovations and fresh ideas will remain private.

To keep measurement systems from becoming associated by performers either with extinction (no one cares) or with negative reinforcement (do just enough to get by), they need to be supported by positive reinforcement. This reinforcement may grow out of natural consequences in the work itself or come from others in the performers' work unit. *Natural consequences* are similar to intrinsic rewards—meaning that the performers find greater satisfaction in their work. Measures can make this possible by providing them with new information that enables them to greatly improve the quality of their work. The external sources for positive reinforcement can come from their supervisors, peers, employees, or customers. In such cases, measurement systems become associated with developments that enrich the value and contribution the performers associate with the work they do. (Chapter 3 discusses various forms of reinforcement in more detail.)

To summarize, measures can accomplish several important tasks:

1. *They add focus to the work.*   After a work process, procedure, or desired practice is explained to performers, measures aligned with these priorities can provide necessary information on how well the employees are performing in these areas. The measures add meaning and concrete reality to the directives given to individuals or work teams. If something is worth doing, its worth measuring.

2. *They provide a source of feedback to performers.*   Measures are meaningful only when they generate useful feedback. In fact, it is difficult to separate measures from feedback. In this context, feedback is not a judgmental assessment of performance but actual, real-time data about work done. Measurement information that is not given to the performers involved is misdirected. While managers may be the beneficiaries of the information, the performer is and should be the primary customer of the measurement system. (In the author's experience, misdirection of feedback is the root cause of the inability of many organizations to realize any value from measurement systems.)

3. *They create opportunities for providing positive reinforcement.*   In terms of compensation or recognition programs, measures are the most important element in their design. They define the areas in which improved performance is sought and determine the basis for additional pay. In pay-for-competencies-employed systems (see Chapter 5), they form the basis for assessing competencies and rewarding growth. In gain-sharing or team incentive plans, they define the results the team must achieve to receive incentive payments or equity-based awards. In individual pay-for-performance programs, they define the expectations and contribution requirements. In special recognition programs, they form the basis for giving recognition. Finally, they define the difference between positive reinforcement and a mere "ata boy/ata girl" response.

Summary

Under the old paradigm of command-and-control management, the role of the manager was to use measurement and information systems to find out which employees were not performing their assignments correctly in order to mete out punishment. Information was used to play "gotchya" with the employees. In fact, many of today's employee safety programs work by encouraging employees to report on their coworkers—a way of using fear to manipulate behavior in the workplace. This is not collaboration, and it does not produce desired behaviors. People may in fact simply go underground or display undesired actions in more subtle and damaging fashions.

Measures in a collaborative environment are used to provide performers with information on performance as quickly as possible, to empower them to correct or celebrate desired achievements, and to create opportunities for communicating the value and importance of their efforts. The customer for measures is the performer, not management, and the individuals involved are set up for success rather than for punishment. They view their work as creating value, as contributing to something greater than themselves, as an opportunity to benefit the customer, and as a means of gaining something personal and important from the process. This is the foundation of collaboration and for a new and meaningful use of measurement systems.

Notes

1. Deming, W. E., *Out of the Crisis.* Cambridge, Mass.: MIT Press, 1986.
2. O'Byrne, S., "EVA and Management Compensation." *ACA Journal,* Summer, 1994, p. 60.
3. Ticky, N. and R. Charan, "Speed, Simplicity, Self-Confidence: An Interview with Jack Welch." Harvard Business Review, September–October, 1989, p. 112.
4. Kaplan, R. and D. Norton, "The Balanced Scorecard—Measures that Drive Performance." *Harvard Business Review,* January–February, 1992.
5. Loafman, B., "Envision Your Priorities—The Focus Board Alternative." *Performance Management Magazine,* Tucker, Ga., Vol. 8, No. 1, p. 35.

11

Changing from Control to Contingency

Nothing endures but change.
—HERACLITUS, FIFTH CENTURY, B.C.

Too much of a good thing is wonderful.
—MAE WEST

Building collaboration, commitment, and customer focus in an organization is fundamentally a process of changing behaviors. According to a survey reported in the July 26, 1993, issue of *USA Today*, the central issue in total quality management efforts is human behavior. Of the CEOs participating in the survey, 91 percent agreed that "the biggest challenge in TQM involves changing human behavior, not mastering technical skills." Only as organizations realize that the key to their organizational change lies in creating different conditions for human behavior will change become permanent. While perhaps not the only important factor contributing to those conditions, reward systems are certainly a powerful element in the pattern of changes an organization needs to make to remain competitive and prosper in the future.

The previous chapters have addressed various aspects of reward systems. We have seen that what makes them effective is tied to the SMART criteria. (Note: The opposite of SMART is DUMB: Doesn't

Understand Managing Behaviors!) This chapter will describe how to develop a strategy for achieving desired change. No idea, however brilliant and needed by the organization, will succeed if it is not integrated into an effective process for change, and being right does not mean being effective. Creating conditions that will minimize resistance and maximize acceptance of new ideas is a central challenge for the agent of change.

Understanding the Context of Change

Virtually every industry, and therefore every organization, is experiencing increased pressure to change. Whether the changes are to focus on customers, increase services, introduce new products, reduce costs, reduce cycle times, improve delivery performance, build alliances, or eliminate waste, people need to do things differently. In traditional, hierarchically based organizations, change usually means a fundamental shift in the way business is conducted and behaviors are managed.

In the book *Danger in the Comfort Zone,*[1] Bardwick describes this challenge of change quite well. In traditional organizations, employees traded loyalty for job security. Workers were told what to do and where to work (which sometimes included moving to a different city), and they were expected not to question the decisions of those in authority. Employees were expected to perform according to the accepted norms and practices of the firm. In return, they received a job for life, protection from fluctuations in the marketplace, and regular pay raises that kept pace with inflation. Although operational employees were sometimes laid off, they were expected to return to work when needed as part of their employment contract. This sense of entitlement worked both ways—the organization and its employees each got what they expected.

As Bardwick points out, people do not appreciate what they have when they are enjoying an entitlement environment. Their advantages are expected, taken for granted. The irony is, they want more. They feel they deserve more. They expect the organization to protect, provide, and promote them. The roots of this management philosophy, as Bardwick indicates, go back to many organizations' sincere desire to address the pain of the Great Depression of the 1930s. As individuals who had been affected by that national crisis succeeded to positions of authority in organizations, they wanted to protect their employees from the risks of an uncertain and devastating business environment. This approach grew out of paternalistic values, and had the associated positive and negative impacts.

A sense of entitlement is created when people receive something they want without having to do anything special for it. They receive regular pay increases. They receive their annual management bonus or stock option awards. They participate in the annual awards dinner. The sense of entitlement creates an expectation that is not associated with performance or taking certain actions. This is a noncontingent environment.

In contrast, in an achievement-oriented environment, people are frequently rewarded for achievements and feel they have earned what they receive. In this context, people feel confident, and empowered for taking risks and succeeding. Empowerment occurs when people have the opportunity to take risks—to fail or succeed—and *want* to take the necessary actions. If they fail, they may be disappointed or depressed, but they can also seek to learn why and how to prevent it in the future. If they succeed, they feel confident, powerful, and valued.

In this context, *success* can be defined as contingently receiving positive reinforcement. When people receive reinforcement for taking risks, they are likely to be willing to take such risks in future. If they fail often enough, they will experience extinction or punishment consequences (see Chapter 3), and the frequency of desired behaviors will decline. Success builds confidence. If a person is frequently called upon to make presentations and receives significant positive reinforcement each time, he or she will gain confidence. The root of success and confidence therefore is positive reinforcement.

In contrast, when people receive punishment or extinction (non recognition) for their work, they come to believe they are not very good at it. Failure that is not turned into a learning process or made into an opportunity to find or receive reinforcement will be regarded as a punishing event. It is also true that when people receive something not actually contingent on their actions, they may appreciate it for a while, but soon grow to expect and want more (entitlement). A classic example is annual pay increases that are common to all, and given regardless of performance.

Chapter 1 described the process of change in the environment and the implications for the organization's attempts to do things differently. Fundamental to this process is the creation of a "stake in the business" for the employees. Creating a stake means sharing the risks of failure and success with the employees rather than protecting them from the forces of the business environment. Nothing is certain in an environment where people share in the risks of the firm. This means *moving from a paternalistic to a partnership environment.*

The significance of this concept is essential to developing a strategy for implementing change. People who are used to an entitlement environment are likely to *expect* an incentive payout. If they receive the payout however well or badly they do their work, the entitlement environment is reinforced. If, on the other hand, they believe they may not receive the payout unless they take certain actions, the organization begins to operate on the basis of contingency.

Being in a partnership means sharing risks and consequences. Creating a stake in the business or performance of the unit means that there is a risk inherent in what the team does to satisfy its external customers. Measurement and real-time feedback are part of the process of determining whether these results are being achieved. Further, as shown in the chapter on performance appraisals, desired behaviors are encouraged when performers believe that there is a reasonable opportunity for achievement. If they feel they can win, watch out, here they come!

In many organizations the stated policy of "pay at risk" or "pay for performance" is actually misleading, particularly when the determination of pay is based on the subjective assessment of managers using little precise performance measurement. In this situation the "risk" is viewed as being dependent on how a manager evaluates employees' performance, not on how the marketplace (internal or external) values their actions. This means control, not contingency. As shown in the last chapter, few managers have the ability to judge performance accurately without precise measures. Therefore, judgment-based assessment of performance is often quite ineffective despite being called "pay at risk" or "pay for performance."

Rewards that are indeed contingent have a clear element of risk associated with them. If the risk is too great, a performer will not put forth the effort, but if the risks are perceived as within reason, desired actions are likely. In an *entitlement environment,* people simply expect that they will receive what they want, and the general atmosphere is likely to be one of lethargy and boredom. In a *compliance environment,* people receive little reinforcement for their efforts. In fact, they may be punished in very subtle ways for taking certain actions. But in an *achievement environment,* people perceive the risks and opportunities as doable. (See Figure 11-1.)

Measurement and feedback are the tools that enable rewards to be associated with achievement and demonstrate that they are contingent on performance. The balance between risk and security is related to that between success and failure. Risks will be taken when people feel there is a reasonable probability of success. Security will be sought when the forces that determine success are perceived as outside the control of the performers. The probability of success or failure is what defines the extent of the risk. In the pure entitlement environment, people never experience failure nor do they experience the joys of success. Success means accomplishing something that was not certain—that was *at risk.*

In a risk-*averse* organizational culture people do not necessarily

	Descriptions	Root Cause
Entitlement	• People expect to be protected, provided for, and promoted. • They want more, feel they deserve more. • They focus on the threats to stability and security.	• Increases in pay levels are non-contingent. • Things work according to a time schedule, not performance. • There is little perceived need to change the way things are done.
Compliance	• They do what is expected and seek clarity of goals. • There is limited desire to take risks or do things differently. • They focus on the actions of the leader.	• Increases in pay are based on achieving specific, personal goals. • Consequences primarily are extinction and negative reinforcement • The focus is on the threat or prevailing practices.
Achievement	• They do what is necessary to achieve desired results. • They challenge conventional practices, unless they work. • They focus on the tasks to be done.	• Measurement is used to identify winners. • Feedback is welcomed because it is used to aid improvements. • Positive reinforcement exists at a greater level than other consequences.

Figure 11-1. The impact of consequences on the culture.

receive rewards without earning them; instead, they are likely to experience punishment or extinction consequences for taking actions that are not the "way we do things around here." As stated in Chapter 3, the culture of an organization is a function of what behaviors are rewarded and punished. The more individuals fail to realize the importance of change and continue to operate in this "expectancy entitlement environment," the greater will be the challenge when change is attempted.

The task of achieving change through alternative reward systems is usually very dependent on the historic role of consequences within the organization. If the consequences are basically noncontingent, the organization is functioning in an environment of entitlement. If the consequences entail being ignored (extinction) or punished for not achieving specific standards or working outside prescribed patterns, the organization is functioning in an environment of compliance. If the consequences involve rewards and reinforcements for accomplishing desired results, the organization is functioning in an environment of achievement.

Understanding the Personal Experience of Change

If there is one critical lesson for today's executives, it is that "Quality is not an act. It is a habit." A habit is a set of behaviors that are a regular part of an individual's practices. A habit is created by a history of reinforcing consequences in the workplace or in an individual's life. Knowledge and skills are retained when their use leads to the achievement of desired results (i.e., positive reinforcement). The effectiveness of these consequences, or their impact on the individual's beliefs about what works, will determine how ingrained are the habits the individual displays. This historical pattern of consequences defines the paradigms within which the individual operates.

To change behaviors we must first understand the history of consequences and the impact they have had on the individual. If the current actions are rooted in long-established habits, we need to utilize consequences that address the historical consequences, assumptions, and expectations of the individual. We need to create a desire for change that is based on a combination of understanding clearly that current practices are no longer acceptable and seeking to acquire new skills and practices because they offer attractive reinforcements. This is using a combination of negative reinforcement and positive reinforcement. To challenge an individual to abandon current habits without giving him or her reason to be confident of reinforcement for new practices will almost certainly lead to resistance.

The degree of change required in people's habits will determine the difficulty of the change process. This is often referred to as *resistance to change*. If we are looking for a minor, incremental refocusing of existing practices, the change effort may be relatively simple. If we are looking for a major breakthrough, a fundamental redirection of actions, the process of change will be quite involved.

In Chapter 6 I discussed the seven key questions that determine whether an organization is ready for a variable pay program. In developing a broader strategy for change, we should understand the factors leading to readiness and those that indicate resistance to change. This will enable us to develop a strategy with a high probability of success.

When a change is viewed as entirely positive, it is unlikely to encounter resistance. The reason most change is resisted is that people have to give up a perceived level of reinforcement for a different type of reinforcement. This "giving up" or "letting go" implies that certain behaviors will no longer be reinforced and that the consequences of extinction or punishment will be in operation. These consequences are frequently not perceived as positive by the individual. If, on the other hand, performers can perceive the changes as better than continuing to do what they currently do, the resistance will be minimized.

Organizations that are struggling with resistance to change are often making the mistake of emphasizing antecedents as the major drivers for the change efforts. These antecedents may be special training, communication programs, and speeches by the top executives. In such cases, one is asking the employee to give up a well-known and established relationship between certain actions and their reinforcement for a yet-to-be-realized new consequence. If the employee perceives the new consequences to be better than the existing ones, he or she may be willing to listen.

The likelihood of change will be enhanced or diminished by the organization's track record. In other words, if previous management efforts to bring about change have not been associated with positive reinforcement, it can have a negative effect on employee response to *new* efforts.

Campaigns associated with quality circles, merger integrations, and reorganizations, for example, have often been driven by antecedents— training, job descriptions, organization charts, communications, meetings, etc.,—rather than by positive consequences. Hence, when executives begin new efforts, such as self-managed teams, empowerment, and quality management, employees are justifiably skeptical that any meaningful change (i.e., positive consequences) will result. This can lead to such comments as: "Why should I do this? What's in it for me?" (an employee) and "How do I do this on top of everything else I have to do?" (a manager).

Reward systems that offer change that is perceived as positive by the employees and managers and seen as meaningful to them personally are the first major steps to providing positive consequences for change. The risk of not receiving the reward (e.g., negative reinforcement) ensures that a entitlement mentality will not be created. Although such reward systems offer an opportunity, there is no guarantee that they will be successful.

The Fibers Division of DuPont disbanded their gain-sharing program because of negative reactions by employees when the program was beginning not to pay out. Employees were unwilling to share in the risks associated with a deteriorating organizational performance because there were no other positive consequences for doing so. The stake in the business and the creation of a partnership-oriented organization mean that there will be elements of risks. The challenge in the design and management of a reward system is to minimize the risks associated with the operation of the plan while retaining the risks that are associated with performance.

Much has been researched and written about the impact of change on the individual. Perhaps one of the more important works in this area is that done by Elizabeth Kübler-Ross in her work on understanding the stages an individual experiences when going through the cycle of death and dying.[2] The stages are illustrated on in Figure 11-2 and described in the context of organizational change below.

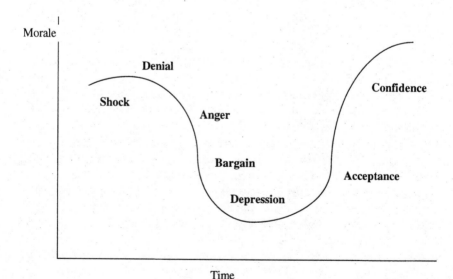

Figure 11-2.   Stages of resistance to change.

When introducing a change in a reward system, there should be a strong business need behind it. The need is often based on a change in the environment of the business such that continuing to operate in traditional ways will lead to a serious, if not a threatening, situation. Employees need to understand this. The creation of a business partnership means that all parties need to understand and appreciate the impact of the risks they share in common.

When employees or others within an organization are told that things cannot go on as always, there is often a *shock*. The work of Grayson and O'Dell[3] indicates that many American businesses are operating under a "two-minute warning." The public media is full of articles about companies that are facing major survival issues or threats to their future. Employees need to know how and why external conditions are impacting the prosperity or survival of the organization. The value of the shock is that it indicates what needs to change and why.

After the basic shock has worn off, the next expected response is one of *denial*. Employees offer excuses as to why *their* actions have not contributed to the problems and why they don't really need to change. They may question the validity of the data, or need to have the information confirmed by outside parties or by internal resources. They may insist that the process is likely to affect competitors before it affects them. In some cases, whole organizations may isolate themselves and withdraw to situations that were known and reinforcing in the past. Each of these responses is an attempt to return to the previous situation so that changes are not necessary.

Once the reality of the situation begins to sink in, the expected response is one of *anger*. There may be major complaints about other departments, blaming them for the current situation. People may lose faith in senior management, be angry at the engineering department, blame the lack of effort in marketing or sales. The response may turn in on itself and be directed at other members of individual teams. Every effort should be made to discourage this essentially futile venting of rage and fault-finding. The source of these feelings is the realization that the reinforcements people are used to will no longer exist in the future and that there is no absolute certainty as yet regarding the replacement reinforcement.

If anger doesn't work, the next process is one of *barbaining*, as people seek to negotiate with those in authority to retain some semblance of the "way things were." This may involve collective actions or individual attempts to circumvent the system so that their own environment can be protected. For example, a group that was having its piece rate incentives replaced by team-based incentives sought to have the measures for team performance be the same as those used in their individually-based plan. Not being successful at this, the group sought to delay the implementation date by either offering to produce more products or threatening to slow work down immediately. Each of these proposals was an attempt to bargain a way out of the decision to change the pay systems.

Once such attempts have been unsuccessful—the process cannot be denied, the anger gets no response, and all efforts to negotiate a better deal fail—the next stage is *depression*. In this condition, people give up hope. They say they don't understand why the change is occurring or what is really being done (though in truth they really do). There is often a sense of longing for the "good old days" or uncertainty and fear about the future. Nevertheless, people begin to try things differently, hoping against hope that they may be successful.

From the effort to try a few things comes a level of *acceptance*. This involves people seeking to understand what the new requirement will involve. It may entail their taking some steps to move in the desired action, and to do so with sincerity. The extent to which they receive a good response (i.e., positive reinforcement), will determine whether their new behaviors are reinforced. As positive responses gather momentum, and the performers accept the replacement of the "good old days" with the "good days *today*," the process moves forward.

If new efforts continue to be reinforced, employees begin to experience a level of *confidence* as a result of their experience of success. As this grows, an achievement-oriented environment, characterized by focusing on the desired tasks, knowing how one is doing, and celebrating incremental and breakthrough accomplishments, becomes a reality.

The length and breadth of this process of change can vary dramatically in relation to several factors. First, the *degree* of change is important in the impact of this process. If the change is minor—limited in the extent of its "newness" to the workforce—the process usually goes through easily. People may question why they need to change, while they recognize that it is important. If they are swiftly reinforced for exercising the new behaviors, they will see that the new approach is better than the old. But when major changes in physical structures, working conditions, or power structures are involved, the process may take longer and encounter more resistance.

Second, the effective use of *data* is important in managing resistance to change. Data is needed to demonstrate the reason for change. Employees have all heard the generalized preaching of doomsayers, either within or outside the organization, and they usually discount their words. But specific data that indicates declining market share, declining competitiveness, increasing costs, lower profitability, reduced staffing, etc., lends credibility to analyses. Data that is used to reflect progress, reinforce the actions people are taking, and show improvements in important areas can also minimize potential fear and build an achievement environment.

Third, *reinforcement* of desired actions can demonstrate that the new way is better than the old. Part of the process of change is letting go of old habits that were reinforced in a certain way and reinforcing new, desired actions. Reinforcement can both minimize the negative impact of change and shorten the time needed for people to experience a better situation than they had before. Reinforcement that is insincere and not based on valid data, undermines the credibility of the intent. Therefore, measurement, feedback, and celebrations tied to incremental improvements in achievement are critical to attaining the desired change.

Typical Reactions to Changes in Pay Systems

Although this process is described in terms of major change, there are common reactions of employees to changes in their rewards systems. These will likely be encountered when a new reward system is being introduced.

1. *Why are you doing this? (Am I at fault?)* This question is about understanding the true reasons for instituting a change in a reward systems. An employee's initial concern usually involves looking for ways in which the new program is really intended to punish them for something. This will be all the more true if past changes, particularly ones involving measurement, were associated with efforts to identify who was not living up to the performance standards. Or, they want to see how the program will support other strategic or organizational changes currently being employed. They may also wonder about the sincerity of the effort.

2. *What do I need to do differently? (Will it be worth the effort?)* Most organizations that implement team-based variable pay plans with operational or administrative employees encounter a suspicion that this new program is just intended to get them to do more work or manipulate them in some other way. There is a suspicion that the true emphasis is to get them to work extra hard, with little true appreciation of what they do now. They then judge the potential rewards in relation to the extra efforts they need to expend, indicating their belief that the payout is merely a bribe. It is very important at this stage to get people to see the value of working differently, of working smarter rather than harder, and of working with an opportunity to share in the success of the unit.

3. *What will you be taking away? (What do I have to give in exchange?)* Although the American Compensation Association study indicated that 84 percent of the group-oriented incentive plans were instituted

on top of current base pay programs,[4] most employees feel that these plans will be used to reduce or eliminate their base pay increases. From the organization's perspective, why should they increase their compensation costs with no change in performance? Employees are concerned that something will be taken away, and they want to understand what and how. They will then judge the value of the plan in relation to the opportunity to do better, discounted by the risk inherent in the plan and experience over time.

4. *If we are truly successful, will you take it away? (Is this just a more sophisticated way to punish us?)* If employees believe that management's response to their success will be simply to raise the performance bar and thus make them "unsuccessful" again, the proposed change will fail. People are skeptical of change because their experience (i.e., reinforcement history) has been that the new efforts did not live up to expectations. We need to address the level of expectations people have for the new plan, as well as build their confidence that the value of the plan will be sustained. This latter point can only be achieved through repeated actions consistent with the stated purpose and principles of the plan.

5. *Are you sincere and committed to make this work? (What will happen to the plan when this senior manager/sponsor moves on?)* People are often concerned with continuity and the unknown future. When a plan looks attractive on the surface and then has as a positive impact on the employees, people are concerned about losing it. People simply do not like to lose a source of positive reinforcement. In an era of continual change, most of which people find has a negative impact on their work experience, there is a natural suspicion that "this too, will soon pass." Nothing can be guaranteed, but assurances and action to support these words are an essential element of a successful plan. Herman Miller Furniture and Lincoln Electric Company, for example, have had their incentive plans for more than 50 years. Their managers have continued to be committed to the success of these plans. The employees have continued to benefit economically from the firm's performance, and each company has continued to be a leader in a highly competitive business environment.

In summary, in order to minimize the negative impact of the change, there are several important actions to take. These are:

- Explain why the program is necessary; make the explanation data- and facts-oriented.

- Clearly state what people specifically need to do differently and what they do not need to change.

- Don't back off from the commitment; listen to the resistance but do not yield if you believe the plan is the right thing to do.

- Focus positive attention on those supporting the changes and ignore—i.e., use extinction to silence—the complainers and skeptics.

- Use measurement and feedback to track progress.

- Reinforce every aspect of performance; don't rely on the payout to provide the reinforcements necessary to achieve change.

The essential objective in implementing changes in reward systems is to demonstrate how the new programs will make people better off than before for doing the necessary actions. The emphasis needs to be on strategies to improve performance and how people will be able to share in the results based on their achievements.

Developing Strategies for Change

As discussed above, the process of change can be a relatively straight-forward effort or involve considerable time and effort. The challenge is defined by the degree of change, the history of reinforcement, and the credibility of management. Further, selling the program to senior managers may also involve overcoming resistance. You need to develop a strategy of selling the program "upward" as well as "downward." The overall strategy will need to include several priority elements: dissatisfaction with the status quo; a vision of how things could be; a plan of action; a structure to support the change; and reinforcement that shapes and celebrates progress.

Dissatisfaction with the Status Quo

People must understand that there is a problem and the reasons underlying it. The information needs to come from a reliable source and be backed up with facts. Data is essential to establish the credibility of any concern about the current situation. If people do not accept that there is a problem, they will be unlikely to support a change. This is particularly true of executives, who usually have to sponsor and/or approve changes to reward systems. They will give only marginal support to a suggested change unless they see exactly how it can solve a problem.

A sense of dissatisfaction with the status quo can also develop as a result of a crisis or a continual deterioration of a firm's ability to compete. The crisis can be regarded as a fight for survival for the firm. In this situation the continued prosperity of the company is in doubt. The risks are very present and very great. This type of condition often demands a *re-creation* strategy of change. This requires the firm to totally rethink its current strategy, structure, and business processes. Actions need to be swift, bold, and targeted to keeping the organization alive.

Another pressure for change can arise from the need for continuous improvement to be more effective than one's competitors. This can amount to an *incremental* change, but one that engages large elements of the organization. Many total quality management efforts that are not driven by survival needs are this type of change. Overall, this approach implies that there is no immediate threat to survival but that the organization needs to anticipate and adjust to developments.

These two categories of change reflect differences on a continuum. Re-creation needs immediate, decisive action by all members of the organization. Incremental change means focusing on creative, innovative ways to improve the firm's competitiveness. Re-creation change often implies a reengineering of basic work processes, restructuring the organization at a fundamental level, and implementing efforts to enhance the firm's ability to survive. Layoffs, downsizing, divestitures, etc. are often examples of re-creation change. In contrast, incremental change involves thoughtful, analytical assessments and the development of the firm's core capabilities. (See Figure 11-3.)

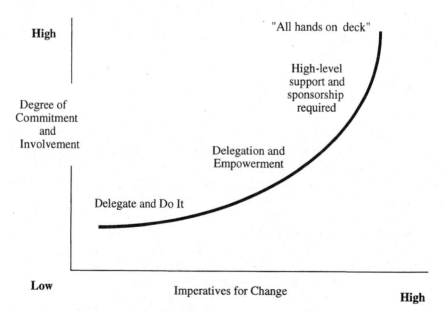

Figure 11-3. Determining the degree of involvement necessary.

The degree of dissatisfaction with the status quo has a major impact on the nature of the change required. Obviously, re-creation change can be fueled only by a major level of dissatisfaction, while incremental change depends on a sufficient level of dissatisfaction to keep the pressure for change alive.

The issues at stake are the most compelling if they are recent and derived from sources external to the organization. When the pressures for change are related to past practices of the organization, its members are likely to be defensive and treat the information skeptically. People generally do not like being punished, especially for something that occurred in the distant past. For example, a chief executive of a large health maintenance organization wanted to spur action to increase productivity and attention to customers by the physicians. He hired a consulting firm to conduct a benchmark study comparing the organization with others in the industry, and used the data to demonstrate the organization's poor performance. Instead of getting the desired response, he encountered tremendous resistance to change, and the process of improvement was set back for several years. Had he discussed how the market characteristics had changed and how the organization needed to adapt to remain competitive, the outcome would have been very different.

Dissatisfaction with the status quo needs to be expressed in terms that are important to the listener. If the audience is direct labor, one might stress the risk to job security. If the audience is executives, one might stress the costs associated with current practices or increasing the chances of survival, competitiveness, and continuity for the organization. In marketing, the emphasis might be on competitive pressures or a loss in market share. In engineering, the emphasis might be on the loss of technical leadership. In human resources, the emphasis might be on increased turnover, employee relations issues, or a decreasing ability to compete for talent in the marketplace.

Finally, the degree of change needs to be comparable to the level of dissatisfaction. If there are few risks to survival, the change needs to focus on incremental improvements. If the risk is primarily future-oriented, the change needs to focus on increasing the capacity to respond to emerging threats. If the risk is the core survival of the firm, the change needs to involve an "all-hands-on-deck" strategy, with a strong and firmly directed campaign.

A Vision of How Things Could Be

The primary utility of a vision is that it can draw people to it. Unlike dissatisfaction with the status quo, which is essentially negative, a vision of the future can describe an attractive alternative. The vision creates in the mind of the target group a view of how things can operate, should operate, and will operate if certain changes are made. It needs to relate to the values and concerns of the target group. Therefore, what may be attractive to an executive group may not be attractive to an operational group. The vision needs to inspire, attract, and offer a meaningful opportunity for reinforcement. In other words, "We are not bricklayers. We are builders of cathedrals."

Much has been written about the value of vision and leadership.[5] In terms of our focus on reward systems, the vision can describe a context that will enable the organization to improve its competitiveness and work life. Then the changes in the reward systems will provide a means to that end. In selling the changes to the pay systems, the task is to demonstrate how the new program will produce a strong return on investment in terms of compensation costs (to executives) as well as work effort (to participants).

A Plan of Action

Once people understand the risks for the status of quo and share a vision about how things could be, there needs to be a plan for how to close the gap. The action plan should include:

- What needs to be done
- How will it be done
- Who will do it
- What and when they need to do it
- What it will cost, in what time frame, and with what return on investment

The action plan provides the road map for taking action and defines the short- and long-term steps necessary for the program to be successful. It needs to define accountabilities as well as identify the resources necessary to achieve success. Further, it defines a way to measure progress and reinforce the improvements desired. Finally, for an action plan to be truly meaningful, it needs to define the specific next steps necessary to start the process going.

A Structure to Support the Change Effort

Great ideas and good plans are important to achieving necessary change, but they need to be supported by a specific structure. By *structure*, I mean that roles need to be defined, people need to assume these roles, and action needs to be taken. The literature on organizational change is helpful in understanding three key roles. These are described below.

Sponsor. The *sponsor* is the one who authorizes and sanctions the change effort. He or she needs to be someone with sufficient power to set the change effort in motion. (In consulting terms, it is usually the client whose decisions determine whether the change effort will be engaged.) The role of sponsorship is a key focus for top executives of an organization. By their actions, they support the process as well as reinforce efforts. They provide support when resistance is encountered by those within or outside the unit. Finally, the active commitment of the sponsor is necessary for efforts requiring moderate to large-scale change.

As has often been said, management commitment is an essential prerequisite to organizational change.[6] The focus needs to be on relating the level of commitment necessary to the degree of change required. For example, if one simply wants to develop a different salary increase guide to reflect teamwork, a major public display of commitment by senior executives is probably not necessary. But if one is shifting pay systems from individual- to team-based as part of an overall corporate strategy to increase interdependencies within the firm, then senior managers' active involvement will definitely be necessary.

Management sponsorship and commitment can be gained in two ways. First, there can be a "leap of faith" on the part of management that what is being developed and implemented will produce the desired effect. Although a similar change may have worked for other organizations, there is no guarantee that it will produce the desired impact in this case. Thus, management will need to "trust" that these changes are worth the effort.

The second way of gaining management sponsorship is through "earned commitment." In this case, the organization tries pilot or demonstration sites and analyzes the impact of the changes. As initial success is achieved and can clearly be related to the new program, management commitment increases. Commitment that is earned is usually more lasting and valuable than that gained in a leap of faith, though a "leap" swiftly followed by supporting results is perhaps the best combination. In my experience, executives are reluctant to attempt any major change unless they are confident that it will achieve the desired results.

Champion. This is the person who leads the change effort within the organization. The *champion* is often very knowledgeable about the specific technology for change and may serve as an internal consultant or project manager. This role is often referred to as that of *change agent*. The champion needs to believe sincerely in the new technology or process, and will be accountable for making it successful. Hence, it is important that he or she fully understand what is needed and have the skills (or access to the skills) necessary for the change to be successful. The champion's commitment is closely tied to his or her inner values and personal objectives, but the individual must have credibility and influence within the organization so that his or her efforts are valued by other members of the organization.

Target Group. This is the group that will be the focus of the change effort. The target group is the unit within the organization in which the change effort will be initiated, established, and demonstrated. This may be a division, a department, a selected team, an organizational level, or the entire company. The sponsor needs to be related organizationally to this group, but should not be part of the group. This is the unit most likely to express the resistance, in that it will be the one whose actions need to change first. In planning the change effort, this group needs to be well understood in terms of the degree of impact it will experience, the extent of change required of it, and the reasons for its members' potential resistance.

Reinforcement that Shapes and Celebrates Progress

This final area of the change process addresses the need to understand the concept of *shaping*. Simply stated, people will begin to try new actions when they feel reinforced for them. The tasks should initially be relatively small. Then, as success is experienced, the focus can change and new levels of performance can be achieved. In essence, we need to create "early wins" in order to create a positive momentum for change. Further, as we learned about behavior research in Chapters 2 and 3, people continue to excel when they receive positive reinforcement for improvements in their performance at a level greater than just achieving a goal.

If more change is required than the organization can tolerate, people will experience an extinction consequence, in that they may feel more punished than reinforced for their efforts. Breakthrough change efforts can be achieved when people associate significant reinforcement with taking required actions or necessary risks. This concept is illustrated in Figure 11-4.

The expectation of change in behavior needs to correlate with the capacity to measure and reinforce these efforts. If people are successful, they must feel a sense of celebration. This reinforcement needs to occur frequently at first. Then, as results are achieved and need to be sustained, the reinforcement can occur less frequently and on a more variable basis. This strategy relates to the behavioral concept of schedules of reinforcement.[7]

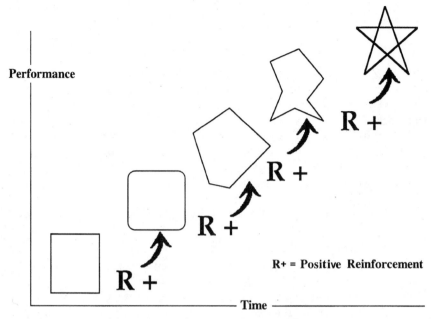

Figure 11-4. Shaping is the process of reinforcing change.

If the desired behavior begins to decline, the cause may lie in one of several areas. First, there may be insufficient reinforcement to enable people to feel valued for their achievements. The key is to increase the rate and variety of reinforcements. Second, the reinforcements may no longer be perceived as meaningful to the employees. This is the concept of *satiation*.[8] In one large technology firm, employees were given ham and biscuits whenever they achieved a goal. While this was nice at first, it soon seemed meaningless and mechanical. A similar syndrome has been experienced in organizations that have made frequent use of ball caps, T-shirts, dinner passes, or pizza parties. The challenge is to use *creative* reinforcers, ones that are experienced as pleasant, welcome surprises.

Third, the individual or group may be reaching a level of maximum capacity in which obstacles within the system are preventing them from achieving expected levels. There are ultimate levels of capacity for individuals, teams, and organizations. The problem may be barriers within the organization or systems surrounding the work that cause certain goal levels not to be achieved. The task is to understand why this is happening and what should be done—and then do it.

Finally, organizations that experience change as exciting often increase the number of priorities to the point at which people cannot focus. For example, a heavy industrial manufacturing company experienced a decline in the change efforts after thirty separate major programs where initiated. While executives often feel that more is better, the reality is that at some point the change efforts actually begin to slow down. This problem is illustrated in Figure 11-5. The solution is to refocus on the critical priorities, perhaps showing how actions in some areas will have a multiple impact on other areas. Although there is little valid research to demonstrate it, the conventional wisdom is that people can handle only two to three major initiatives at one time. The level of change employees can tolerate is often directly tied to their history of reinforcement in similar efforts.

To recap briefly, the process of successful organizational change requires understanding and action in each of the five areas noted above. The degree of effort required in each is a function of the gap between the current situation and the desired situation. The extent of involvement in the change process and the level of sophistication required by the areas noted above are determined by the change gap. Otherwise, the time required to achieve the desired results will the significantly extended or the level of success will be compromised. If the objectives are important to the organization, if they represent an financial, competitive, or survival impact on the firm, it cannot waste the time or costs on half-hearted or overly ambitious efforts. These dimensions of organizational change should offer some guidelines for achieving the desired goals. (See Figure 11-6.)

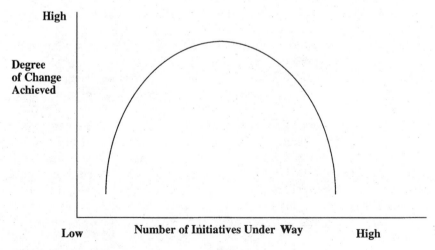

Figure 11-5. The impact of too many things to do.

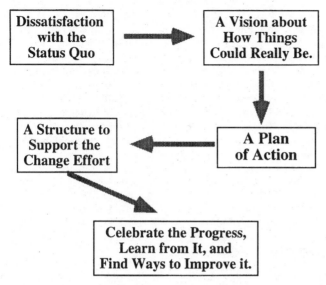

Figure 11-6. Key dimensions of achieving desired change.

Situational Strategies of Selected Case Studies

Thus far this chapter has provided the conceptual and process dimensions for achieving organizational change. We will now examine several specific case studies to help the reader understand how these principles can be applied to various reward systems.

Case Study: Shifting from Piece Rate to Team Incentives

The Mustang Manufacturing Division (a fictitious name but an actual company) was facing increased competitive pressures as patents on its key products began to lapse. In order to survive this threat, the company needed to reduce manufacturing costs—primarily materials usage and scraps rates—introduce new products, and improve its product delivery performance. Mustang had a piece-rate incentive system that basically paid workers additional money when the number of units produced exceeded an expected standard on an weekly basis. Many regarded this program as a major contributor to the firm's productivity.

On closer examination, several problems in this incentive plan emerged. First, the standards had not kept pace with the investments in process, and employees were receiving clearly above-market pay levels. Second, the amount of scrap, rework, and remake was excessive. There was little concern about material usage since it was not measured in the plan. Third, the firm was late on its shipments between 10 percent and 15 percent of the time. Finally, the plan served as a surrogate for management. Supervisors basically felt incapable of managing performance because of the restraints of the incentive plan.

The senior executives decided that to address the changes needed in the manufacturing area they would eliminate the piece-rate incentive system and establish a team-oriented, gain-sharing program. (Wilson provides a full description of how this kind of plan was put in place.[9])

The process of change involved several important elements. First, the senior executives began holding meetings with all employees on the current status and future of the business. They discussed specifics and displayed data indicating that the market environment was changing rapidly and that, if the firm did not respond effectively, it would face certain decline. Second, they decided and informed employees that the piece-rate system would be terminated at the end of the current fiscal year. The reasons, they explained, were that the measures and inherent characteristics of the system were no longer compatible with the firm's competitive response strategy. They indicated that while there was a need to decrease costs, they sought to do this through materials and not labor costs. They would guarantee a portion of the workers incentive pay (i.e., add it to a base rate); another portion would be guaranteed for one to three years (declining over time); and another portion would need to be earned through a team-based, gain-sharing plan.

As expected, there was a significant negative reaction, particularly from the high-earners in the incentive system. They expressed denial and anger and a number of times tried to negotiate the plan. Senior managers understood their concerns and met with many of them individually. These meetings sought to explore the potential impact on the individuals' earnings and show how they could earn comparable levels through the new plans. But there were no side agreements and the elimination of the piece-rate incentive plan went on as scheduled.

It was important in this communication to explain the pressures for change in terms of external factors and to focus attention on the need to respond to a major crisis. It was also important to reassure people about what was *not* going to change and to indicate that change would follow a clear road map. Much of the communication was done in small groups in which the executives could meet and discuss issues face-to-face with their employees.

The process of developing the new gain-sharing plan involved a task force of operational, management, and technical professionals. The measures were directly tied to the competitive strategy, and progress was reported on frequently. As the firm implemented the new pay system and performance in the key areas improved, there were celebrations, at which people discussed how they took certain actions to retain customers, increase savings, cross-train others, improve the process, and strengthen the firm's competitiveness. The very real threat to their survival was translated into a spirit of change that was truly remarkable.

Case Study: Implementing Team Incentives in a Low-Trust Environment

Nelson Electric Glass company (a fictitious name but an actual company) manufactured glass panels used in television sets and computer terminals. The quality of its products and their specific features, such as weight, durability, etc., were essential elements of Nelson's competitive strategy. While the demand for its products remained strong, it faced significant internal issues. The firm was unable to effectively implement changes in the manufacturing process because of certain traditional management practices. Nelson had major walls between departments within the manufacturing site.

There were even rules that employees could not go to other departments without written permission from supervisors. The environment could have easily been characterized as one of "low trust."

The senior managers wanted to change the culture in the firm to enhance teamwork, communication, and responsiveness across departments. The goals were to decrease all costs, increase productivity, retain competitiveness, and attract new customer orders. While a team-incentive plan works well in a high-trust environment, could it work to *create* trust in this setting?

With an understanding of this organizational context, the design process and the plan itself were focused on improving teamwork within the firm. While the employees were very excited by the prospects of greater teamwork, the managers and supervisors felt very threatened. Their concern was centered on how they had managed in the past and on their potential loss of control or authority. They were unclear about what they needed to do differently, or how to increase teamwork while still meeting their production goals. They were skeptical that a team-oriented process would enable them to achieve their business goals. They not only needed to be convinced, they needed to be reinforced for their efforts to these ends.

The design process included creating a cross-functional team of managers, operators, and functional specialists (finance, marketing, engineering, human resources, etc.). They met periodically with the senior management team (a new expression within this environment) to review their progress. The senior managers expressed their complete support to the team and sought to reinforce each member for his or her contribution throughout the design process.

When the plan was being finalized, the design team met with senior managers, supervisors, and employees in focus group settings. They presented the plan and discussed how to change the process of working together. They sought reactions and answers to specific questions from each focus group. The data from these meetings was then summarized and integrated into the final design plan and implementation strategy.

One of the key components that lead to the success of this plan was the feedback obtained on results at a total division and unit level. The weekly results were communicated in a large display for all members to see. Each department had its own charts and graphs in its work area that tied directly to one or more of the key measures for the total division. The plan paid out on the total divisional results, but significant reinforcement and celebrations involved the work of each team. There were frequent surprise visits by senior managers to each work area to discuss the ways achievements had been made. For example, one group developed a very creative solution to the hand-off process between shifts. This idea was then communicated to other teams with similar needs with the hope that they could build on the idea.

The results included improvements in productivity, quality, and reduced costs. Employee grievances went down by 50 percent, and employee safety problems were virtually eliminated.

Although trust was an overriding issue in this case, it was not the focus of the intervention. Instead, the process and the resulting reward systems concentrated on improving performance and increasing the celebration, reinforcement, and financial reward of all performers. Trust was the *result* of these efforts, not the aim. In this way, people could respond and adjust their actions to understand and value their fellow employees.

Case Study: Implementing Team Incentives with Skeptical Management Commitment

Landmark Medical Center (a fictitious name but an actual company), is a major teaching hospital and like many of its counterparts in the health care industry, faced increasing competitive and financial pressures. It had implemented numerous actions to reduce head count, delay pay increases, and minimize purchases. The results were always productive initially, but the cost pressures soon returned. The vice president of human resources felt that implementing team incentives at the departmental level would provide a much-needed push to reduce costs and enhance the quality of services. However, the chief executive and several other senior executives were concerned that such programs might create undesired disruptions in the organization. They were concerned about increasing costs or conflict within the medical center.

The strategy was thus to develop pilot or demonstration sites that would be meaningful to the organization and yet not commit it to an undertaking it could not handle. Three departments were selected because they represented a variety of different operations—clinical, administrative, and operational. Further, the supervisors in all three departments were quite strong and highly committed to this effort. The medical center completed the "Readiness Analysis" described in Chapter 6, and the three departments were approved as pilots.

The design process focused on three principal areas. First, sound and effective plans had to be developed for each department. Second, as the plans were being developed, the medical center had to develop its approach and guiding principles for team incentives; the process needed to be compatible with other areas of the hospital that might be interested in developing similar plans in the future. Finally, the process had to increase Landmark's internal capacity to design, implement, and manage such programs. There was an important learning process required from both a content and an experiential point of view.

To accomplish this there was a steering council made up of

representatives from each of the three pilot groups as well as several of their key customers—the nursing and finance departments in particular. After training in the design of incentive plans, the council broke into three design teams. Each team was composed of the manager over the target group, a primary customer, and an independent third party (i.e., human resources). The steering council met periodically to review status reports by each of the design teams. There were important reinforcement meetings because of the effort involved. The meetings also ensured that organization-wide design issues could be addressed effectively. The steering council presented the final plan recommendations to the hospital's senior management and the compensation committee of the board of trustees.

The results were very impressive. Not only did each plan yield a significant return on investment for the medical center, but employees in the pilot groups felt very special. They were members of the cutting edge and they received significant attention for their efforts to improve the quality of their functions and services to customers. Finally, the pilot projects were expanded to many areas throughout the organization and the new areas, too, achieved remarkable improvements in their performance.

Lessons to Be Learned from Successful Change Efforts

These three case studies illustrate several key concepts related to implementing change.

1. *Focus on the vital few.* Change efforts that are not clearly focused on addressing specific issues are seldom successful. The need for change has to be explained, as does what can be expected in the way of results. People need to understand what needs to be different and why.

2. *Tie changes in the reward systems to the needs of the business.* While this may seem obvious, it is essential that people see that the reason the changes are being introduced is to support the needed changes in the organization. I often say to executives, "If you can achieve the same results in the same time frame without changing the reward systems, do it." Reward systems simply offer a better way to achieve certain objectives than do current methods of management. Furthermore, they may serve as a catalyst to other changes needed within the organization—in systems, management practices, and working relationships.

3. *Clearly communicate what will be done.* The program, whether focused on changing the organization or implementing reward systems, should state the purpose clearly. It often needs to be presented within the context of broader change efforts. Provide examples to help people understand. Demonstrate the sponsor's commitment and

involvement. This will tell people that the process is going to happen and there is no turning back.

4. *If you don't have the support you want, find the support you need.* Individuals are often promoted to senior executive positions for reasons other than their management philosophy of collaboration, teamwork, and customer focus. They may have a reinforcement history that leads them to conclude certain paradigms are truth. If these are inconsistent with the champion's objectives, don't waste time trying to "move a mountain." Instead, find pilot or demonstration sites in which strong sponsorship *is* available. Then, as results are achieved, use this as compelling evidence to gain broader or higher-level sponsorship. If the change plan is valuable to the organization, then the more time that is spent trying to "sell up" or gain extensive management commitment, the more likely it is that costs will become excessive, competitiveness will decline, and the firm will lose much-needed assets (i.e., people).

5. *If appropriate, involve the target group in the design process.* Each of the three case studies involved plan participants in the design process. The value of this is threefold:

- You increase the chance that there will be support for the changes by the target group.
- You increase the probability that the plan will be effective, relevant, and understood by the participants.
- You enhance the level of confidence and trust in the new system.

However, not every situation requires target group involvement. For example, the decision to eliminate the piece-rate incentive system was not accomplished through a consensus decision-making process. Decisions that are right for the business are sometimes best made in an executive fashion. While input to a decision may be of value, the decision needs to be made by someone who has ultimate accountability for its impact. Another consideration in limiting involvement is time. When there is a deadline for a union contract, fiscal year, or some organizational changes, a design team process may not be appropriate. Design teams may take from three to six months to complete their tasks, depending on the complexity of the assignment. If they are not included in the process, the target group participants will have to be persuaded by how the plan is communicated, implemented, and managed over time.

6. *If others are involved, give them the freedom to design the right plan.* Executives who are excited and impatient about designing changes to reward systems often want to prescribe numerous dimensions of the new plan. For example, they may stipulate who will be eligible and

who will not, the level of payout or additional compensation, the types of measures, the frequency of payouts, etc. If a design team is used, they must be given the freedom to consider all the facts and develop the best plan possible. Otherwise, if the executives prescribe the plan provisions or ignore/deny the team's recommendations because of personal values, the chance of a successful plan will be severely limited. The executives may express their desires and wishes, and the design team should consider them. The design team needs to consider many perspectives, and the ultimate design plan needs to support a variety of constituencies. In this way, the use of a design team can be legitimate and sincere.

7. *Define what people need to do differently and how they will benefit.* Personalizing the measures and the reinforcement process will enable people to see how they will benefit from the proposed change. Describing what people should continue to do as well as what needs to change will give individual performers a strong sense of direction. These antecedents need to be supported by the reward system and underlying management practices (i.e., performance management). Describe the opportunities for reward, recognition, and reinforcement in terms that will be meaningful to them.

8. *Design the best possible plan and realize that it will need improvements over time.* A frequent concern of many design teams is that the plan they create needs to remain untouched for at least five years or that it must somehow be perfect. While in theory one does not want to change the basic features of a plan too frequently, plans do need to be improved as they are implemented. It is important for the target group and sponsors to realize that improvements should be made, consistent with the basic plan purpose and design principles. Each of the design teams in the above case studies stayed committed to do the very best job they could, and each plan has become better over time. In this way we realize that we truly do live in a world that requires "continuous improvements."

9. *Monitor and reinforce the process of change.* The measures inherent in the new reward system offer an opportunity to monitor the progress of the change. However, they often need to be supported by more detailed and unit-specific measures. These numbers indicate the true process of change. By monitoring them, one creates additional opportunities to reinforce progress. By using feedback and reinforcement, people can become excited by the small, everyday wins. When issues emerge, the solutions can be developed on a real-time basis. This supports the process of continuous improvement discussed above.

10. *Get started!* The process of analysis, design, and testing can be very reinforcing. The key task is to turn ideas into action. Take action

as soon as possible. In some cases it is often more appropriate to ask for forgiveness than to ask for permission. If one truly believes that the changes will produce the desired changes, then the longer one waits, the greater will be the cost, the further market share will decline, and the more alienated the workforce will be. As the Nike commercials say: "Just do it."

Implications for the Human Resource Function

These strategies for change offer an opportunity to fundamentally alter the role of the human resource function. In many organizations the human resource function serves in an advisory and watchdog capacity; it administers programs and seeks to keep legal or employee-relation problems at a minimum. As the requirements for change increase, the HR function has an opportunity to become a major contributor. The scope of this book clearly goes beyond the traditional considerations of compensation systems and right to the heart of the management process itself. Therefore, the HR function can perform the following new activities in reshaping their impact on the firm:

1. Instead of reviewing documentation, the HR professional can monitor, aid, and facilitate line managers in setting up systems and practices to manage performance. In fact, waiting to review materials is a command-and-control model of management. Viewing line managers and employees as customers of the HR function is a mind-set critical to making their functions more successful.

2. The pressures for conformity (by legal, financial, and administrative functions) need to be balanced with the requirements to serve each business entity as a unique and important function. The HR function should not collude in retaining the practices of command and control, but should instead seek creative and innovative strategies to serve the needs of each business unit as if it were a paying customer.

3. The HR function needs to use technology to handle administrative matters and direct its resources to that of being a change agent or business partner. As discussed earlier, a change agent is the champion of a cause. A business partner works with other executives in setting strategic directions and making investment decisions for the organization. In this role, the business partner can also serve as a sponsor if he or she has sufficient credibility and power to exercise this function.

In summary, addressing organizational change and using reward systems as a primary vehicle for this change is an emerging role for the HR function. This implies that one needs to fully understand the strategic variables of the business and the factors critical to its success, as well as being able to persuade and present facts and data to the executive round table. When the HR function fulfills this role, it can serve as the bonding force within the firm, the conscience and the champion for true progress.

Building a Bridge from Here to There

This chapter has addressed the need to develop a game plan for implementing changes to reward systems. While the fundamental reason for these changes is to support a redirection in the business, one needs to develop a strategy for implementing change to specific programs. While we need to realize it will not be perfect, it should be the very best possible strategy that can be drawn up at that time. Then, as successes are realized or problems encountered, adjustments can be made from a foundation of understanding and commitment.

The process of organizational change, especially in making changes to reward systems, is never easy. However, not to take action is also a form of taking action, *not* to decide is to decide. Change is not always bad. Resistance exists not because people do not support change, but because they have a history of reinforcement that makes them feel they would be better off with the old ways. Not everyone will benefit from the change, or at least be able to retain their current role or reinforcers. As Robert Palmer, chairman and chief executive of Digital Equipment Corporation, stated as he examined the prospects of between 15,000 and 20,000 layoffs, "My task is to save 65,000 jobs."

The primary task needs to be increasing the rate of change that is focused on areas of success critical to the business. People will adapt to change when they realize that it is more reinforcing to exercise the new behaviors than to retain the old ones. Further, not everything is going to change. We have to pinpoint what needs to alter and how everyone can benefit from the process. If individuals do not choose to participate, at least they have been given the opportunity to do so. As one executive stated, "I need to either change the people or change the people."

Reward systems create the opportunity for reinforcement; people take those actions necessary to take advantage of the opportunities. When reward systems are developed, planned, and executed in ways that build collaboration, we enhance our probability of success. There is no certainty of reward when people have a stake in the business. They operate in a partnership of common fate. Without this relationship, the firm is at a competitive disadvantage vis à vis those who *have* achieved it. With this relationship in place, the possibilities are almost endless.

Notes

1. Bardwick, J. M., *Danger in the Comfort Zone.* New York: AMACOM, 1991.

2. Kübler-Ross, E., *On Death and Dying.* New York: Macmillan, 1969.

3. Grayson, C., Jr., and C. O'Dell, *American Business: A Two-Minute Warning.* New York: Free Press, 1988.

4. McAdams, J., and E. Hawk, *Capitilizing on Human Assets.* A research project of the American Compensation Association, Scottsdale, Ariz., 1992.

5. Bennis, W. and B. Nanus, *Leaders: The Strategies for Taking Charge.* New York: Harper & Row, 1986.

6. Lawler, E., *Strategic Pay.* San Francisco: Jossey Bass, 1990.

7. Daniels, A., *Performance Management: Improving Quality Productivity through Positive Reinforcement.* Tucker, GA.: Performance Management, 1989.

8. Daniels, op. cit.

9. Wilson, T., "Is It Time to Eliminate the Piece-Rate Incentive System?" *Compensation and Benefits Review,* March–April, 1992, pp. 43–49.

12

Case Study: A Total Approach at WILCO ELECTRONICS, INC.

(*Author's note:* This is a case study about a fictitious company. Many of the previous case histories have paralleled those of the author's clients. This one, however, is to illustrate how an integrated system of rewards can be developed and applied to an organization needing fundamental change. It reflects a model of the way things can be. It is based on real situations and reflects ideas being implemented by many companies. It describes an ideal—but one that could be real.)

Background of the Company

Wilco Electronics (WECo.) manufactures highly sophisticated electronic diagnostic and monitoring equipment for the healthcare industry. It produces noninvasive devices used to monitor patients in surgical and critical care situations. This equipment is sold through distributor networks or to some large hospital network companies. They are frequently marketed directly to physicians who then ask hospitals and medical centers to purchase WECo. products.

WECo. was founded in 1955 by Robert J. Armistead and grew rapidly as part of the medical electronics expansion in the 1960s and 1970s. It is a privately held company. John Armistead, son of the founder, is the chairman; 80 percent of the stock is owned by the family and 20 percent is owned by senior management. Mr. Armistead serves in an oversight role for the family's investments and does not get involved in operational matters. He and the major shareholders have significant confidence in Robert Johnson, the cheif executive officer, and his senior executive team. See Figure 12-1 for an overview of WECo.'s organizational structure.

WECo. had a reasonably sound product base and cost structure. It's sales were $200 million. There were approximately 2200 employees in its three plants and one large distribution warehouse. Each plant has between 350 and 500 employees. WECo.'s products were perceived as having the highest quality in the marketplace. Nevertheless, its competitors, primarily Japanese firms and large U.S. electronic firms, were steadily gaining ground. Because of its product quality, WECo. had been able to retain a comfortable premium pricing strategy in the market, but senior managers were aware that this might soon disappear.

For two years, WECo. had been attempting to implement a quality improvement process (QIP), primarily in its manufacturing areas. Significant automation investments had been made in its manufacturing process and greater skills were being required of its workforce. Many routine jobs had been replaced by computer-driven robotic equipment whose operators needed well-developed skills in problem analysis, preventative quality analysis, and production planning and control. Most managers and employees in manufacturing had been trained in various performance-measurement and control procedures (e.g. statistical process control), but few practices had actually been implemented. Only 15 percent to 20 percent of the operators maintained charts in their work areas.

The company had also been attempting to develop self-managed teams. As in WECo.'s QIP program, people had been trained to work in teams, but few teams actually existed except in some cross-functional, new-product development areas. The company had attempted to reduce cycle time for new products, increase operational productivity, and reduce management layers. To date, however, these efforts had been disappointing.

Finally, the company had conducted an employee opinion survey (see Figure 12-2) and the results had clearly reflected several major issues, including a lack of real teamwork and integration across areas, a lack of a clear direction about the firm's strategy, and a lack of follow-through by supervisors regarding the changes wanted by senior management. The survey data had been presented to management, and a summary report, along with a personal response by the CEO, had been sent to all employees. Though very disappointed in the results, senior managers were interested in using them to bolster their efforts to make the necessary organizational changes.

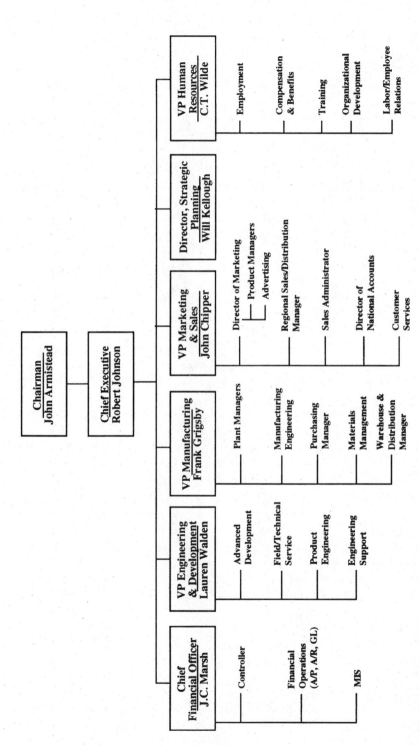

Figure 12-1. WECO.'s organizational structure.

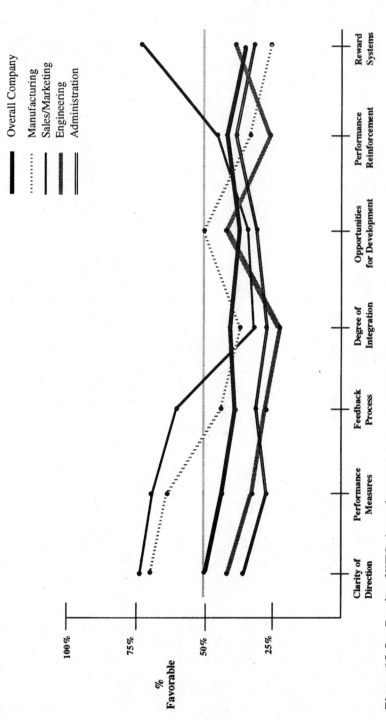

Figure 12-2. Results of WECo.'s employee opinion survey.

Overview of WECo.'s Strategy and Priorities

WECo. had a well-articulated mission-and-values statement. (See Figure 12-3.) The senior managers developed these statements in a series of off-site meetings. They enjoyed both the business focus and team building nature of this work. Their sense of humor was reflected in these values (see point 6).

The company had begun to experience rather flat sales. This was due to an increasing level of competition, primarily from quality-oriented foreign firms, in a marketplace with little absolute growth. WECo.'s future market leadership was being threatened as the competitors increased their product and service quality and as customers steadily increased cost pressures. The financials appeared fairly strong, but they reflected only what was, not what would be. (See Figure 12-4.)

After a thorough study of the marketplace, WECo.'s competitive position, and its capabilities, senior management had developed a set of key success factors as part of the firm's overall strategy:

OUR MISSION:
>   Contribute to saving lives by providing our customers with the information they need, when they need it, on their patients' vital signs through superior technology and supporting services.

OUR VALUES:

1. Adhere to the highest ethical standards in everything we do.

2. Know that we exist to serve others—customers, peers, and employees.

3. Continually seek new, innovative ways to improve the quality of what we deliver.

4. Act responsibly in matters related to our financial, material, and human resources.

5. Work as a team, with each other, our suppliers, and our customers in order to be better than the competition.

6. We love to rock and roll.

Figure 12-3.   WECo.'s mission and values.

	19XX	19XX	19XX
Net Sales	$160,000	$176,000	$188,000
Cost of sales	$130.000	$142,000	$152,000
Materials	80,000	84,000	87,000
Payroll/Benefits	30,000	34,500	36,000
Overhead	20,000	23,500	29,000
Selling and Administrative Expenses	20,000	24,000	25,200
Research and Development Expenses	7,200	8.500	8,000
Total Expenses	157,000	177,500	185,000
Operating Income	3,000	1,500	3,000
Other Income	1,400	1,500	3,000
Interest Expenses	1,600	1,700	1,700
Net Income Before Taxes	2,800	4,700	6,000
Return on Sales	1.8%	2.7%	3.2%
Return on Equity	5.0%	7.6%	12.6%
On-Time Delivery	84.5%	85%	88%
Scrap Rate	12.2%	11.9%	11.2%
Employee Turnover	8.90%	8.6%	7.1%

Figure 12-4. Overview of WECo.'s financial operating statements ($000).

1. We will continue to *focus* on offering physicians and healthcare providers the highest-quality monitoring devices. Our markets will be primarily in the United States, but we will penetrate international markets through joint ventures and strategic alliances.

2. Our products need to be *highly reliable* to meet or exceed the specifications of the customers. They also have to be *very easy to use*. The accompanying instructional information should be easy to read. Products must have an attractive price.

3. We will stay at the forefront of our technology, our industry, and the preference of our customers by *continuously finding ways to improve* our products and the process of our work.

4. We will *expand our product line* through working with our key customers, identifying what they need and being the primary source for the fulfillment of this need. We must build on our technical expertise and provide additional products that strengthen the capabilities of our core products.

5. The *delivery* of our products and the *quality of our services* need to exceed customer expectations.

6. Our *profitability* will come from increasing our market share, reducing all low-value-added activities, and investing in process and product technology.

7. We will *build and manage an organization* in which employees:
   - Are partners with all of us in retaining our market leadership
   - Have opportunities to grow and find areas to add value
   - View WECo. as their employer of choice

To implement the basic strategy implied in these statements, the company had begun to focus its efforts on several important initiatives.

1. *Increasing the links* with primary customers so that products could be developed, engineered, manufactured, and delivered in a manner that truly built a strong relationship with them. This would mean frequent and intensive interactions with physicians and healthcare providers.

2. *Reducing the time* required to market all aspects of WECo.'s products. This would include new product development as well as the manufacturing lead times. To reduce time to market, the firm would fully integrate its product development process and eliminate the standard sequencing of tasks. Work processes would be examined for ways to reduce steps, costs, and time.

3. *Decreasing the costs* of developing and manufacturing products so that prices could be made more competitive. Costs would be lowered by minimizing unnecessary tasks and optimizing the use of materials. Reducing human resource costs and/or the quality of products was not an option.

4. *Increasing responsiveness* to opportunities in the marketplace and within the organization. People would know what they could do and be encouraged to work with others within and around their natural work setting. Collaboration across functions, vertically within the company, and with the customers would become a common pattern of behavior in order for WECo. to survive and prosper.

WECo.'s Existing Reward Programs

WECo.'s compensation programs could best be described as traditional. (See Figure 12-5.) The base salary program had a set of ten non-exempt and twelve exempt grade levels (excluding the company executives).

Base Pay

Point factor job evaluation, 10 nonexempt, 12 exempt levels
Standard job descriptions (out of date) reflecting levels of responsibility, budget, and authority
Uses national surveys to target 60th percentile for entire company
12 percent difference between midpoints in salary ranges (50 percent
  spread)
Merit increases based on individual performance (via anniversary
  date performance appraisals) and position in salary range
5 percent average increase budget in base pay (avg. 5.2 percent)

Variable Pay

Senior and Mid-management Incentive Plan

  Payout once 90 percent of profit budget is achieved

  Payouts range from 10 percent to 25 percent of base pay

  Payout dependent on personal MBOs and grade level

  ■ Target is 40 percent for senior executives
  ■ 15 percent for mid-management
  ■ 10 percent for supervisors

Gain-sharing plan in one plant; awards tied to increases in number of
  units/hour over last four quarters average (rolling)
Average gain-sharing payout last year was 5.8 percent
Senior managers (VP and above) all have stock grants and options

Performance Management

Annual performance appraisals—MBOs and traits—scale of 1–5
Special cash awards given to top 10 percent "Super Stars"
VPs recognition quarterly to "Top Performer" in division

Figure 12-5. WECo.'s compensation program.

The grades were based on a job evaluation system that used the factors
provided by an external consulting firm—narrative job descriptions that
reflected levels of responsibility, budget, and decision-making authority. Most job descriptions were used to evaluate jobs and assign them to
the right grade level. Hence, managers frequently looked for the "magic
words" that would enable them to get a job upgraded or positioned
similar to perceived peers in other functions of the company.

Managers were supposed to perform annual performance appraisals for all employees on a job-anniversary basis. Merit increases could be held up pending the human resource function's approval of the performance appraisal document. The purpose of the appraisal was to review performance against annual objectives or performance factors and determine the rating of the employee on a 1 (marginal) to 3 (competent) to 5 (outstanding) scale. Merit pay increases were then calculated on the basis of this performance rating and on the basis of where the individual's pay fell in the salary range. People low in the salary range got a higher merit increase percentage than did people high in the range, and higher performers were supposed to get a higher percentage than did average or lower performers. In reality, 90 percent of the employees had received between a 4.5 percent and 5.5 percent pay increase for the last three years.

There was a management incentive program based on MBOs for each executive and midlevel manager. If the company fell short of 90 percent of its projected profit targets, no bonuses were paid. If the company exceeded the profit goals by more than 25 percent, the bonuses could be increased by up to 25 percent. In the seven years since the program had been introduced, the firm had only once failed to pay out the bonus and had never exceeded the 25 percent level. In over 80 percent of cases executives and managers had received the targeted bonus for their level (e.g., from 10 percent of salary for supervisors to 40 percent for top executives).

There was a gain-sharing program in one of WECo's plants. The program included everyone in the plant, except the plant manager and those who reported directly to her. (They were on the management incentive program.) The gain-sharing program was based on a single index of productivity: the value of goods shipped divided by the total number of employee hours for the given period. The value of goods shipped included products manufactured as well as goods taken from inventory. The products were assigned a value that in most cases reflected the market prices. Products that required rework or replacement by the customer were redone with no revenue credit. The employee hours involved were those of all the plant workers and included their overtime, vacation time, and time spent on special projects. The payout was made when there was an improvement over a rolling baseline of performance of the previous four quarters. The program paid out on a quarterly basis, and used a percentage of total pay. The payout had been an average of 7.8 percent in most quarters, although over the previous few years the percentage payout had been declining to around 5.8 percent.

The company maintained several important special-recognition programs. First there was a "President's Club," membership in which was reserved for departments that had exceeded their goals for a year. The work unit was presented with a special trophy for display, and its employees were given a free lunch for some day during the month in which they received the award. The group could choose to have its lunch brought in or go out at the company's expense. Also on an annual basis, senior management designated the top 10 percent of its employees as its "Super Stars." A special cash award was given to these employees, amounting to 10 percent of their base salary. Senior mangers devised their own strategy for nominating the Super Stars, and the final selections were made by the total senior management team.

In addition, the vice presidents selected a "Top Performer" from their area on a quarterly basis. The individual could be nominated by any employee, and the managers of the department discussed and selected the person based on these nominations. The employee received a $100 check given by the vice president and the immediate manager. Although this program had been in place for two years, the participation of the employees had declined. There was a feeling that the same employees were nominated each month, and the number of nominations was declining.

Creating a New Reward Strategy for WECo.

When one examines all WECo.'s compensation and recognition programs, it becomes apparent that they did not fit its key success factors. The job descriptions and job evaluation process reflected the power of the manager or function and did nothing to encourage people to focus on their customers. The management incentive plan did little to link managers together except to meet the profit threshold, nor did it link the managers to the outcomes achieved by their staff. The merit increase plan was basically ineffective in rewarding its high performers however deserving they were. The special recognition programs focused on a limited number of employees and fundamentally put high-performing employees in competition with each other. Most employees saw little chance of receiving an award, and those chosen seldom really understood exactly what they had done to merit distinction.

Based on the firm's strategy and key success factors, the following points had been identified as the critical practices needed for success:

1. Focus on serving the needs of our customers, internally and externally.

2. Continuously seek ways to enhance the quality of our products.

3. Eliminate costly, nonproductive activities that add costs, delay our responsiveness, and complicate our working together.

4. Encourage and implement creative ideas.

5. Continuously develop our knowledge and skills; put them to use as quickly and efficiently as possible; learn what we need and learn from what we do.

6. Optimize the use of our financial, material, facility, and talent resources.

7. Promote teamwork within and across the company; work together to achieve more.

8. Reinforce others for their contributions and for the assistance they provide us.

9. Be highly responsive to the needs of others, the demands of our tasks, and the changes occurring in our markets.

10. Integrate new technologies, processes, and resources into the way we fulfill our responsibilities to each other and to our customers.

To reinforce these actions, the organizataion needed a portfolio of reward programs that not only directly impacted the behaviors the firm desired but also served to compliment one another. These programs needed to be tailored to each employee group while maintaining an overall sense of fairness and equity across the company. (However, it was more important that the programs be effective with the target group than that they be the same across the company.) Finally, the reward programs needed to be integrated with and serve the role of the managers within the organization. Centralized control had to be discouraged, and administrative duplication had to be minimized. In this way, the various programs of rewards could operate as a system that created value for the employees for their contributions to WECo.'s competitiveness. Within this context, the basic reward programs had the following objectives:

- *Base salary.* This would be the secure pay—the wages and salaries of employees of WECo—and would enable the company to retain its overall market competitiveness and focus on rewarding individuals for their contributions and capabilities. The levels of base salary would correspond to the value-added nature of jobs and the degrees of knowledge and experience necessary to fulfill the responsibilities. Further, the base salary would promote opportunities for individuals to have careers within the organization and pursue those careers in a manner that utilized their talents, potentials, and desire to serve the organization. Internal equity would be ensured in terms of talent and contribution, not responsibility to control resources.

- *Variable compensation.* This would include all incentive compensation programs and would ultimately include everyone in the organization. It may be referred to as "opportunity pay" for it is based on the possibilities, not the guarantees, of performance. The unit of focus would be teams within the organization and their use of resources to contribute to the success of their customers. The measures used would focus on performance factors that directly related to each team's role within the company. The variable compensation programs would create opportunities for individuals to share in the success they achieved in improving WECo.'s competitiveness and improving its ability to serve customers.

- *Performance recognition and reinforcement.* This would include the fundamental work of managers in creating an environment in which people were reinforced for their actions on a real-time basis. The company would eliminate annual performance appraisals and replace them with more frequent feedback and reinforcement of performance. It would try to enable everyone to receive special recognition for their contributions, and would discourage competitive or meaningless programs. WECo. would help all its workers focus and measure their performance, receive timely, data-based feedback on the results, and celebrate incremental and continuous improvements. In this way, WECo. would create an environment that sought to bring out the best talent and contributions of each individual and provide genuine opportunities for personal and professional development. This would be WECo.'s primary competitive advantage in attracting, retaining, and utilizing talent.

WECo.'s Strategy for Rebuilding Its Reward Systems

If you compare WECo.'s new reward strategy with its current programs, you will notice significant differences. Its old pay practices were developed at a time when the management philosophy used a command-and-control approach rather than one focused on the customer. But current reality and emerging challenges demanded a change in thinking. The firm needed to implement various basic alterations in the way it did business, and these required changes in the way its employees worked and the way they were rewarded for their contributions. New behaviors need to be developed and reinforced. Changes in the reward system would be the cornerstone of a new approach to implementing the company's fundamental goals and initiatives.

To support this process of change, the senior managers began an important communication campaign. The purpose of this campaign was to increase employee awareness of the need for change and to provide a sense of direction. The employee opinion survey had indicated significant problems with the clarity of direction, and senior managers wanted people to fully understand the new strategy and how each individual could contribute to its implementation.

The communication process began with managers telling people about what had changed in the marketplace and the threats posed by new competitors. They described the firm's declining market share and how its delivery performance and revenue growth were declining in terms of industry performance. They showed the differences in WECo.'s product prices and those of the competitors. They made no attempt to blame employees, but instead pointed out that unless the company engaged in a serious improvement process, it would face its growing competitive challenges from a very weak position. The message got through.

The next element in the communication strategy was to outline what was necessary for the firm to be successful. The managers emphasized the key success factors described above. While these factors were important to the entire company, each senior manager led discussions with individual departments to translate the general factors into specific points that were important to each function. As these new lists were being developed, there was an increased sharing of information across departments. In particular, when the emphasis was on understanding and serving the needs of the customers, senior managers brought internal and external customers and suppliers together to react and refine their mutual interdependencies. These discussions were eye-opening experiences for their participants and led to much clarification and renegotiation on the things that were important to each sector of the company. Every level of employees was involved in these meetings, and the results of their activities were published throughout the company.

While the emphasis for some units was on internal relationships, the company encouraged teams to visit customers to discuss the needs of the physicians and the health care providers, and to see their products in actual operation. The insights gained from these visits were brought back to others in the organization and widely communicated. The firm was breaking down the wall between customers and management and between the two functions that had traditionally "owned" the customer—marketing and sales. The same process was also occurring with suppliers as they were invited to see how their materials, equipment, and services were meeting or not meeting, the needs of the organization. These contacts also brought in new perspectives and a strong sense of alliances with the firm.

The third element of this change strategy involved redefining and redeveloping WECo.'s reward systems. This was accomplished through a series of special task forces, each of which included a cross section of people and, where appropriate, established subgroups to examine selected areas or develop specific programs. The task forces concentrated on the following four areas:

1. *Base salaries.* Here the focus was on setting up the basis for establishing salaries, the levels of pay, the desired market position, and the salary administration process.

2. *Variable compensation.* The focus here was on all variable pay programs from the gain-sharing program to the management incentive program. A primary concern was building team-based variable pay programs for all employees in the company and driving the key economic linkages throughout the organization.

3. *Special recognition.* Here the focus was on revising current programs and developing creative programs to celebrate achievements made by units, teams, or special groups in the company. Whether or not these were an executive's pet programs, nothing was out of bounds. The focus in this area was also on developing ways to involve WECo.'s suppliers and customers in the process.

4. *Performance reinforcement.* The focus here was on replacing the current performance appraisal program with practices and support systems that would provide people with meaningful feedback and reinforcement. In this area, the focus was also on the leadership process, with a particular emphasis on utilizing positive reinforcement to encourage the desired contributions of both individuals and teams.

A central part of the company's approach in accomplishing these objectives was the creation of a steering team made up of individuals chosen from throughout the organization to guide the work of the task forces. The steering team's role was to sponsor the work of the task forces; to monitor and reinforce their progress; to ensure that their activities were consistent with WECo.'s overall mission, values, and key success factors; and to examine ways in which the innovation and creativity of one group could be used by others. Further, if additional resources were necessary, the steering team could ensure that they were made available. The human resources department, played an important part, both in the steering team and in each of the task forces, but overall, the steering team performed the critical coordinating and sponsorship role. The CEO, steering team, and HR department used an outside consulting firm to educate, facilitate, and initially guide the effort. However, their role diminished as the task forces were able and committed to achieving the desired ends.

As a result of these activities, employees at all levels of the organiza-tion began to see that there was a major threat facing WECo. They also began to understand some of the areas that needed changing and they started exploring what each person could do to make a difference. Finally, they saw a corporate commitment to taking action that was dif-ferent from previous attempts at change. The process was not viewed as "just another new program," but rather as a fundamental step in redefining how the firm was going to conduct its business and revise its systems and practices. The changes were implemented as they were developed. There was a strong sense of urgency to get things done. Although everyone took on extra work, it was viewed as a top priority because the future of the company was at stake. The process became one of renewal in an enthusiastic spirit that had once been a hallmark of WECo's. As a result of this revitalizing "winds of change" through-out the organization, WECo. would be forever different.

Base Salaries

"Building the talent we need to serve our customers."

WECo.'s base salary program was reconstructed using a different set of principles. The major shift was to transform this program from one founded on the command-and-control approach to one focusing on customers and on the talent necessary to serve them.

Several important barriers were apparent in the company's existing pay program that tended to:

- Create competitiveness between people in terms of job opportuni-ties and merit pay increases

- Reinforce the acquisition and control of resources

- Define a pecking order that was more oriented to control than to service

- Create barriers between people in terms of their job responsibilities and functional focus

- Require significant resources to maintain and control

Needless to say, these conditions were often in direct conflict with the new requirements of the firm. The base pay task force focused its efforts on several specific areas. First, it examined the basic criteria for developing levels of pay. The criteria was judged to be incompatible with current desired behaviors. Second, the task force examined the salary administration process. This, too, was viewed as creating more competition than teamwork. While the cost of base pay increases would need to be controlled, a more team-oriented, results-oriented process needed to be created in support of the success factor of reducing costs. Finally, the task force examined the need for career-based and pay-for-competencies-employed (PACE™) programs so that the base pay could reinforce the acquisition and utilization of new skills.

The focus of the base pay programs was on the individual. However, it was important not to create competitive situations. Costs needed to be controlled, but from an investment philosophy. If the firm increased base compensation costs, it needed to increase its capacity to serve customers. The marketplace considerations were important only to the extent that the firm was able to attract the talent it needed and not lose people because of pay. Several market surveys of pay practices provided general guidelines for administering pay, but they were not the primary determinants. The final determinant of pay had to be what employees were able to contribute, given their roles and the needs of their customers.

This overall understanding of requirements provided the necessary framework for making a number of fundamental changes in the base pay systems.

1. *Prepare customer-focused descriptions of accountabilities.* WECo. decided to ask each individual or small team to prepare a set of *role* descriptions (not *job* descriptions) that encouraged a focus on the customers rather than on authority and control. The format for the description was as follows:

- Who are your customers and what do they want or need?
- Who do you receive resources from and what do you use in your work (e.g., materials, information, services, supplies, etc.)?
- What are the primary areas in which you add value (i.e., how do you use the resources supplied you to serve your customers)?
- How do you know whether your are meeting your customers' needs (i.e., what are the primary performance factors or measures)?
- What specialized knowledge, skills, or abilities are necessary for you to perform this important function?

This process of preparing a description of one's value-added role was presented in the context of ways to clarify and improve the functions of the organization, not as a way of determining increases in pay. (See Figure 12-6.)

2. *Create pay bands based on competencies, contributions, and competitiveness.* The firm decided to consolidate the number of pay grade

Role Title:_____	Team/Unit_____	Reviewed:_____
Name:_____	Job Code:_____	Approved:_____

Customer Profile:
    Who are your customers?   What do they want or need?

Resource Profile:
    From whom do you receive   What do they provide you?
    resources (e.g., materials,
    information, money, etc.)

Value-Added Profile:
    How do you utilize these resources to serve your customers (i.e.,
    primary accountabilities)?

Performance and Capability Profile:
    How do you know if you are performing your services well (i.e.,
    primary performance measures)?

Capability Profile
    What is necessary for you to perform these functions at an opti-
    mal level (i.e., primary capabilities)?

Figure 12-6. WECo.'s new role-definition format.

levels into seven bands. Four of these would apply to nonexempt, operational, and clerical roles and three would apply to exempt, managerial roles. The bands would define the pay opportunity for people; the minimum would correspond with the lowest acceptable rate of pay and the maximum would reflect the highest. These bands would vary in width from minimum to maximum, from 50 percent for the lowest level to 200 percent for the highest level roles. This would permit people to move around the functions of the organization without the stigma of work at a lesser grade.

An individual would be placed in a band depending on their role and their competencies. The role was defined by the value-added nature of their work; their competencies were defined by a set of criteria within this role or function within the firm. Each band had a set of criteria that defined these roles and competencies. Because there were much fewer levels, the differences were significant from one band to another.

In order to ensure pay was competitive, managers were provided target rates or guidelines of pay for those roles or functions that could be validated with external market surveys. There was good market information on the compensation levels for assembly technicians, secretaries, systems analysts, financial analysts, etc. The manager would determine whether this information was relevant to his or her people. The market information was important to the firm so that it could attract and retain the talent it needed, but it was not the primary determinant of pay. Instead, competencies and performance were the drivers of pay.

This structure to compensation had to serve several important purposes. First, it ensured that individuals with comparable levels of competencies and contribution responsibilities had similar pay opportunities. Second, it provided managers with general guidelines as to how to administer pay fairly and equitably. Third, it provided specific guidelines for hiring people into the organization consistent with their roles and abilities. And fourth, it gave employees a sense of their opportunities and of the critical milestones in their career progression. As people increased their ability to add value to the organization, they needed to see some degree of progress financially, and when major thresholds were reached, as defined by their progression to the next band, there should be some form of celebration to mark the occasion.

3. *Establish pay increases based on contributions and competencies.* Increases in base pay needed to be based on the core principle of service to customers. The variable pay programs would focus on the results produced by the team; therefore, the base pay system needed to reward individuals. However, the traditional individual pay-increase guidelines had created win/lose situations and conditions of competition among employees. WECo. needed to take a different approach.

Its first step was to develop a variable merit pay pool in those areas where team performance clearly had an economic benefit to the firm. In this context, a set of dollars would be budgeted for increases in base pay. These dollars would reflect a general movement in pay within the markets for people in that function, whether internal or external. Pay increase dates would be consolidated to the first quarter of the fiscal year. If the performance of the overall group was on par with plans, the budgeted dollars could be allocated. If the performance exceeded plans and was clearly above expectation, dollars would be added to the merit pool. These funds would come from the increased economic benefit (i.e., increased profit contributions) of the group. If the performance fell short, the merit pool would be reduced. It could even be eliminated entirely for a given year if performance was significantly below expectation. Hence there would be an opportunity for people to receive amounts equal to, more than, or less than budget, based on the performance of their division, region, or plant.

The second step was to establish a set of salary increase guides that reflected a relationship between team performance and individual contributions in those cases where teams existed and performance measures were more focused on service and quality (and thus had less direct economic impact). If team and individual performance were on par with plans, the individual would receive a planned pay increase amount. If the performance of the team or the individual exceeded goals, pay would be above the planned amount. If the performance of either was below plan, the increase would be below budget. The performance measures of the team could be the same as their incentive plan measures or could be focused more on improvements in work process, teamwork, or special projects. The individual's performance would be judged in relation to its contribution to the team goals. As teams developed their ability to judge performance accurately and fairly, this performance assessment would be conducted by the team. Until that time, supervisors would make the determination, based on their own observations and on hard evidence provided by the team, their suppliers, and customers.

4. *Develop specific pay-for-competencies-employed programs for technical, knowledge-based functions.* While the pay levels as described above would apply to most people, certain functions needed specifically tailored pay programs to reinforce individuals for acquiring and applying special new knowledge, skills, and abilities. These areas included manufacturing and the engineering and development functions. In each area the levels would be defined within the band in terms of the diversity of skills needed to perform the responsibilities or the critical depth of specialized skills needed. As individuals clearly demonstrated a sustained application of the required competencies, they would receive a pay increase. Pay increases were not tied to time (e.g., annual), but to demonstrated performance. The frequency would reflect the learning curve. As higher levels of skills were acquired, there would be a higher level of work accomplished by a fewer number of people. These milestones would reflect career progression, and pay actions needed higher levels of management approval for higher level talent. A motivational challenge would be created when there were too many people qualified to perform the functions necessary at a given level.

The firm was committed to avoiding layoffs. However, if the firm could not provide meaningful work at a certain level, the individual would have to seek employment elsewhere. WECo. could not afford to pay additional dollars to people just because they were qualified.

5. *Monitor pay competitiveness to attract and retain the necessary talent.* The company would monitor the competitiveness of pay from several perspectives. First, it would monitor the movement of people. As people were hired, note would be taken of their previous employer and at what level they entered. As the firm lost people to other companies, note would be made of where they went and from what level they left. Most important, the company would monitor its own internal promotions and transfers of people to ensure that sources of talent were always being developed as needed by the firm.

Additionally, existing and special surveys would be conducted for the markets in which WECo. competed for talent. This information would provide useful guidelines for setting target pay rates. Finally, WECo. would monitor its ability to attract and retain the talent it needed. If the time to fill certain jobs became extremely long or there was a mismatch between the talent wanted and appropriate pay levels, a "red flag" would go up to identify the problem. If certain individuals with a particular talent were at risk of being recruited away from the firm for more pay, their situations would receive special study and action.

WECo. did not want to lose people because of inadequate pay or reinforcement. Turnover was acceptable if there were insufficient opportunities for an employee to use his or her talent, or if the person's skills no longer fit WECO's requirements, or if an individual wanted to work at a different location for personal reasons.

Overall, the compensation function shifted its role from that of control agent to that of change agent and advisor to line management.

In summary, the base pay program was established to link pay levels with the nature of the work and talent required. It served as the foundation on which other reward programs would be established. While the marketplace was important, the strategy was to create rewards that clearly valued the contributions that resulted from individual talents and efforts. The control of expenses in compensation became a financial function, not a human resource management responsibility. By linking pay with the performance of the team, by viewing pay as an investment in the resources of the firm, and by managing base pay with a focus on reinforcement, WECo. established a fundamentally different form of rewards. Now their base pay system could serve to support the values and key success factors of the business and be integrated into their new approach to utilizing resources.

Variable Compensation

"Creating a share in the success of the team."

WECo. senior managers quickly saw that a variable pay program could have an immediate impact on the behaviors of all members of the organization. These programs could be timely while not adding to the fixed costs of doing business. Furthermore, they could create a sense of having a real stake in the economic performance and competitiveness of the firm through giving employees a share in the risks and rewards that came with performance. While base pay could provide stability in an employee's economic life, variable pay could provide additional income when a high level of performance was sustained. Moreover, unlike base pay, variable pay could break down the walls between employees and the marketplace. The risk would lie in the company's ability to succeed in the marketplace. Sometimes there would be wins and sometimes losses. The impact on behavior would stem from the creation of a game that people could win by performing well.

Seen in this light, the variable compensation program would ultimately involve all members of the organization. The emphasis would be on the performance of teams. Their measures would derive directly from meeting the needs of their customers and fulfilling the criteria necessary for the team's success. They would need to make an optimal use of their resources in order to achieve the results desired. They would need to create measurement systems and monitor performance closely so that people could respond effectively. Regardless of the unit, these programs would need to have the common purpose of creating a share in the performance of the team to fulfill the needs of its customers by reinforcing and rewarding performance that:

- Focused on serving the needs of the customer
- Provided the highest quality products and service possible
- Sought new ideas to achieve improvements
- Eliminated costly nonproductive activities
- Encouraged risk-taking and change
- Increased the use of talents and resources
- Promoted teamwork and the integration of activities

In terms of process, the task force on variable compensation took accountability for designing a series of incentive plans throughout the organization. It reviewed and revised the management incentive program and the sales incentive plans. It analyzed the gain-sharing program and made modifications to align it with the overall purpose. It created similar plans for other areas of the organization through a series of interlocking measures and matrices. Finally, it integrated the implementation and management of these programs with the task forces focused on special recognition and performance reinforcement.

The specific features of the team incentive plans were as follows:

1. A team would be defined as a natural work group with common customers and technology. The scope would need to be large enough to capture the desired level of integration but small enough so that the measures could be meaningful to the individuals.

2. Performance measures would be a combination of financial and operational factors. More specifically, each team would seek measures that addressed issues of quality, quantity, timeliness, and resource utilization (i.e., expenses). The measures would be limited to between three and six areas, and the performance levels would need to reinforce improvements in baseline levels or sustaining levels of high performance. Further, the measures would need to be defined in terms of:

- Minimum acceptable performance
- Baseline or current reference performance
- Target level of desired performance
- Outstanding or distinguished levels of performance

These four levels would need to be further grouped into milestones to monitor and reinforce progress. Finally, the customers of the unit would need to be involved in identifying the measures and establishing the desired levels. In this way, the measures would serve to integrate the team with their customers and provide focus to their efforts.

3. In most cases a performance matrix would be used. (See Figure 12-7.) This matrix would display the key measures, weight them, and provide a process for determining an overall score. The weighting would reflect the importance of each measure on the overall results, reliability in tracking progress, and the ability of the team to influence the outcomes. The scoring would translate performance into payout as shown in Figure 12-8.

4. The matrix would provide opportunities to recognize special contributions, particularly those made by members of cross-functional process improvement teams. The matrix would also provide an opportunity to recognize teams that provided special assistance to other departments or enabled other departments to gain from their innovations and creativity. The team could receive extra "Special Achievement" points.

5. The payouts would be on a quarterly basis with a final payment equal to a quarter's total opportunity, based on annual or cumulative

TEAM/UNIT _____   DIVISION _____   Performance Period _____

MEASURES	X Weight	50	60	70	80	90	100	110	120	130	140	Points
		Minimum		Baseline	Points		Target					Outstanding

Special Achievements

SCORE _____

Approved _____

Figure 12-7. Performance incentive matrix.

Range of Performance		Quarterly % Payout	Annual % Payout
From	To		
Below	75	0%	0%
75	89	2%	0.5%
90	99	3%	0.75%
100	110	4%	1.0%
111	120	5%	1.5%
121	140	6%	2.0%

Figure 12-8. Matrix points keyed to incentive payout opportunity.

results. The first four quarters would be paid out based on the results of the quarter. There would be no cumulative affect. The fifth annual payout would be based on cumulative performance.

6. The payouts would be based on the total earnings—total salary (for exempt) or total wages plus overtime (for nonexempt)—for the performance period, one quarter or the year.

7. If someone left the organization during the period, they would not receive any payout. If an individual transferred, retired, or became disabled, he or she would receive a pro rata amount based on earnings for the period.

8. The human resource department would be responsible for administering the program. It would ensure that the results corresponded with performance levels, and would provide incentive checks in special envelopes to managers so that they could distribute them in special and celebratory ways.

The variable compensation plans were tailored to each department through the performance measures and operation of the plan. In some cases, payout opportunities were adjusted in line with the performance of the entire division. When the firm's profitability exceeded the plan, the senior managers could increase the payouts to all teams based on their performance matrix score. In this way, the plans could focus on the work of the team, provide a clear line of sight between the results and the behaviors, and reinforce collaboration across departments. The teams would not be in competition for the payouts; they would each be competing against their own historical best. As ideas in one area were applied and improved upon by another, the "giving" team could be reinforced through the special achievement points or by being invited to participate in some special activity for the "receiving" team.

Finally, a "level playing field"—comparable performance expectations across levels—was achieved in three ways. First, the customers of internally focused teams were involved in setting the measures and levels. Second, the measures and matrices were reviewed by senior managers in an open session. Third, the measures were displayed prominently in the work area, and people passing through from other departments could see what the team was working on. Payouts were seen as ways to celebrate achievements. If a team did not achieve desired results, they could focus on how to do better next time. Criticism of other departments was seriously discouraged. Everyone was given an opportunity to win and share in the gains, but this was contingent on desired performance.

Special Recognition

"Making everyone a winner."

The task force that focused on special recognition sought to create programs that were fun and reinforcing, with little emphasis on win/lose or internal competition. This was particularly difficult because many of the senior managers were used to being reinforced by giving out awards. Even though the measures were unclear, the awards often did not fit the performance, and employees seldom understood what they had done to merit their awards, senior managers at WECo. loved these programs. The challenge was not to further refine the measures, but to transform them into programs that truly reinforced desired performance.

To begin with, the special recognition task force developed several standards and principles according to which they would develop programs and practices within the organization. In terms of standards of performance, an achievement worthy of special recognition need to:

- Serve the special needs of the unit's customers
- Be innovative, creative, and usable by others
- Enhance the ability of the firm to use its resources well
- Have enduring impact on others
- Be regarded as something special

In terms of underlying principles, it was decided that special recognition awards needed to:

1. Be available to all with a basic threshold level that all members achieve
2. Reflect the contributions made by all to the process
3. Be personally meaningful to the recipients
4. Be awarded as close to the time of the achievement as possible

After an analysis of the current special recognition programs—the "President's Club," "Super Stars" and the "Top Performers"—several modifications were made. First, membership in the President's Club was awarded on a quarterly basis and was open to any team that exceeded its target performance as defined by the incentive performance matrix. Any team could achieve this level and have its achievements celebrated with free lunches, free coffee/donuts from its division, and/or funds to provide gifts to one another. There would be a significant ceremony when a team first came into the President's Club. WECo.'s president and several members of senior management met with the group, and the discussion centered on learning how the group had overcome obstacles to achieve this level of performance. At the meeting, the senior managers devoted most of their time to listening and reinforcing the efforts that led to the achievements.

When a group had been in the club for several quarters, the senior managers provided surprise visits and celebrations, like serving ice cream sundaes, giving special hats to everyone, and taking the group out to some special activity. While a team would not know when this would happen, but it would know that it had to have been in the club for more than three quarters before it could. Membership in this club became an important symbol of achievement for a team. Those who had not reached this goal were involved in analyzing the barriers to their success, as well as in identifying and implementing strategies to improve their performance.

In this context, the Super Stars program was disbanded. It was felt that it was too much a function of "looking good to senior managers" than of doing good for WECo.'s customers. Meanwhile, the Top Performer program was reformulated into a monthly process for team members to recognize one another. Participating teams displayed charts on the wall featuring the achievements of members who had made a special contribution to the team during a given month. The team decided whose names should be posted, what a team member needed to do to be eligible, and how the chart should be done. Sometimes a chart featured every member of a team. Managers from other areas, customers visiting the facility, and senior managers often asked to meet the individuals listed. The program provided an opportunity for teams and managers alike to recognize and reinforce those making the greatest contributions. This program was retitled "Our

Top Contributors," but each team could create a different name for the recognition if they so wanted.

The task force on special recognition sought to refocus the company's attention on fewer programs that increased the rate of reinforcement going to everyone. The funds used in previous programs were used for the new programs, but the monetary awards were deemphasized. The focus needed to be on providing a meaningful reinforcement to the individuals that made a difference to the team, group, division, or total company. The awards could go to teams or to individuals. The most important element was on creating a memory in those individuals that the organization valued the efforts of everyone. It served to create an environment in which people felt honored for their contributions. The organization realized important results from these efforts.

Performance Reinforcement—Bringing Feedback and Development into Real-Time

The mission of the task force on performance reinforcement was to replace the performance appraisal process with one that provided people with more immediate feedback and reinforcement for their efforts. The task force needed to develop the process, identify the skills needed by managers, and oversee the transition process. It sought to create the conditions in which managers could earn the right to stop doing performance appraisals because they were implementing a better process to manage performance.

The company's existing approach to performance appraisals reinforced the manager as the judge and jury. The "data" involved usually amounted to no more than personal assessments of performance. Although high performance was supposed to be rewarded, the appraisals often resulted in employees feeling more alienated than reinforced. From almost every point of view, the existing process of performance appraisals was counterproductive.

This task force faced a difficult challenge, one that involved more than merely preparing new forms or developing new policies. Such antecedents would be of little value. The task force had to redirect the fundamental practices of managers to create an environment in which people felt truly reinforced for accomplishing desired actions. Moreover, this reinforcement had to be provided on a real-time basis, not according to some predetermined time schedule.

In designing WECo.'s new performance reinforcement process, the task force prioritized the following four main objectives:

1. *Focus.*   Critical areas for change and improvement had to be identified; these must be aligned with the strategic priorities of the business.

2. *Measurement.*   A system had to be developed for judging performance in these areas.

3. *Feedback.*   Performers needed to know how they were progressing
   on as frequent a basis as possible and multiple sources were preferred.

4. *Positive Reinforcement.*   Performers needed to be valued for their
   contributions consistently so that they would want to continue.

The task force identified several critical steps for achieving these four
objectives. To get the program started, the managers and supervisors
were trained in a special workshop on performance reinforcement.
They then began applying their new skills to actual performance
issues facing each area. As the managers began implementing visible
feedback and reinforcement systems within their work areas, they
were no longer required to perform annual performance appraisals. In
fact, managers used quarterly and sometimes monthly meetings to
review the performance of their work units and to understand the barriers as well as the opportunities being encountered. Initially, these
meetings were conducted on an individual basis, but later grew to
include entire teams. Some teams began including their internal customers in these review sessions, and sought feedback and suggestions
for improvements from them. A multi-rater feedback process emerged
over time; it was created through a demand-pull rather than a mandat-
ed process.

The teams provided feedback and coaching to their members, and
the managers began to play a more facilitating role. When the situation warranted it, managers met with individuals to review either general issues or particular achievements. These sessions tended to be
summarized in writing so that there was adequate documentation for
managing performance. For employees with significant performance
issues, a specific corrective action plan was prepared with commitments documented by the employee and manager. When the employee did not live up to his or her commitments, there were grounds for
dismissal.

These review meetings were important "calibration sessions" to
make sure that the efforts were in fact leading to improved performance for the company. Senior managers attended some of the meetings, using them as further opportunities to learn how achievements
were accomplished and present a strategic perspective to the team
members. The human resource function also reviewed the meetings,
the managers' documentation, and the performance information to

ensure that the four critical objectives were being met. The HR reviews assisted the managers in improving their skills in managing the performance of individuals and teams. The HR function did not perform a control role, but rather served to coach, encourage, and facilitate the management process.

While not all managers progressed at the same rate, there was significant participation by senior managers in reinforcing the process. More attention was paid to managers who implemented the process well than to those who did not. There was excitement over the results, which were often communicated throughout the organization. Managers who were unwilling to take serious steps to implement the process were moved out of managerial roles and into technical-contributor functions or other positions more in keeping with their abilities. The commitment by senior managers was highly visible and was reinforced by the results and improvements that they could see happening within the organization.

Summary of WECo.'s Results

WECo. has been able to retain its market leadership despite complex competition. The marketplace continues to change and the need for highly reliable, easy-to-use health monitoring equipment is increasing. WECo.'s battles for survival are not over and may never be. Everyone realizes this. However, the spirit of achievement is strong and is providing WECo. with a strong competitive advantage.

The organization has been able to achieve impressive results due to the effective implementation and reinforcement of its strategy. WECo. has been able to retain valuable talent. Its new products, especially those using wireless network technology, are entering the market in record time. Its variable costs have dropped significantly in relation to its growth in revenues. This increased throughput has increased WECo.'s yield from fixed investments and improved its operating financial performance. Delivery performance has gone up to near 98 percent on time, and scrap rates are well below 3 percent. Sick leave, turnover, and employee accidents have been cut by 50 percent. The credibility of senior managers has grown rapidly as people have seen a positive, active, and direct relationship between what their managers say (i.e., antecedents) and what they do (i.e., consequences). The managers' active leadership has been felt throughout the organization as their role has successfully shifted from command and control to working with employees to serve customers better.

All these results did not come quickly, and WECo.'s ultimate objectives have yet to be fully realized. However, the process so far is viewed as very positive and important to the organization. Moreover, it has been fun and rewarding. Senior managers have taken the necessary steps to bring their employees into the process of the business to share its risks and successes. They have broken down the walls of entitlement and bureaucracy by providing their people with both direction and a stake in the outcomes. The process has not been easy, but it has truly been worth the investment.

13

Reward Systems for the Emerging Company

*There is nothing more difficult to take in
hand, more perilous to conduct, or more
uncertain in its success than to take the lead
in the introduction of a new order of things.*
—NICCOLO MACHIAVELLI
The Prince

Why do people go to work for small companies? For some it is because the company is located near their home, or because they know someone at the company, or because it is simply the first job they can find. For others, working for a small company offers a chance to escape the impersonal or overly structured environment of a large organization, a way of staying close to the customer, or an opportunity to handle a wide variety of responsibilities.

Some people start their *own* company to pursue their own ideas and reap the rewards if the firm is successful, to call the shots, not have to work for others, and not "make money for the other guy." Each of these reasons can also define a reinforcer for the individual involved.

At the beginning of this book we examined how entrepreneur's move toward the military or the Catholic Church organizational models when faced with growing management issues. We also examined the various reward systems that have been developed in corporate settings. Many of these systems were founded on a command-and-control philosophy rather than on a customer-focused approach. We saw how these reward systems have tended to reinforce employees' relationships with their bosses rather than with their customers.

Today we face complex competitive times. Many organizations are attempting to change the fundamental premises on which they have operated for years, perhaps for decades. These changes are necessary to survival, but some will be successful and some will not. The challenge for the emerging company is how to *prevent* the problems experienced by so many of the larger companies that took the command-and-control path.

In this chapter we will examine the developmental cycle of the small business and seek to understand what reward system would be most appropriate. We will review some of the common issues that plague organizations as they grow and develop, and focus on the steps necessary to develop effective reward systems. We will conclude by examining some dos and don'ts to guide the reader in implementing a reward strategy that will continue the spirit of the small business. The aim is to provide the reader with guidelines to create reward systems that truly support the long-term viability of the organization and help it avoid the problems now facing many larger firms.

Much as been researched and written about the stages of growth for small companies.[1] Perhaps the most useful way to summarize this research is to explore five stages of growth as organizations progress from a start-up to a mature, operating company. The concepts will provided a basis for understanding how reward systems can support the developmental process of companies at different stages in their life.

Stage One: The Start-Up

In the beginning, the entrepreneur has an idea. This idea may come from research or experience with an employer or from seeing a need in his or her community that has not been met. Some of the greatest entrepreneurs had an vision about a technology or service where there wasn't an expressed need. Once introduced, the market came to them. Kenneth Olsen of Digital Equipment, Tom Monaghan of Domino's Pizza, Fred Smith of Federal Express and Bill Gates of Microsoft are examples of such entrepreneurs.

This first stage is truly the beginning of the company. Here the owner does everything—provides the vision, the technical know-how, the energy, the capital, the housekeeping, and the marketing drive.

The company is built on the talents of the owner and is often a manifestation of his or her personality. The owner hires and supervises everyone in the organization. He or she is a doer-manager.

The challenge at this stage is to obtain customers and maintain sufficient cash flow from operations to cover expenses. The focus is often on making what one delivers and keeping expenses to a minimum. The customers' impact is supreme, and all members of the organization know the importance of each customer.

In these organizations systems to manage the business are informal or nonexistent. Planning is focused on ensuring that there is adequate inventory to meet customer orders and managing cash flow to cover operating expenses. Budgeting is also basically nonexistent because the firm needs to remain opportunistic about the situations it faces; it cannot be held to a budget. The structure is informal; almost everyone reports directly to the owner. Recruiting is built on people known by the owner or to close members of the organization. Compensation is in a "Let's make a deal" mode (see Chapter 4, Rewards Strategy).

The spirit of these companies is one that can be characterized as fast-paced, action-oriented and "living on the edge." People tend to move faster, stay task-focused and feel significant emotional ups and downs based on the way the business is going. There is little time for internal politics. Teamwork and cooperation by all the firm's members are essential building blocks to success. The feedback is often quickly felt. The consequences are usually clearly derived from the customer and the effective manager. These environments have many characteristics that their larger counterparts envy.

These firms offer an environment in which people can have a direct impact and see that impact right away. In fact, if is often the frequency and amount of positive reinforcement in a small organization that brings people into it and keeps them there as the firm celebrates the crossing of such important milestones as the first customer order, the first payment received, the first time sales exceed $100,000, etc.

There are often few formal reward systems. Pay is usually less than that paid by larger companies. Base pay may not even exist, and variable pay is often very contingent on revenues and profits (i.e., cash flow). The incentives are paid weekly or monthly; there may be some longer-term (i.e., annual) variable pay agreements. Often a profit sharing plan is appropriate as a substitute for large base salaries. In terms of equity participation, many simply seek a piece of the action, or want to get in on the ground floor in order to have opportunities for significant wealth later. The stock is usually of little value in current terms. Its value is established by its long-term future opportunity. This is a situation that can offer high rewards for high risk and high reinforcement for high levels of energy and effort.

Stage Two: Survival

This stage has many of the same qualities as the start-up stage, only now it is clear that the original idea is viable. Customers come back for repeat business or tell their associates or friends about the company. But the firm remains in a survival mode because if it does not continue to produce high-quality, reliable, and valuable products or services and manage its cash effectively, it will not survive. The primary challenge for companies at this stage is one of sustaining customers and building a reputation in a particular niche. They need to ensure that there is adequate cash to grow the firm and meet the investment needs for upgrading equipment, facilities, and marketing programs. As a result of being opportunistic about customer demand, product lines are expanded and are usually closely related to the core technology.

The owner still makes all the decisions, only now there are other competent individuals who can implement the decisions. At this point the firm has added so many members that they cannot all be supervised by the owner. A void is created, one based on the lack of his or her direct leadership. The new people often do not fully share the vision of the owner and the original founders of the company. Firms that achieve this level create structures and define work responsibilities into roles that are usually organized around some functional or geographic areas.

Internal conflicts often emerge when the founding employees do not accept the emergence of a new managerial class. These new managers often receive high compensation or stock-related rewards commensurate with their roles. They are sometimes seen as receiving special treatment or special favors from the owner. Often the founding employees, believing that the owner would never "desert" them in this way, come to think that he or she is being manipulated by someone on the staff. There is a general resistance to change from the "good old days" of the start-up company.

Rewards and reinforcements are often at the heart of many issues. Pay levels are different; special incentives or stock programs reflect preferential treatment. All this is different from when the company was small and everyone shared in the profits. Attention by the owner is viewed as scarce and highly valuable—perhaps more so than when the firm was "one happy family." If people were to really relive those times, they were probably seldom really happy *or* a family, in fact, those times were probably characterized by stress, resource constraints, and pressures to produce. The "one happy family" memory tends to emerge only when the firm has moved on to a different stage.

Reward systems at this stage need to take a more structured approach. "Deals" need to be documented. This may be as simple as a letter of agreement from the owner or the description of an incentive program. The challenge is to create opportunities for people to be compensated for their contributions toward building the business, not for their previous role in the start-up company. There will be differences in roles and accountabilities, and the reward systems need to reflect them.

At this stage there is perhaps sufficient cash flow to introduce base compensation as long as there is a strong reliance on incentives. Some roles, such as those in sales, service, and management, will rely heavily on incentives. Certain support functions can have base salaries, but linking these individuals with the growth and profitability of the company is a way to continue to reinforce a "common fate" philosophy. The incentives should be short-term (monthly or quarterly), and each individual needs to be reinforced for actions that support critical objectives related to the firm's survival.

At this stage the firm is likely to experience several primary issues. First, the "special treatment" for individuals with new roles within the firm will need explanation and strong support from the owner/founder. These roles will need to be documented and reflect the way the individuals are treated within the firm. It is important not to pursue traditional job descriptions that focus on command-and-control accountabilities. Rather, role descriptions should serve as a means to provide clarity of direction for serving the customer (see Chapter 5). They may be developed and communicated by people involved in or affected by those in the particular role. A problem may emerge if the owner is not willing to delegate decision-making authority and reinforce desired performance. It is essential that the consequences (i.e., rewards) support the antecedents (i.e., the role).

Second, as the demands of the firm become more complex, there is often a mismatch between the performance requirements and the capabilities of the individual. While many will be able to rise to the occasion because of a change in the consequences, not everyone will succeed. Therefore, the owner will need to give people with new roles sufficient time to adjust and achieve the desired results, but not continue to countenance poor performance because of past loyalties. This may present a major personal challenge to the founder.

Finally, the measures that determine the rewards need to be focused on the strategic issues of the firm's survival. Long-term considerations can be provided for by equity-based programs, such as performance stock programs or stock options. If too much emphasis is placed on profitability, decisions may become too short-term oriented and fail to take advantage of market opportunities. If there is too little emphasis on profitability, the firm may not survive unless it is highly capitalized. In these cases the emphasis should focus on revenue and revenue growth while sustaining a desired profit margin over a longer time period. Additional investments should lead to increased revenues, which should in turn lead to improved profitability. (This is the way things *should* work, but seldom do in the dynamic world of a survival company.)

Stage Three: Stability

Firms that achieve this stage have clearly demonstrated that they have a product or service desired by the market and that they can manage their resources to achieve sustained profitability. At this point there is a choice in direction: *stability or growth.* The choice is one that involves both a strategic risk and a personal decision by the owner. To sustain the firm in its current form means not seeking new markets or new product opportunities outside a particular niche. To grow the firm means making investments, taking risks, and bringing in new talent. The primary risk in sustaining the business is that the markets may change radically in terms of customer's demands or competitor's technology. The primary risk in growing the company is that new ventures may not be accepted in the market or generate sufficient return on investments. Growth and stability each require a different model of management and a differrent approach to rewards.

The stability path requires the firm to manage its revenues and expenses so that survival is ensured. In high-revenue periods, capital will need to be accumulated to cover periods when revenues are down. The firm is focused on sustaining its market position and will need continual improvements in products, processes, and marketing. This improvement needs to be at a faster rate and qualitatively better than that of the firm's competitors in order for it to survive. The marketing strategy must be more defensive than offensive. The organization should be based more on retaining customers and continuing to be their preferred provider of products and services than on acquiring new markets. The firm may continue in this stage for many years, perhaps for its entire existence.

From an organizational perspective, functional managers usually assume day-to-day responsibilities for the organization. Systems are created to manage the profitability and quality of services for the organization. This includes production planning, scheduling, inventory control, advertising and promotions, forecasting and budgeting, and other such practices that provide stability to the organization. Business plans are created so that the firm is able to adjust to market demands and make planned investment in the business. The focus is often on sustaining profit margins and ensuring an adequate return on sales, equity, or investments.

From an owner's point of view, the firm may be used as a platform for other activities. These may include new ventures with other companies, a political career, community activities, or the pursuit of personal interests. Managers are in place, freeing the owner to disengage from the operations of the firm, to prepare it for sale, simply to retain a positive cash flow to make other investments. The firm may stay in this situation as long as its products and services continue to serve the needs of its customers better than its competitors do.

In terms of reward systems, the firm needs to maintain and reinforce stability, service to customers, continuous improvements, and prudent use of resources. Roles can be clarified in relation to their service to customers. Base pay levels can become sufficiently competitive to attract and retain talent, replace people who terminate, or improve the level of talent within the firm. Incentives can focus on financial results or key operational measures. If the firm is small enough and people can relate their actions to the measures, profit sharing may provide a strong common-fate perspective. Performance measurement and feedback need to occur on a frequent basis, with celebrations centered around achievements in customer satisfaction and continuous improvement.

Stage Four: Growth

Firms that take the growth-oriented path will face significant risks as well as potentially great rewards. The central challenge is to maintain sufficient cash or investment sources (debt or equity financing) to cover increasing expenses. Such firms often need to sustain the profitability of the core business and utilize this capital to finance growth in other areas. They will need to make considered and opportunistic decisions on growth-oriented investments. Further, as the organization adds staff, it will need to address the issues of assimilation, diversity, and talent utilization.

The owner in the growth-oriented firm needs to clarify accountabilities, delegate responsibility, and reinforce performance achievements. Managers can focus on functional roles or on market, customer-oriented operations. Often the organizing concept will determine the nature of the growth and the ability to optimize market opportunities. Firms that assume a functional-control form of governance may be unable to implement plans except through directing and controlling the operations and through the use of negative reinforcement—factors that may limit their ability to see opportunities and capitalize on them. However, firms that organize around markets or core technology need to generate sufficient cash flow to finance investments. This can enable them to balance economic viability with an growing presence in the marketplace. The tension between control and risk lies at the heart of the challenge facing firms in this stage.

The growth strategy may involve a variety of directions. First, the firm can seek expansion of its current core technologies into new marketplaces. (A U.S. domestic firm might open operations in Asia or Europe, for example.) Second, the firm can capitalize on its existing customer base and expand product lines to better serve a current market. These strategies can be achieved either through acquisitions or through the application of the firm's own internal skills and resources. Some firms try to do both, only to find themselves short of resources or looking for creative financing strategies. Key performance indicators in this overall growth strategy should relate the revenue increases to the achievement of strategic marketing objectives, such as milestones in a new product launch, achievement of market share, or expanding account penetration.

Once a firm has established a strong reputation and seeks growth in new markets, it is likely to experience some customer resistance and a great deal of competitive pressure. A very experienced chief executive client of mine once said: "If we are successful in our growth strategies, watch out for the competitors, for they will surely come."

When you create markets through advanced technology or innovative products or services, both customers and competitors emerge. Of the two, the more crucial to the firm's survival is its customers. Being the first to market is not always the best strategy. Many firms have lost their competitive edge because they took customer loyalty for granted. The challenge for the company's leadership is to understand the dynamics of the competitors while maintaining a focus on customer acquisition and retention. Both new customers and long-term customers are the result of the kind of products or services that enable them to be more competitive in their own struggles.

In terms of reward strategies, firms in a growth stage need to keep fixed costs at a minimum and reinforce a sense of urgency. The heavy use of variable compensation plans tailored to the unique needs of each role or function within the competitive strategy can provide the catalyst for responsive actions. The firm should also seek to build long-term value. Equity-related plans enable the participants to share in this gain. There are a variety of creative equity-based plans, such as nonqualified stock options, reload options, and phantom share plans (see Chapter 7).

Firms at this stage offer an unusual form of career opportunities. Because they are still small, there are few traditional upward movement possibilities, but the "ladder" itself is likely to move up. Managers will be able to assume activities and responsibilities that should continue to challenge and enhance their professional development.

Hence the growth stage offers significant opportunities for creative, high-potential reward programs. What is needed is a dynamic balance between rewarding the contributions of individuals and rewarding the contributions of the team. The focus must be on investing in those efforts that yield immediate growth, managing cash to sustain the growth, and building long-term worth of the company. The essential demands on the leadership are to build market share with a core technology, to work together with common values, and to remain committed to the firm's success.

Stage Five: Maturity

Firms that have achieved this stage of their development see a decline in growth rate. They have reached a saturation point in their markets or full capacity in terms of what the firm can handle from a resource and managerial perspective. They have characteristics similar to those of firms at the stability stage, only they have more diversity and more complexity. The firm can continue in this present "steady flight" mode, or experience yet another round of growth through acquisitions, technological breakthroughs, or marketing initiatives.

Companies at this stage of their development can withstand many of the pressures of the external marketplace. They may have an entrenched customer base or a set of resources that enables them to be basically unaffected by the short-term winds of the marketplace. Firms at this level usually develop sophisticated planning, development, and control systems. Their human resource strategies often do not entail heavy recruitment, but rather emphasize development and application of skills. Succession planning, for an example, may be a valuable strategy at this point, enabling the firm's top executives to discuss and shape the core competencies necessary for the future of the firm.

When a firm reaches a size at which it becomes self-sustaining, it is often because there are a variety of units within the firm that are at earlier stages of their development. Some units are clearly in a growth mode while others have achieved a level of market maturity that limits rapid growth patterns. Systems and practices become more routine, and pressures on survival fade. There are many voices from the marketplace. The challenge is to understand those that make a difference at the unit level. One issue that often emerges is how the firm can manage such diversity and organizational complexity without the focused pressures of a single marketplace.

When the firm reaches a state of maturity, it faces circumstances that can lead to its failure. First, people may come to expect their rewards. This is the era in which entitlement can become a characteristic of the firm's environment. Second, managers or functional heads may create systems that serve their own need for control rather than what is good for the company. Such systems can create "bureaucratic barnacles" on the organization, slowing its responsiveness to change. Finally, management may become overconfident and arrogant, unwilling to listen to other voices within or outside the organization. Executives may come to believe they are the true model of leadership—after all, didn't they grow the company to its present size? They can become used to hearing only what they want to hear: those things that reinforce their preferred perceptions of reality. This process, very evident throughout the high-technology industry of the 1980s, was epitomized by the behavior of Kenneth Olsen and his senior management team at Digital Equipment Corporation, An Wang of Wang Laboratories, and Edward DeCastro of Data General.

A primary root cause of these problems is reinforcement. While reinforcement is desired, it can also narrow the individual responses. If managaers are frequently reinforced for what they *have* been doing, without being driven toward continual improvement, they can come to believe that they control destiny. A paradigm is created. As long as the actions fit the needs of the environment, the executive will be successful. When the market changes and the paradigm does not, major trouble lies ahead. This overconfidence can produce the seeds of a company's destruction. The risks to survival for firms at this stage in their growth are often more subtle, more long-term, harder to pinpoint, and more potentially destructive than the simple loss of a customer. Organizations (or executives) that do not succeed may never really understand why.

Therefore, when introducing new reward systems, care must be taken not simply to adopt what other firms do or what would best serve the "masters" of the organization. Reward systems need to be based on a strategy that reinforces actions that support the firm's key success factors and its core competencies as they apply to its customers and markets. At this stage the firm has the ability to introduce a wide range of reward systems. It should guard against plans that treat all people within the firm the same. Everyone should have equal opportunities, but the system should reflect an achievement orientation rather than an entitlement one.

For example, a midsize health maintenance organization implemented significant base pay increases when it discovered that it had fallen seriously behind the rest of the market. Employees were told that these increases were to enable the firm to be more competitive in terms of salaries. Senior management then expected that its people would perform at a higher level, because of the higher levels of pay. This is a "management by guilt" philosophy. While the employees were very appreciative of the pay increase, they kept doing as they always had. There was little need to change. Ultimately, senior management felt betrayed by the employees and attempted to remedy the situation with salary freezes and control oriented incentive plans. These actions had the effect of making the firm less able to attract and retain desired talent, and it became competitively weaker.

Companies at this stage often find they are behind the market in terms of pay. They also tend to uncover serious internal equity issues as they attempt to formalize pay systems. The typical response is to "throw money at the problem," usually through special pay adjustments. An alternative strategy should be to:

- Provide clearly above-market pay increases reflecting the performance of individuals or teams

- Create retention awards—cash or stock paid out over time based on sustained employment and performance—for individuals who are clearly at risk of going over to the competition and who are important to the firm's continued success

- Introduce incentive plans with moderately aggressive payout opportunities, paid on a frequent basis and tied to strategic performance measures of the unit or team

- Create and use funds to promote celebrations for teams, individuals, or the entire company for achieving important results

The primary emphasis should be on addressing issues of compensation by creating opportunities for individuals to earn more than their counterparts in other companies. The payout should be modest but frequent. Large payouts, made infrequently, have the potential to create an extinction pattern of consequences and an entitlement mentality that says, "What will you do for me now?"

Firms at this stage can create a portfolio of reward systems that open a large number of opportunities for recognizing individual and team contributions. The systems should be tailored to fit each particular business unit so that specific behaviors important to the success factors of each unit can be reinforced. While there will be fundamental differences, everyone can participate in several programs. This can and should produce a sense of excitement about achieving results. The measures should be related to the central themes of the key success factors of the firm and the overall reward strategy. This strengthens the alignment of strategy to measures of behaviors. In this way, the firm achieves its desire to be more competitive with pay, but does so by creating opportunities for people to win.

Issues Common to Emerging Companies

As a firm becomes successful, so it become more at risk. Growth and market acceptance open new challenges that are often more subtle and more fundamental than when the firm was small. Growth means change. Size by its very nature creates problems that need to be

addressed in order for the firm to remain viable. The company needs
to address the strategic, structural, and managerial challenges of
growth in order to become stronger in its marketplace. Alternatively,
the owner may choose to keep the company at an earlier stage, prefer-
ring the values and the culture of the small firm. In this case, as the
firm grows, it subdivides itself back into a collection of small firms
bonded together only through an ownership structure. Thermo-
Electron of Waltham, Massachusetts, is an example of this management structure. While the overall company is several hundred millions
dollars in size, it is really just a network of small firms.

In this context of growth and change, several fundamental issues
emerge. While the reward systems cannot solve these issues, they can
create conditions in which answers can be found.

1. *The owner has been so reinforced at one stage that he or she will not let
go.* As stated above, the problem with reinforcement is that it
becomes habit-forming! Some executives of successful small companies believe that they are uniquely endowed with leadership qualities
and that they know everything that is to be known. This attitude can
be reflected in a pattern of "all-knowing-and-all-powerful" behavior.
The problem is that such executives often control all the resources of
the firm. Sometimes only an outsider who has a strong personal relationship with the owner can open the door to change. Individuals
working for this type of owner often have no choice but to cope,
ignore, or act. "Acting" may involve finding new ways to influence or
finally leaving the company.

2. *The reward systems become focused on control.* As stated in earlier
chapters, many large companies have become saddled with reward
systems based on a command-and-control philosophy. This approach
gets conveyed in job descriptions that reflect power and authority, and
in incentive systems that basically reinforces management needs for
control and power. The pay system may be so complex and cumbersome that individuals cannot understand it and the plan has minimal
impact on behaviors. Finally, the reward systems may become so
focused on what others are doing outside the firm that fundamental
internal requirements are ignored. Such pay systems then become
mere distributions systems for cash. They simply determine how dollars are allocated and stop being a meaningful process for rewarding
achievements.

3. *Executives seek to "buy" a solution.* Companies experiencing rapid
growth simply do not have the time to implement new programs.
There is a level of impatience, a sense of urgency, that is important to
their survival but that often leads to wasted efforts. An executive in a
rapidly growing light manufacturing firm indicated that his firm had

no time to plan or prepare but was willing to apply lots of resources to fix problems. This preference for speed and simplicity over thoroughness and effectiveness can show itself in almost every decision. When it comes to reward systems, particularly performance appraisals, such firms want a new form or a training program that will act as a cure-all. They seek incentive programs that are simple to understand and administer. These executives are vulnerable to outsiders who offer quick-fix solutions. The new programs may make the executives feel good for a time and create the illusion that the problems are solved, only to create more fundamental alienation in the workforce. While outside expertise is often required to achieve desired change, the process needs to be internally based.

4. *Because of past success, executives fail to listen.* One of the traps of success occurs when organizations fail to listen to the customer, the competitors, or outside advisors. Executives and senior managers begin to believe that what was right in the past will be right for the future. The "not invented here" syndrome emerges, and a once-flexible, once-responsive organization becomes slow, structured, and resistant to change. Once again, the seeds of success lead the organization to ultimate vulnerability.

5. *People become incapable of handling new challenges.* As the organization grows, especially if it does so at a rapid pace, the current staff may not be equipped to handle the emerging challenges. It is often difficult to distinguish between a lack of true capabilities and a pattern of habits reinforced by earlier successes but no longer appropriate. When new people are hired and assimilated into the organization, they often challenge conventional wisdom. Sometimes these confrontations are exactly what the firm needs. At other times they reflect a fundamental misfit in values. The behaviors may be the same but the root causes are not. These challenges often present serious personal dilemmas for the owner. He or she must choose between opposing viewpoints, each seemingly committed to the well-being of the organization. It often takes a wise and courageous individual to discover the truth.

These problems can represent a pattern that inhibits an organization from developing from one stage to another. The future viability of an organization is often at risk—perhaps at high risk—when the capabilities and habits of the organization are no longer appropriate to address the current issues. The task therefore is to continue learning, challenge the assumptions, and take actions that have not been taken before. If based on a clear commitment to the customer, continual improvement, and the celebration of achievements, the process of change and renewal can become a characteristic of the successful firm.

Some Dos and Don'ts for Reward Systems

The stages of development for the emerging company and the common issues that often confront the firm, set the backdrop for managing reward systems. The following pages will examine a variety of dos and don'ts that the reader may find helpful. They are intended to prevent the bureaucratic syndrome from emerging within the firm as it grows and develops. These guidelines are keyed to each of the elements of the total reward system.

Base Salary: Try These Ideas

The primary purpose of the base salary program, if there is one, is to attract and retain the skills and talent needed by the business. While the focus may appear to be on external competitiveness, the real message is understanding how the firm should align its pay structure with the roles, contributions, and value-added nature of work. To this end, the following are preferred actions.

1. *Establish pay levels based on the importance of the tasks to creating value for the firm.* Value is defined as providing what the customer wants, with the optimal use of resources. Therefore, pay levels need to reflect the roles and/or talent individuals bring to the organization, not what they control or manage.

2. *Calibrate your pay levels to the right market.* The right market is the sources of the human resources the firm needs to do its business. It is often defined by the companies from which people are hired and to which they move on. This flow of talent often determines where the company needs to focus its attention to remain competitive.

3. *Review your situation annually, but don't necessarily make pay adjustments annually.* Adjustments in pay should be based on several related factors. These include:
   - The continual value of the role within the strategy of the firm
   - How the market is paying for similar talent
   - The ability of the firm to pay (i.e., affordability)
   - The performance and contributions of individuals within this role

   When a role is assessed from these perspectives, the firm may or may not make adjustments to base salary.

4. *Stay flexible and make adjustments to base salary contingent on the performance of the individual, the unit/team, and the company.* If the performance is comparable to marketplace performance, make marketplace adjustments with confidence. If the performance is above or

below marketplace performance, alter the adjustments to reflect this. Avoid the trap of having to make salary adjustments just because that is what is done by competitors or because of cost-of-living factors. But don't withhold pay increases that may exceed competitors' if performance has been demonstrated.

Base Salary: Avoid These Pitfalls

1. *Don't tie pay levels to the resources a position controls, is responsible for, or manages.* Instead, link pay levels to positions making the greatest contribution to customers, including internal customers.

2. *Don't try to keep pace with inflation.* In the 1970s and 1980s, many organizations attempted to keep people's increases in step with inflation, only to see the costs of living escalate beyond ability to pay. Pay levels almost always exceed increases in inflation except in periods of very high rates or at times when the rates are increasing rapidly. Cost-of-living pay raises should be abandoned because they do little for the organization and create an entitlement mentality within the workforce. Instead, create opportunities for people to earn additional compensation through performance and achievements.

3. *Don't pay for seniority.* While organizations need people who are loyal and committed, this does not mean the organization needs to be held hostage to the long-timers. Instead, equate pay levels with contributions and impact. Let people earn the right to receive additional pay and provide many opportunities for this to occur. Reinforce people's long-term service with personal, immediate, and contingent reinforcement.

4. *Avoid the zero-sum game.* Many organizations have used traditional merit guidelines as a means of controling pay increases (see Chapter 5). If someone were to get more than the budget amount, someone else would have to get less. This is the zero-sum game. (It's no wonder that people think pay does not reflect performance.) Instead, relate pay to achievements or the application of increased capabilities. Use the financial budgeting system to control compensation expenses and reward/punish managers for using the system well/not well. Consider making the merit budget flexible, based on team or company performance (see Chapter 5).

5. *Don't depend on the base pay system to motivate people.* While in theory the base pay system should reinforce performance, current practices make it basically ineffective. Since, by its very nature, the pay system has a built-in delay between action and reward, it cannot be an effective system for rewarding performance. It should therefore

serve to support other reward systems that do have more meaning-ful, immediate impact on performance. Don't expect the base pay system to do all you want it to do. It can assist, but it cannot score.

Variable Compensation: Try These Ideas

The fundamental purpose of the variable pay system should be to cre-ate a stake in the results of the business. If the firm or unit/team does well, the rewards should be forthcoming. If the firm or unit/team does not do well, the financial rewards will not be there. It is essential that variable pay programs be truly contingent on performance. Otherwise, they reflect entitlement management.

1. *Focus the measures on what defines the success of the firm.* Variable pay should be linked to a few high-priority measures of perfor-mance. Therefore, they need to define results that will enable the firm to be competitive in the present and in the future. This is per-haps the most important task of developing a variable pay program.

2. *Support the program with regular, meaningful feedback and frequent, valuable reinforcement.* When variable pay programs fail, it is often because people cannot see what they should do to impact the num-bers. Thus, any variable pay program needs to be translated into personalized measures that provide guidance to action. Then, feed-back and reinforcement of achievements can encourage people to try harder, do better, and be successful.

3. *Make the payouts as frequently as possible, as long as they support the cycles of the business.* When variable pay programs have a long time hori-zon, they are basically nonfunctional for two-thirds to three-fourths of the performance period. Frequency can be an important element of the reward system. However, programs that have very frequent pay-outs can lead to an oversimplification of measures like production goals. In these cases the actions may not support the competitive strategy or the real role of units in making the firm successful.

4. *Consider using a pool based on revenues or profitability to modify unit/team performance incentives.* In small companies, a profit-shar-ing program can provide an important means to create the sense of a shared fate. As the firm grows and roles become more differenti-ated, the usefulness of profit sharing may diminish. It may be valu-able for the executives but have little impact on the performers. A transition strategy can use the profit-sharing plan to create a fund-ing pool for incentives, but team-based measures should define the payout opportunity and levels. Care must be taken not to create competition for the pool. This can be achieved by using the pool to modify the planned payouts given for performance.

5. *Link the managers with the performance of their units.* One fatal flaw in some incentive plans is a plan for managers that is different from the plan for their performers. This can create a situation in which the performers receive small payouts while their managers receive large payouts. There are few devices that undermine the collaboration and common spirit of an organization more than this. Therefore, set at least—or, better yet, *all* of a manager's incentives—on the same basis as those of their unit. This way, their incentive payouts will be dependent on those they are expected to supervise. This situation creates mutual consequences in direct and meaningful ways.

Variable Pay: Avoid These Pitfalls

1. *Avoid/eliminate discretionary incentive plans.* This type of program serves to undermine the leadership of an organization in several ways. First, everyone quickly figures out that the key to an award is looking good to the supervisor/manager. The customers' needs take a back seat to the boss's approval. Second, such programs reinforce the executives' need for power rather than a companywide focus on the customer. These plans create a series of power-based relationships with all the trappings of dependency and arrogance. While flexibility may be necessary because of ongoing changes in business conditions, discretionary plans divert people's attention from the most important part of the game: the customer.

2. *Don't wait until the game is over before giving them the score.* Regular feedback on the progress of performance is essential to winning the game. Most people can understand good news/bad news if they hear it on a regular basis. The data becomes believable, credible. They should hear how they are doing at least three if not five or more times during a performance period. People begin to take important actions when the feedback points toward the possibility of achieving desired goals.

3. *If incentives work for some, they can work for others. Don't be too restrictive.* The problem for many small companies is their fear of including too many people in an incentive plan. They worry that additional money may be paid out when people have not earned it. They complain that a base salary is for an expected level of performance, so why should it be necessary to pay more? The reality is that people respond very effectively to incentive plans that they feel are fair—that pass the SMART tests. Furthermore, amounts within a 3 percent to 5 percent of salary have been shown to be sufficient to optimize performance. The issue is not the amount, but the way in which an incentive plan is structured and managed. To

this end, if incentives work well to motivate managers, they can also work well for other performers within an organization.

Performance Management: Try These Ideas

The primary purpose of the performance management process is to provide real-time feedback and reinforcement to performers. This includes day-to-day management involvement, team celebrations, special recognition programs, and performance reviews. Small companies have perhaps a greater opportunity than do large companies for providing these reinforcement events if they understand that they do not need to cost a lot of money. Small companies often hold back on these practices because they feel they cannot afford them. Dinner for everyone at a big downtown hotel or some resort outing may indeed be out of the question. But small firms can find or create other ways of celebrating the contributions of their staff. In fact, they may be better equipped to do so than their large-company counterparts. The limitations are often more a state of mind than of resources.

1. *Focus on the variables critical to the firm's success.*   It is often easier for small firms to explain customer priorities to their staff than it is for large firms. All directives should point in this direction, and people should see many opportunities where they can individually and collectively contribute to these ends. This is a fundamental role of the firm's leaders regardless of where they sit in the organization.

2. *Create a real-time, chart-oriented feedback system.*   Using the critical measures, display charts that reflect where the firm is heading. This visual display should create performer interest and excitement as achievements are recognized. A shop that provides mail services displayed its performance on a daily basis in the stockroom. It also listed its key customers and placed gold stars by their names when they were being served well.

3. *Create celebrations that mean something to the performers.*   Often the more meaningful celebrations are the ones done on a shoestring budget. This requires creativity, ingenuity, and true resourcefulness. One will know if these events are meaningful if the talk the morning after reflects a desire to "do it again" (i.e., achieve the desired performance).

4. *Use performance reviews as an opportunity to reflect "how we won" and "how we lost," make them as often as necessary to cement in the learning.* Performance reviews that give employees judgment-based feedback from the supervisor quickly undermine the desired relationship. The manager may have opinions, but they need to be integrat-

ed as just one perspective in a process of learning. The focus should be on understanding how the employee was able to overcome obstacles and achieve good results (i.e., positive reinforcement) and on examining what can be done differently next time to avoid or handle difficult situations (i.e., learning). In both cases, the individual should get the message and the manager should understand the facts, not just his or her perceptions, of the situation.

5. *Anchor the memory of achievements.* An organization that becomes oriented toward entitlement does not know when or how to celebrate. People seldom turn down awards, and they may grow to expect them regardless of performance. Achievement-oriented firms measure a lot, accomplish milestones frequently, and do much celebrating. There is a lot of energy and excitement, surprises and special events, and people enjoy working there. They see results from what they do and they feel valued for their contributions. This practice is not dependent on the work or the nature of the business, but rather on the leadership and the process of managing performance. The greatest celebrations are those that firmly anchor the memory of an acknowledged accomplishment. Such occasions encourage people to believe they can do it again, and they will make every effort to try.

Performance Management: Avoid These Pitfalls

1. *Don't rely on annual performance appraisals.* For many of the above reasons, annual appraisals delay feedback and establish confrontational situation between managers and employees. If there is little or no real-time feedback to performers, the company may actually be worse off than before.

2. *Avoid recognition programs that honor only the individual—employee of the month, the top 10 percent, etc.* These programs seldom yield desired performance and tend to reinforce the role of executives as all-knowing, all-powerful. I wish executives could hear what people say about them after some awards ceremonies. If they did, they would never put on such a function again.

3. *Don't force-rank individuals for purposes of awarding merit or incentive pay.* This process assumes that performance is based on individual actions alone or that individuals all have the same performance opportunity. Neither is the case, and such actions give executives a misleading picture of their true stars. This does not make poor managers good, but it does make good managers do poor things.

4. *Avoid "doing what the Joneses do" and the "let's make a form" game.* While organizations can learn a great deal from benchmarking others and learning the practices of successful companies, this information needs to be interpreted in the light of the firm's own history, business circumstances, and reinforcement practices. As a client executive of mine once said: "While there is no clear road to success, not every road will get you there. We have to understand and apply the principles that work. When we get results, we have to know why." He meant that there are principles of truth that need to be understood and practiced within a firm for it to be successful. Further, although impatience is often a virtue in small companies, it can also lead a firm to approach tasks in a wasteful and trivial manner. The form is not the answer; rather, the key to success lies in the process. Learning what one does by learning what others do can be of some value. But the best learning process is the one that discovers the gains one can create at home.

Sustaining the Value of an Emerging Company

Perhaps the most important message of this chapter to those in emerging companies is to utilize the opportunities you possess to create and sustain an organization in which people achieve because they feel valued for doing so. Emerging companies have many advantages over their larger counterparts. First, the customer is often known or dealt with by almost everyone in the firm. Second, people tend to know each other, and personal relationships may span the entire organization. This enables reinforcers to be more personalized and meaningful to the individual. Third, the pace of change is fast, and the risks of failure are great. Therefore, actions that slow the ability of the firm to serve or respond to customers often have serious consequences. Finally, people do not need the permission of some distant authority to take action and celebrate achievements. They do not have to wait until external auditors have completed their assessments. They usually don't have to wait till the end of the performance period to know how they are doing. The pace and sense of urgency can create an environment that is oriented toward action.

Risks to the survival of small companies can arise in several areas. First, an organization may fail simply because it does not have the resources or financial flexibility to compete with larger, financially better-endowed competitors. In such cases, failure is due to factors outside the firm's control. Second, a few individuals in key positions of power and influence may be more interested in supporting their own egos than in serving customers or building an effective organization. They may present major barriers that cannot be worked around. Third, the firm may not take advantage of its size and inherent flexibility to utilize the opportunities available. These opportunities may include making decisions about meeting a customer's unique needs, measuring and displaying results of business outcomes, and reinforcing people who have made a difference.

This chapter has attempted to provide a road map for how to prevent the problems currently experienced by large companies. Reward systems for an emerging company cannot be separated from the process of managing. This is both a virtue and a challenge, one from which large firms could well learn a lesson. The effectiveness of a system lies in how it is used, not in its design. Therefore, small companies have the responsibility and the ability to use reward systems to their advantage. While they often cannot pay as high as the larger firms, they can create an environment in which people want to excel. While they may not have the systems to track critical performance data, they can make the measurement and feedback systems more personal, more real-time, and more meaningful to their performers. While they may not have the resources to create fancy special events, they do not have to wait till the game is over and the fans have gone home to celebrate.

The fundamental message is to keep the focus on serving the customer, to use measures and feedback to create opportunities for reinforcing desired actions, and to continue to adjust the reward systems as the firm develops. One size does not fit all; what is right for today may not be so for the near future. Hence, continual improvements need to become a hallmark of reward systems in small companies. In this way, they can create an environment in which people excel, customers keep coming back, and the firm not only becomes truly successful but able to create a new order of things within the marketplace it holds dear.

Notes

1. The reader may choose to selection from the following for an excellent description of the stages of growth of small companies:

   Churchill, N. C., and Lewis, V. L., "The Five Stages of Small Business Growth," *Harvard Business Review*, May-June, 1983, p 30.

   Greiner, L. E., "Evolution and Revolution as Organizations Grow," *Harvard Business Review*, July-August, 1972, p. 37.

   McGuire, J. W., *Factors Affecting the Growth of Manufacturing Firms*. Seattle, Wash.: Bureau of Business Research, University of Washington, 1963.

   Rostow, W. W., *The Stages of Economic Growth*. Cambridge, England: Cambridge University Press, 1960.

14

Reward Systems for the Giant Learning to Dance

How do you do more with less? Do less!
—FRANCES C. GRIGSBY
Motorola Codex

I saw great businesses become the ghost of a name because someone thought they could manage just as they (always) were managed.
—HENRY FORD

There is perhaps no challenge so broad in its impact as that of changing a large organization. The work of Rosabeth Moss Kanter, who wrote *When Giants Learn to Dance*[1] and the foreword to this book, Michael Beer,[2] Richard Beckhard,[3] and many others has discussed the dangers and opportunities of creating change in large organizations. The complexity is immense. The task is monumental. The opportunities are enormous. And the need is very real.

In the *Fortune* magazine article "Nothing is Impossible,"[4] Noel Tichy states: "You're walking a very lonely road. Life in a large corporation is easier if you go with the flow and don't support major change....The corporate environment just doesn't reward people for changing the status quo."

Understanding Resistance to Change

The reasons for the resistance to change are complex, but they can be understood by reviewing some of the core concepts in this book. Companies grow in the first place because of their successes. Customers want their products or services, and the organization prospers. At this point, companies have traditionally adopted the organizational models of the military and the Catholic Church because they have been effective and enduring. This command-and-control mentality has become the prevailing philosophy for the successful company.

But as organizations grow and the command-and-control management model increases, managers tend to become isolated from the external marketplace in general, and from their customers in particular. Managers spend more time working on internal issues than on dealing with the impact of their firm's products/services on the customer. They are often rewarded and promoted for their strong abilities to manage or lead internally.

Finally, *employees* become isolated from the marketplace as well. Their attention turns from pleasing the customer to pleasing their supervisors. They receive regular pay increases, steady promotions, and job security regardless of what they do or what is happening in the marketplace. The employee-employer contract of entitlement and loyalty emerges as a natural order of things.

Because of this dependable growth and prosperity and because of the lack of any significant link or interface with the customer, employees have become accustomed to the conditions that define their world. They believe that annual merit raises are simply a natural part of working life. For their part, managers believe that discretionary bonus programs and employee-of-the-month clubs are an appropriate way to reward individuals; they don't even think about other feasible ways of managing rewards.

The Trouble with Success

The trouble with reinforcement, or success, is that it creates paradigms. When we believe we will receive certain reinforcers for certain actions, we come to believe that this cause-and-effect is reality. Unless experience refutes this impression or we arrive at a better understanding of the basis of success, we naturally believe that certain things are fact.

In Plato's *Republic,* the allegory of the cave provides a very important lesson. The story corcerns a group of people who have been chained to the walls of a cave for their entire lives. They see shadows moving on the cave walls as people walk past a fire burning behind them, and the cave people believe that these shadows represent reality. Then, one day an individual gets free. He leaves the cave to explore the world outside, and what he discovers astounds him. He comes to realize that the shadows are only images created by firelight. He understands that the sun produces the seasons and is the ultimate cause of all that he and his companions experience. But when he returns to the cave and tells the others, they cannot believe him. They laugh at him and say his venture has ruined his eyes. They ridicule his stories as fabrications bent on destroying the values of their cave society; he is a person gone crazy. In the end if his cohorts in the cave could get to him, they would kill him.

Large organizations in many industries are stuck in their own paradigms. These paradigms emerge because executives are reinforced for traditional practices. The command-and-control mentality that results comes to be viewed as real. The trouble is that the outside world has changed. The change has not been sudden; no earthquake has shaken the world. It has just become steadily more difficult to be successful.

Responding to the Pressures for Change

The normal response by organizations—and by managers in particular—is to try harder, to do more, to increase the number of "special projects." When we explored the four types of consequences in Chapter 3, we learned about *extinction,* which occurs when people do not receive something they were expecting for something they have done. They increase their activities, hoping that the problem is really just one of extra effort. It isn't, of course, but they don't yet know this. Despite all their efforts, their contributions continue to go unnoticed. They go from frustration to burnout and eventually cease to make much of an effort at all. The extinction process is complete.

An example of this sydrome occurred at a division of a large industrial company that was attempting to address a major decline in market share that had occurred over a ten-year period. Initially, the focus was on reducing costs and increasing productivity. The general manager had more than 30 major projects underway, including reducing a head count, eliminating piece-rate incentives, implementing a materials-planning system, establishing self-managed teams, investing in new equipment and technology, developing new products, and training managers. But there were no central themes to guide these projects, and most people felt that they were just a series of unrelated programs. The announcement of yet another program just seemed like more mashed potatoes on an already overladen plate. In a similar situation, the CEO of a large health insurance company instituted more

than 250 different major projects for her senior executives to implement. The focus was around a series of vague issues calling for
"change," but there were few central themes.

Such approaches can actually slow the rate of change because
employees are accountable only for implementing programs, not for
changing the organization, while managers are recognized only for
implementing changes, not for improving the business. Employees
begin to lose confidence in the leadership of the firm. They see a lot of
activities, but very little progress in any clear direction.

What Has Changed?

We discussed a series of pressures and trends for change in Chapter 1.
The most fundamental is that the market has changed. The customer's
needs and opportunities have altered, and the competitive landscape
has become more complex. Organizations that were built on the old
model need to understand the changes in order to respond to them
effectively. To make these changes more concrete, let's briefly examine
three industries.

In the retailing industry, Sears once dominated the landscape of
America. Sears is now facing survival issues arising from the emergence of discount stores like Wal-Mart and various catalog and direct
sales networks. Furthermore, consumers' preference has changed from
one-stop shopping to specialty shopping. They are buying on the basis
of both price and quality; they are seeking value. Shopping malls provide both convenience and specialty in one location.

Sears is currently undergoing major strategic and organizational
repositioning. This includes changing its pricing strategy and using
sales instead of everyday low pricing. The company is implementing
various strategies to simplify its stores and its supporting infrastructure. Regional and district offices are disappearing, and the store managers are being provided with more on-line services through the use of
technology and greater control over their stores. Finally, Sears is
divesting itself of many of its holdings outside the consumer products
retail market (e.g., Dean Whitter, Allstate Insurance, Caldwell
Realtors, etc.) in order to generate the cash necessary to support business investments and a return to its roots. The organization is seeking
to become more competitive both through its business portfolio and
through re-engineering and structural change.

IBM and Digital Equipment are fighting for survival because of a
change in the demands of their customers. The major buyer is no
longer the chief technologist or management information systems
executive, but the line manager and consumer. They are buying computer systems that are easy to use, personalized, decentralized, flexi-

ble to specific needs, and fun to work with. They are interested in networking with others, in communication, and in mobile flexibility. Why should you have to be hardwired to tap into a mail or communications network, when you can walk down the street talking on the phone?

Both IBM and Digital Equipment are implementing wholesale structural and process changes in the way they do business. Layers of control and internal competition are being replaced by focused accountabilities and cost reductions. IBM is experimenting with changing the incentive program for their sales staff by weighing 40 percent of the payment on customer satisfaction measures. Whether they are successful in the long term will largely depend on whether they can change their cultures and return to their roots in customer service and market sensitivity.

The big three U.S. automakers—General Motors, Ford, and Chrysler—have been engaged in a battle for survival for almost twenty years. General Motors has seen its market share drop from more than 50 percent in the mid-1950s to less than 35 percent in 1992. In the mid-1960s foreign imports accounted for approximately 10 percent of the market; by 1992 this market share had grown to almost 35 percent. This decline is well documented and each firm has pursued a change strategy focused on customers, costs, and employee commitments.

Each of these organizations is undergoing massive restructuring. General Motors has tended to emphasize investments in plant, equipment, and technology. Ford has emphasized management and teamwork. Chrysler has focused on research, development, and product redesigns. How successful they are in achieving market leadership will depend on the effectiveness of their strategies and on the actions of people within their firms to implement change.

In 1963 Thomas J. Watson, Jr., then chairman of IBM, reported in a lecture series at Columbia University that only two of the companies that appeared on the *Fortune* top 25 list in 1900 still existed. (The two remaining companies were General Electric and U.S. Steel/USX.)[5] This was truly a warning to all that once an organizataion reaches the top of an industry, its greatest challenge is to remain there.

The Rise of Managerial Fads

Organizations have been responding to these threats with change initiatives. If one were to examine the litany of change efforts over the past 15 years, we would find an amazing array of initiatives. Some of these include:

Sensitivity Training	Vision and Values
Quality Circles	Benchmarking/Best In Class
Synergy/Portfolio Management	Total Quality Management
Mergers/Acquisitions	Continuous Improvement
Centralize/Decentralize	Cycle Time Reduction
Management by Walking Around	Downsizing
Corporate Culture	Self-Managed Teams
Leadership Development	Employee Empowerment
Management by Objectives	Re-Engineering
Strategic Alliances	Focused Customer Service

The rise of these initiatives comes from a need to find the holy grail, the answer to the question, *what should we do differently?* Each tends to begin with one or more executives who believe that there is a problem deep within the organization. They then read about a successful company, see a presentation of particular interest, or hear about a new initiative. After reading more about the program and perhaps sending a representative to a training session or visit a successful company, they become convinced that this program is the answer to their problems. Managers, supervisors, and others are trained in how to implement the particular practices required by the program. (People go along because it would clearly be "career limiting" to resist such efforts, but their quiet hope is that "this, too, will pass.") Then the executives sit back and wait to see the return on their investment.

The whole "new initiative" cycle can really be characterized by the following statement: "Having lost sight of our objectives, we redoubled our efforts." There is a sense of urgency on the part of the top executives. There is an impatience to get people through the programs or get the teams up and running. At times there are wonderful surprises that emerge from deep inside the organization. One operator trains another and the results are a dramatic drop in the scrap rates. A team restructures its work and is able to cut cycle time. There may be celebration, but there is also a general mumbling about why this wasn't done before, and some middle managers become the scapegoats for resistance to change.

The Saturn plant of General Motors in Spring Hill, Tennessee, has a unique opportunity to form an organization with a different set of traditions. The plant was formed to break the mold of traditional manufacturing technology within GM. It had the luxury of starting from scratch. GM involved many employees in the design and construction processes, and has continued to emphasize this involvement now that the plant is fully functional. Saturn regularly communicates to people about the business, its competition, and its concerns about product design, manufacturing, delivery, and marketing. Many elements of the plant are involved in running the business. Saturn pays its employees slightly less than the equivalent base wage in other GM facilities. However, it provides an additional 7 percent of pay to those who complete training requirements of 92 hours per year. Saturn also offers employees a profit-sharing/gain-sharing incentive based on quality and financial performance.

While the Saturn experiment has been highly successful, issues still remain. The challenge is one of continuing the improvements at a rate that is faster than the competition's. There is no end point at which GM can stop investing in Saturn; its continued success lies in GM's continual efforts.

The Common Themes in Implementing Change

Each of the "giants learning to dance" is facing a marketplace that has changed, not gradually, but radically. These pressures for change tend to revolve around one or a combination of factors that include:

1. *Quality.* Customers want increased reliability, convenience, personalized features, and commitments that are met.

2. *Service.* Customers want their requests listened to and acted on in a timely, caring, and effective manner. Their problems need to be understood, taken seriously, and dealt with *swiftly*.

3. *Time.* Time to market is increasingly differentiating competitors. The issue is a combination of getting the product or service to the customer more quickly, and being sure that it is there *when the customer wants it*.

4. *Cost.* The price of a product is measured in terms of its value, and often this value is established by factoring in quality, service, and time and then comparing the product's cost with that of the competitors' products. In many industries quality or service is less a differentiating factor in the eyes of customers than is price.

These changing requirements in the marketplace are causing large organizations to seek and implement many changes in the way they do things. The primary themes that emerge when one examines the wide variety of change efforts tend to fall into six areas, which will be described as they affect the survival and future prosperity of the large corporation. (See Figure 14-1.)

1. *Focus on what is valued by the customer.* Perhaps the greatest stimulus to change comes from bringing teams of people closer to their

1. Focus on what is valued by the customer.
2. Break down the walls that impede responsiveness and change.
3. Build strong partnerships with suppliers and customers.
4. Reduce all low-value-added activities.
5. Increase speed in all aspects of work.
6. Continually seek improvements.

Figure 14-1.   Common themes of implementing change.

customers. In Chapter 10 we explored how to develop performance measures so that they reflect the needs of the customer rather than the needs of management. This drive to understand and build a strong relationship with customers is key to breaking down the walls that divide people. Paul Allaire, CEO of Xerox, stated: "I have to change the company substantially to be more market-driven. If we do what's right for the customer, our market share and our return on assets will take care of themselves."[6]

Xerox, for example, had always prided itself on shipping the product to the customer faster than its competitors. The problem was that the customers wanted to know when to expect the product so that they could be prepared to install it, with as little disruption as possible in their operations. Allaire asked a team of midlevel managers and staff to find a way to do this. The team developed a tracking system for each copier through the distribution process, with a focus on meeting the *customer's* deadline. The measurement system, feedback, and reinforcement practices helped Xerox improve its customer satisfaction score from 70 percent to 90 percent.

2. Break down the walls that impede responsiveness and change.   AT&T focuses its people on identifying with its four core businesses: telephone networks, telecommunications equipment, consumer products, and computers. The organization utilizes an operations committee, made up of the business heads, the CEO, and the CFO, which meets for two days monthly and rotates chairmanship annually. In line with Rosabeth Kanter's emphasis on seeking synergies,[7] AT&T utilizes cross-functional business teams to explore and develop capabilities that will potentiate the competencies of each business. AT&T's greatest collaborative opportunities are with video, wireless communication, data transmission, voice recognition and processing, and messaging.

But interlacing businesses with matrices and interlocking directorates can potentially direct people's attention away from customers to problems of role clarification and conflict resolution. One needs to explore the value-added nature of these activities and ensure the activities retain the customer performance focus and create new opportunities for people. As Jack Welch, CEO of General Electric, has stated: "For a large system to be effective, it must be simple."[8]

In this era of breaking down the traditional roles and decentralizing business functions, managers are challenged to address these areas. First, managers need to understand the environment in which their businesses operate. Second, managers need to understand what the competitors are doing and what impact they are having. Third, managers need to outline the actions of their businesses to capitalize on market opportunities, fight the competition, and respond to threats.[9]

The key issue in successful decentralization is determining the organizing concept of the firm. Should it be around customers, markets, products and services, geographic markets, or functional capabilities? The resolution of these structural issues is often strategically imperative; it will drive the reward systems and the actions of the people within the firm.

3. *Build strong partnerships with suppliers and customers.* Organizations can be more flexible when they create alliances, partnerships, and joint ventures that complement their own core competencies. Toshiba has made a practice of creating such strategic alliances. It forms alliances with companies that give it a competitive edge in the design, manufacturing, distribution, and marketing of electrical/electronic products. Of the search for synergies with other organizations within and outside the company, Fumio Sata, president and CEO of Toshiba, has said: "It is no longer an era in which a single company can dominate any technology or business by itself. The technology has become so advanced and the markets so complex that you simply can't expect to be the best at the whole process any longer."[10]

North American Tool and Dye Company (NATD) makes sheet metal components for computer manufacturers like Apple and Hewlett Packard. It regularly involves engineers, operations, and quality people in its product review and problem-solving meetings. It has built such good relationships with its customers that it is often hard to differentiate NATD employees from its customers on the shop floor.

4. *Reduce all low-value-added activities.* The emphasis on re-engineering had its roots in the early 1930s, when industrial engineers developed concepts of workflow analysis—documenting the process of work in order to develop more efficient procedures. At the Vanderbilt Owen Graduate School of Management, research studies have identified some very interesting patterns in value-added work. Especially notable is the dramatic "wait-times" in most organizations. Vanderbilt's research has shown that less than 5 percent of the time is typically spent on a prod-

uct from initial order to delivery. The other 95 percent of the time, the product is waiting for someone to get to the tasks necessary to ship it to the customer. (Figure 14-2 shows these value-added activities.)

The challenge of re-engineering work is to find ways in which employees can improve their responsiveness to the customer without working harder, a task that requires understanding and removing barriers to quality, service, speed, and cost. This is the central focus of many total quality management efforts and re-engineering or transformation change initiatives.

5. *Increase speed in all aspects of work.* If a competitor can get the customers what they want when they want it (i.e., on time) and at a price they are willing to pay, the competitor will be victorious (and so will the customer). In an increasing number of industries, speed, not quality, is defining the competitive edge. If a product or service is not of the highest quality, the company will not even be able to play the game. Elements of quality may be of limited value to the customer. Removing the wait-times and other barriers is an important element in increasing speed.

Speed is an important determinent of success. McKinsey & Company completed a study of the high-technology industry and discovered an interesting fact: products that come to market six months late, but on budget, will earn approximately 33 percent less profit over five years. In contrast, products that come out on time with a 50 percent budget overrun, see a decline in profits of only 4 percent.[11]

John Young, CEO of Hewlett Packard, says, "Doing it fast forces you to do it right the first time." Further, products that can be manufactured with great speed enable the organization to yield a greater return on their fixed assets (i.e., capital equipment and facilities) and

Tasks	Industry	Average Cycle Time	Value-Added Time	Average Wait Time
Policy Application	Insurance	10 days	7 minutes	4793 minutes
Patient Billing	Healthcare	10 days	3 minutes	4797 minutes
Consumer Loan	Banking	2 days	34 minutes	1886 minutes
Claims Processing	Blue Cross/ Blue Shield	17 days	12 minutes	8148 minutes

Figure 14-2. The time it takes to do things.

inventory. Speed is the product of reducing low-value-added activities and creating a positive sense of urgency. Establishing work processes that minimize the tasks, distance, and wait-time for products increases the speed of the workflow. However, firms that emphasize speed in order to cut costs are seldom successful. Those that emphasize speed to accomplish market advantage are better positioned to win, and their costs are reduced as a side benefit.

To illustrate, General Electric used to take three weeks to deliver a custom-made industrial circuit breaker. It now can accomplish this in three days. At Motorola it use to take three weeks to deliver an electronic pager. Now the product can be assembled in two hours. A bicycle shop in Tokyo can produce a completely customized product to fit your shape, size, interest, and color preferences in less than two hours. Each of these companies has a unique and powerful competitive advantage.

6. *Continually seek improvements in everything you do.* Executives, managers, and team members who are unable to think outside the current way of doing things will continue to miss opportunities. By living in their own cave of paradigms, they will be limited to defining problems and solutions as they have been defined always in the past. Asking simple questions like, "Why does it have to be this way?" or, "If we could start over with a blank sheet of paper, how would we do it?" are essential to continuing the process of change.

Sony and JVC engineers envisioned a videotape recorder that could be delivered for one-thousandth of the then-market price: $500 versus $500,000. Fidelty Investments created a market of investor services for the average person. Fred Smith rejected his professors at Yale and created a package delivery system called Federal Express. Hal Sperlich could not get the executives at Ford to buy into the minivan, but found a home at Chrysler. George Fisher, the former CEO of Motorola, reflects his management vision when he says: "As you drive your business, you focus on the cause, not the result. You focus on the quality segment. Those are the right things to focus on in a business. But if you're doing all those things really well, your profits are going to be there, your market share is going to be there, and your customer satisfaction is going to be there."[12] An executive of a large southern insurance company sought to clarify accountabilities for his employees when he stated: "Your job is not just to do your job, but to improve it."

What's Missing?

On reviewing these six major themes for improving the competitiveness of a firm, what we find missing is an understanding of the dynamics of human behavior. As Steward put it at the conclusion of a *Fortune* magazine article on re-engineering: "When the consultants move on and the process map comes down from the wall, the painfully won gains will leak away unless the employees who have to live with the new work design had a hand in creating it and unless the human systems of the company—compensation, career paths, training—reinforce the changes."[13]

Each of the points Steward touches on indicates the need for people to do some things differently. Many traditional change efforts involve re-engineering work, restructuring reporting relationships (i.e., removing layers within an organization), training, communication campaigns, and setting up special task forces to study the problems (e.g., General Electric's workout sessions). We have three choices to get people to change:

1. Change the people—terminate those you don't want and hire those you do want.

2. Inform and train people to do what you want.

3. Create an environment in which people take the initiative to achieve the changes needed.

Although the third strategy is obviously the preferred one, most change efforts place only superficial emphasis on creating this environment. Many current thought leaders urge that people be given the freedom to create, pursue, or explore new ways to improve the firm's performance. While the ultimate objective is to create an environment in which people naturally achieve desired outcomes, the realization of this goal usually requires a process of transition and shaping (see Chapter 10). Reward systems can play an important part in this process.

Creating the Strategy for Rewards

In order to focus and develop the reward programs necessary to reinforce desired behaviors, one needs to formulate a reward strategy. This reward strategy will require a set of important preparation steps.

1. *The organization needs to get its strategy clear.* This means identifying the desired markets that build on the organization's core competencies and planning how the firm will establish a desired position in this marketplace. This analysis is critical to fully understanding the key success factors of the target group.

2. *Determine the role to be played by the reward systems in the change process.* Is it more important for the reward systems to *support* the

process of change or to serve as the *catalyst* or *driver* of change? The answer is often predicated on the nature of the change effort: re-creative or incremental change. The reward strategies will need to be tailored to the particular situation.

3. *Establish the necessary support for change among those who control the consequences.* Sponsorship is needed in order to create and manage organizational change. The degree of sponsorship and active involvement required are directly related to the degree of change required by the organization. The greater the sense of urgency and the need for change, the more active support and commitment will be needed from senior management in order to achieve success.

These three elements form a foundation for establishing a strategy for change using reward systems. As pointed out in the quotation from Steward's *Fortune* article on re-engineering, the gains will gradually disappear unless we change the conditions that influence the behaviors.

Rewards for Re-creative Change

Imagine a firm whose future survival is in doubt. It may not be facing immediate liquidation or bankruptcy, but there has been such an erosion of its market leadership that its competitors are regularly winning away its customers. The cost structure is very out of line with revenues. The products or services are outdated, given what is available on the market. The organization is tangled up in a set of bureaucratic strangleholds that slow down decision making. There are numerous turf battles going on. And waste is apparent is almost every area—materials, facilities, time, and human potential.

Now imagine that this firm gets a new leader, one who either comes from outside the firm or is an insider with an outsider's perspective. This leader recognizes the challenges facing the company and is very concerned about its near- and long-term prospects. Articulate and decisive, he or she has a vision of the firm as it could be and has already replaced some of the senior managers going down several levels within the organization and has made major shifts in accountabilities and reporting relationships. Employees may be both concerned about their job security or thankful that someone is finally taking action, or both. Managers are concerned about their role, their future, and whether or not they will be blamed for the failures of the firm. They are also hopeful that some desired changes are finally beginning to happen.

In terms of the strategy for change, imagine that the new senior management team has decided to focus on three critical objectives:

1. *Identify the firm's core competencies and devise a business strategy to regain the leadership in specific markets.* This includes translating the vision into a business strategy that focuses on the customer and the particular strengths of the organization. Senior managers need to communicate the critical importance of changing in this new direction if the organization is to survive. They must highlight the fact that the reason for these changes is the need to meet a changed external marketplace, not the need to correct the faults of people within the organization.

2. *Rid the organization of any structural elements that do not actively support these competencies and this strategy.* This includes divesting the company of certain businesses and cutting out redundant operations. This also includes removing unnecessary levels of management and any overcontrolling staff functions that do not add value to the firm's core competencies in the marketplace. Finally, this includes controlling costs and jettisoning some pet projects of the previous management.

3. *Create a culture within the organization that will translate the strategy into action.* This involves a series of critical implementation actions. First, the process of reformulating purpose and strategy must be implemented at lower levels in the organization. This involves an examination of current processes and aligning, developing, or changing work processes so that they are focused on adding value to the customer. Second, this means using cross-functional temporary task forces to examine various aspects of work and recommend ways to implement needed changes. Third, the organization must acquire or develop the necessary competencies to realize the changes needed by the business. This can come from external hiring in selected areas, transferring highly talented people to areas where their skills can be better utilized, and creating stronger alliances with selected suppliers, distributors, and competitors.

Up to this point, most of the company's change efforts have been of an antecedent or competence-building nature. This is critical for providing focus and direction to the change effort. However, the process of change is only beginning. Furthermore, because of the severity of the situation, the senior managers are very involved in providing the leadership necessary to drive the desired changes. This means that they attend critical meetings, make decisions quickly, and provide the resources where they are most needed (note the role of sponsor described in Chapter 11). Imagine that because of these efforts, the organization is gaining momentum and realizing some early successes. What will increase the rate of change as well as sustain it throughout the organization?

The reward strategy for this organization will require a series of integrated, targeted programs to support, if not lead, the process of change. Earlier chapters have outlined specific techniques and processes for building various types of reward systems. Here, we will examine the use of reward strategies in the following critical areas:

1. Reinforce a sense of urgency and a commitment to making changes consistent with the new strategy. This implies that any time frame for incentives or recognition programs needs to be short (on the spot, monthly, quarterly, or perhaps semi-annual).

2. Translate the strategic and competitive plans into measures that mean something important to every individual and to their role (their work) in the organization.

3. Provide a link between people and the future of the business unit to which they relate most closely. Focus the efforts of people on their business units and their immediate customers.

4. Emphasize the importance of implementing those changes that will enhance the use of resources, add value to the customer, and increase the speed at which products and services are provided.

5. Provide many opportunities for people to celebrate both large and small successes in rebuilding the competitiveness and attractiveness of the organization.

The implication of these requirements is that compensation programs cannot be managed from a central point. The emphasis needs to shift from controlling expenditures to utilizing them to reinforce desired actions. Expense control needs to shift to the line manager and the finance department. This means that those responsible for the compensation function need to work directly with the primary business units of the firm. Furthermore, the compensation programs need to be multifaceted and relate to particular target groups within the organization. The external competitiveness of pay levels should not be a primary issue of concern except in those areas where the firm seeks to attract specific functional talent. The focus needs to be on understanding the drivers for success in the particular business units and then on implementing programs that reinforce desired practices. Those practices must be contingent on meaningful measures that reflect the firm's key success factors and competencies and the customers' wants and needs.

In addition to ensuring support from the compensation function, the manager of each target area is accountable for utilizing the resources available to reinforce desired performance. This means viewing employees as customers, not subordinates. It also means taking actions that will enhance the probability of success by the team. Finally, it means reinforcing individuals for taking desired actions and reinforcing teams for achieving desired results.

To summarize, this imaginary organization is attempting to regain its competitiveness by redirecting the business and utilizing a variety of strategies to identify and develop needed changes. The reward systems should support as well as lead the change process in every corner of the organization.

Given the immediate nature of the changes, increases in base pay may not be appropriate. The organization needs to control escalating costs and investments that are not performance-specific. Since annual merit increases have little lasting impact on reinforcing performance, other pay and reinforcement programs will need to drive the desired change. This process needs to be applied to all levels and areas within the organization. A turning point on the path of change, when strong teamwork is important, is no time to play favorites. Finally, the message about controlling costs is important to the organization, and freezing salaries communicates a consistent action. If this is done without providing other forms of reinforcement, the workforce will react very negatively at first and be less committed to implementing desired changes. Thus, incentives and special recognition will be of critical importance to counter the negative effects of no base pay increases.

The only area in which base pay needs to continue a focus on the market is the human resource function. When the organization needs to hire specialized talent or when the firm is at risk of losing certain key contributors, considerable thought must be given to the use of base pay, and the results need to be monitored closely. In times of critical pressure, the organization should make it very expensive for a competitor to cherry-pick its key human resources.

The reward systems should focus efforts to implement desired changes. This can be achieved through a variety of team-oriented incentive compensation plans or other specialized reward programs. Individual incentives may be appropriate in sales situations in order to increase the sense of urgency to acquire new business. This will depend on what it takes to achieve sales and on the degree of interdependency required to positively impact sales.

One question that often emerges in times of change is whether team incentives should be given to the task forces that identify and recommend changes or to the natural work groups responsible for implementing their ideas. In most circumstances, the best use of incentives is to reward the work groups that implement changes. They must integrate the ideas of the task forces into their daily operations. They have to assess the impact of the change and determine whether it is feasible. (This assessment must be made in light of possible rewards for performance improvements rather than with the idea of getting reinforcement for continuing past habits and practices.)

Those involved in the task forces to identify and recommend changes should be heavily reinforced but not compensated for their contributions. Team celebrations, special-equity or similar awards, and visibility in other areas of the organization are often appropriate types of reinforcement. Further, the team that has contributed someone to serve on the cross-functional task forces should be recognized for its ability to achieve results with one less staff member. This combination of reinforcement and rewards is essential for creating an all-round reinforcement-oriented environment.

One can tell if the process is effective when appropriate action is taken both to analyze situations and to implement changes. The primary aim is to keep the focus on implementing change and on realizing improved results, not on analyzing problems and developing creative solutions. However, if the development process is not effectively supported and reinforced, it will not remain a priority focus for many areas of the organization. In the ideal model, those involved in identifying the changes needed participate fully with those involved in implementing the changes in a total rewards environment.

The implementation of some variable pay programs may need to wait until most of the major restructuring, re-engineering, and resource-realignment efforts have been completed. It is very problematic to introduce incentives when an organization is undergoing tremendous change, especially when that change is driven by major external threats. These situations often change the focus of performance measures, obviate baseline performance data, and require new relationships between people. Once the direction has been set, the variable pay plans can serve three purposes:

> Providing an opportunity for the "survivors" to realize something of value for rebuilding the organization and implementing the needed changes

> Locking in the primary changes by rewarding individuals for producing greater results through the application of new practices, procedures, or systems

> Keeping the pressure for achievements focused and very real to each individual to encourage the team to look forward instead of backward

In terms of recognition and reinforcement, the rate needs to increase dramatically throughout the organization. Measures and feedback will create opportunities for providing positive reinforcement. Until such time as the urgency of the crisis has been reduced, the firm should probably delay implementing any special-recognition programs. They tend to require a delayed decision-making process and give executives a false sense of doing something important. Special-recognition programs, as shown in Chapter 8, have little value to most people in an organization. Instead, special recognition should be provided by managers and teams on a real-time basis. This requires managers to be actively involved in the work of their areas, taking actions to remove barriers or acquire resources needed by the teams, reinforcing high-performance individuals, sponsoring team celebrations, getting data to performers from their customers, and taking the other actions necessary to create an environment of achievement and success.

An executive at a large telecommunications company complained that the problem with its re-engineering efforts was that more attention was being focused on making changes than on achieving results. Managers who were successful in creating change were transferred to other areas only to be replaced by people who "undid" many of their changes in their own efforts to create change. The problem with managers as change agents is that creating chaos is so enticing. The risk inherent in more and more change efforts is that the actual process of improvement slows down.

In this imaginary company, the challenge is to regain the "share of mind" in the marketplace and the confidence of the workforce. The marketplace needs to view this organization as focused on its needs and able to offer an increasingly attractive array of products and services. The firm needs to be viewed as strong and successful—a survivor and a winner. The firm's workforce should believe the same thing. This goal can be achieved by producing results in a way that builds strength and confidence. The road to this commitment and confidence can be paved by the reinforcement practices of the organization.

Reward Systems for Continual Change

Imagine a firm that is doing fine today, but facing increasing competition. As always, risks exist, but they are not threatening the immediate survival of the firm. There is no need for drastic action, but there is a need for continual action.

In many ways this organization is facing more difficult changes than the firm addressing re-creative change. It is often difficult to even express a credible dissatisfaction with the status quo when the firm is generally successful. Most organizations are more likely to reward people for handling a crisis than for preventing one. But if the executives and employees come to believe themselves invincible, they soon will *not* be. Therefore, the primary challenge of this organization is to promote continuous improvements at *a rate that is faster and better* than its competitors.

In terms of strategy for change, imagine an intact senior leadership team. There may be individual units that are facing competitive struggles, but there are resources available to assist their efforts. Employees and managers feel somewhat reassured that the firm is not yet facing the kind of survival struggles that are described in the public media.

But they are probably worried about the possibility that the tide may turn on them. They are confident and hopeful that senior management is watching the situation, and they wonder what they can do to prosper in this organization. The strategy that needs to be employed will involve three basic elements:

1. Understand the dynamics in the marketplace and the actions of the competitors and be prepared to take preemptive actions.

2. Monitor the changing needs of the customers and implement actions that enhance relationships with them.

3. Continually take actions to encourage quick action, avoid unnecessary costs, and make improvements to process and products/services.

The focus of this organization must be on building ever-stronger relationships with its customers by removing barriers, increasing the number of contacts, and responding to their needs in an effective manner. Everyone in the organization has a part to play in this strategy, which should include such actions as the following:

- Senior managers meeting frequently with customers and sponsoring events between the organization and its customers

- Functional/business unit managers meeting frequently with their specific customers to promote frequent contact between their staff and the customers (including visits by operator/support personnel), making investment decisions in collaboration, and implementing process improvements that can be linked to customer needs

- Operational employees meeting with customer representatives to discuss issues, examine how products are developed or used, and build relationships of mutual support and respect

- Support employees meeting with customers to better understand how the organization serves the customer and examine ways in which services and communication can be enhanced with and across the firms

The basic strategy behind these actions is to create a closer working relationship between the firm and its customers. While many of these activities may relate to the firm's key accounts, they set a model of working relationships that should apply in some manner to all customers. Furthermore, they set in motion a process by which employees of the organization see themselves as members of a firm that is closely wedded to its customers. Retention of both customers and employees will be an important benefit from this strategy.

In terms of reward systems, the basic strategy is one that focuses on continuous improvement. Because there is little need for a sense of crisis, the reward systems can serve to build a workplace environment that is attractive for recruiting and developing desired talent. Being competitive in the marketplace will be important, but this can be accomplished by creating a reinforcement-oriented environment rather than by leading the market in pay levels. The reward systems will need to perform the following functions:

1. Reinforce a commitment to the customer and to taking actions that enhance the firm's ability to acquire, serve, and retain them
2. Translate the requirements of the customers into performance measures that are specific, meaningful, and important to all areas of the organization
3. Reinforce actions that continually increase the speed of improvements, fully utilize the resources of the firm, and enhance the competencies of the firm

As in the case of the firm facing re-creative change, the role of the compensation function is to support the process of change within the organization. This is done by fashioning pay strategies and reinforcement practices that enhance the ability of the units to serve their customers, both internal and external. This will involve them in working with managers to set the right performance measures by providing customized reward programs and by increasing the ability of the managers and teams to reinforce desired actions.

From a line management perspective, the focus must be on serving customers and on celebrating the achievements made by people within the unit in the three areas noted above: customers, measures, and action. This means that managers must use the reward systems to their fullest potential. Waste in products or processes, in people or money, in time or effort are the devils to be rooted out of the organization.

In this context, base pay can perform several roles. In areas of the firm where it needs to create new competencies, a pay-for-competencies-employed type of program may be appropriate (see Chapter 6). This depends on the business reasons for hiring advanced or more flexible (i.e., cross-trained) talent. The process may entail paying people an increased level of compensation for acquiring and utilizing abilities needed by the firm. If the work is not available or the firm is not able to capitalize on this new talent to improve productivity, such a plan will only increase costs with little true benefit.

Base pay can be oriented to reinforcing career progressions in management information systems, engineering, research and development, and other highly technical fields. In this case, the organization can offer career paths for people that are consistent with the human resource requirements for its future. As people progress in their chosen field, there should be associated pay opportunities commensurate with the value-added nature of their work.

Pay levels should be externally focused in areas where the firm needs to acquire a number of people. These pay levels should be based on an analysis of the flow of people through the organization—identifying the entry, the "leakage" or turnover points, and the progression of people within the firm. The strategy for the base pay system needs to be based on the strategic requirements for human resources within the organization today and in the future. In this way base pay can be used to make the necessary investments to build the human resource capabilities for the future.

In terms of incentives, the use of team or unit plans can offer a powerful reward program for achievements. The measures need to be grounded in the requirements of the customers (See Chapter 10 on performance measures). They need to support the continual improvement of the unit's competitiveness and the use of its resources and encourage ways to improve the speed and value-added nature of work. The emphasis must be on people working smarter, not harder.

The best form of special recognition is one that is as personalized and as close to the achievement as possible. This means that managers and employees alike need measures that create opportunities for reinforcement—team celebrations, for example, that are really focused on reinforcing individuals for making their contributions to the team's success. The corporation can support special recognition by encouraging the occurrence of such celebrations (it is important to measure this), by involving senior level people in the events (to listen, not talk), and by providing the funding for these programs.

Performance appraisals can shift from being judgment-based (or merely mechanisms to determine ratings) to emphasizing review of performance, learning about what went well and what didn't, and building relationships within the firm. The form is not as important as the process, which should be based on collaboration and reflection. Collaboration can involve managers and employees, peers and working partners, customers and others within the firm. It is an opportunity to summarize all the data for a performance period and examine it with an eye to primary themes, threats to future performance, and priorities for the next period. The timing should reflect the natural cycles of the business, such as quarterly results and project milestones. In most cases, annual reviews are simply not frequent enough to do any good. (See Chapter 9, for a further discussion of this point.)

In this imaginary company the priorities are to strengthen its leadership in the marketplace by building strong relationships with its customers. This process brings every member of the organization into the act. Rather than looking upward within the firm for guidance, the members should talk with their customers. Rather than limiting costs to create bigger profits for someone else, they should look for ways to enhance the value of each expenditure, increase savings, and share in the successes that are achieved. Rather than blaming others for not pulling their weight, they should integrate the feedback and reinforcement in ways that improve performance.

This imaginary company has a competitive advantage because of the way it operates. Customers are valued by the organization, and so are its employees. Resources are used wisely, even though there are mistakes. A crisis is viewed as a sign of weakness; both preventing problems and making continual improvements are valued. People as well as the firm progress because of what they are able to achieve and how they achieved it. This is a balanced organization, one that is able to be highly competitive in turbulent times because of its coordination, capabilities, and commitments. This is a very special company, and unfortunately not a common archetype in American industry.

Breaking the Gridlock of Change

This chapter has explored the world of the large organization undergoing change. We have seen how most strategies are focused on the structural and process elements of the firm. Some are driven by survival imperatives and others face growing challenges to leadership. Tools and techniques to analyze the organization abound. The challenge is to create an environment in which people take the initiative to use these processes and improve the competitiveness of the organization.

The task of changing the culture is often an excuse for not taking action. People wait until senior managers provide the leadership they are seldom capable of displaying. Senior managers try one set of initiatives only to become impatient with the results or angry at the costs. They introduce new initiatives or restructure the organization. Employees see all the programs come and go, and wonder if there will ever be a time when they won't need to do something differently. Simply stated, they've created a "change gridlock" in which change is desperately needed but seldom sustained.

This chapter has offered reward strategies for large organizations facing either a crisis or a challenge. We have explored how to drive the themes of renewed competitiveness down into the organization and provide people with an opportunity to participate. If managers and employees alike redirect their efforts in ways that enhance the firm's capabilities to compete, the only variable will be the effectiveness of the strategy itself. The emphasis is on implementing change and reinforcing individuals for taking the actions needed by the firm now.

Collaboration is not just about peers working together in teams; it is about building an environment in which the organization and all its various parts work closely with its customers to enhance value. When the customer receives greater value from its suppliers, it can create greater value for *its* customers in turn. This creates win/win situations, not only at the individual and organizational level, but throughout the value chain of industries as well.

Notes

1. Kanter, R. M., *When Giants Learn to Dance: Mastering the Challenges of Strategy, Management, and Careers in the 1990s.* New York: Simon & Schuster, 1983.
2. Beer, M., *The Critical Path to Organizational Renewal.* Cambridge, Mass.: Harvard Business School Press, 1990.
3. Beckhard, R., *Changing the Essence: The Art of Creating and Leading Fundamental Change in Organizations.* San Francisco: Jossey-Bass, 1992.
4. Henry, K. and R., "Nothing Is Impossible," *Fortune* magazine, Sept., 23, 1991, p. 134.
5. Loomis, C., "Dinosaurs?" *Fortune* magazine, May 3, 1993, p. 36.
6. Dumaine, B., "The Bureaucracy Busters," *Fortune* magazine, June 17, 1991, pp. 37–50.
7. Kanter, op. cit.
8. Tichy, N. and R. Charan, "Speed, Simplicity, Self-Confidence: An Interview with Jack Welch," *Harvard Business Review,* September–October 1989, p. 112.
9. Tichy, N., *Managing Strategic Change: Technical, Political, and Cultural Dynamics.* New York: John Wiley, 1983.
10. Schlender, B., "How Toshiba Makes Alliances Work," *Fortune magazine,* October 4, 1993, pp. 116–120.
11. "How Managers Can Succeed Through Speed," *Fortune* magazine, February 13, 1989.
12. Cook, F., "An Interview with Motorola CEO George Fisher: Compensation Strategies and People Philosophies," *ACA Journal,* Autumn 1993, p. 14.
13. Steward, T., "Re-Engineering: The Hot New Managing Tool," *Fortune* magazine, August 23, 1993, pp. 41–48.

15

The Winds of Change

The winds and the waves are always on the side of the ablest navigators.
—EDWARD GIBBONS
The History of the Decline and Fall of the Roman Empire

Throughout this book we have explored various aspects of organizational change. Much has been written about the pressures for change and the strategies for survival in other books and periodicals. Many writers have presented compelling advice about what one should and should not do and what other firms have done. Further, many other writers have indicated that in order to fully realize or sustain its recommended approach, the organization needs to change its reward systems—compensation, recognition, and career paths. However, they do not indicate *how*, and we are left wondering what to do.

Enter this book. The fundamental element in all aspects of change is getting people to do some things differently. They do not have to modify every aspect of their performance, nor do all the people have to change. The organization needs to target people's efforts so that desired conditions are realized and the rate of change can grow and multiply. This change must be rooted in human behavior. It is the behaviors, the actions, the activities of people that determine whether a firm will continue to survive and prosper in these challenging times.

The Pressures for Change

In the 1960s, Bob Dylan wrote a song in which he said: "And the times, they are a changin.'" Little did he know that these words would be more a prophecy than a description of those times. We are facing challenges of global competition and global development. The political barriers that have divided peoples are coming down. The acquisition of companies and the operations of firms are crossing international boundaries at an incredible rate. Information is becoming almost instantaneous around the planet. Capital can be acquired from many sources, not just from one's local bank. The complexion of the population is changing in the United States as well as in many other countries. We are truly becoming a global village, or, as Buckminister Fuller would put it, "Spaceship Earth."

The Chinese symbol for crisis has two figures. The first means *danger*. We are facing a situation in which the forces of change are threatening our way of life. When we resist change, we decrease our ability to survive. But while stiffening ourselves against the pressures that face us may work for a time, it creates a false sense of confidence in our ability to survive as we are. In the end, our lack of flexibility may actually render us incapable of addressing the dangers we face.

The second Chinese figure for crisis means *opportunity*. The drive for survival is very strong. This can be seen in a forest a few months after a fire has apparently destroyed it. New shoots emerge from the ashes, and the life that returns becomes stronger and more resilient. Similarly, there are crisis opportunities in which a firm can use its talents and competencies to reshape the marketplace or its role in it. This requires an investment in the way things are done within the organization. It also requires risk taking, bold action, and a determination to overcome adversity. At the beginning of Chapter 2, I quoted a famous old saying that goes: "If you always do what you've always done, you'll always get what you've always gotten."

The pressures are different for every industry and every organization. Our task is to see where the forces of change present danger and where they offer opportunity; both are always present. Then we can begin to marshall our resources—the people, capital, materials and core competencies we have to address the situation. Unfortunately, however, this is only the beginning; merely launching a process of change does not guarantee its success however reinforcing it may be to the senior executives who enjoy strategic thinking and planning. The outcomes of executive planning sessions may be very meaningful strategies but they serve as antecedents only. Even after these strategies are communicated throughout the organization, they only serve to get certain desired behaviors *started*. Whether or not they will *continue* will depend on their consequences for the people who enact them. Executives often either forget this element of the change process or cannot see the importance of the forces that drive human behavior.

The problem is that we often use only what we know or what we have been reinforced for doing in the past. Traditionally, negative reinforcement and punishment have been the consequences that gave managers what they wanted. Using these tools, they achieved the desired results immediately. Therefore, when facing similar situations, managers are likely to use similar strategies again. Other managers tend to use inspirational antecedents—vision, values, or strategy statements—to motivate their staff, or they "hold people accountable"—which in most cases means that if individuals do not do their part, they will suffer adverse consequences. "Holding people accountable" seldom means that they will be *rewarded* for doing their part. So desired actions are often ignored (i.e., extinction), and undesired actions are punished in sophisticated ways, like attacking people's ideas, embarrassing them in public, or threatening them with even greater negative consequences (e.g., "You may be next in our downsizing program").

It is clear that we must adapt to the changing forces in our environment. Inherent in these forces are both threats to our survival and opportunities for triumph. If we focus our change efforts on antecedents (strategy formulation, reorganizations, and communication), we provide the necessary *direction* for change. If we invest in training and development, we can enhance the *capabilities* to respond. The problem is that most change efforts stop there. We wait for results. We wonder why spending continues to overrun budgets. We wonder why service and deliveries are not achieving the desired improvements. We see people continuing to stay in their functional roles or do their jobs in the same old fashion. We hear complaints about all the work that has been piled on. We get ourselves trapped in a "change gridlock" from which there appears to be no possible way out.

When an animal is caged or trapped, it becomes aggressive and strikes out at its captors and friends alike. Many executives and managers feel similarly; there is often a lot of stress and defensive action. We deny the existence of threats. We attempt to fight or bargain our way out. We become cynical. We wonder when the next crisis situation will occur. Only by surviving an actual crisis or fighting a fire do we feel valued for our contributions. But there is a nagging sense that there must be a better way.

Creating the Achievement Workplace

In organizations that are winning the competitive struggle of the marketplace, there is a clear strategy that fits the opportunities of the marketplace. Further, there are usually wonderful developments taking place deep inside the organization. For example, a large electrical utility that has been undergoing re-creation-level change for several years celebrated the work of a supervisor who was able to create savings in excess of $50,000 per year. In the same company a team in accounting was able to reduce account receivables exceeding 90 days by 90 percent. In a high technology company, an accounting clerk was conducting a routine phone call to a customer when he learned about a major problem in a recent delivery. He called the sales representative, and he was able to take immediate action. The customer was so impressed with the firm's responsiveness that they turned all competitors away.

In every organization there are marvelous events occurring every day. People cover for each other when one is overwhelmed with work. Shipments are sometimes hand-delivered by people in the firm when it is not part of their job but the product is desperately needed by the customer. The talent within a firm is sometimes just incredible, a potential reserve that few executives truly understand or believe. In this book I have presented tools for implementing change. The roots lie in understanding the forces that drive human behavior. As we have studied, human behavior is a function of three forces: The *antecedents* (what needs to be done), the *competencies* (how it needs to be done), and the *consequences* (what will happen if it is done).

Antecedents come before the behaviors and, if effective, get them started. The competencies are the skills and abilities people have to perform the desired functions. But the most powerful force is the consequence of their actions, which determine whether or not people will continue/increase the desired behavior or discontinue/decrease it. Will people find value in the effort or find it unfulfilling or frustrating? Are they doing the desired actions because they have to or because they want to? Our challenge is to use consequences in a sincere and strategic manner to create a win/win situation.

Achievement comes from doing something of which one can be proud. It requires some concentrated or extra effort. The reinforcement, whether it comes from inside oneself or from someone noticing the value that is created, is positive. The feeling is that one *wants* to do it again. In the achievement-oriented organization, this relationship between action and consequence occurs thousands of times every day. The ongoing practices of managers and employees reinforce the desired actions of others as a regular habit. The beauty of this process is that it is simple to understand and clearly valuable to all.

There are those who believe that rewards set up a "carrot-and-stick" relationship between managers and employees. They contend that the best alternative to rewards is to let the relationship between actions and consequences emerge naturally from their jobs. According to this view, people should not expect external rewards for doing the work of the organization; the work should be inherently satisfying. If it is not, then it is the responsibility of the organization to make it so. This approach amounts to leaving people alone to do their jobs and/or finding ways to make their work more inherently meaningful. It is an approach based mostly on research simulations in which people did not perform as desired when different consequences were used. The proponents of this approach seem to have a problem with the premise that our environment influences our behavior through the consequences we experience. This is essentially a rejection of behavior-based research in favor of more cognitive theories of human behavior. The reader will need to determine the value of these opposing theories for achieving desired changes within a work setting.

The ideal situation, of course, is one in which the work is full of natural reinforcers and people do find inherent value in the work they do. In such cases there is little need for organizational "interference" except to provide direction and resources to performers who already know what to do and do it because they want to. In such cases there is little or no need for supervisors or managers, nor any need for feedback external to the immediate tasks of the work. Unfortunately, however, these ideal conditions are not always possible, and when they are, they can take years of workplace engineering to achieve.

Instead, we are looking to create conditions in which people find a wide variety of reinforcers for their contributions. Some of this reinforcement comes from the work itself, some from their peers, some from their customers, and some from their managers or supervisors. We are seeking to create conditions within the workplace that encourage and reinforce people for serving their customers in a manner that achieves a win for the customers and a win for themselves.

Driving these reward systems is a desire, not to manipulate people into taking actions, but to provide them with an opportunity to share in the achievements of their contributions. The process does not imply that people are not already performing at a fully competent level. Rather, it is aimed at continually improving performance at a rate that is faster than the competitors'. Sincerity is key to the effective use of consequences. If reward systems are established as a way to manipulate people, they are likely to fail. If, on the other hand, they are established to reinforce progress, achievements, and service to the customers, they are very likely to succeed.

There are those who will not respond to positive pressures for change. They will complain about it, criticize it, or encourage others not to respond. These individuals find their reinforcement in pushing against desired change. The more attention they receive, the more they are rewarded for their negative efforts and the less reinforcement goes to those that *do* respond well. The best strategy is to ignore (extinguish) the resisters and focus attention and rewards on those who do respond, adapt, and become energized.

Consequences are effective when they are:

- *Specific*—clear as to what was accomplished
- *Personalized* so as to be meaningful
- *Contingent* on what was actually done
- *Sincerely* given
- *Immediately* available

In this way performers can feel truly valued for what they accomplished that enabled the firm to be more competitive and successful.

Utilizing Reward Systems

So far we have discussed the change gridlock and the need to find a different path to success. We have examined the characteristics of the organization that is oriented toward achievement and success. We have explored many ideas, concepts, and examples of reward systems that are directed to supporting the change process. From the five factors above that determine the effectiveness of consequences, we have built a model for an effective reward system. These criteria are:

- *Specific.* A line of sight is maintained between results and actions.
- *Meaningful.* The opportunities provide an important return on investment to both performer and organization.
- *Achievable.* The goals are within the reach of the performers.
- *Reliable.* The system operates according to its principles and purpose.
- *Timely.* The awards are provided frequently enough to make performers feel valued for their efforts.

These criteria provide the SMART way of doing things. Within this context, we have examined a wide variety of reward systems. We have explored how to re-direct and re-engineer them so that they are better able to influence behaviors and reinforce the focus on the needs of the customer.

Reward Strategy

Traditional thinking about reward strategies focuses on the external marketplace and what is necessary to be competitive in attracting and retaining people. The guidelines presented in this book focus the reward strategy on those actions needed by people to implement a firm's competitive strategy. This means that we need to understand the strategy in terms of the organization's key success factors, then translate these factors into describing the types of behaviors or actions required of people within the firm. The resulting description may define what the firm currently does well and what needs to be increased or introduced. The reward strategy that is developed must include the types of measures or describe the capabilities needed by the firm. The basic premise is that people should be performing actions that are in accord with the strategy of the firm. This strategy will enable the organization to succeed in an increasingly complex and competitive marketplace.

Once the reward strategy is defined, we can describe the purpose and desired requirements of the various reward systems. This will enable us to manage a portfolio of reward programs as an integrated system. Each of these is summarized in the following pages.

Base Salary

The fundamental purpose of the base pay system is to enable the company to acquire and retain the human capabilities it needs to perform its business. By its very nature, the system can support the values of the firm that are critical to the implementation of the firm's strategy. This includes understanding the needed competencies and either buying the resources (through competitive pay structures) or developing the capabilities (through pay-for-competencies-employed™ type programs). Base pay systems are oriented to the individual and should be personalized to reflect the individual contributions and talents of the person. In this manner, we can create a system that is not zero-sum but reinforces collaboration, continual growth, and competitiveness in acquiring the talent the firm needs to succeed.

Variable Compensation

The fundamental purpose of the variable pay system is to create a share in the success of the team, unit, or company. By its very nature, variable pay can support the economic process of the organization. This includes the way it achieves its revenues, uses it resources, and performs its operations. As these areas are improved, individuals will have an opportunity to gain financially and the firm will gain both financially and competitively.

In this area we have explored the use of cash incentives as well as equity-related incentives. In all cases the measures are targeted on meeting the needs of the customer and improving performance. The performance dimensions include revenues, costs, resource yields, timeliness, accuracy, reliability, service, and customer satisfaction. Taken in combination, these measures enhance the competitiveness of the firm by building a closer relationship with its customers.

Performance Management

While base salary can reflect *values*, and variable can pay reflect *economics*, performance management reflects *the process*. The process includes how the work gets done between the points in time at which compensation awards can be given. It also creates the environment in which people feel valued on a daily basis for their achievements. This includes four critical elements:

- *Focus* on what is important to change or be improved
- *Measures* to determine whether and how much progress is being achieved
- *Feedback* so that performers will know whether and how much progress is being achieved
- *Reinforcement* so that everyone celebrates achievements as they are unfolding

Performance management is therefore the ongoing process of managing people and the conditions in which they work. We have reviewed a wide variety of applications, including special recognition programs, performance reviews, and management practices. Performance management is not a single program, but an array of actions, a process taken by managers, teams, or individuals to monitor and reinforce desired actions. When desired actions are taken, desired results will be achieved. What could be more important to a firm?

Some Summary Dos and Don'ts

Throughout this book I have attempted to offer alternatives, concepts, and guidelines from which the reader can select to build a system of rewards that will work in his or her environment. I strongly believe that, while there is no *single* right way to do things, not *every* way is right. In selecting an approach, it is necessary to understand some fundamental principles that have worked over time. The principles I offer are based on solid research in both academic and industrial settings, as well as on personal experience gained through seeing results and analyzing the reasons for them.

These principles boil down to ten basic guidelines that I would like to leave you with as you finish this book. They are not presented in any order of importance, but do follow a logical flow.

1. *Do it now!* If you believe that the practices of building reward systems in support of implementing strategic priorities will benefit your business, the longer you wait, the longer it will be before you realize any true results. One large financial institution, discovered that it was wasting over $100,000 a day in excess costs and missed revenues. While you debate whether or not change is needed, your competitors are losing no time in approaching your customers or gaining an advantage.

2. *Keep your eye on the needs of the customer.* Throughout this book, the customer has been at the center of all the measures and the focus for actions. By building value for customers and strengthening relationships with them, a firm creates a critical value chain. Suppliers should treat *you* as a customer, and you in turn can enhance their ability to serve you by treating *them* as a customer. The customer's needs have been the primary focus because they provide a positive point for guidance to all activities.

A wise old cowboy told the author an interesting strategy for riding one's horse through a raging river. Focus your eyes on a mountain, a tree, or something in the distance. Don't look at the waters swirling around you. If you do, you will likely lose your balance. Keep your eyes focused on the object in the distance, stay responsive to the currents, and continue to push ahead in rhythm with the horse. Eventually you will reach the other side, safe and reasonably dry.

3. *Take action, be proactive, and continue to go for it.* There is a commonly held belief that if the organization can establish the right reward system, it can replace the process of management. In fact, the opposite is true. Well-designed reward systems actually require more management, not less. But the management required is different. It is more focused on providing people with meaningful measures, real-time feedback, and on-going reinforcement. It demands that managers break down the walls, get actions to occur, and strengthen the relationships between the team and its customers. It is more positive, action-oriented, and results-focused than traditional management practice.

4. *Personalize rewards to their recipients.* One of the values of having multiple reward systems is that everyone has an opportunity to receive the benefits of the system. An essential tenet of effective consequences and reward systems is that the rewards are valued by the performer. The performer needs to see that the reward opportunities are directly linked to the effort and results taken and that there is an appropriate return on investment. This occurs not only through the amount of

award; it comes through in how it is delivered. By personalizing the reward, you can anchor the meaning of the achievement more deeply than if you simply treat the reward as a mechanical administrative task.

In an earlier chapter, we reviewed an example of a firm that took a creative approach to awarding incentive checks. It is appropriate to review it again because it is a good example of how to personalize rewards. When it came time to distribute incentive checks, the general manager brought everyone into the employee cafeteria, he spoke briefly about the value of the achievements, and then distributed the checks. Only instead of giving each person his or her own check, he gave them someone else's. Each person's task was to find the recipient, and tell him or her something special they had done to make this payout possible. If the check giver was not able to mention a specific achievement, he or she was just to thank the person for their efforts. This occasion was discussed for weeks and became an important symbol of the firm's efforts to build a more mutually supportive and competitive organization.

If you want to know how to make a reinforcer meaningful, notice what people do when they have free time, go on vacation, or enjoy a weekend outing. People tend to do things that are meaningful and valuable to them when they have choices. Create reinforcers that are similar to what employees do when they make the choice themselves.

5. *Make sure everyone can win.* Reward systems built on the principles of competition or compliance are counterproductive, if not downright destructive. As we discussed in Chapter 2, collaboration can only be achieved when benefits are maximized and affect as many people possible. Many traditional systems seek to pit one team or employee against another, a technique that undermines the credibility of the organization as well as the commitment of its members. The kind of strategies that should be pursued instead are those discussed in Chapter 8, Making Special Recognition Special. Everyone should have the opportunity to achieve the desired goal, not just the top 10 percent. The challenge for management is both to get people over the goal and to maximize the payouts—not by lowering the performance levels, but by providing whatever assistance is necessary for people to achieve. This creates a new role for management and leads to the creation of a true win/win situation.

6. *Make sure that awards are contingent.* Reward systems become entitlement systems when they lose their contingency on performance. A sense of entitlement is created when people are automatically and regularly rewarded for not doing anything special. They grow to expect their awards, and want even more. People appreciate surprises and benefits, but when they are noncontingent, people come to think of them as their right. This has become a major issue in the current struggle over

employee health insurance programs. Employees feel that something is being taken away when they are asked to make copayments. They feel it is their right to receive the present level of benefits, even though the nature of the game has changed radically. This is the central issue with entitlement. Each award should be fully earned and people should understand exactly what they have done to achieve it. If payouts cannot be made, the progress people *have* made should be reinforced.

7. *Don't expect it all at once; shape into it.* The process of developing effective rewards is one of change and continual improvement. While it is not productive to change the nature of the game during the process, few plans are perfect the first time out. Create the expectation among the participants that problems will be identified and improvements will be made. Present the design and management of the reward system as one that is still being shaped as the abilities and capabilities of the organization are increased. Solicit employees' ideas about ways to improve or enhance the effectiveness of the reward system. This is the spirit of continuous improvement and collaboration.

8. *Remember that you are in competition with other consequences.* An organization has thousands of consequences happening at every moment of every day. While management is a very powerful source of consequences, it is not the only source. People are influenced by their peers, their staff, and their customers. Behaviors are influenced by people's outside interests, personal history, and personal work activities. Because reward systems are constantly in competition with other consequences for the hearts and minds of the workforce, they need to be effective and meaningful to the performer in order to have an impact. This is both the risk and opportunity whenever one introduces changes in the chemistry of consequences.

9. *Do it from the heart.* People will not respect or respond favorably to consequences that are intended to be manipulative or aversive. The fundamental purpose of reward systems is to build a powerful partnership between the individual and the organization. That is why I view collaboration as an essential theme of success. The general manager of a division that recently introduced a team incentive plan, took personal responsibility to manage the actions that would maximize the payout. He knew that if the plan paid out to the maximum, everyone would be a winner, the firm would improve its financial performance and be a stronger competitor in the marketplace and the members would gain a great deal financially. This was not based on a "carrot" philosophy, but on a sincere interest in building partnerships within the organization. The drive was to win, and everyone felt the same commitment.

10. *Have fun while you are doing it.* The process of developing new reward systems, whether they be through the compensation system,

through special-recognition programs, or through new performance management practices, is always a difficult one. Don't underestimate the amount of work necessary or the resistance that will be encountered. If a job is worth doing, it is worth measuring progress and celebrating achievements. Therefore, examine every aspect of the process to see what can be done to make it more satisfying and exciting. We are seeking every avenue to bring purpose and meaning into the workplace because that is the spirit of reinforcement and achievement. Special-recognition occasions can range from an ice cream sundae party for a gain-sharing design team that has reached a major project milestone, to a special visit by an executive who is enthusiastic about the work of the managers in developing new measurement and feedback systems, to a surprise party by employees for their supervisors who are attempting new ways to reinforce performance. These all add to the excitement and fun of making change. One needs to reinforce the reinforcers if one wants to see an increased rate of reinforcement.

Thoughts about the Winds of Change

The quote at the beginning of this chapter is by the nineteenth-century author Edward Gibbons. It offers a unique insight into the message in this book. When one travels on a sailing ship, one cannot see the wind or the forces of the waters, but the navigator can. Yet they have a powerful influence on the speed, direction, and fuel needed to achieve the ultimate destination. The ablest navigator uses these forces to take maximum advantage of the capabilities of the ship. In this book we have looked at the forces that influence human behavior within organizations. We now know that those forces exist, impact behaviors in significant ways, and we have examined a variety of strategies to use them effectively. Like the navigator, we can utilize this knowledge to steer our ship. Without this knowledge, we are blind. With this knowledge, we can see what others cannot. We have a competitive advantage. But knowledge without application remains unpotentiated. Our task is to use this knowledge to achieve our mission: a workplace in which everyone wins. In this way we can leave our world a little different and a little better than when we arrived.

Bibliography

"ACA: Skill-Based Pay: Practices, Payoffs, Pitfalls, and Perscriptions." A study sponsored by the American Compensation Association. Scottsdale, Ariz., 1992.

Albrecht, K., and R. Zemke. *Service America: Doing Business in the New Economy.* Homewood, Ill.: Dow Jones–Irwin, 1985.

Balcazar, F., B. Hopkins, and Y. Suarez. "A Critical, Objective Review of Performance Feedback." *Journal of Organizational Behavior Management*, Vol. 7 (Fall 1985/Winter 1986).

Bandura, A. *Principles of Behavior Modification.* New York: Holt-Rinehart & Winston, 1969.

———*Social Foundations of Thought and Action.* Englewood Cliffs, N.J.: Prentice-Hall, 1987.

Bardwick, J. M. *Danger in the Comfort Zone.* New York: AMACOM, 1991.

Barrett, K., and R. Greene. *The Man Behind the Magic: The Story of Walt Disney.* New York: Viking Press, 1991.

Beckhard, R., and R. Harris. *Organizational Transition: Managing Complex Change.* Reading, Mass.: Addison-Wesley, 1987.

———and W. Pritchard. *Changing the Essence: The Art of Creating and Leading Fundamental Change in Organizations.* San Francisco, Calif.: Jossey-Bass, 1992.

Beer, M., R. Eisenstat, and B. Spector. *The Critical Path to Corporate Renewal.* Cambridge: Harvard Business School Press, 1990.

Belcher, J. G., Jr. *Productivity Plus.* Houston: Gulf, 1987.

Bennis, W., and B. Nanus. *Leaders: The Strategies for Taking Charge.* New York: Harper & Row, 1986.

Bernardin, H. J., and P. C. Smith. "A Clarification of Some Issues Regarding ... Behaviorally Anchored Rating Scales." *Journal of Applied Psychology*, Vol. 66 (1981): 458.

———and R. W. Beatty. *Performance Appraisal: Assessing Human Behavior at Work.* Boston: Kent, MA, 1984.

Black, F., and M. Scholes. "The Pricing of Option and Corporate Liabilities." *Journal of Political Economy*, 81 (May–June, 1973): 637.

Blasi, J. R. *Employee Ownership.* Cambridge, Mass.: Ballinger Press, 1988.

Churchill, N. C., and V. L. Lewis. "The Five Stages of Small Business Growth." *Harvard Business Review* (May–June 1983): 30.

Cohen, A., and D. Bradford. *Influence Without Authority.* New York: John Wiley & Sons, 1990.

"Compensation and Performance Management Pracitices in Companies with Total Quality Management." A study conducted by the Wyatt Company for the U.S. General Accounting Office (Fall, 1991).

Cook, F. "An Interview with Motorola CEO George Fisher: Compensation Strategies and People Philosophies." *ACA Journal* (Autumn 1993): 14.

Cooper, W. H. "Conceptual Similarity as a Source of Illusory Halo in Job Performance Ratings." *Journal of Applied Psychology,* Vol. 66, (1981): 302.

Covey, S. R. *The 7 Habits of Highly Effective People.*, New York: Simon & Schuster, 1989.

CSRA (Civil Service Reform Act), Public Law 95–454, 1978, 92 STAT.

Daniels, A. *Performance Management: Improving Quality Productivity Through Positive Reinforcement.* Tucker, Ga.: Performance Management Publications, 1989.

———"Parties—With a Purpose." *SKY* (December 1992).

———*Bringing Out The Best in People: How to Apply the Astonishing Power of Positive Reinforcement.* New York: McGraw-Hill, 1993.

Davidow, W., and B. Uttal. *Total Customer Service: The Ultimate Weapon.* New York: Harper and Row, 1989.

Davis, S. *Future Perfect.* Reading, Mass.: Addison-Wesley, 1987.

Deci, E. L., and R. M. Ryan. *Intrinsic Motivation and Self-Determination in Human Behavior.* New York: Plenum Press, 1985.

Deming, W. E., *Out of the Crisis.* Cambridge, Mass.: MIT Press, 1986.

Dertouzos, M., R. Lester, and R. Solow. *Made in America: Regaining the Productive Edge.* Cambridge, Mass: MIT Press, 1989.

Dickinson, A. M. "The Detrimental Effects of Extrinsic Reinforcement on 'Intrinsic Motivation'." *The Behavioral Analyst,* Vol. 12, No. 1 (Spring 1989): 1–15.

———"Exploring New Vistas: Performance Management Research Laboratory at Western Michigan University." *Performance Management Magazine,* Vol. 9, No. 1 (1991): 27–31.

Dickinson, A., and K. Gillette. "A Comparison of the Effects of Two Individual Monetary Incentive Systems on Productivity: Piece Rate Pay versus Base Pay Plus Incentives." *Journal of Organizational Behavior Management.* Vol. 14, No. 1 (1993).

Doyle, R., and P. Doyle. *Gain Management.* New York: AMACOM, 1992.

Dumaine, B. "How Managers Can Succeed Through Speed." *Fortune* (February 13, 1989).

———"The Bureaucracy Busters." *Fortune* (June 17, 1991): 37–50.

Drucker, P. F. *The Frontiers of Management.* New York: Harper & Row, 1986.

———*The Practice of Management.* New York: Harper & Row, 1954.

Farrell, C., and J. Hoerr. "ESOPs: Are They Good For You?" *Business Week* (May 15, 1989): 116.

Fein, M. *Improshare: An Alternative to Traditional Managing.* American Institute of Industrial Engineers. Norcross, Ga., 1981.

Fuller., R. B., *And It Come to Pass—Not to Stay.* New York: Macmillan, 1976.

Galbraith, J. *Designing Complex Organizations.* Reading, Mass.: Addison-Wesley, 1973.

Garbor, A. "Take This Job and Love It." *New York Times* (January 26, 1992): 1.

Garfield, C., and H. Bennett. *Peak Performance: Mental Training Techniques of the World's Greatest Athletes.* New York: J. P. Tarcher, 1984.

Gilbert, T. F. *Human Competence—Engineering Worthy Performance*. New York: McGraw-Hill, 1978.

Goldratt, E., and J. Cox. *The Goal: A Process of Ongoing Improvement*. New York: North River Press, 1986.

Graham-More, B., and T. Ross. *Productivity Gainsharing*. Englewood Cliffs, N.J.: Prentice-Hall, 1983.

Gray, R. "The Scanlon Plan: A Case Study." *British Journal of Industrial Relations*, 9, (1971) 291–313.

Grayson, C., Jr., and C. O'Dell. *American Business: A Two-Minute Warning*. New York: Free Press, 1988.

Greiner, L. E. "Evolution and Revolution as Organizations Grow." *Harvard Business Review*. (July–August 1972): 37.

Gupta, N., G. Ledford, Jr., G. Jenkins, and H. Doty. "Survey-Based Prescriptions for Skill-Based Pay." *ACA Journal* (Autumn 1992): 48.

Hamilton, R. H. "Scenarios in Corporate Planning." *Journal of Business Strategy*, 2 (Summer 1981): 82.

Hammer, M., and J. Champy. *Reengineering the Corporation*. New York: Harper, 1993.

Hayes, R., and S. Wheelright. *Restoring Our Competitive Edge*. New York: John Wiley, 1984.

Herrnstein, R. "On the Law of Effect." *Journal of Experimental Analysis of Behavior*, 13, (1970): 243–266.

———"Behavior, Reinforcement, and Utility." *Psychological Science*, Vol. 1, No. 4 (July, 1990).

———and D. Prelec. "Melioration: A Theory of Distributed Choice." *Journal of Economic Perspectives*, 5, No. 3 (Summer 1991): 137–156.

Hogarth, R. M., "Beyond Discrete Biases." *Psychological Bulletin*, Vol. 90, (1981): 197.

Huey, J. "Nothing Is Impossible." *Fortune* (September 23, 1991): 134.

Imai, M. *Kaizen: The Key to Japan's Competitive Success*. New York: Random House, 1986.

Johnston, W. "Global Workforce 2000: The New World Labor Market." *Harvard Business Review* (March/April 1991): 115.

Kanter, R. M. "The Attack On Pay." *Harvard Business Review* (March–April 1987): 60.

———*The Change Masters*. New York: Simon & Schuster, 1983.

———When Giants Learn to Dance: *Mastering the Challenges of Strategy, Management, and Careers in the 1990s*. New York: Simon & Schuster, 1983.

———, B. Stein, and T. Jick. *The Challenge of Organizational Change*. New York: Free Press, 1992.

Kaplan, R., and D. Norton. "The Balanced Scorecard—Measures that Drive Performance." *Harvard Business Review* (January–February, 1992).

———"Putting the Balanced Scoreboard to Work." *Harvard Business Review* (September–October 1993): 134.

Kohn, A. "Why Incentive Plans Cannot Work." *Harvard Business Review* (September–October 1993): 54.

Kotter, J. P. *The General Manager*. New York: Free Press, 1982.

Kreitner, R., and F. Luthans. "A Social Learning Approach to Behavioral Management: Radical Behaviorists 'Mellowing Out'." *Organizational Dynamics* (Winter 1993).

Kübler-Ross, E. *On Death and Dying*, New York: Macmillan, 1969.

Laabs, J. "Ben & Jerry's Caring Capitalism." *Personnel Journal* (November 1992): 50.

Land, G. *Grow or Die*. New York: Dell, 1973.

Latham, G., and K. Wexley. *Increasing Productivity Through Performance Appraisal*. Reading, Mass.: Addison-Wesley, 1981.

Lawler, E. *Strategic Pay*. San Francisco, Jossey-Bass, 1990.

Lawrence, P., and J. Lorsch. *Organization and Environment: Managing Differentiation and Integration*. Cambridge: Harvard University Press, 1967.

Levering, R. *A Great Place to Work*. New York: Random House, 1988.

Levitt, T. "Marketing Myopia." *Harvard Business Review* (July–August, 1960): 26.

Likert, R. L. *New Patterns of Management*. New York: McGraw-Hill, 1961.

Loafman, B. "Envision Your Priorities—The Focus Board Alternative." *Performance Management Magazine*. Tucker, Ga., Vol. 8, No. 1: 35.

Longenecker, C., and S. Goff. "Why Performance Appraisals Still Fail." *Journal of Compensation and Benefits*. (November–December 1990): 36.

Loomis, C. "Dinosaurs?" *Fortune* (May 3, 1993): 36.

Luthans, F., and T. Davis. "Behavioral Self-Management—The Missing Link in Managerial Effectiveness." *Organizational Dynamics* (Summer 1979).

———"Managers in Action: A New Look at Their Behavior and Operating Models." *Organizational Dynamics* (Summer 1980).

Mager, R. F., and P. Pipe. *Analyzing Performance Problems, or "You Really-Oughta-Wanna."* Belmont, Calif.: Fearon-Pitman, 1970.

Maslow, A. H. "A Theory of Human Motivation." *Psychological Review* (July 1943): 370–396.

Mawhinney, T. C., A. M. Dickinson, and L. A. Taylor. "The Use of Concurrent Schedules to Evalute the Effects of Extrinsic Rewards on Intrinsic Motivation." *Journal of Organizational Behavior Management*, 10, (1989): 109–129.

———and C. R. Gowen. "Gainsharing and the Law of Effect as the Matching Law: A Theoretical Framework." *Journal of Organizational Behavior Management*, Vol. 2, No. 11 (1992).

McAdams, J., and E. Hawk. *Capitilizing on Human Assets*. A research project of the American Compensation Association. Scottsdale, Ariz., 1992.

McClelland, D. "Achievement Motivation Can Be Developed." *Harvard Business Review* (November–December 1965): 6.

———*The Achieving Society*. Princeton, N.J.: Van Nostrand, 1961.

———,J. Atkinson, R. Clark, and E. Lowell. *The Achieving Motive*. New York: Appleton-Century Crofts, 1953.

McGuire, J. W. *Factors Affecting the Growth of Manufacturing Firms*. Seattle: Bureau of Business Research, University of Washington, 1963.

McWhirter, D. *Sharing Ownership*. New York: John Wiley, 1993.

Michel, W. *Introduction to Personality*. New York: Holt, Reinhart & Winston, 1976.

Milkovick, G., and C. Milkovich. "Strengthening the Pay-Performance Relationship: The Research." *Compensation and Benefits Review*. November–December 1992): 53.

Mintzberg, H. *The Structure of Organizations.* Englewood Cliffs, N.J.: Prentice Hall, 1979.

Morse, E. "Contingent Compensation: Pay for Performance as Pie Comp." *Performance Management Magazine.* Vol. 6, No. 2 (Spring 1988): 21–31.

Nelson, B. *1000 Ways to Reward Emoloyees.* New York: Workman Publishing, 1994.

O'Brien, R. M., A. M. Dickenson, and M. P. Rosow, eds. *Industrial Behavioral Modification: A Management Handbook.* New York: Pergamon Press, 1982.

O'Byrne, S. "EVA and Management Compensation." *ACA Journal* (Summer 1994): 60.

Odiorne, G. *Management by Objectives: A System of Managerial Leadership.* Belmont, Calif: Fearon-Pitman, 1965.

O'Rourke, L. "Redesigning Performance Evaluation and Compensation Systems to Support Total Quality." *The Quality Letter for Healthcare Leaders,* Vol. 5, No. 3 (April 1993).

Ott, E. "Team-Based Pay: New Wave Strategic Incentives." *Sloan Management Review* (Spring 1990): 19.

Prahalad, C., and G. Hamel. "The Core Competence of the Corporation." *Harvard Business Review* (May–June 1990): 79–91.

"People, Performance and Pay." A study by the American Productivity Center and the American Compensation Association on Non-Traditional Reward and Human Resource Practices, Scottsdale, Ariz., 1986.

Peters, T., and R. Waterman. *In Search of Excellence.* New York: Harper & Row, 1985.

Peters, T. *Thriving on Chaos.* New York: Alfred A. Knopf, 1987.

Porter, M. *Competitive Strategy.* New York: Free Press, 1980.

Premack, D. "Toward Empirical Behavior Laws: I. Positive Reinforcement." *Psychological Review,* 66: 219–233.

Reich, T. B. *The Next American Frontier.* New York: Penguin Group, 1983.

Riggs, J. L., "Monitoring with a Matrix that Motivates." *Performance Management Magazine,* Vol. 4, No. 3 (1986).

Rock, M., and L. Berger. *The Compensation Handbook: A State-of-the-Art Guide to Compensation Strategy and Design.* New York: McGraw-Hill, 1991.

Ross, T. and R. Ross. "Productivity Gainsharing: Resolving Some of the Measurement Issues." *National Productivity Review* (Autumn 1984): 382.

Rostow, W. W. *The Stages of Economic Growth.* Cambridge, England: Cambridge University Press, 1960.

Savage, C. *Fifth Generation Management.* Maynard, Mass.: Digital Press, 1990.

Schlender, B. "How Toshiba Makes Alliances Work." *Fortune* (October 4, 1993): 116–120.

Scholtes, P. "An Elaboration on Deming's Teachings on Performance Appraisal." *Performance Appraisal,* a publication of Joiner Associates, Madison, Wisc., 1987.

Schuster, J. R., and P. K. Zingheir. *The New Pay.* New York: Lexington Books, 1992.

Senge, P. *The Fifth Discipline: The Art and Practice of the Learning Organization.* New York: Doubleday/Currency, 1990.

Skinner, B. F. *Science and Human Behavior.* New York: Macmillan, 1953.

————*Contingencies of Reinforcement: A Theoretical Analysis.* Englewood Cliffs, N.J., Prentice-Hall, 1969.

Smith, A. *The Wealth of Nations,* 1776.

Snyder, G. "Incentive Pay at St. Elizabeth's Hospital." *Performance Management Magazine,* Vol. 9, No. 3: 18–24.

————"Top Gun Performance at Allied Systems." *Performance Management Magazine,* Vol. 8, No. 4: 32–34.

————"May I Make A Suggestion?: Dow Chemical Canada Says 'Yes'." *Performance Management Magazine,* Vol. 8, No. 2: 10–15.

Spratt, M., and B. Steele. "Rewarding Key Contributors." *Compensation and Benefits Review,* (July–August 1985).

Steward, T. "Re-Engineering: The Hot New Managing Tool." *Fortune* (August 23, 1993): 41–48.

Taylor, A. III, "U.S. Cars Come Back." *Fortune* (November 16, 1992): 52–85.

Taylor, F. W. *Principles of Scientific Management.* New York: Harper & Brothers, 1911.

Thomas, B., and M. Olson. "Gain Sharing: The Design Guarantees Success." *Personnel Journal* (May 1988).

Tichy, N., and R. Charan "Speed, Simplicity, Self-Confidence: An Interview with Jack Welch." *Harvard Business Review* (September–October 1989): 112.

Tichy, N. *Managing Strategic Change: Technical, Political, and Cultural Dynamics.* New York: John Wiley, 1983.

Tully, S. "Your Paycheck Gets Exciting." *Fortune* (November 1, 1993): 83.

Ulrich, D., and D. Lake. *Organiztional Capability.* New York: John Wiley, 1990.

Vreon, U. H. *Work and Motivation* New York: John Wiley, 1964.

Vroom, V. *Work and Motivation.* New York: John Wiley and Sons, 1964.

Watson, D., and R. Tharp. *Self-Directed Behavior.* Pacific Grove, Calif.: Brooks/Cole, 1989.

White, J. K. "The Scanlon Plan: Causes and Correlates of Success." *Academy of Management Journal,* 22 (1979): 292–312.

Wilson, T. "Changing the Purpose of Pay Programs." *Performance Management Magazine,* Vol. 9, No. 2: 29–32.

————"Group Incentives: Are You Ready?" *Journal of Compensation and Benefits."* (November-December 1990): 25–29.

————"Is It Time to Eliminate the Piece-Rate Incentive System?" *Compensation and Benefits Review* (March–April, 1992): 43–49.

————"Making Negative Feedback Work." *Personnel Journal* (December, 1978): 680.

————"Why Self-Managed Teams Work." *Industrial Management* (February 1993, special supplement).

Index

ABOUT THE AUTHOR

Thomas B. Wilson is President of The Wilson Group, Inc. in Concord, Massachusetts. With more that 20 years of hands-on business experience, Mr. Wilson has helped hundreds of companies develop reward systems to achieve change and improve their competitiveness. Prior to forming The Wilson Group, he was vice president at Aubrey Daniels & Associates, vice president and partner with the Hay Group, and director of Consulting Services for the Forum Corporation. His clients include Analog Devices, St. Elizabeth's Medical Center, GTE, Norton Company, Fidelity Investments, Titleist & Footjoy Worldwide, and Harvard Community Health Plan.